William Morris on Socialism

Edinburgh Critical Editions of Nineteenth-Century Texts

Published titles

Richard Jefferies, After London; or Wild England
Edited by Mark Frost

Marie Corelli, A Romance of Two Worlds: A Novel
Edited by Andrew Radford

Sensation Drama, 1860–1880: An Anthology
Edited by Joanna Hofer-Robinson and Beth Palmer

Agriculture and the Land: Richard Jefferies' Essays and Letters
Edited by Rebecca Welshman

Maxwell Gray, The Silence of Dean Maitland
Edited by Julian Wolfreys

Jane Porter, Thaddeus of Warsaw: A Novel
Edited by Thomas McLean and Ruth Knezevich

Hubert Crackanthorpe, Wreckage: Seven Studies
Edited by David Malcolm

Catharine Sedgwick, Redwood: A Tale
Edited by Jenifer B. Elmore

Philip James Bailey, Festus
Edited by Mischa Willett

William Morris on Socialism: Uncollected Essays
Edited by Florence Boos

Forthcoming titles

William Barnes, Dialect Poems in the Dorset County Chronicle
Edited by Thomas Burton and Emma Mason

Geraldine Jewsbury, Critical Essays and Reviews (1849–1870)
Edited by Anne-Marie Beller

George Gissing, The Private Papers of Henry Ryecroft
Edited by Thomas Ue

The Plays of Charles Dickens
Edited by Joanna Hofer-Robinson and Pete Orford

Visit the Edinburgh Critical Editions of Nineteenth-Century Texts website at: edinburghuniversitypress.com/series/ecenct

William Morris on Socialism

Uncollected Essays

Edited by Florence S. Boos

EDINBURGH
University Press

Edinburgh University Press is one of the leading university presses in the UK. We publish academic books and journals in our selected subject areas across the humanities and social sciences, combining cutting-edge scholarship with high editorial and production values to produce academic works of lasting importance. For more information visit our website: edinburghuniversitypress.com

Edinburgh University Press Ltd
13 Infirmary Street
Edinburgh EH1 1LT

First published in hardback by Edinburgh University Press 2023

Typeset in 11/12.5 Baskerville by
IDSUK (DataConnection) Ltd

A CIP record for this book is available from the British Library

ISBN 978 1 4744 5808 5 (hardback)
ISBN 978 1 3995 4851 9 (paperback)
ISBN 978 1 4744 5809 2 (webready PDF)
ISBN 978 1 4744 5810 8 (epub)

Contents

List of Figures vii
List of Abbreviations x
Acknowledgments xi
Series Preface xii

Introduction: William Morris's Uncollected Political Essays: Equality, Nonviolence, and "One Socialist Party" 1

Part I From Liberalism to Socialism, 1878–1881

1. Early Political Essay, Untitled ["Against War with Russia"], 1878 31
2. Address at the Cambridge School of Art Prizegiving ["Art for All"], February 21, 1878 41
3. "Our Country Right or Wrong," January 1880 49
4. A Lecture Delivered to the Men's and Women's College ["Art and Inequality"], 1880 74

Part II Socialism: The Middle Phase, 1883–1889

5. "An Invitation to Join the Democratic Federation," 1883 91
6. "The Relations of Art to Labour," April 1884, 1890 94
7. Address at the Opening of the Fourth Annual Loan Exhibition, Whitechapel, April 1884 119
8. "Misery and the Way Out," September 1884 133
9. "Introduction to *A Review of European Society* by John Sketchley," September 29, 1884 153
10. "Commercial War," 1885 159
11. "Socialism," 1885 179
12. "The Political Outlook," 1886 203
13. "Equality," 1888 221
14. "How Shall We Live Then?" March 1889 243

15. Address on English Socialism on Behalf of the Socialist League: Report to the First Congress of the Second International, Paris, July 1889 263

Part III Some Tempered Warnings: A Final Phase, 1891–1896

Nonviolent Revolution, 1891–1894

16. "Socialism Up to Date," 1891 277
17. "Communism—i.e. Property," 1892 289
18. "Town and Country," 1893 307
19. "How I Became a Socialist," June 1894 315
20. "Why I Am a Communist," 1894 323

Valedictory, 1895–1896

21. "What We Have to Look For," 1895 337
22. "Change of Position—Not Change of Condition," 1895 355
23. ["One Socialist Party"], 1896 359
24. "Against the Abuses of Public Advertising," January 1896 367
25. "The Present Outlook of Socialism in England," April 1896 373
26. "The Promise of May," published in *Justice*, May 1896 385

Appendix: List of Morris's Anthologized Essays 389
Index of Titles 394
Subject Index 396

Figures

Frontispiece	William Morris, 1887. Courtesy of the National Portrait Gallery	xiii
Figure I.1	One Socialist Party	19
Figure I.2	Jane Morris, 1879 (1839–1914). Courtesy of the National Portrait Gallery	27
Figure I.3	May Morris with musical instrument (1862–1938). Courtesy of the William Morris Gallery, London Borough of Walthamstow	27
Figure 2.1	"Pink and Rose," 1883. Courtesy of the Metropolitan Museum of Art, Edward C. Moore Jr. Gift	40
Figure 3.1	"Our Country Right or Wrong," British Library Add. MS 45,334	48
Figure 7.1	*Manifesto* of the Socialist League. Courtesy of the William Morris Gallery	118
Figure 8.1	Henry Hyndman (1842–1921), Joe Burgess, *John Burns: The Rise and Progress of a Right Honorable* (Glasgow: Reformers' Bookstall 1911)	132
Figure 8.2	"A Summary of the Principles of Socialism," 1884, by Henry Hyndman and William Morris	132
Figure 9.1	Socialist League Membership cards, front and back. Walter Crane. Courtesy of Special Collections, University of Maryland	152
Figure 10.1	Andreas Scheu (1844–1927). Courtesy of the National Trust	158
Figure 10.2	Philip Webb (1831–1915). Courtesy of the National Portrait Gallery	158
Figure 10.3	James Tochatti (1852–1928). Courtesy of Stephen Williams	158
Figure 10.4	John Carruthers (1836–1914). Courtesy of *Economic Studies*	158
Figure 10.5	Frederic Harrison (1831–1923). Courtesy of the National Portrait Gallery	158
Figure 11.1	London Survey Hammersmith Map, 1896. The Morris house is marked by an arrow.	178

Figure 11.2	Kelmscott House, Upper Mall, Hammersmith (WA1941.171.6). © Ashmolean Museum, University of Oxford	178
Figure 11.3	The Coach House of Kelmscott House, site of Hammersmith Branch Social Democratic Federation, Hammersmith Branch Socialist League, and Hammersmith Socialist Society meetings. Courtesy of William Morris Gallery	178
Figure 12.1	May Morris, G. B. Shaw, H. H. Sparling, and Emery Walker, 1889. Courtesy of The Wilson, Cheltenham	202
Figure 12.2	Charles Faulkner (1834–92). Courtesy of the National Portrait Gallery	202
Figure 12.3	John Bruce Glasier (1859–1920), *Labour Annual*, ed. Joseph Edwards, 1895	202
Figure 12.4	Fred Henderson (1868–1957). Courtesy of the Norfolk Public Library	202
Figure 13.1	"Alfred Linnell: A Death Song," 1887	220
Figure 13.2	"The Riot in Trafalgar Square," *The Illustrated London News*, 1887	220
Figure 14.1	Invitation to Socialist League Meeting, 1890. Courtesy of Special Collections, University of Maryland	242
Figure 14.2	*Manifesto of English Socialists*, 1893. Signed by William Morris, G. B. Shaw, and others. Courtesy of Special Collections, University of Maryland	242
Figure 15.1	William Morris, 1884. Courtesy of the Victoria and Albert Museum	262
Figure 16.1	Hammersmith Branch of the Socialist League, ca. 1888. Courtesy of the Victoria and Albert Museum	276
Figure 16.2	Eleanor Marx Aveling (1856–98), member of the Bloomsbury Branch of the Social Democratic Federation and Socialist League (Source: Wiki)	287
Figure 17.1	Frontispiece, *A Dream of John Ball* (Kelmscott Press, 1892)	288
Figure 18.1	Kelmscott Manor, front view. Morris co-leased Kelmscott Manor in 1871 and spent much time here during the 1890s. Photo credit: Julia Griffin	306
Figure 19.1	Frontispiece, *News from Nowhere* (Kelmscott Press, 1892)	314
Figure 20.1	Peter Kropotkin (1842–1921). Courtesy of the Gallica Digital Library	322

Figure 20.2	Charlotte Martin Wilson (1854–1944). Charlotte at Newnham College, Cambridge; she is seated in the middle row, left. Courtesy of The Principal and Fellows, Newnham College	322
Figure 21.1	Orchard Tapestry, 1890. Courtesy of the Victoria and Albert Museum	336
Figure 22.1	"Blackthorn" wallpaper, 1892	354
Figure 22.2	"Double Bough" wallpaper, 1890	354
Figure 23.1	Newspaper clipping for *One Socialist Party*, *The Labour Leader*, January 1896	358
Figure 24.1	"William Morris Speaking from a Platform in Hyde Park," May 1894, Walter Crane	366
Figure 25.1	"May Day 1890," Walter Crane, published 1890. Courtesy of the Victoria and Albert Museum	372

Abbreviations

Bacon	Alan Bacon, ed., *The Relations of Art to Labour* (London: William Morris Society, 2004)
Cole	G. D. H. Cole, ed., *Selected Writings of William Morris* (London: Nonesuch Press, 1946)
CW	May Morris, ed., *The Collected Works of William Morris* (London: Longman's, Green, and Company, 1910–15)
Holland	Owen Holland, ed., *How I Became a Socialist* (London: Verso, 2020)
Jackson	Holbrook Jackson, *On Art and Socialism: Essays and Lectures by William Morris* (London: John Lehmann, 1947)
Kelvin	Norman Kelvin, ed., *The Collected Letters of William Morris* (Princeton: Princeton University Press, 1984–96)
LeMire	Eugene LeMire, ed., *The Uncollected Lectures of William Morris* (Detroit: Wayne State University Press, 1969)
MIA	Morris International Archive (a subdivision of the Marxists International Archive), marxists.org/archive/morris/index.htm, transcribed by Nicholas Salmon, Graham Seaman, and others
MM1 and MM2	May Morris, *William Morris: Artist, Writer, Socialist*, vols. 1 and 2 (Oxford: Basil Blackwell, 1936)
Morton	A. L. Morton, *Political Writings of William Morris* (London: Lawrence and Wishart, 1973)
Thompson	E. P. Thompson, *William Morris: Romantic to Revolutionary* (London: Lawrence & Wishart, 1955)
WMA	Florence S. Boos, ed., William Morris Archive, http://morrisarchive.lib.uiowa.org

Acknowledgments

This edition has benefited from the helpful suggestions and insights of many friends and Morris scholars. I am grateful to Frank C. Sharp for valuable tips on manuscript locations and background information, to Martin Stott for alerting me to the importance of Morris's "Town and Country," and to Mark Samuels Lasner for his provision of scans of original manuscripts. Stephen Williams located the newspaper report of "One Socialist Party" as well as other relevant items, and Graham Seaman provided helpful transcriptions of several essays on the Morris International Archive, located texts for several of Morris's periodical publications, and constructed the composite text of Morris's important speech to the 1889 Second International. I owe a special debt to Owen Holland for his helpful reviewer's suggestions on both the original proposal and the completed text for this edition.

I was also pleased to be invited to give an early version of my thoughts on these essays to the William Morris Society at Kelmscott House in March 2019. I thank the librarians at the British Library, the Society of Antiquaries, the Wilson Art Museum and Library, the International Institute of Social History in Amsterdam, and the Beinecke, Morgan, and Huntington Libraries for many forms of assistance, and the *Journal of Pre-Raphaelite Studies* and the *Journal of William Morris Studies* for permission to reproduce material previously published in their pages. It is also a pleasure to thank Sheila Jalving of Hampstead for her gracious hospitality during my visits on behalf of this collection, and Kimberly A. Maher, the Project Manager of the William Morris Archive, for her expert help in preparing the illustrations for this volume. I am grateful for the enthusiasm and meticulous help provided during the stages of publication by acquisitions editor Julian Wolfreys and the editors of Edinburgh University Press Michelle Houston and Susannah Butler. Finally, until his death earlier stages of this edition were aided by William Boos's editorial skills and commitment to the values inherent in Morris's works.

Florence S. Boos
Iowa City, Iowa and Gibsons, British Columbia, May 2022

Series Preface

The nineteenth century saw an unprecedented, prodigious production of literary texts. Many of these, often best-sellers or offering vital commentaries on cultural, political, and philosophical issues of the period engendering debate, did not survive in print long into the twentieth century, regardless of putative quality, however measured. Edinburgh Critical Editions of Nineteenth-Century Texts seeks to bring back to the reading public and the scholarly eye works of undeniable importance during the time of their first publication and reception, which have, often unjustly, disappeared from print and readers' consciousness. Covering fiction, long and short, nonfiction prose and essays, and poetry, with comprehensive critical introductions and carefully chosen supporting appendices, germane to the text and the context of the volume, Edinburgh Critical Editions of Nineteenth-Century Texts provides definitive, annotated scholarly reprints.

Frontispiece William Morris, 1887. Courtesy of the National Portrait Gallery

William Morris's Uncollected Political Essays: Equality, Nonviolence, and "One Socialist Party"

In addition to his work as artist, designer, poet, translator, fantasy writer, entrepreneur, and pioneer of the book arts, William Morris (1834–96) was also one of Britain's foremost campaigners on behalf of socialism from the time he joined the Social Democratic Federation in 1883 until his death in 1896. Nicholas Salmon, the modern editor of his essays for *Justice* and *Commonweal*, observes that Morris's "lecture campaign of 1883 to 1890 remains one of the most impressive ever undertaken by a British politician. In a seven year period he addressed over 1,000 meetings and was heard by as many as 250,000 people."[1] As the headnotes to these uncollected socialist essays confirm, these dates could be extended even further, from 1878 to 1896. Moreover, Morris brought to his political speeches and essays the same stylistic grace, exactitude, and sense of varied audiences that characterized his poetry, romances, and (in another register) his work as the proprietor of Morris & Co.

Morris was a prolific author whose works, despite extensive efforts, have never been entirely catalogued or published, and of his writings, his lectures and journalism remain perhaps the least fully represented in print. Morris published two volumes of his essays on art and politics in 1882 (*Hopes and Fears for Art*) and 1886 (*Signs of Change*), and had the Socialist League not broken up in 1890 or had he not died so early, he might well have issued another volume. By 1890 his health was failing, so that it is impressive that he managed as much effort for the socialist cause as he did during the 1890s, especially when one recalls that during this period he also continued residual work for Morris & Co., created designs for and directed the Kelmscott Press, composed and printed his late prose romances, helped prepare the *Saga Library*, managed a translation of *Beowulf* with A. J. Wyatt (1895), and systematically pursued the collection of incunabula and illuminated manuscripts as a legacy for his family.

Since Morris's death several efforts have been made to gather and publish a larger selection of his prose writings. May Morris was pressed by Morris's executors to limit the number of volumes in the *Collected*

Works, and so she only reproduced his already published essays in volumes 22 and 23 (1914–15). She therefore tried to pack all she could of the remaining material into the two volumes of her *William Morris: Artist, Writer, Socialist* (1936). All who study Morris owe much to the extensive compilations and background information in her 1334-page opus, which provided additional poems, translations, and many essays, but on occasion omitted the titles and opening passages of the latter in order to weave them into her narrative.

In addition, as Yuri Cowan has noted in "Morris as Book Collector,"[2] in their inventory of Morris's estate his executors failed to enumerate autograph and literary manuscripts, since these were seen as of limited financial value. May—trained chiefly as an embroiderer—was thus left largely on her own to organize Morris's writings. She omitted preparation of a full inventory before selling or giving away many autographs, with the result that in her editorial remarks she sometimes changed her mind about dates of composition after viewing previously displaced material, noted her lack of access to relevant manuscripts she had once owned, or parceled out her comments on earlier drafts in more than one place, obscuring their sequence.[3] In addition, several manuscripts of essays and lectures were sold to collectors and have ended up in repositories in New Haven, Connecticut, Pasadena, California, and elsewhere. In view of the great wealth of material Morris left behind, however, we can only be grateful that these disorderings were no worse. Without a key to what had once existed, dispersal could only add confusion, as occasional poems or essays were orphaned; complete works were fragmented into parts; successive early drafts of a work were separated from fair copies, printer's proofs, and published texts; and individual illuminated pages and even entire calligraphic manuscripts were distributed as gifts and eventually sold.[4]

Additional Morris essays have been gathered in *Architecture, Industry and Wealth* (1902), a collection of previously published articles chiefly on art and architecture edited by Sydney Cockerell and Robert Proctor; in *The Unpublished Lectures of William Morris* (1969), edited by Eugene LeMire; in *The Ideal Book: Essays and Lectures on the Art of the Book* (1982), edited by William Peterson; and in *Political Writings: Contributions to Justice and Commonweal, 1883–1890* (1994) and *Journalism: Contributions to Commonweal, 1885–1890* (1996), both edited by Nicholas Salmon; as well as several scattered individual essays mentioned in the bibliography. The meticulous checklists of Morris's speeches and essays in Eugene LeMire's *Unpublished Lectures* deserve special mention as a *sine qua non* for this collection, and I have tried to follow all his leads. Moreover, several volumes have made selections of Morris's essays available to the public, including G. D. H. Cole's *Selected Writings of William Morris* (1943); Holbrook Jackson's *On Art and Socialism: Essays and Lectures by William Morris* (1947); A. L. Morton's *Political Writings of William Morris* (1984); Gary Zabel's *Art and Society: Lectures and Essays by William Morris* (1993), Norman Kelvin's *William Morris on Art and Socialism* (1999), and Owen Holland's *How I Became a Socialist* (2020).[5] Many of Morris's essays are now also available digitally on the William Morris Archive (morrisarchive.lib.uiowa.edu) and the Morris Internet Archive (marxists.org/archive/Morris/index.htm).

William Morris on Socialism: Uncollected Essays gathers twenty-six anti-imperialist, socialist, and environmentalist essays, all but one of which are previously unpublished or not published in full in the collections of May Morris, Eugene LeMire, and Nicholas Salmon. Sixteen of these have been transcribed in whole or part from the original manuscripts, and others are taken from essays Morris published during the 1890s in *Justice*, *Liberty*, *Freedom*, *The New Review*, *The Forum*, the *Journal of Decorative Art*, and *Our Beautiful World*. I have also included "How I Became a Socialist," although reprinted elsewhere,[6] for its eloquence and importance, and one newspaper report, the *Labour Leader*'s account of Morris's last known socialist lecture, "One Socialist Party," delivered in January 1896. Morris's essays on art and architecture (both those published in periodicals during his lifetime and those remaining in manuscript) would ideally comprise another volume, as would his writings for the Society for the Protection of Ancient Buildings. Since Nicholas Salmon's *Political Writings . . . 1883–1890* and *Journalism . . . 1885–1890*, despite their combined 1342 pages, exclude many of Morris's *Commonweal* contributions as well as his later brief commentaries in the Hammersmith Socialist Society Record, a volume could also be gathered of his further political journalism. In addition, some Morris lectures not otherwise preserved were summarized at length in contemporary newspapers, and these accounts have likewise never been fully gathered and reprinted. A potential *Collected Essays and Journalism of William Morris* might therefore comprise many volumes. As mentioned, here I have chiefly concentrated on writings still in manuscript or published after Salmon's volumes leave off in 1890, since Morris's opinions on the contemporary political landscape in the final years of his life would seem of special interest. For reference, as an appendix to this volume I have included a checklist of Morris's already published political essays, excluding the indices of his *Justice* and *Commonweal* publications 1883–90 provided by Salmon.

After Morris's death his friend Edward Burne-Jones remarked to his studio assistant Thomas Rooke, "Top was all sunlight, he didn't have anything to hide, he wanted everything to be out in the open."[7] Accordingly his uncollected political writings lack startling or scandalous content. They do, however, chart the significant progression in Morris's thought, style, and public manner as he developed from an admittedly not very inspiring if earnest Liberal Party speaker in 1878 to an unillusioned but still-hopeful socialist in 1896. Often the innocuous titles or descriptions of early essays obscure quite revolutionary content, as in "A Lecture Delivered to the Men's and Women's College" ("Art and Inequality," no. 4) or "Speech at a Picture Show" (no. 7). They reveal that as early as his first essays he considered the condition of art chiefly as a reflection of contemporary social problems and advocated drastic change in the fundamental structures of society. The later essays moreover suggest, if they do not entirely clarify, what he believed would be the best means of achieving a socialist transformation of society in the altered political environment emerging at the time of his death.

* * *

Many years ago I published a small edition of Morris's unpublished manuscript poems, *The Juvenilia of William Morris*, and innocent of editorial practice, I normalized his punctuation and spelling. This evoked a rather blunt rebuke by a later editor of one of its poems, with my renderings chided as devoid of "manuscript authority." Some years later I issued Morris's "Our Country Right or Wrong" in a small William Morris Society edition, complete with all of Morris's punctuation omissions and spellings carefully noted, and this in turn evoked an online review by a British reader who commented, in effect, "Morris's essay itself is worth reading, but the text is deformed by the editor's constant pedantic intrusions." On balance I think the second critic was also correct, for the purpose of a modern edition is to render Morris's writings as readable as possible. It goes much against the grain for me to alter Morris's texts, the more so as his often nonstandard punctuation and paragraphing are arguably elements of his style. Thus I have largely followed the example of Eugene LeMire's *Unpublished Lectures* in lightly normalizing, correcting spellings, inserting paragraph breaks, and adding some necessary punctuation marks.

A further issue arises in that Morris often wrote two versions of a lecture with the same title but with a partially or substantially different text, only one of which has been published; for example, an early manuscript of "Gothic Architecture" overlaps some portion of the later text but seems of interest in its own right, even if not appropriate for separate publication, and these twinned versions appear in the

Essays section of the William Morris Archive. "The Relations of Art to Labour," a revised version of "Art and Labour," has been carefully edited by Alan Bacon and is included in this volume.

Consistency and development

Although as one might expect, Morris's speeches and essays over an eighteen-year period reflect an increasing sophistication of analysis and mark his responses to each stage of the socialist movement, they also reveal surprising consistencies. Anyone who would argue that Morris radically altered his principles or priorities in his last decade has not followed the nuances and qualifications of his thought as revealed in these essays. Over time he developed a more systemic analysis of injustice and emphasized the need for working-class leadership of any rebellion against the class system; he altered his predictions about whether the desired revolution would (not *should*) entail violence; he came to place greater hope in local elections and local political efforts in general; and as the socialist and labor movements of the 1880s and 90s became increasingly fractured, he devoted his final years to the advocacy of "one socialist party." However, several features of his thought seem constant throughout his political writings, and although his emphases alter and evolve with context, these guiding convictions and preoccupations remain. In what follows I will consider four consistent themes exhibited throughout these essays: Morris's anti-imperialism; his identification of socialism with radical equality; his warnings against destructive violence and commitment to peaceful revolution; and his preoccupation with the need for socialist unity, "one socialist party."

Anti-imperialism and opposition to colonial war

Morris's first three surviving political speeches ("Address to English Liberals," *AWS* 2, 370–82; no. 1, ["Against War with Russia"]; and no. 3, "Our Country Right or Wrong") were framed in opposition to a possible British war with Russia over the latter's seizure of land claimed by the Ottoman Empire. In this he closely followed the lead of W. E. Gladstone, who in 1876 had published an anti-interventionist treatise, *The Bulgarian Horrors and the Question of the East*, and who in 1880 campaigned strongly against British adventurism in Eastern Europe on both pragmatic and moral grounds. Addressed to Liberal Party audiences on behalf of the Eastern Question Association between January 1878 and January 1880, each of Morris's early talks exhibits an advance in organization and persuasiveness over its predecessors and manifests passionate opposition to the injustices of war. Disraeli biographer Paul Smith has characterized the Liberal Party's platform in the period leading up to the 1880 elections as an attack on Disraeli for involving Britain in "immoral, vainglorious and expensive external adventures, inimical to peace and to the rights of small peoples,"[8] subversive of domestic liberties and antithetical to reform, and Morris's speeches track these views. They also begin to formulate a more general argument against British foreign adventurism in the service of profit which remained a consistent feature of his later analyses of "commercialism" and the roots of inequality.

In ["Against War with Russia"] Morris attacked those fomenting an unjust war as well as those attracted to war in general: "I say that there is a war party. Nay a party of war at any price. . . . [T]he successful result of [a Tory War] would be the restoration of absolutism over people[']s armies in just insurrection." The war party is moreover composed of "a set of men whose interest it is either that we should sustain Turkey at any price, or that we should have a war with some one or another." He recalls the recently publicized 1876 Bulgarian massacre of Batak, in which 5,000 persons had been slaughtered by Ottoman troops, and suggests that to the "residuum of reactionists" a foreign war to prevent the liberation of Bulgaria would be welcome, "all the more as they and we well know that amid the confrontation and excitement of such a war many things will be forgotten here at home[,] many reforms put off: nay they may well hope that reaction will flourish amidst the rank growth of unreason and violence that is sure to spring up in the heart of an unjust war."

Morris's final surviving talk in opposition to an Anglo-Russian war, "Our Country Right or Wrong," was signed by him on January 30, 1880, directly before the March–April elections which returned the Liberal Party to power and Gladstone to five years of prime ministership. By 1880 he has broadened his attacks on British imperialism to include its treatment of Ireland ("a plain account of all our dealings with Ireland from Strongbow's time to Beaconsfield[']s . . . would not be either short or pleasant reading I fear"), as well as further ongoing wars in Afghanistan—"if ever war was waged for war[']s sake that has been"—and Africa—the Zulu war was "a war of which the very soldiers are heartily ashamed." Once again he sees imperial wars as an attempt to shore up reaction by diverting attention from domestic reforms: "I think history will put down [National Vain-Glory] to its right cause, an attempt to amuse the people with dramatic events abroad, while the drag is being put on democracy at home." A few years later he would follow Marx in also viewing such wars as a necessary byproduct of capitalism's hunger for expanding markets.

Although like its predecessor, this essay attacks jingoism as a compound of ignorance and self-conceit, Morris brings a new specificity and empathy to the topic as he appeals in personal terms to his audience:

> Yes, yes, how we wrap up facts in meaningless phrases till we forget most often what the facts are that they represent. Take . . . for example a very common sort of phrase that is used in dispatches of battles . . . 'the enemy's skirmishers annoyed us a little as we advanced.' . . . if you had been among the 'annoyed,' a life-time would not wipe it out from your memory: an army-surgeon would interpret the words for you best perhaps, yet we as we sit here can imagine it all pretty well if we try: . . . .

Britain's wars transgress basic fairness:

> Say 3 men shot stone dead: no great harm to them perhaps: but how would your hearts have been frozen with horror if you had seen that done in the New Road this afternoon, or if their bodies with the ragged holes in them through which the life had ebbed away had been brought into the place where you were at work and resting, and laid among the familiar things of common life: or was there no one waiting for them to come home again?

Though it ends with a brief appeal to his audience to vote for "Peace, Retrenchment and Reform," echoing current Liberal Party slogans, "Our Country" passes beyond the partisan concerns of Morris's earlier talk to mount a case against foreign invasions and needless violence more broadly. Striking, too, is his early formulation of "what all political action should tend towards in the long run":

> I think of a country where every man has work enough to do, and no one has too much: where no man has to work himself stupid in order to be just able to live: . . . where every man's work would be pleasant to himself and helpful to his neighbour; and then his leisure from bread-earning work . . . would be thoughtful and rational: for you understand he would be thoroughly educated, whatever his condition. . . . justice to himself & all others would be no mere name to him, but the rule of all his actions, the passionate desire of his life. . . .

Though this is not the egalitarian socialism Morris would later espouse nor the fully developed communal template of *News from Nowhere*, "Our Country" nonetheless presents a holistic vision which presses firmly against the limits of "peace, retrenchment and reform."

Several lectures of Morris's early socialist period emphasize the systemic connections between competition, inequality, and foreign war. His 1885 essay "Commercial War," for example, reflects a new emphasis on the interrelatedness of contemporary social problems, likely intensified by his readings in Marx and other Marx-derived texts.[9] Here he seeks to identify the motive force behind human exploitation; no longer is this merely the greed of individual men, or even of a class of men and their corrupt mouthpieces, but the entire *system* which organizes all economic life. His remarks are infused with autobiographical resonance:

> While this commercial war lasts we are all the slaves of it, not the working-classes only, but all of us[,] however grand we may think ourselves; men of science, literary men, artists, we all wear the chain. I know by sad experience that intelligence, enthusiasm, knowledge of history, patience, years of hard work can contrive or accomplish nothing outside that charmed circle of slavery. . . .

Such "commercial war" is all-engulfing, creating massive waste, destroying nature and art, enslaving domestic laborers, and motivating "the frequency[,] persistency and bare-faced cynicism of these wars of exploitation of barbarous countries . . . these last few years":

> For once again I tell you that our present system is . . . a tyranny: one and all of us in some way or another we are drilled to the service of Commercial War; . . . it is for this that we are overworked[,] are made to fear starvation, live in hovels, are herded and jammed up into foul places called towns, while the houses in the countryside fall into ruins, and once fertile fields go uncultivated. . . . : it is for this that we let our money, our name, our power, be used to drag off poor wretches from our pinched fields & our dreadful slums, to kill & be killed in a cause they know nothing of.

He also provides one of his fuller indictments of the motives of Britain's foreign wars, masked by dishonest pieties and racism:

> [T]his cause of civilization simply means spreading to countries which are developing on their own lines . . . the curse of exploitation which we ourselves are suffering from . . . . Still more noteworthy it is that the Commercial liberals . . . [are] aiding and abetting this war, and crying out for annexation of whatever is annexable, and [are] not ashamed to take up one after another all the old jingo cries, finishing up with a grand scheme for

> creating a new fanaticism, a new religion, the foundation of a holy race, mongrel indeed in fact, but in theory and name Anglo-Saxon, which should be prepared to contend for the mastery of the whole world against all comers.

Perhaps his most dramatic statement on imperial wars, however, is his eloquent tirade against the wastefulness of capitalism in his 1885 "Socialism":

> At Manchester lately I was told that it was the general opinion . . . that the one thing needed to amend the Depression of Trade was a great European war so that some of the surplus wealth might be destroyed. One's brain whirls at the enormity of the confession of helplessness or stupidity in the present system which this involves. What! You have created too much wealth? You cannot give away the overplus; nay you cannot even carry it out into the fields and burn it there and go back again merrily to make some more of what you don't want; but you must actually pick a sham quarrel with other people & slay 100,000 men to get rid of wares which when [got rid?] of you are still intent on producing with as much ardour as heretofore.

The speeches of Morris's last decade are more preoccupied with outlining the features of a socialist, communal society ("How Shall We Live Then," 1889) and with advocating socialist unity ("What We Have to Look For," 1895) than with reiterating the relationship between capitalist domestic exploitation and foreign wars. However, in his last public lecture on a political topic, "One Socialist Party," delivered to a Social Democratic Federation audience, he reproves the injustices and overreach of British adventurism. The choice of topic for this venue may not be accidental, since the S. D. F.'s leader, Henry Hyndman, was an opponent of Irish Home Rule and a supporter of England's colonial expansion who believed England's colonies were "the special heritage of our working class."[10] E. P. Thompson observes that "the response of the S. D. F. to imperialism was contradictory" (777), and Morris's remarks address this ambivalence frontally in a reminder of the need for international solidarity.

As reported in the *Labour Leader*, he first notes that anxiety about a British war with the United States over a Canadian boundary line is groundless, for the two imperialist powers share a vested interest in capitalist trade. Moreover, any difficulties Britain may face in defending Canadian land claims are entirely self-imposed, for England has no business in maintaining a North American colony. Worse is British hypocrisy in claiming moral superiority to the Boers in their treatment of South Africans; the Boers had stolen the land from its people and welcomed British help in "developing" what they had stolen, and "if they could manage it, [the English] would steal from the Boers in turn." Moreover Europeans were "developing" Africa with a vengeance, resembling "a pack of thieves quarreling over their booty." These insights seem sadly prophetic in the light of Britain's future relations with its colonies in South Africa, Ghana, Gambia, Southern Cameroon, Lesotho, Nigeria, Swaziland, Kenya, Sierra Leone, and what are now Tanzania, Zambia, Malawi, Botswana, and Zimbabwe. Morris's basic abhorrence of both violence and injustice thus caused him to oppose consistently all the colonial wars of his era and to proclaim an anti-imperialist stance as an integral part of socialist internationalism.

Radical equality

Morris's socialism and communism were grounded in a conviction of radical human equality; that is, he was unable to conceive of the existence of socialism in any meaningful sense without true equality between persons of all abilities and personal qualities. In this intransigence, he was of course temperamentally different from many reformists of his day, such as the Fabians, and it was this interpretation of socialism as a doctrine of egalitarian fellowship which motivated his views on specific socialist tactics. As he said in his eloquent 1894 retrospective, "How I Became a Socialist":

> Now this view of Socialism which I hold to-day, and hope to die holding, is what I began with: . . . nor when I had become conscious of the wrongs of society as it now is, and the oppression of poor people, could I have ever believed in the possibility of a *partial* setting right of those wrongs. In other words, I could never have been such a fool as to believe in the happy and "respectable" poor.

The motivations of his socialist commitment were emotional and moral, as seen in the troubled discomfort of such early pre-socialist essays as his 1880 ["Art and Inequality"], in which he deplores the gulf between classes: "a difference not of title, position, or the like, but of manners, habits of thought and aspirations." So great is this inequality that it would have been better had society never evolved from a more primitive state; and Morris urges his audience to hope for radical change, for "so also are we best preparing the arts for that greater equality of Society to which I am sure the world must come at last. . . ." Similarly, in April 1884 he appealed to an audience of philanthropic and working-class attenders at an East End art exhibition:

> I am told that serious people of good will amongst the cultivated classes have been used to attend here of evenings to explain these works of art to the uncultivated who come to see them: a sad business, a woeful admission that seems to me. . . only I must ask what must be done before we can meet before a wall covered with pictures on an equality . . . . ("Speech at a Picture Show")

Morris first public lecture to include the word "socialism" in its title was delivered in January 1884 ("Art and Socialism"[11]), and his lectures from 1884 onwards appeal for socialism as a condition of equality and the provision of due work and leisure for all. In his 1885 "Socialism," for example, he notes the distortions of class hierarchy:

> In sober earnest I say that no man is good enough to be master over others; whatever the result to them, it at least ruins him: equality of fellowship is necessary for developing the innate good and restraining the innate evil which exists in every one.

A Benthamite "happiness of the greatest number" is too low a standard; socialism must instead

> offer a chance of happiness to every one; that is to say, an opportunity for the full development of each human life: it denies the title of society to any system which degrades one class to exalt another; . . . an injury to one will be an injury to all. . . .

It may be surprising that only one of Morris's speeches was explicitly titled "Equality," though he delivered it eight times between 1888 and 1890. In this lecture Morris sets out his most stringent requirement for a truly socialist society:

> Let me begin then . . . by telling you what the nature of my ideal as a Socialist is. . . . it is complete equality of condition for all. That is to my mind the aim of Socialism stated in the fewest possible words: any sacrifice that is necessary for its attainment is worth making: no further mastery over the powers of nature that we may gain can be a substitute for it; without it freedom, education, happiness, in one word, progress, is impossible. . . . we *must* attain it, there is no second course open to us, whatever great change as yet undreamed of lies before the world must be reached through this . . . .

It would be difficult to be more emphatic—for Morris socialism demands the complete eradication of all classes and hierarchies, what he will later call "communism":

> . . . I must now tell you what I mean by *equality* . . . I have advisedly used the phrase equality *of condition:* for of course I admit that it is no more possible that men should be equal in capacity or desires or temperament than that they should be equal in stature or weight: but in fact if there were not this inequality in this sense I doubt if we could have equality of condition . . . .
>
> No one can expect to find the virtues of free men in slaves . . . . That is the reason why I am here speaking to you about equality; I do not speak to you about it as a mere abstraction, but as a thing quite practical, and indeed the *only* practical political matter, that which lies at the root of all our politics.

Moreover, equality is a necessary precondition for authentic human relationships:

> Do we not understand the pleasures of fellowship, the joy of converse with our equals: the advantage of the give and take which ought always to be between two [persons] good-tempered and useful to society, whatever the different caliber of their minds may be?

And in his 1889 lecture "How Shall We Live Then," he addresses head-on the issue of sustainability: 'We may have in appearance to give up a great deal of what we have been used to call material progress, in order that we may be freer, happier and more completely equal.' Finally, compromise is impossible, for "[s]urely there are but two theories of society; slavery on the one side; equality on the other."

The essays and speeches of Morris's final years increasingly probe the issue of values: why should he and his audiences espouse a radical socialism rather than any of the more palliative reformist movements of the day? In his 1894 article for the anarchist publication *Liberty*, "Why I Became a Communist," he defines his subject clearly:

> It remains to ask what real Communism is, and the answer is simple: it is a state of Society the essence of which is Practical Equality of condition . . . . This is its economical basis; its ethical basis is the habitual and full recognition of man as a social being, so that it brings about the habit of making no distinction between the common welfare and the welfare of the individual . . . . In short I can see no other system under which men can live together except these two, Slavery and Equality.

In addition, he looks forward to a stage beyond what is now meant by socialism to a classless society, since in "a [socialist] society tending toward equality," over time "the position of complete equality as to condition will be accepted without question."

Morris delivered "What We Have to Look For" twice in 1895, the year before his death. Here he warns that immediate politics are only a necessary means to an end. If one's sole aim is a less burdensome life for oneself under the present system, there is no need to resist one's "masters," but those with a "wild fancy" for freedom will seek something far better:

> to have their affairs under their own control; . . . to work happily and unwastefully, restore what of the earth's surface which is spoilt and keep that which is unspoilt, to enjoy rest and thought and labour without fear or remorse, . . . let them say, . . . let us use [our wages] now as best we may, yet not so much for the present profit we may get out of them as for hastening the realization of the new Society, the time when at last we shall be free because we are equal.

A *Justice* article published the same year, "Change of Position – Not Change of Condition," acknowledges the difficulty of persuading desperate workers to seek long-term goals: "it is so hard for them in their miserable condition to have any vivid conception of what a life of freedom and equality can give them that they can scarcely . . . turn their hopes to a future which they may never see." Yet ironically, Morris argues, it is only by "the abolition of privilege and the realization of equality" that workers can actually effect a change in their immediate circumstances.

Finally, in his last political essay published before his death, his 1896 "The Present Outlook of Socialism in England," Morris returns to the issue of what constitutes a true socialism. As often his words intertwine encouragement with admonition and the sense of darker possibilities. He first celebrates a recent change in public sentiment that "points toward a new society founded on equality of condition, and the association of equals." An authentically socialist party can have but one basis, however: "a simple text in accordance with one aim, the realization of a new society founded on the practical equality of condition for all, and general association for the satisfaction of the needs of those equals." Such an outcome is only prospective, however, and dependent on a not-yet-achieved socialist unity; for "unless [these egalitarian principles] are once again to become the root principles of a true society, I for my part can see nothing for it but a continuous degradation of our false society until it disappears in a chaos caused by greed and suffering." Morris's religion of socialist equality, then, is closely tied to his views on another important topic, the relationship between violence and "the Social Revolution."

Disruption, violence, and the social revolution

"Social Revolution" was a term Morris employed throughout his writings, from his "Speech at a Picture Show" in 1884 to "How I Became a Socialist" in 1894. Not surprisingly after the revolutions of the twentieth century, it has been assumed retrospectively that the events that Morris envisioned in the term "revolution" would be violent, or at least, like the Paris Commune, an essentially peaceful, democratic assumption of power later brutally repressed by the reactionary governments of its day. This accords with the events of the prospectively retrospective chapter "How the Change Came" in Morris's 1890 *News from Nowhere*; here, after democratically chosen representatives have become a de facto government of the people, the official upper-class government initiates an extended guerrilla-like war against the supporters of the people's "committees of public safety."

Morris's essays and lectures, however, present a generally apprehensive view of violence and manifest increasing uncertainty over the issue of whether this may be avoided. Despite his conviction of the need for radical transformation, he fears that in the absence of a coherent worker-led socialist party with principled aims and broad support, any social explosions precipitated by injustice may lead to yet greater evils, suffering, and even setbacks for the socialist cause. As early as his 1880 "Art and Inequality," he enjoins his hearers to help England palliate or, at best, cure its social divisions, for "history has taught us what happens to nations that do less and worse than this: and the terrible vengeance that time stores up for them . . . ." Though present-day Europe may be spared, "the prospect must remain dark and doubtful before us."

Indeed, the forces of commerce may even propel a destructive war, with uncertain although potentially somewhat hopeful results, as he suggests in the 1885 "Commercial War": "And if by chance the great capitalist and despotic communities are to meet in a huge all[-]embracing conflict, I don't believe . . . that the new heavens and the new earth . . . will turn out to be the paradise of exploitation which the Imperialist liberals have figured to themselves." However in "Socialism," also in 1885, he reminds a working-class audience that, although he believes the reactionary forces of society would be compelled to yield to a widespread threat of revolt, it remains equally imperative to prevent "the waste and misery of civil war":

> [R]emember that it can only be avoided by the combination and organization of all that is most energetic, most orderly, most kindly, most aspiring among the working classes. . . . Take note then, working men, that the Revolution, the change in the basis of society, must come, and choose whether there shall be a transition period of violence, confusion and chaos, or whether we shall glide into the great [change] peaceably because obviously irresistibly.

In his 1888 "Equality," perhaps chastened by his experiences in the Socialist League and the slow progress of "making socialists," Morris assesses the difficulties which will impede his fellow socialists in attaining their aims. Regretfully he notes that the workers as presently constituted seem unprepared to lead a transformed society:

> [T]hough the workers are more useful than the idlers, yet they too are corrupted and degraded by their position. No one can expect to find the virtues of free men in slaves. No, if the present state of Society merely breaks up without a conscious effort at transformation, the end, the fall of Europe, may be long in coming, but when it does come it will be far more terrible, far more confused and full of suffering than the period of the fall of Rome.

A so-called populist uprising without guiding principles would be revolution betrayed, and as one thinks ahead to twentieth-century Europe and beyond, Morris's warnings seem prescient.

In an essay delivered five times during 1889–90, "How Shall We Live Then," Morris likewise expresses apprehension about an immediate cataclysm, however desirable its ultimate effects. In the present competitive system one must live "in one or the other of two opposed camps of enemies, which we feel certain must one day fall upon each other, ruining many a hope and many a quiet life in the process." He returns to similar warnings in several essays of the 1890s, most urgently in the wake of several incidents of alleged anarchist violence. In the 1892 "Communism, i.e. Property," he responds to the fact that earlier in the year several anarchists had been arrested in Walsall and London and charged with attempting to construct a bomb:

> In short I do not believe in the possible success of revolt until the Socialist party has grown so powerful in numbers that it can gain its end by peaceful means, and that therefore what is called

> violence will never be needed . . . . As to the attempt of a small minority to terrify a vast majority into accepting something which they do not understand, by spasmodic acts of violence, mostly involving the death or mutilation of non-combatants, I can call that nothing else than sheer madness. And here I will say once for all, what I have often wanted to say of late, to wit that the idea of taking any human life for any reason whatsoever is horrible and abhorrent to me.

The argument for nonviolence is made not only on moral but also pragmatic grounds:

> There is no royal road to revolution or the change in the basis of society. To make the workers conscious of the disabilities which beset them; to make them conscious of the dormant power in them for the removal of these disabilities, to give them hope and an aim and organization to carry out their aspirations. Here is work enough for the most energetic; it is the work of patience, but nothing can take the place of it. And *moreover it is being done*, however slowly, however imperfectly.

When invited to publish in an anarchist periodical, *Liberty*, Morris used the occasion to promote peaceful resistance. In his 1894 "Why I Am a Communist," he asserts that the final goal of socialism is a condition in which operatives own the markets and means of production, so that a "period of incomplete Socialism will, I believe, gradually melt into true Communism without any violent change." This he expects may be obtained peacefully "by using the vote," rather than by precipitating a single, cataclysmic event:

> In the first place I do not (who does really) believe in Catastrophical Communism. That we shall go to sleep on Saturday in a Capitalistic Society and wake on Monday to a Communistic Society is clearly an impossibility. Again I do not believe that our end will be gained by open war; for the executive will be too strong for even an attempt at such a thing to be made until the change has gone so far, that it will be too weak to dare to attack the people by means of direct physical violence.

By contrast he again underlines his objection to violence: "I am opposed to Anarchism then (among other reasons) because it forbids the use of the only possible method [persuasion] for bringing about the great change from privilege and inequality and property to equality and general wealth."

Morris returns to these points in his 1895 essay, "What We Have to Look For," a reassessment of the current prospects of socialism addressed to socialist audiences. He notes sarcastically that "the idea of successful insurrection within a measurable distance of time is only in the heads of the anarchists, who seem to have a strange notion that even equality would not be acceptable if it were not gained by violence only." Nonetheless "[a]lmost everyone [else] has ceased to believe in the change coming by catastrophe," a noticeable change from a period in which

> [he and others] thought that the change we advocated would be brought about by insurrection; and this was supposed even by those who were most averse to violence: no other means seemed conceivable for lifting the intolerable load which lay upon us.

Morris next states the current dominant position carefully: "Socialists hope so far to conquer public opinion, that at last a majority of the parliament shall be sent to sit in the house as avowed Socialists and the delegates of Socialists." On balance he accepts that this change represents progress:

> Well, since battle also has been made a matter of commerce, and the God of War must now wear a mantle of bank-notes and be crowned with guineas, since human valour must give way to the longest purse, and the latest invention (which I do not much complain of since it makes it more difficult to exercise the accursed art of destruction and slaughter), since war has been commercialized, I say, we shall as above said not be called upon to gain our point by battle in the field.

As his tone suggests, however, Morris has reservations. In contrast to his message in "Why I Am A Communist," delivered the previous year to an anarchist audience, he here expresses the fear that so profound a revolution in social relations cannot be entirely peaceful:

> But the disturbance and the suffering – can we escape that? I fear not . . . . Can that combat be fought out again I say without loss and suffering? Plainly speaking I *know* that it cannot.

Any true change would provoke resistance from the current masters, and might even temporarily disrupt the livelihoods of workers who at present engage in "the production of useless articles." Once again Morris appeals to his audience to seek realistic as well as long-term goals; for, though their aim may be to "gradually get a majority in the House of Commons," this cannot be done until "the thinking part of the population will have gone Socialist." To attain this requires "a genuine Socialist Party," and until this entity exists, "we had better confine ourselves to the old teaching and preaching of Socialism pure and simple, which is I fear more or less neglected amidst the said futile attempt to act as a party when we have no party."

Once again, revolution can only be reached by persuasion, what in "Why I Am a Communist" he had called "mak[ing] Socialists," and in "Communism, i.e., Property," "the work of patience." His final recorded statement on this subject is preserved in the transcript of his 1896 speech to a Social Democratic Federation (SDF) audience. The SDF had on occasion seemed supportive of violence, and Morris enjoins his listeners instead to wage revolution by peaceful means and eschew counterproductive attacks:

> In conclusion, he would urge upon them the necessity for ever keeping before the people the broad, deep, reasonable side of the question, otherwise it would one day come upon them all with suffering, misery and violence, in ways which would be worst instead of best.
>
> Let them gain their cause by reason, i.e. the force of principles and the force of intelligence.

Thus, although Morris's predictions regarding how socialists can most likely gain their ends varied slightly over the years, he consistently advocated against "cataclysm" and in favor of an orderly and peaceful revolution. His views on violence are thus quite consistent both with his opposition to imperialist militarism as a form of unjust oppression and his view that the basis of revolution must be equality itself within a society of fellowship.

Socialist unity: one socialist party

The issue of socialist unity seemed less urgent in the early period of modern British socialism, when, as Morris notes in his address to the International Socialist Workers Conference in Paris in 1889, "Just six years ago there was no socialism in England except some remnants of the old Chartist movement." And in his 1895 "What We Have to Look For," he recalled that "[i]n the early days of our movement we had nothing to think of seriously except preaching Socialism to those who knew nothing of it but the name, if indeed they knew that."

For Morris the Socialist League itself would have been the best candidate for a unified socialist party between 1885 and 1890. However as the League fractured, on the one hand losing its influential

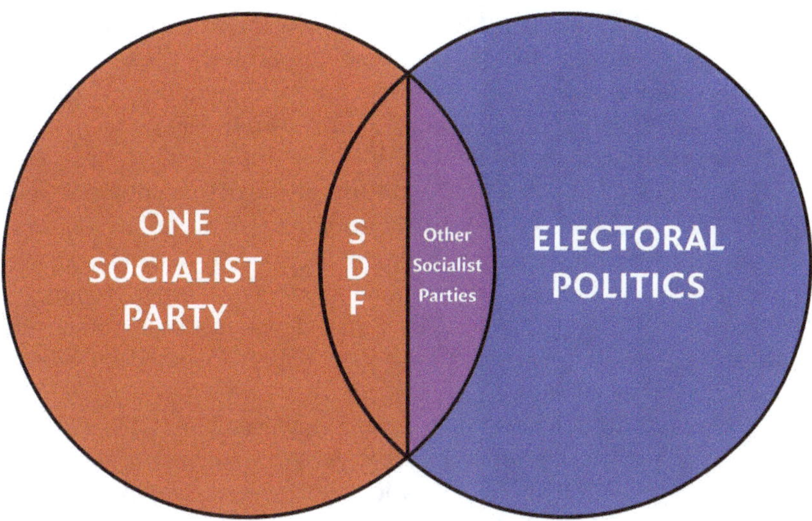

Figure I.1 One Socialist Party

Bloomsbury Branch as the latter pursued a more electoral strategy, and on the other succumbing entirely to an "actionist" variant of anarchism, Morris was left without a central socialist organization with which he could identify, though he remained active on behalf of the former Hammersmith Branch of the Socialist League, now reorganized as the Hammersmith Socialist Society. It is to his credit that, although in failing health, he initiated efforts to promote cooperation between as many of the remaining disparate socialist groups as possible.

In late 1892 the Hammersmith Socialist Society delegated Morris and others to meet with representatives of the Fabian Society and the SDF "to promote the alliance of Socialist organizations in Great Britain." Perhaps realistically, after the recent factionalizations among socialist groups, Morris proposed a federation of autonomous organizations and drafted a proposed manifesto.[12] In the end, however, the Fabians rejected the manifesto, and although Morris argued for the inclusion of the newly formed Independent Labour Party (ILP), Hyndman refused to permit its representatives to be invited, and so by summer 1893 the effort had lapsed. During the next three years Morris followed the electoral activities of the ILP with distant interest, but by contrast actively sought friendly relations with the SDF, which he praised for its continued commitment to socialism defined as the control of resources by workers. On the electoral front he supported his daughter May Morris's 1894 candidacy for the London Vestry on a united "Progressive" platform, and, more importantly, spoke on behalf of George Lansbury, an SDF candidate for Parliament from Walworth (and later Labour Party leader 1932–5) in 1894 and 1895.

Between 1891 and 1896 Morris gave approximately nineteen political lectures,[13] and in addition contributed articles to political periodicals such as *Justice*, *Freedom*, and *Liberty*. As mentioned above, these speeches and articles were targeted to his specific audiences, as he repeatedly urged them to seek common ground with other socialists—not to negate their individual efforts and viewpoints, but to focus on common pragmatic goals and long-term efforts to empower worker autonomy and ownership.

In October 1891 Morris delivered "Socialism Up to Date" to an audience of workers organized by the Ancoats Recreation Committee in Manchester. His final peroration is preserved only as a series of notes, but it seems pointed that he does not advocate for his listeners to join any particular socialist organization as such. Instead he merely asserts that workers should combine to support "the new labour party-agitation" and "take their own business in hand including all responsibilities." A further reference to a more general movement reappears in his August 1892 talk, "Communism, i.e. Property," in which Morris asserts that claims to private property are a form of theft from the laborers who create all wealth. In arguing for the necessity of education rather than violence as the means to revolution, he appeals to socialists in general as "the Socialist party": "I do not believe in the possible success of revolt until the Socialist party has grown so powerful in numbers that it can gain its end by peaceful means."

As we have seen, in 1893 Morris led efforts to unite England's explicitly socialist parties, and his desire for the ultimate inclusion of all socialists in a cooperative effort is reflected in his March 31 address to the Hammersmith Socialist Society, "What We Have to Look For." His message is nonetheless multitiered and qualified: although there should be a united socialist party in Britain, this can only occur after "the thinking part of the population will have gone Socialist," whereas at present the socialist movement consists of sometimes opposed factions as well as other amorphously "unattached socialists and semi-socialists." The question then arises, "are we to be a sect or a party?" Surely the answer must be the latter:

> . . . you see we have settled that we want to go into parliament, and for that it seems to me a party is definitely necessary; . . . such a party once formed which would not break up any existing bodies but include them, would, it seems to me, have a claim

> on all genuine socialists, and one thing at least I am sure of, that until it is formed, though we may do good propagandist work we shall do nothing worth speaking of in the political way. My hope is, and if people really care for socialism enough, it will be realized, that we shall do so much propagandist work, and convert so many people to socialism, that they will insist on having a genuine Socialist Party which shall do the due work . . . .

This would seem to settle the matter, but not so: contemporary socialists are too fragmented and disorganized to have achieved significant results. Moreover, the task of "making Socialists" remains incomplete:

> Well, it may be some time before we can have that party, because we shall have to wait till the general body of socialists see the futility of mere sections attempting to do the work of the whole mass properly organized. Meantime . . . I think that until we can do our party-work effectively, we had better leave off the pretence of doing it at all.

Instead, "we had better confine ourselves to the old teaching and preaching of Socialism pure and simple, which is I fear more or less neglected amidst the said futile attempt to act as a party when we have no party." Thus, although the claim that Morris came to support electoral campaigns on behalf of socialist parliamentary candidates is largely accurate, as we have seen, yet this support also came with distinct qualifications as to the realism, timing, and necessary principles for such political efforts. As in past years Morris seeks consistently to energize a movement rather than merely to promote electoral candidates.

In the last year of his life Morris returned twice to the subject of a united socialist party. On January 3, 1896 he delivered a talk to the SDF on the topic of "One Socialist Party," a transcription of which was published in the ILP newspaper *The Labour Leader.* It is possible that the transcription is somewhat incomplete, for Morris's words as recorded do not identify the "one socialist party" of the title. Although he praises the SDF for "holding aloft the real flag of revolution" and agrees that electoral political action is necessary, he notably fails to identify the ideal of "one socialist party" with his SDF audience. Instead, he reiterates his own priorities—"after all he was of the opinion, and always had been, that the main thing Socialists had to do was to make other socialists"—and he urges his hearers to be more active, "to hit out, and show they were alive," to avoid side issues and pedantry, to maintain socialist principles more broadly, and to seek to "gain their cause by reason" rather than force. In short, he challenges them to develop the qualities needed for a wider future socialist effort.

Morris's final published essay, "The Present Outlook of Socialism in England," appeared in April 1896 only six months before his death. That the article had been solicited for an American periodical, *The Forum*, may have encouraged him to frame his remarks in the most explicit and definite terms for a wide audience. He finds in the recent elections which had brought electoral gains for the "reactionists" (the Conservative Party)[14] a sign of the consolidation of the hitherto dominant parties, a shift which will leave room for a new, more socialist party to arise:

> the answer to [the reactionists'] attack should be to organize a real definite Socialist party. . . . It is true that a wide-spread opinion cannot be defeated, and need not fear the temporary decision of the ballot-box; but to such a decision it must come at last. . . . Socialism has not yet formed a party in Great Britain, but it is essential that it should do so.

His conclusion blends prescription and contingent hope:

> This Socialist party must include the whole of the genuine labour movement, that is, whatever in it is founded on principle, and is not a mere temporary business squabble; it must also include all that is definitely Socialist amongst the middle class; and it must have a simple text in accordance with one aim, – the realization of a new society founded on the practical equality of condition for all, and general association for the satisfaction of the needs of those equals.
>
> The sooner this party is formed, and the reactionists find themselves face to face with the Socialists, the better. For whatever checks it may meet with on the way, it will get to its goal at last and Socialism will melt into society.

In this final essay Morris has not altered his conviction that a true progressive party must be socialist, and that without a change in public opinion a socialist society cannot come into being, but he is hopeful at the recent signs of an increased desire for change emerging in the political landscape. As in his presentation of his other desired political goals—peace, internationalism, equality, and nonviolent revolution—Morris thus balances the presentation of an ideal with realism in assessing the current progress made toward its realization. Moreover, his opinions are very carefully nuanced, so that without hostility he continues to prod his various audiences forward toward a more unified, more activist, more realistic, and, above all, a more socialist electoral and post-electoral future.

Coda: religion

An aspect of Morris's thought less often considered is his view of religion. He found meaningful elements in medieval religion, as presented in the moving central figure of *A Dream of John Ball*, whose sermon on fellowship as life remains one of its author's most eloquent statements of his own convictions; and among his publications at the Kelmscott Press he included medieval religious texts such as the *Biblia Innocentium* and *Psalmi Penitentiales*.[15] In the coauthored *Socialism: Its Growth and Outcome* he and Ernest Belfort Bax suggested that a future socialist society would practice a "Religion of Humanity."[16] Nonetheless passages in these uncollected essays from the late 1880s onwards indicate his clear view that at the present time institutional religion constituted a retardant on progressive thought.

Morris's 1888 lecture on "Equality" introduces this new strand of thought, the identification of religion with political reaction, a view largely absent from his published collections. According to this interpretation, society's original sin was a belief in hierarchy, with its ultimate Hierarch a postulated supreme being. For Morris radicalism had at least been useful in eliminating the feudal idea "of a divinely appointed government," though its modern descendant remained, "the claim of an aristocracy of intellect to govern the average man for his own good, even if he suffers by it." The latter phrases seem a swipe at the increasingly influential Fabians, who since their inception in 1884 had agitated in favor of meritocratic government by an educated elite.

Morris returned to the topic of religion again in 1892 in his "Communism, i.e. Property," a talk delivered to the Hammersmith Socialist Society that at his death remained unpublished and in somewhat rough and informal form. After noting that the changes brought by greater "conquest over material nature" have actually worsened rather than improved life by exaggerating the contrasts between rich and poor," he notes another irony. Even the decline of religious authority with its claim of a divinely ordained natural order has similarly failed to improve social conditions:

> Religious tradition also hampers us but little; or need not, save the double-faced hypocrisy has now another double face, . . . for atheism stands by its old foe orthodoxy to strike a blow together with it, against true freedom & in favor of monopoly. . . .

> Religion is gone down the wind, and will no more cumber us unless we are open fools.[17]

Morris might well have clarified or revised this passage had he prepared the essay for publication, but here it stands.

A final deprecatory mention of religion appears briefly in his final political essay, the 1896 "The Present Outlook of Socialism in England." The first section of Morris's article provides a retrospective of British political history since the Whig revolution, in which Morris finds the seeds both of the French Revolution and of the modern "factory organization of production amidst the ruins of handicraft." What might have seemed progress in the political sphere was advancing, and "modern democracy, on the basis of irresistible, nay unquestionable, commercialism, seemed to be on the very point of being firmly established." British democracy faced a check, however:

> It is true that in Britain religion lagged behind, and the "free-thinking," which had long been accepted as an essential part of the Whig revolution on the continent, was here revolutionary and unrespectable, as an open and expressed opinion, though even then almost universal amongst intelligent persons. For the deep-seated hypocrisy of our nation (and perhaps race), which has often, wrongly as I think, been dignified with the historical title of "Puritanism," would not allow facts to be faced openly on this side of things.

These are strong words, especially when placed in the opening paragraph of an article intended to attract converts to socialism, and apparently reflect Morris's long-standing distaste for the social censure of "open and expressed opinion(s)" of religious skepticism.

* * *

In conclusion, throughout these essays we have seen Morris develop from a formal and conventional, if sincere, political speaker with an abhorrence of British imperial wars into a fierce opponent of an encompassing "commercial system," a congeries of profit-driven processes which limit and embitter the lives of all. At this middle stage he also posited the need for radical equality, later to be called "communism," and this emphasis remained central and nonnegotiable in his pronouncements to the end. As he turned his mind to tactics, he continued to remind audiences that only workers could achieve their own equality, that palliatives were not true socialism and might even impede its attainment, and increasingly, that violence without equality would not be revolution, but rather a reckoning of "suffering, misery, and violence" ("One Socialist Party"). Only the transformation of desires, "the making of Socialists," could create a new society.

Freed from the constraints of Socialist League factionalism and slowed by deteriorating health, throughout the 1890s Morris attempted to fulfill his own dictum, "let us . . . be at peace amongst ourselves, that we may the better wage war against the monopolist" ("The Socialist Ideal," *CW*, 276), and his remarks often became personal as he reached out to his varied audiences to assert common ideals. These later essays adjust to changing political times in their hopeful but still-qualified suggestion that partial reforms may be a first step toward wider social transformation, their satisfaction at the electoral victories of socialists in local councils, and their support of candidates put forth by the Socialist League's former competitor, the SDF. In advocating firmly for "one socialist party"—a broad tent inclusive of those traversing different paths but with common aims—rather than for a particular strand among the several emerging social and political movements of the 1890s, Morris acknowledges that he cannot predict which of the many potential paths to socialism may prove effective in the new century.

Yet honest uncertainty regarding tactics enabled him to focus with unwavering conviction on the sole ends of political effort, an equal and unfettered life for all. In his 1889 Paris speech Morris had praised the "idealism" of the British socialist movement, which in his view had protected it from narrow aims. Accordingly, in his final speeches and essays Morris left an eloquent legacy of balanced warning and hope, one likely to remain relevant for as long as humans strive for a more just and equitable life both within and outside of the political structures of their day.

Notes

1. William Morris, *The Political Writings: Contributions to* Justice *and* Commonweal, *1883–1890*, ed. Nicholas Salman (Bristol: Thoemmes Press, 1994), xlviii, xlvi. I have reversed the order of sentences.
2. *Routledge Companion to William Morris* (New York: Routledge, 2020), 489–500.
3. For example, in MM2, May Morris notes of the drafts of *Sigurd the Volsung*: "Some of the drafts are in the British Museum and others in private hands and not available to the public . . . . I have already shortly described the British Museum MSS, (*Collected Works*, Vol. XII) which consist of the fair copy of the poem and two note-books of great interest as showing how the work was built up. They should really be considered together with the six note-books and loose leaves now to be described, which came into my hands later" (478–9).
4. For the dispersal of Morris's manuscripts, see my "Where Have All the Manuscripts Gone? Morris's Autographs in Diaspora," *Journal of William Morris Studies* 24.1 (2018): 4–14.

5. *How I Became a Socialist* includes "The Political Outlook," "A Report on the Progress and Condition of English Socialism," and "The Promise of May," also published in this edition.
6. Included in Cole, 655–9, Morton, 240–5, Jackson, 275–8, and Holland, 168–72.
7. Mary Lago, ed., *Burne-Jones Talking: His Conversations 1895–1898* (Columbia: University of Missouri Press, 1981), 168.
8. Paul Smith, *Disraeli: A Brief Life* (Cambridge: Cambridge University Press, 1996), 198–9.
9. E.g., Henry Hyndman, *The Historical Basis of Socialism in England* (London: K. Paul, Trench & Co., 1883). By April of the same year Morris was reading Marx's *Das Kapital* in translation, and in February 1885 he advised John Carruthers: "On the whole tough as the job is you ought to read Marx if you can: up to date he is the only completely scientific Economist on our side."
10. Thompson, 293. In radical contrast with Morris, Hyndman had supported a British war with Russia in defense of Turkey, defended the conquest of Afghanistan in the Anglo-Afghan War, opposed Home Rule for Ireland, and generally accepted claims of British superiority. Since he was an anti-Semite who blamed "imperialist Judaism" for the Boer War, Morris's remarks on the origins of the Boer War may have been an indirect response.
    Until his death in 1921, Hyndman led the National Socialist Party (1916–24), an offshoot of the British Socialist Party (1911–20) formed in support of British involvement in World War I. The NSP later merged into the Labour Party, and the BSP joined in forming the Communist Party in 1920.
11. "And the price to be paid for so making the world happy is Revolution: Socialism instead of laissez-faire." "Art and Socialism," January 23, 1884, *CW*, 23, 194.
12. Thompson, 605–6.
13. LeMire, 317–22.
14. Robert Salisbury and his Conservative Party, allied with the Liberal Unionists, had made sweeping gains in the July–August 1895 elections and were to remain in power until 1908.
15. Published in 1892 and 1894, respectively.
16. William Morris and Ernest Belfort Bax, *Socialism: Its Growth and Outcome* (London: Swan Sonnenschein, 1893), 289–90. "But the religion of socialism will be but the ordinary ethics carried into a higher atmosphere. . . . socialistic religion would be that higher form of conscience that would impel us to actions on behalf of a future of the race, such as no man could command in his ordinary moods."
17. Morris enunciated this view with increasing bluntness in his late lectures and essays. In "Waste," as reported in *Justice*, March 17, 1894, he is quoted as saying that "Religion nowadays hampers us but little," and in "The Present Outlook of Socialism in England," published in 1896 in an American periodical, he states that "It is true that in Britain religion lagged behind, and the 'freethinking' which had long been accepted as an essential part of the Whig revolution on the continent, was here revolutionary and unrespectable, as an open and expressed opinion, though even then almost universal amongst intelligent persons. For the deep-seated hypocrisy of our nation (and perhaps race), which has often, wrongly as I think, been dignified with the historical title of "Puritanism," would not allow facts to be faced openly on this side of things."

Figure I.2 Jane Morris, 1879 (1839–1914). Courtesy of the National Portrait Gallery

Figure I.3 May Morris with musical instrument (1862–1938). Courtesy of the William Morris Gallery, London Borough of Walthamstow

Part I

From Liberalism to Socialism, 1878–1881

1

Early Political Essay ["Against War with Russia"], 1878

Editor's introduction

Morris's political career arguably began with his interest in the "Eastern Question," a long-standing quarrel over the fate of the Balkans manifested in the late 1870s as a dispute over whether Britain should declare war against Russia on behalf of its nominal ally, Turkey, then head of the Ottoman Empire.[1] Turkey's repression and mistreatment of its subject peoples—including those in Bulgaria, Serbia, Montenegro, Bosnia-Herzegovina, Albania, Macedonia, and parts of Greece—had been exposed in several recent British accounts, including journalist J. A. McGahan's *The Turkish Atrocities in Bulgaria* (1876) and William Gladstone's *The Bulgarian Horrors and the Question of the East* (1876). When Russia invaded several Ottoman territories to defend local independence movements and protect its interests in the Balkans (the Russo-Turkish War, 1877–8), Conservative Prime Minister Benjamin Disraeli advocated entering the war in support of Turkey. Alarmed at the thought that Britain might fight to prop up a murderous regime, in December 1876 Morris joined members of the radical wing of the Liberal Party and other antiwar and workingmen's groups to form the Eastern Question Association, dedicated to opposing the projected Anglo-Russian war (Thompson, 210). In the event, Britain would join Germany, Austria, France, and other powers at the June 1878 Berlin Congress, which curtailed Russia's war victories, granted limited independence to certain Balkan territories, and ceded Cyprus to Britain, an uneasy resolution of regional tensions that would continue to fester until World War I.

Morris's first contribution to the cause was likely a long October 24, 1876 letter to the *Daily News* (Kelvin, 1.323–6), but his first impromptu speech on the issue was not delivered until more than a year later, when he spoke on the topic at a December 19, 1877 Eastern Question Association meeting in Lambeth.[2] Of this Morris wrote to Jane Morris the next day, "I even tried to fit a few words at a small meeting we had at Lambeth yesterday. I can't say I got on very well, but I did manage to get a few words out & get to the end" (Kelvin, 1.421).

Morris is also known to have prepared three further speeches on the topic in 1878 and 1880, and for these the likely texts have fortunately been preserved.[3] The manuscript for the text May Morris published as "An Address to English Liberals" (*Artist, Writer, Socialist*, 2.370–82) is now housed in the Wilson Library as MS. Z6, and May notes that it was delivered at the Chichester Liberal Association in January 1878. This description would accord with a Morris letter of January 4, 1878 in which he tells Jenny that on the next Monday (January 7) he plans to travel to Chichester to speak to a Chichester Liberal Club (Kelvin, 1.430), and the talk itself appropriately begins, "In speaking to you as English Liberals. . . ." (*AWS*, 2.270).

A second manuscript, now also housed in the Wilson Library as Z6b, is reproduced below under the title, "Against an Anglo-Russian War." A January 17, 1878 *Times* report confirms that this is the speech Morris delivered the afternoon of January 16, 1878 in Willis's Rooms, King Street, St. James,[4] directly before a mass meeting at Exeter Hall the same evening (LeMire, 235).[5] For the latter Morris had composed a five-stanza hymn, "Wake, London Lads" (Kelvin, 1.436–7), which provided emotional resonance to the case against war:

> From out the dusk, from out the dark,
> Of old our fathers came,
> Till lovely freedom's glimmering spark
> Broke forth a glorious flame:
> And shall we now praise freedom's dearth
> And rob the years to come.
> And quench upon a brother's hearth
> The fires we lit at home?
>
> O, happy England, if thine hand
> Should forge anew the chain,
> The fetters of a tortured land,
> How were thy glory vain!
> Our starving men, our women's tears,
> The graves of those we love,
> Should buy us curses for all years,
> A weight we might not move. (sts. 2–3)

Morris's January 19, 1878 letter to Jane (Kelvin, 1.434–6) briefly described his speech, noting unrepentantly that he had been admonished by the chairman for criticizing the Queen ("You will have got the newspapers by this time with a sort of report of our proceedings including the speech of me, and its—may I call it amicable indiscretion: of course I said more connected words than that. . . ."). By contrast he lingered lovingly on the emotional effect of his song: "It went down very well, & they sang it well together: they struck up while we were just ready to come on to the platform & you may imagine I felt rather excited when I heard them begin to tune up: they stopped at the end of each verse and cheered lustily . . ." (435).

The last of Morris's known early antiwar speeches, "Our Country Right or Wrong," is preserved in a manuscript dated January 31, 1880, and is reproduced as the third selection in this volume.

Since all three of these preserved lectures were designed as Liberal Party campaign speeches, they directly address audience members as potential voters. The following January 16 speech against an Anglo-Russian war is more compact and less digressive than the preceding week's "Address to English Liberals," and it displays the extent to which Morris's views were initially framed in response to political journalism. An earnest speaker, he is nonetheless more concerned with refuting other political stances than enunciating grand principles, and his expressions of disgust for Benjamin Disraeli ("a man with scarce any qualities in him except shiftiness and ambition; a man without genius but with a sort of galvanic mockery of it") and appeal to an alleged history of Liberal Party anti-imperialism ("we Liberals, we radicals, do not seek to humiliate the Russia that is now freeing her brethren from anarchy sustained by massacre") were tailored to his specific audience.

Nonetheless this early speech displays a few features which reappear in Morris's later essays: an opening observation based on personal reflection or experience ("Only at the end of last week"), its use of battle metaphors to describe political conflict ("so that we may know where and [on] what our strokes are falling"), and its appeal (in this case, ironic) to an imagined future: "Ah well, I suppose tis wrong to wish an artificially long life even to one[']s enemies: and yet I sometimes wish some of them could live for a few hundred years to see what will happen to the world after our time." As in his next preserved political essay, "Our Country Right or Wrong," he observes that internal reforms are unlikely in wartime: "amid the confrontation and excitement of such a war many things will be forgotten here at home[,] many reforms put off: nay they may well hope that reaction will flourish amidst the rank growth of unreason and violence that is sure to spring up in the heart of an unjust foreign war."

Notes

1. See Florence Boos, "Dystopian Violence: William Morris and the Nineteenth-Century Peace Movement," *Journal of Pre-Raphaelite Studies* 14 (Spring 2005): 20–41.
2. LeMire, "Appendix 2: A Bibliographical Checklist of Morris's Speeches and Lectures," 292. LeMire's claim that "no text remains" (292) is confirmed by the fact that the December 20, 1877 *Daily Chronicle* report (p. 6) matches no yet identified text. Morris wrote his wife on December 20, 1877 that he believed Disraeli and Queen Victoria would attempt to force a war ("the Jew wretch and that old Vic forcing us into the war: you will see how the sprightly widow went to Hughenden [Disraeli's home] & then said she would stay at Windsor Christmas over: & now Parliament is to meet for business. . . ." [Kelvin, 1.421]), and this matches Morris's reference in the January 16, 1878 text reproduced below to the "dangers" of the past three weeks.
3. LeMire notes that a manuscript in the Emery Walker House, Hammersmith appears to match what he titles as "A Speech on the Opening of the Dardanelles," but "the published account is not sufficiently detailed for positive identification" (292); however, the speech was reported in January 17, 1878 editions of *The Times*, p. 6 (Kelvin, 1.436), the *Pall Mall Gazette* (p. 19), and the *Daily Chronicle*, p. 5 (LeMire, 235), and *The Times* report is sufficiently full to enable identification. Manuscripts from the Emery Walker House were later transferred to the Wilson Museum and Art Gallery in Cheltenham, England; and of its two autograph drafts of Morris's speeches, as mentioned above, the other corresponds to May Morris's published text of "An Address to English Liberals."

   LeMire's "Appendix 2" apparently reverses the dates for the delivery of these two early speeches, "Address to English Liberals" and "A Speech on the Opening of the Dardanelles" (January 7, 1878 and January 16, 1878).
4. The January 16, 1878 date is also consistent with Morris's reference to "the dangers we have passed through in the past three weeks" (that is, the extension of Parliament in anticipation of a possible war declaration). Less accurate seems his claim that a week previously the *Pall Mall Gazette* had denied the existence of a war party, since such a statement had appeared in the December 27, 1877 issue. Perhaps I have missed a later statement, or he had drafted the talk somewhat earlier.
5. Further reports in the *London Daily News* (p. 2) and the *Leeds Mercury* (p. 8) are reproduced on the Morris International Archive, www.marxists.org/archive/morris/works/1878/dardanelles.htm

Only at the end of last week a writer in the Pall Mall Gazette said that there was no war-party:[1] how we must all wish that this were true even though many of us should seem to have been striking strokes in the air of late if it be true: but it is of no use deluding ourselves; it is worse than no use, it is dangerous: and I must needs say it is untrue that there is no war party in England, and that we all know it as well as the man who wrote that article in the P. M. or the editor that allowed it to be published.

I say that there is a war party. Nay a party of war at any price: let us look at it thus, tearing from our eye any veil of hypocrisy that might

1. December 27, 1877.

hide the real nature of things from us: let us see what composes this party so that we may know where and [on] what our strokes are falling: trust me not on air, but on a danger real and substantial enough: let us look on our foes and count them: not that we may be discouraged but that we may be encouraged, that we may strike heartily against the things we hate, and now at last it may be make an end of it for ever: let us make those words of the Pall Mall Gazette as true of the future as they are untrue of the present or the past—let us return good for evil, and make that gentleman of the P[all] M[all] G[azette] a prophet.

Could we but first push out of our way a sort of friends; good Liberals or radicals, who are still lions in the year 48, and think that Russia is no less; who still perhaps have serious hope of the regeneration of Turkey by means of the Ottoman and are the one people in the world, I suppose, who do: what can we say to these men who wish to see Russia the great absolutist power humbled, even at the expense of their allying themselves to all that is reactionary in this country, to men who for their part have no doubt whither their instincts should lead them: I say what can we say to Liberals who would involve us in a Tory War, the successful result of which would be the restoration of absolutism over people[']s armies in just insurrection in a Tory War in order that Russia might be humiliated: I think they ought to listen to us when we say, we who wish that we may never speak again rather than say one word in favor of absolutism in any country, in Russia in Turkey or in England, we Liberals[,] we radicals, do not wish to humiliate the Russia that is now freeing her brethren from anarchy sustained by massacre[,] which is carrying order and civilization into wasted and barbarous Asia: and once more I think they ought to listen to us when we bid them look who are their fellows, and what motives what tactics they have: for the others compose but part of the war party, the existence of which the Pall Mall denies[,] are soon told over: first I blush to have to name them a set of men whose interest it is either that we should sustain Turkey at any price, or that we should have a war with some one or another: a knot of men whose mouthpiece is the D[aily] T[imes].

These are the men who have allied themselves with all that is ignorant and senseless in the country[,] deluding them with bawling out about the decadence of England and the like: these are they whose tireless industry has so sickened us for the last eighteen months, who are so devoid of any show of reason in their arguments that we have all been inclined to pass them by in contempt; thinking can such rubbish as this be dangerous? Unluckily it seems it can be: it appears that there is still a lingering feeling in the country capable of being whipped up into a froth by the geniuses [?] of the D[aily]T[imes]. A feeling that it is necessary for England to have an enemy[,] and which seeing no other country that it can put in that position must needs fix upon Russia: I do believe that the loudly expressed hatred of Russia so common in peoples mouths, people of all the ignorant classes you understand has just this base to stand upon, and nothing firmer: and yet we must not think it otherwise than dangerous for all that: Sirs it is this many varied instrument that the D[aily]T[imes] plays upon daily making such sweet music as you all know, and doubtless deceiving people abroad who believe that sound to be the voices of England.

Again Sirs this ignorance and rampant lionism if I may so call it that cries out for an enemy a rival on any terms is played upon by another set of men: the set of the cultivated reactionists: they I think believe in the singular virtues of the Ottoman the irreclaimable vices of the Russian to exactly the same extent as those who are fanning the flame of war for the sake of interest but they are genuine in one matter I suppose: that is a deep hatred for all that is on the face of things generous and high minded and at the same time popular: I suppose a great many of us must have acquaintances among these men nor will it be a great effort of our memories to recall the hatred and loathing they were eager to express at the outburst of popular indignation that followed the revelation of the horrors of Batak[2] and the rest: they were forced to keep pretty quiet in the public prints, they revenged themselves and let out their bile in private: these are the men whose hatred for a great and single hearted statesman, for our leader Mr. Gladstone rises to the dignity of a passion, nor can I wonder at it remembering his career, and how he had cast aside prejudice after prejudice in favour of naked truth and justice: for these men these Pall Mall Fanatics seem to be influenced by no hereditary prejudice, but have been drawn into their position, by a littleness of soul and narrowness of vision, that I know no parallel for, perhaps I am saying too much about them: perhaps they are not very dangerous enemies: their influence is chiefly over a class of society too cowardly and shamefaced to be either of much harm or good: you remember their representative journal is written by gentlemen for gentlemen[,] nevertheless their malice worries me, and I think it is a shame for us that all we should have to bear it[.]

Ah well[,] I suppose tis wrong to wish an artificially long life even to one[']s enemies: and yet I sometimes wish some of them could live for a few hundred years to see what will happen to the world after our time.

So much for the blind Liberals, for those whose private interests, lead them to cry out for war, for those whom little-minded and narrow

2. J. A. McGahan reported that 5000 of the 7000 inhabitants of the Bulgarian town of Batak had been slaughtered by Ottoman troops in 1876, and in many cases raped, beheaded, or burned alive.

pride of would[-]be[-]intellect constrain to take up that cry: there are left us the great party of the Tories, who, with some, nay I dare say many, honourable exceptions, who as a party in short have taken up what has turned out to be the side of war.

One says sometimes that they need not have made it a party question: and yet their instincts are right; if they had forgone the occasion, they would no longer have been Tories, they must have fraternized with the Liberal party: take rather the general behavior of their rank and file in Parliament; or better still the common talk of the people they represent: and I repeat you will soon find that their instinct was right, that they were bound to love the poor Turks (as I have heard them called of late) unseemly as that love appears to us: I believe and rejoice in believing that the fall or the curtailing of the Ottoman power in Europe, the success for insurrection of oppressed peoples will be a blow to that spirit which still exists among us; nay is so strong that it is possible to have in parliament not merely a cautious and conservative party, but even a majority of the very residuum of reactionists, a party whose actions if they durst could be represented by the words[,] keep them down: I say that to such a residuum the fall of irresponsible and corrupt rule in Bulgaria, the confirmation of the freedoms of those peoples who have already revolted[,] will be a heavy blow, and if they could prevent the blow falling they would do so as we know by entangling us in foreign war: all the more as they and we well know that amid the confrontation and excitement of such a war many things will be forgotten here at home[,] many reforms put off: nay they may well hope that reaction will flourish amidst the rank growth of unreason and violence that is sure to spring up in the heart of an unjust foreign war.

One more element I must mention as composing the war-party, since I have engaged to speak without hypocrisy; that element is the court; I say we must face the fact, not to me a very dreadful one, that it has thrown what misfortune it possesses into the scale against the influence it possesses against the thoughtfulness of the English Nation.[3]

3. The January 17, 1878 *Times* reported: "Mr. W. Morris spoke in strong terms against the 'war-at-any-price-party'. . . . He praised Gladstone (Three cheers were heartily given, while in response to a similar call in the case of Lord Beaconsfield . . . cheers mingled with hisses). . . . He . . . also [said] . . . that the Court was using all [its] influence . . . (Cries of 'No, no,' and 'Three cheers for the Queen'). [Morris then being] reminded by the chairman that it was undesirable in a Constitutional Country in which Ministers were responsible to the people to introduce the name of the Sovereign into political discussions, he concluded by expressing his regret that fortune had placed at the head of affairs in England a man without genius (Cries of 'Oh! oh!') but only a galvanic imitation of it, to whose shiftiness . . . the nation mush oppose a steady resistance. (Renewed cries of 'Oh, Oh')."

Let me recapitulate for a moment: let us see what we have against us: first those Liberals who fear and hate Russia unreasonably. Next all those who are primarily interested in a war; next the would[-]be intellectual hierarchy, the cultivated reactionists—then the man of ignorance and Philistinism that the industry of these two last have worked upon. Then the Tory residuum, the confused reactionists: finally what is called society and the Court. This is a long list and comprises I doubt [not] some very stubborn and thick-skinned persons: yet I do believe there is so great a body of intelligence in the country, so many people that can be moved by an appeal to their love of freedom and sense of justice, that formidable as our list sounds it would not have been very dangerous but for one circumstance: indeed the great mass of that ignorance and prejudice would scarcely like to take the responsibility of making war on their shoulders[,] pleased as they would be if somebody would declare war for them: now that dangerous circumstance is that our stupidity has put a man over our heads who is perhaps of all men with any pretension to be called statesmen the most unfit to be there at a critical time: a man with scarce any qualities in him but shiftiness and ambition: a man without genius but with a sort of galvanic mockery of it, that makes him the most fantastic object in Europe: it is a shame to us to have to have to talk about such an inconsiderable man: but I say our own stupidity our own sloth have set him where he is and in that position it is he who is the heart of the war-party: if he says yea all his henchmen in the papers write flaming war articles; if he says nay then there is no war-party and all the rest of it: it is hard to believe that he really has any policy in spite of all the hints that have been thrown out from time to time: any policy but one [–] to wear us out and our resistance to folly by shifting about[,] going on the same ring or ground and forever coming back to the same point again [–] that is the point of the whole thing: it is just that which I chiefly want to say to you: we have nothing for it but to oppose steady patience in resistance to his shiftiness: neither he nor any other ministers I believe would dare to make war with even a large minority strenuously resisting it: but if we tire and show an appearance of not caring about it; out will fly insults to Russia: she will be irritated into something rash; some cause of quarrel will be found[,] something that Lord B[eaconsfield] will get people to raise a shout over—and—the worst will come perhaps: and who will be able to mend matters after the first shot is fired? Who knows where we shall drift to then.

But you above all things I beseech you not to drift: make up your minds to what is fair and right, and stick to that: above all things let us have courage, and believe that every man whether he be what is called political or not may be of some use: do not let any of us allow either down-heartedness or false shame stop him from doing his utmost to get rid of the burden our own folly has laid on our backs: I hope [–] I think that all those meetings held all over the country ending with what we are doing today, what we shall do this evening[,] will do their work and finish with the party of war at any price: what dangers that we have passed through during the past three weeks we shall probably never know[,] the dangers that lie ahead we shall know in a few days: let us meet them calmly and with all determination in the name of peace, good will, and justice[.]

Note on MS.: Given by Morris to Emery Walker

Figure 2.1 "Pink and Rose," 1883. Courtesy of the Metropolitan Museum of Art, Edward C. Moore Jr. Gift

2

Address at the Cambridge School of Art Prizegiving ["Art for All"], February 21, 1878

Editor's introduction

Morris delivered this speech February 21, 1878 at the award ceremony of the Cambridge School of Art held in the Guildhall, Cambridge, with Sydney Colvin, Slade Professor of Art, presiding as chairman. The previous December Morris had given a talk on "The Decorative Arts," later published as "The Lesser Arts" in *Hopes and Fears for Art* (1882), but with this exception the Cambridge School of Art address was his first oration on the subject of art in general. Its direct and heartfelt eloquence merited the concluding remarks of one of the examiners, Dr. Bateson, who as noted in the *Cambridge Chronicle and Journal* (February 23, 1878, 4–5), remarked that "the address they had heard from Mr. Morris was a sort of weekday sermon, and seemed to come home to them. He hoped such a valuable address would prove profitable to them, and proposed a hearty vote of thanks to Mr. Morris for his admirable discourse." I am indebted to Graham Seaman for locating this text, which, as he states, "appears to have been copied directly from William Morris's manuscript (which has not survived) but with some minor copying errors by the typesetter" (MIA), who has inserted the paragraph breaks lacking in the newspaper version.

Here Morris introduces themes which were to preoccupy him for the rest of his life: his view that the significance of art lies in its interrelations with society at large—so that without a flourishing popular art there can be no healthy society and the reverse; his dismay at the basic inequalities which underlie contemporary life; and his belief that all must share equally in social well-being, conceived as the right to free and pleasurable employment. Characteristically Morris's attachment to a living and organic history shapes his ideals—we should "look[] backward with gratitude and forward with hope." His remarks are carefully addressed to his student audience, as he tactfully includes those who study art as well as its practitioners as equally able to further its designs, "to make men's labour a pleasure to them and a pleasure to those for whom they labour."

Morris first shares his anxiety that art itself will decay under the conditions of modern civilization, becoming "effete rubbish"—"Where is this art now? . . . Has it died out? And if so, can the dead live again?" At this point he mounts his critique of the radical inequality of contemporary society, already entwined with his conviction that members of his own class are inextricably linked with those less fortunate. Noting that despite their privileges the wealthy generally lack appreciation for anything beyond vulgar show, he continues:

> I should doubt the existence of any possible justice in the world if while 999 thousandths of the people, say, of London, are living in such a state that it is impossible for them to have any idea of beauty at all, the thousandth part were not oppressed by the mere brutality, unconsciously if they did not share it, as they verily do.

As a solution, Morris appeals to his audience as a community of like-minded persons to join with him in preparing for a new future, even as a few years later he appealed to audiences on behalf of a not-yet-achieved socialist vision. This community and shared identity extend beyond present lifetimes: "Like enough the youngest of us all will not live to see one of those new days, and yet I say the hope of their coming even now makes me a part of them, even as memory makes me a part of the great works of the past." Notably these are the emotional ties which will later underlie the historicist/futurist ethos of Morris's other later romance and political writings, as in *A Dream of John Ball*, whose time-traveler proclaims: "That though I die and end, yet mankind yet liveth, therefore I end not, since I am a man," chapter 9).

Morris then makes his major leap, from art seen as crucial to society, to art understood as a type of all labor, for "to be an artist or a handicraftsman seems to me to be the only quite satisfactory way of living." If this claim might seem a bit extravagant in its literal application, it nonetheless enables him to define a goal for all his auditors/readers, the making of pleasurable labor available to all men. Though the effort may be arduous, yet "it will be a changed world indeed and a world that will have cured many and many an evil when every man's share of daily toil is dignified with pleasure, good will, and hope."

It is startling to see so many of Morris's future convictions neatly embodied in this short address to graduating students: the embedded nature of aesthetics; the noncommercial sources of value; the need to create a different future guided by a consciousness of the past; the moral imperative of radical equality; the duty to strive for a better social order; and the inevitable obstacles which will delay the latter's realization. When transferred to the specific terminology and concrete goals of the cause of socialism, these beliefs would shape Morris's political writings for the next eighteen years until his death.

❧

In these days, when even those of us who love art most are apt sometimes to be discouraged by the carelessness for art that surrounds us, it is not wonderful that people should ask, some in triumph and some in sorrow, is the desire for beauty, and even fulness of form that produces art, an essential part of man's nature? or is it only one of the fleeting outcomes of the necessary energy of life, like many another fashion that has now passed away for ever?

That is an anxious question for you and me, whose lives are being spent now in dealing with that art. For indeed, I conceive that, to put it in another way, it means, are we merely trifling over the cast-off hobbies of former ages, and weakly trying to spin out the time a little before all these toys are looked upon with clear eyes and priced at their proper value; or are we working diligently, looking backward with gratitude and forward with hope, expecting while we toil to see some glimmer of the new light beginning to shine upon neglected art, on the creative powers of man, that as in the latter days shone so fully on science, on man's analytical powers. I say it is a most serious question to us, whether art has become a mere rag of past history or is still a living fibre of our present days. For if we must say yes to the first part of the question, then we artists are wasting our time, or worse; we by our trifling are helping to make the age effeminate and trifling and we had better at once make an end of what we call art and hope to see some new thing take the place of it.

And now I must say that the very fact that such a question can be put by any one that loves the Art[s], is a sign that some great change is at work in these matters. Who could have thought of such a thing once except a few devotees or grumbling philosophers,[1] with whose contempt

1. Plato's *Republic* had famously argued (Book 10) that poetry, as a form of mimesis, corrupted the soul by weakening its rational powers and should be banned from the good society.

of Art, indeed, I imagine there was mingled not a little affectation. The most of men worked on, letting their hands follow the instinct of their brains, and producing abundant beauty either simple even to childishness, or sublime and mighty, according to the measure of the mind that guided their hands. There has been accomplished all that great body of Art that we in these latter days have the pleasure and advantage of studying, if we have no other pleasure and advantage. [I]t rose from mere barbarism, how or where we know not: it changed, it wavered, grew faint, rose up again, lost on one side, gained on the other, fitted itself to all races all creeds, and through everything was still the same Art, with one unbroken though varying life.

Where is this art now? Where is the life of so many thousand years? Has it died out? And if so, can the dead live again? Indeed, in appearance, I should say it has died; or rather, we must at least say that the link that binds the imitative conscious art of today with that progressive unconscious art of the past is hard to find, if indeed it can be found at all. Yet somehow we artists must find it if we are not to call ourselves triflers over effete rubbish, even as I said before. If you are astonished at my taking what must at first seem such a gloomy view of art, I can only say many people, I know, think or rather feel that that link is clean lost.

I am forced to say that beyond a very small circle now-a-days, I find people living in a world that does not know art at all. For the most part even highly cultivated people eager for the good of the world with all kinds of sensitiveness, nevertheless are utterly blind on this side of things. True, they may think it necessary or rather desirable that something should be known of art as a matter of education, but they would not miss it if it were to disappear; they do not really care about it at all; they will live amidst the most frightful ugliness quite blandly and happily: though some of them, at least, make a profession of loving the country, the mountains, the sea, and so on, all the things that inspire art in those that produce it. I say "make a profession to do so," since I rather more than suspect they are not a little blunt to these impressions also. This, I am sure, can never have been the case in those past times I have been talking of, and it is a puzzle to me, how it can be now.

A puzzle to me in one way: yet in another way I must acknowledge the justice of it, yes and rejoice in it even. I say I must rejoice in it when I think of the mass of squalor and misery, the unhelped and apparently unhelpable hideousness, which surrounds the greater part of our big towns. I should doubt the existence of any possible justice in the world if while 999 thousandths of the people, say, of London, are living in such a state that it is impossible for them to have any idea of beauty at all, the thousandth part were not oppressed by the mere brutality, unconsciously if they did not share it, as they verily do. For I declare to you that though in this as in all else the rich have the advantage over the poor, the advantage in matters of taste, in appreciation of and longing for beauty, I would rather say, is but small. Glitter show and vulgarity are copiously paid for by the rich. Into such strange byways of folly has civilization strayed at whiles.

I must ask you not to think that I am wandering from the point, for let us consider. These unconscious artists of past days were thinking of something more than art when they wrought wonders that we rejoice in. They were earning their bread, they were glorifying their creeds, they were struggling with difficult and intricate prizes[2] of knowledge while they wrought them. Their life was in those works of art and showed in them their ways of life. But with us the life of our great cities, the places, you understand, in which the arts must always mostly flourish, is so distasteful and disgusting to every man—I will not say of taste, but of heart rather,—that we who work in the arts cannot by any means help striving to escape from all that into some unreal world, in which nothing but art exists; and the result is that all we do is weak, isolated, wanting in abundance and spontaneity.

Now I do not stand before you as a mere praiser of past time. I also know the injustice, the ignorance, the violence, and unreasoning passion of those past ages. I know what the world has won since then. But I ask what it seems to have lost. Has it lost it past recovery? My discontent of the present of art is bred by the hope of its future. I am speaking [so] hardly [of] what we do, not for our discouragement, but for our encouragement. For, look you; the arts have gone so far in one direction as they possibly can go: say 300 years ago it had come to that at last. Then people tried to push it further in the same direction, and failed, as might have been expected. Hence three centuries of trifling, of eclipse, and neglect of the arts coinciding with the enormous increase of riches and consequent luxury, which has been, is, and will be, I most solemnly affirm, the very bane of all the arts.

I say the arts have gone as far as they can go in one direction. By some means or other new scope, new life, must be found for them. Go into our museums, and look at the works there, and if you mean imitation you will despair if you know anything about the matter; so complete, so miraculous you will find them. But if you are looking for instruction, if you are seeking insight, you will hope and rejoice rather at the sight of that unapproachable excellence, [t]hinking the mind of man that brought such things to pass is still alive in its vehement and

2. Possible typesetter's error for "pieces."

partly successful struggles for other good things. [I]t has been blind to these hopes for a while, but when those matters that it has of late desired have been some of them attained to, some of them found out not to be desirable, the mind of man will again turn to the embers still as I think kept alive from the old times of art; and will once more carry on the torch to be a light and a glory to the world.

Like enough the youngest of us all will not live to see one of those new days, and yet I say the hope of their coming even now makes me a part of them, even as memory makes me a part of the great works of the past. For, indeed, I cannot seriously think that anything can really permanently take the place of art in men's minds, whatever the seeming outlook may be. Nay, I affirm that looking all over the world, looking at the decay of the East and the tumult of the West, secure as I am that our present civilization in some form must needs be pushed on further afield, so sure I am that elsewhere—yes, I will be [so] bold [as] to say it, especially in brutal America, in brutal England, our civilization must needs be re-civilized; nor do I think that anything but art can do it—I mean real living art, springing as ancient art did from religion. I use that word in no narrow sense, but in the widest imaginable sense, and again I say that in these days our civilization halts and sickens, nay sometimes seems as if it would take some steps on the backward path for lack of an art springing from pure and simple ways of life[;] from the exaltation of soul that comes from the constant practice of courage, kindness, and good faith.

Once more I say that whatever reaction there may be, yet assuredly such art will arise, and in the meantime I am sure also that our task, our pleasure of preparing the path for it, of keeping alive the hope of it may well make for us artists a serious and earnest, and not a trifling life.

To you especially who are studying in this school, I have but little advice to give that your own good sense would not give. You know very well that nature can be your only final guide, your only test of right and wrong. You know very well that as you work no diligence can be too great for the sake of getting a thing right from the outset, that shuffling and pretence will always find you out, and land you in discomfort and waste of time. You know very well, and the more you know of art the more you will know it, that you cannot study the works of the past too much, always on one condition, that you do it for the sake of study, not for the sake of reproduction; for of course it is clear to you that no one can have any call to be an artist, except in virtue of his being able to do something that nobody else can do. Even as in a wider scope [so] it is with the arts. I mean that no words can describe a picture, that no prose analysis can say what a poem means.

I do not mean by saying all this to discourage those of you who are studying for the sake of educating yourselves to know and love beauty rather than for becoming professional artists of any sort, still less those who are or will one day be artists of the lesser kind like myself, designers as they are called. What I say is that however humble a man's walk in the arts may be, any excellence he may be capable of will come from some grain of originality in him, and on what side that may lie he will find out by finding what he really likes, which is not as easy a matter as it seems to be at first sight.

Let me finish these few words by praising the pleasures of an artist's life. Other people work hard and are glad often I am afraid to shake off the thought of their work at the day's end and forget it, nay often if they could and were free they would choose some other work, or no work at all perhaps. But with us every day is a holiday, except perhaps the days when we fail notably. We don't like to leave off at night, and are in a hurry to begin in the morning. Nor if we were the freest and richest people in the world would we lead any other life. I must ask the rest of you to forgive me when I say that to be an artist or a handicraftsman seems to me to be the only quite satisfactory way of living.

Ah, sir[s], might it not come about that by far the greater part of mankind had that happiness. It was so once. Every handicraftsman was once an artist, and I must needs think that our civilization has gone astray in this, that it is no longer so. And once again I say without any condition, without any "if", that one day or other this will be amended, and I call upon all you here present to consider this[,] if this is not the great end of all instruction in the arts[:] to make men's labour a pleasure to them and a pleasure to those for whom they labour. Nay, I think that it is a very good work for us all to help in though we may be long in bringing any great measure of it about, for it will be a changed world indeed and a world that will have cured many and many an evil when every man's share of daily toil is dignified with pleasure, good will, and hope.

(1)
51

Looking down the columns of a newspaper the other day I saw an advertisement of certain songs, and among the titles of them I noted this one: "Our country, right or wrong". That set me a thinking, for though the words were harmless in themselves, or indeed might be so interpreted to mean a noble sentiment, yet I cannot help thinking that what they did mean was something neither noble or even harmless: I don't think I am wrong in supposing them to have been taken as the motto of a banner, as it were: the banner of a tribe clamorous once, now somewhat subdued by the force of circumstances, but which may as circumstances change become clamorous once again, and unless they are well looked after dangerous also: that tribe has been called the tribe of the Jingoes.

Now if that be so, those words are the cry of a false patriotism and I do not think I shall waste your time if I say a few words to warn you to be on your guard now and for ever against this sentiment and what comes of it: for you know how dangerous an enemy is a vice disguised as a virtue; and this particular disguised vice must be called a wolf in sheeps clothing for its danger rather than an ass in a lions skin for its stupidity.

I should say then that when stripped of its borrowed gear false patriotism becomes National Vain-glory, which is both begotten of ignorance and begets it: a legacy of the injustice of past times, it breeds injustice in us in the present that we may be unjustly dealt with in the future: it gabbles of the valour of our forefathers, while it is busy in undoing the deeds that their valiant lives accomplished: it prates of the interests of our country, while it is laying the train of events which will ruin the fortunes, and break the hearts of the citizens: it scolds at wise men and honest men for what it calls a policy of isolation, while itself it would have nothing to do with foreign nations except for their ruin and ours.

Figure 3.1 "Our Country Right or Wrong," British Library Add. MS 45,334

3

"Our Country Right or Wrong," January 1880

Editor's introduction

Some two years after his January 1878 talk opposing an Anglo-Russian war (no. 1), Morris wrote out the text for a speech on "Our Country Right or Wrong," signed "W. M. Jan 30th, 1880, 2:30 a. m., Kelmscott House, Upper Mall, Hammersmith." Although the venue in which this lecture was delivered is unknown, it was clearly intended as a Liberal Party campaign speech, as indicated by its praise of the party's leader William Ewart Gladstone ("We had a great statesman leading us then"), its distaste for the current Conservative Party government ("it is some 6 years that I have scarcely felt like a free man"), and its direct appeal to the party's slogan, "Peace, Retrenchment, and Reform." The election, held March 31–April 27, 1880 brought in a Liberal government as Morris had hoped, and so the lecture may have seemed too topical for publication in one of his later volumes of essays on art and socialism (*Hopes and Fears for Art*, 1882; *Signs of Change*, 1888), and moreover Morris's disappointment with the new administration's imperialist policies and disavowal of Home Rule for Ireland would have precluded further advocacy on behalf of the Liberal Party. After his death Morris's manuscript thus remained largely unregarded in B. L. Add. MS. 45,334(3), and although May Morris excerpted sections in *Artist, Writer, Socialist*, 2.53–62, these are introduced only as a lecture on "War and Peace."

In January 1880 a war with Russia, though still possible, was less likely than it had been in 1878, but as Morris's essay indicates, Britain had recently expanded its efforts at dominance in Africa and the Middle East in the Zulu War (1879) and the Second Anglo-Afghan War (1879–80). In the years since his first antiwar lectures Morris broadened his opposition to specific nationalist aggressions into a theoretical critique of nationalism, imperialism, and predatory violence itself.

Although Morris has received attention chiefly as a writer on topics relating to art, historical preservation, and socialism, the best sections of "Our Country Right or Wrong" also remain relevant as powerful antiwar arguments, and reveal his acuity in deconstructing meretricious rationales for foreign interventions. The essay is also notable for its eloquent concluding statement of his political goals for a just society ("I think of a country where every man has work enough to do . . ."), and for its recognition of the destructive effects of foreign wars, however distanced, on the hopes for progress and liberty at home.

As in his earlier speech opposing an Anglo-Russian war (no. 1), Morris identifies belligerence with hubris and a heedlessness of consequences: "National Vain-glory . . . would have nothing to do with foreign nations except for their ruin and ours: . . . all other nations, it deems, pay the price of war; but we never do, and never can pay it, and never shall." As an alternative, he offers an expanded view of patriotism unbounded by geography and politics:

> After all, what is our country? Is it that part of earth's surface that geographers call the British Islands, or the knot of officials that diplomatists call England? or is it not rather the great mass of the lives of all the men and women and children of our race [i.e., kind]; their hopes and fears and aspirations that we perforce share, their joys and sorrows that we know more of than of any other people's joys and sorrows?

Moreover, he identifies two repeated ironies of history: the traits which make nations powerful also prompt militarism and ultimately self-destruction; and any conquest will over time provoke counter-aggression and merited revenge:

> There is always a danger to great nations of some of their best qualities becoming over-masterful, and urging them first to make slaves of other nations, and then of themselves: . . . if any tendencies to our natural force becoming maleficent are not checked by ourselves they will burst out full-blown one day, and will have to be smothered by men not of our . . . nation; and what widespread ruin will come with that we may perhaps imagine.

He then seeks to make abstract notions of war concrete and personal, imagining his audience's horror had the distant war deaths reported in the newspapers occurred instead in central London and its peaceful suburbs. As often he uses himself as exemplum:

> I can't get out of my head thoughts of how I should like it myself if real war were here in the land . . . . How should I like it: I, a man of peace, a craftsman, with a wife and children to take care of . . . . What a face I should pull for instance when I came back to my house after it had been occupied by our own troops for

> a morning! What words I should use as I hunted for my MSS. and drawings among the ruins of my furniture! How I should cry out at having to begin life over again at 46 because of the stupid whim of a half-educated subaltern! And yet such a thing as this would be such a trifle amidst the great tragedy, that no one could so much as say, "I'm sorry for you."

Although Morris leaves open the notional possibility that there may be wars in self-defense, the fighters in even such theoretically just wars would need care to "leav[e] no revenge behind to fall upon us at some indefinite time"—a virtually disqualifying condition. In fact, however, such wars are not those Britain is prosecuting, but rather fabrications by which we have "over and over again . . . allowed ourselves to be satisfied, to be gulled, by wretched travesties of justice." Such false rationales are needed precisely because "people at large do instinctively feel that a war in which one side at all events cannot appeal to the highest principles of truth and justice, is a scandal to the world, a ruinous blow to the hopes of humanity."

Morris's sarcasm serves him in good stead as he reviews recent imperial wars. Some have been wars on the cheap, as it were, and for political show:

> . . . people at home don't bother their heads what becomes of the rights and wrongs of a set of barbarians: and if an attack were made on Affghanistan it would look like an attack on Russia, without being so dangerous or costly[,] . . . it could be slipped into without notice almost, and would be sure to be successful—*brilliantly* successful it might be called without any extra expense . . . .

Such "wars of choice" are exploited to silence domestic enemies: "On my word I cannot explain the Affghan war otherwise than thus: if ever war was waged for war['s] sake that has been—that democracy might be checked in England." Perhaps the most shameful such aggression has been the previous year's war against the Zulu, who famously repelled British troops armed only with spears, "a war of which the very soldiers are heartily ashamed." A proposed visit by their leader, Cetewayo, to London to plead for his people (this occurred in 1882) evokes Morris's derision:

> Doubtless our once dreaded foe, poor Cetewayo, has learned so much of the blessings of civilization within the last year, that it is hardly worth while to bring him over here to complete the lesson; otherwise we might show him in London some strange things: might he not say: 'poor devils! They treated me ill enough certainly, but I can forgive them since I have seen what a dog[']s life so many of their people lead at home! no wonder it maddens them.'

Morris's final appeal for a just society reaches beyond any single election to encompass the features of a truly peaceful society:

> I think of a country where every man has work enough to do, and no one has too much: where no man has to work himself stupid in order to be just able to live: . . . where every man's work would be pleasant to himself and helpful to his neighbour; and then his leisure from bread-earning work . . . would be thoughtful and rational: for you understand he would be thoroughly educated, whatever his condition might be: such a man as this . . . would never fail in self-respect; he would live honourably, and as happily as external circumstances would allow him, and would help others to do likewise: you may be sure he would take good care to have his due share in the government of his country and would know all about its dealings with other countries: justice to himself and all others would be no more a name to him, but the rule of all his actions, the passionate desire of his life. . . .

Struggling in this essay to articulate nascent socialist ideals in conventional liberal terms ("reform," "free men," "the vote"), Morris also embraced most of the arguments war resisters have repeatedly adduced against militarism, as well as developing perhaps his fullest evocation thus far of a society designed to foster critical solidarity, social justice, and mutual respect.

Looking down the columns of a newspaper the other day I saw an advertisement of certain songs, and among the titles of them I noted this one: "Our country, right or wrong."[1] This set me a thinking, for though the

1. This was the original title of an American song by George Pope Morris (1802–64), first performed in New York in 1861. The song managed to avoid all mention of slavery or emancipation in its summons to the Union cause, in the doggerel of the second stanza, for example:

> It is the duty of us all,
> To check rebellion's sway!
> To rally at the nation's call,
> And we that voice obey!
> We like a band of brothers go,
> A hostile league to break!
> To rout a spoilt encumber't foe,
> And what is ours retake!
> Then come ye hardy Volunteers,
> Around our standard throng!
> And pledge man's hope of coming years,
> Our country, right or wrong!
>
> Chorus:
> Our country, right or wrong,
> Inspires the burden of our song!
> It was the glory of our sires,
> Our country, right or wrong!

words were harmless in themselves, or indeed might be interpreted to mean a noble sentiment, yet I cannot help thinking that what they did mean was something neither noble or even harmless: I don't think I am wrong in supposing them to have been taken as the motto[2] of a banner, as it were: the banner of a tribe clamorous once, now somewhat subdued by force of circumstances,[3] but which may as circumstances change become clamorous once again, and unless they are well looked after dangerous also: that tribe has been called the tribe of the Jingos.[4]

Now if that be so, those words are the cry of a false patriotism, and I do not think I shall waste your time if I say a few words to warn you to be on your guard now and for ever against this sentiment and what comes of it: for you know how dangerous an enemy is a vice disguised as a virtue; and this particular disguised vice must be called a wolf in sheep[']s clothing for its danger rather than an ass in a lion's skin for its stupidity.

I should say then that when stripped of its borrowed gear false patriotism becomes National Vain-glory, which is both begotten of ignorance and begets it: a legacy of the injustice of past times, it breeds injustice in us in the present that we may be unjustly[5] dealt with in the future: it gabbles of the valour of our forefathers, while it is busy in undoing the deeds that their valiant lives accomplished: it prates of the interests of our country, while it is laying the train of events which will ruin the fortunes, and break the hearts of the citizens: it scolds at wise men and honest men for what it calls a policy of isolation, while itself it would have nothing to do with foreign nations except for their ruin and ours: its great office is for ever to cry out for war without knowing what war means: all other nations, it deems[,] pay the price of war; but we never do, and never can pay it, and never shall. The price of war – a heavy price is that; confusion and reaction at the best, ruin at the worst.

Yes, that is National Vain-glory: we, as well as other nations, have suffered heavily enough from it before now: but perhaps some of us had got into our heads the idea that this folly was of late years so much abated among ourselves, that it would scarcely do more in our time than help after dinner orators to a few stock phrases which one sits and

2. MS., mottoe

3. The 1878 Congress of Berlin's repartition of the Balkans temporarily obviated war in the region as an instrument of British mercantile interests. The actual negotiations continued through the following year, ceasing only with the election of a Liberal government in April 1880.

4. *Jingoes*: Political senses of this word apparently derive from the refrain of a ditty sung by proponents of British engagement in the Russo-Turkish War (1877–8): "We don't want to fight, but, by Jingo, if we do, / We've got the ships, we've got the men, and got the money, too!" The word itself seems to have been a corruption of "Jesus."

5. MS., injustly

listens to with one[']s tongue in one's cheek: we know better now: we have found out the power of phrases, even when they do not seem to mean much, when they are used to tickle the longing for excitement and self[-]glorification of thoughtless people: we have found these phrases of little meaning turn into actions that have shamed us all without rebuke from the British nation.

We have found out, in short, that it is still possible to convince John Bull that he must have an enemy abroad whether the Fates will have it so or not: once he had got to think that France and her people had been created to fulfill that office, to satisfy that necessity: and it really ought to encourage us to remember that, dead and buried as that folly is today, it has been vigorously alive (or seemed so) long after our beards were grown—nay[,] after some of them were turning grey: well in spite of warmongers & fools, who more than once in our life-times would have set us by the ears, France can no longer be looked upon as our natural and hereditary enemy; so Russia must serve our turn: our nearest neighbour having so grossly disappointed us, I suppose we have now tak[en][6] the huff with the Fates, and so nothing further off will serve our turn but the furthest. [O]n my word I think that is as good a reason as any I have heard put forward in favour of the new choice of a natural and hereditary enemy.

Well, it was France yesterday, it is Russia today that must serve National Vain-glory for a bogie to hang sham hatred and fear upon, and whoever can guess what or who it is to be tomorrow is a conjuror indeed; but I fear indeed that the bogie will be invented: I fear that there will always be plenty of excuses for a cry to thrust ourselves into positions where neither Nature nor our own real desires ever called us; and it is our duty who think we love our country as well as the best, to get ready to turn the light of day on every new bogie that is thrust forward, to keep fast hold of Nature's hand and to look steadily to [our] own real welfare and our just desires for advancement.

For after all[,] what is our country? is it that part of Earth's surface that geographers call the British islands, or the knot of officials that diplomatists call England? or is it not rather the great mass of the lives of all the men, women and children of our race; their hopes and fears and aspirations that we perforce share, their joys and sorrows that we know more of than of other peoples' joys & sorrows? Yes, this is the country that we love; this is what we must serve lifelong if our own lives are to be the lives of men; yet for all that it is a familiar thing, and not some mysterious unapproachable altar of an unseen God: and so,

6. MS., taking; *tak[en] the huff with*, taken offence at

meseems, we are as much bound to rebuke it when it is wrong, as to cheer it when it is right, since we ourselves, whether we will or no, must share its shame as well as its glory.

To serve our country? Yes[,] that is as plain duty to my mind for each man as to maintain his own family, though doubtless it is a duty much forgotten now a days: but what service can we do worth the having if we shut our eyes and tie up our hands, as our Jingo friends would have us do.

Those lives of our countrymen, and ourselves are what they are by dint of the influences of many past centuries[:] it is that which has made the mass cohere, has made it our country: those influences are various enough, there is light and there is darkness among them: both have been busy in making the England of today: they have made the English character forcible certainly, but, as with all great nations, dangerous also by very virtue of that force: there is always a danger to great nations of some of their best qualities becoming over masterful, and urging them first to make slaves of other nations & then of themselves: such dangers nature will in the end deliver the world from: but woe be to that country that does not look to it in time to guard against them by the forethought of her own citizens: if any tendencies to our natural force becoming maleficent are not checked by ourselves, they will burst out full-blown some day, and will have to be smothered by men not of our race and nation; and what widespread ruin will come with that we may perhaps imagine.

Surely, therefore, real patriotism bids us to be keen-eyed to note whether at any time the public opinion of our country sways towards justice or injustice, and to resist both in ourselves and in others blind and ignorant impulses that drive men on to grasp at phantoms of gain and glory created long ago by follies dead or half dead. Those impulses, indeed, the legacy of past sloth[,] cowardice and compromise among us[,] will stir whenever occasion serves; and one could scarcely dare to think of the danger with which they are rife, of the revenge which they might pull down on our heads, if one did not remember that at each reawakening of them there are to be found more and more of those true patriots, who are ready to brave opprobrium by resisting the windy lies, that on such occasions become, as it were part of the public creed, and who will insist on seeing men and things as they are, not as National Vain-glory has bidden them to be.

Such patriots as this the first word of the motto we liberals inscribe on our banner specially calls on us to be: it bids us in difficult times, in such times as these, instead of bawling out, 'Our country, right or wrong!' to cry rather, 'May the right prevail!' and to act strenuously to bring no less than this to pass.

But if any one should cast in our teeth that in longing for the right to prevail, we are longing for the confusion or defeat of our own country; if in short men chide us, that we do not wish to see our country bring a crime to a successful issue: I can only say, that it is a hard word to have to utter that our country is on the wrong side if even for a while; and yet that if it be so, we as good patriots should choose for the country we love the speedier revenge of check and foil on a wrongful course, rather than that longer delayed and more terrible revenge that comes at last to a long victorious land satiate with glory[,] violence and injustice, long after the victors have forgotten not only why they grasped and conquered, but even almost where and when: rather shame, repentance and fresh hope springing from it in our days, than shame without repentance, and ruin without hope in the days of our children's children[.]

Now you see, I think it is not without reason that we put that word Peace first in the motto of our party:[7] in these days indeed, and to us the heirs of such sore struggles for freedom and civilization, to us, who have learned, or ought to have learned, so much from history and many troubles, it means more, surely[,] than mere ease and comfort to ourselves: patience & industry, forbearance & goodwill, justice at home and abroad; these things I seem to read in that word peace: on the other hand, to us and in these days[,] those three letters, war, mean much more than the death of a few men, the loss of a few millions of money, much more than a mere struggle with no consequences but the immediate and obvious ones. Yet I am not saying that all wars are necessarily and positively indefensible at all times of the world and to every people. There have been peoples, whose life for years has been constant fighting for freedom; the Greeks of the last generation, the Poles, the Montenegrins of our own time[8] will give us examples of these without further seeking: now you may scold at them as you please, call them cheats, brigands, anarchists, what you will; yet prejudice must have knocked a good deal of manhood out of you, if you do not feel some exultation at

7. *Peace, Retrenchment, and Reform*: slogan of Gladstone's Liberal Party.
8. An 1863–5 Polish insurrection against Russian dominance was crushed; Poland remained under Russian control until 1918. Serbia and Montenegro declared war against Turkey in 1876, and their soldiers subsequently defeated much larger Turkish forces in battles extensively reported in the British press. Gladstone praised the Montenegrin insurgents in a *Nineteenth Century* article in 1877, and eulogized them in Parliament as "a bunch of heroes such as the world has rarely seen." Tennyson's poetic characterization of the Montenegrins as a "race of mightier mountaineers" appeared in the same issue of the *Nineteenth Century*, and the Congress of Berlin included a provision for Montenegrin independence subject to Austrian control over the port of Bar.

the triumphs of such peoples, some real sorrow at their overthows: you must admit, that whatever they may be, they have at least an ineradicable love of freedom. I should be sorry indeed even to seem to class together the hero Garibaldi with the scoundrel Napoleon.

Nor can I fail to understand that things may take such a turn even in fully civilized and settled countries, governed by men of their own blood, that actual physical force would have to be used by the rational people of such countries against the irrational: an example again will show better what I mean: take the case of what might have happened in France the other day if Macmahon had allowed himself to be used by the reactionists to the utmost: the great mass of the nation was determined on freedom and republican institutions:[9] the executive and a knot of partisans were merely acting as obstacles to the well-understood will of the nation; but they had or seemed to have the army at their backs, and if they had carried their madness but a little further, they would have carried it into crime; and that crime would have actually forced the reasonable and orderly part of France into mere necessary war. Furthermore I can conceive of some country, a member of Civilization, going crazy and being such a danger to its neighbours, that it would require coercion from the other members of the civilized world; only I should say in this case the craziness should be very undoubted, the danger very clear before any other state had a call to move in the matter. But cases of these kinds of war are not common: with the first kind we ourselves happily can have nothing to do as principals: such wars grow out of outstanding wrong and anarchy become at last unbearable: they belong indeed properly to earlier stages of the world's history, to times when peoples were slowly toiling out of barbarism. With all that, even these long-fought wars of liberation, much as we may sympathize with those who battle for the right in them, are even they unmixed gain, even among the rough populations among whom they are carried on, even when fought by newly born or newly reborn nations?

Look you, when any such war has been brought to a happy end, when, for example the Montenegrins have gained their well[-]deserved freedom, do we not pause in anxious expectation, and ask, what will they do next? They have learned war, can they learn any thing else: our hope is strong that they can, since we can hardly think that it is for nothing that their children are born longing for freedom; but if they

9. Maréchal (Marshall) Patrice de MacMahon (1808–92), French general and monarchist president during the Second Empire, made a vain effort to thwart a Republican electoral victory when he dismissed the National Assembly in May 1877.

cannot, how will they have disappointed our hope; what a woeful, what a poor dull ending it will be to a tale so fairly begun; how will they seem to have been fighting in a land of shadows for nothing! So, you see, it is by their fitness for peace and not for war that we must judge them in the long run: we look to them to make peace out of war.

As to those other kinds of necessary war[,] what is there to say? Who doubts the loss and confusion they bring about? The same injustice that individuals have to bear, the things done in haste that have to be undone at leisure, the slowly earned gains that have to be thrust into the fire of rough & hasty violence. Did we not feel as if we could once again breathe freely when we heard th[at] Macmahon had demitted in those threatening days of France;[10] though indeed that would have been a war in which we should have had such sympathy for one side at least, that it would have been hard for some of us to have sat quietly here at home, if it had gone on as we feared it might, and France had been wrapped in civil war.

Or again was there nothing to be mended after that mighty struggle across the Atlantic, though it ended in a gain so prodigious for the whole human race that we have scarcely realized it yet or what it will grow to?

Whatever the gain and whatever the loss may be of even a necessary war[,] it is obvious that we ought most seriously to count the cost of it; if we do not we shall one of these days be entering with light hearts on some war or other, which before it is over will make the whole world heavy-hearted enough.

And what is the cost, or how shall we reckon it; how get to think about it? Well, as for me, I suppose I am somewhat of an egotist: for what happens to me when I think of the relative gains of peace and war is, that I can't get out of my head thoughts of how I should like it myself if real war were here in the land; and what if it were a war in the cause of which I (and a great part of my fellow citizens) took no particular interest? How should I like it: I, a man of peace, a craftsman, with a wife and children to take care of: a man with longings to bring certain things to pass, which would please me, and as I think benefit my fellows; in short with what people call worthy ambitions and a pleasant life: I can't help thinking what confusion actual war present in the land, in London and its suburbs[,] would make of all this! What a face I should pull for instance when I came back to my house after it had been occupied by our own troops for a morning! What words I should use as I hunted for my M.S.S. and drawings among the ruins of my furniture:

10. MacMahon resigned ("demitted," *démissiona*) the presidency in 1879.

how I should cry out at having to begin life over again at 46 because of the stupid whim of a half-educated subaltern. And yet such a thing as this would be such a trifle amidst the great tragedy, that no one could so much as say, I'm sorry for you.

Yes, yes, how we wrap up facts in meaningless phrases till we forget most often what the facts are that they represent, and thus deaden ourselves to terrible realities. Take to pieces for instance a very common sort of phrase that is used in dispatches of battles, and let us note what it really means: 'the enemy's[11] skirmishers annoyed us a little as we advanced.' There's for you a phrase that does not stick in your memory two minutes as you read your newspaper in the morning train: if you had been among the 'annoyed,' a life-time would not wipe it out from your memory: an army-surgeon would interpret the words for you best perhaps, yet we as we sit here can imagine it all pretty well if we try:

Say 3 men shot stone dead: no great harm to them perhaps: but how would your hearts have been frozen with horror if you had seen that done in the New Road[12] this afternoon, or if their bodies with the ragged holes in them through which the life had ebbed away had been brought into the place where you were at work and resting, and laid among the familiar things of common life: or was there no one waiting for them to come home again?

But what other annoyance would there be: a man with his wrist shattered: a skilful right hand destroyed maybe: another shot through both legs—a wretched cripple henceforth[,] he had better never been born he thinks often afterwards: a dozen such or worse; or tortured with mangling wounds (I remember a doctor once horrifying me with describing some of our last scientific inventions in that line, and I shall never forget it)[,] with hurts that will perhaps finish them off in a week or month of careless (necessarily careless) hospital treatment, or will at any rate and at the best leave them much less than the men they were and ought to be.

And this is an annoyance only, which no man thinks of but the actors in it. Now if people say, as they do, such talk as this is but of commonplace truisms: all men know that such things happen, and think of them seriously; but they are so brave that they are content to risk them; or so wise that in their forethought they will buy advantages to their country at the price of these horrors befalling their friends[,] relations

11. MS., enemies

12. Possible reference to a central London artery south and east of The Regent's Park, now known as "Marylebone."

and countrymen generally: if people say that I answer, It is not true: people do not think of such things:

> "Half ignorant they turn an easy wheel,
> That sets sharp racks at work to pinch and peel."[13]

Men's imaginations do not reach very far in conceiving of the evils that are not likely to happen to themselves: let me give you an illustration:

Of course you remember that man who tried to blow [up] a ship with a dynamite[14] which was ingeniously timed to act when the doomed craft was in mid-ocean, but which exploded somehow as she lay by the quays at Bremen and amongst others wounded the author of the plot himself: now would you not have said that such a man was utterly remorseless, senseless—no man in short?

Yet mark what happened, and how he claimed his share in our common humanity; he had schemed and carried out his horrible crime as a matter of business: he thought he should make money of it, and did not think of anything else: well he was carried to the hospital, and tended there amidst his victims, and when he heard their groans as he was lying amidst their misery, a dreadful lurid light broke in upon him; his own anguish and despair taught him what he had done, what results he had schemed for in his ignorance, and he tore his wounds open, and died in Judas-like remorse.

That is a strange story, and I bear it ever in my mind, as the very type of the blind folly that besets mankind, and makes so many lives hopelessly toilsome and unhappy.

I do believe that the great crimes of nations, as of individual men[,] have been caused [by] stupidity chiefly, not by malice. Therefore, I say, enlighten the minds of men on war; let them understand all that it means; let them see its worst details uncloaked by conventional words; let them know what they are doing by it: in other times, or in other

13. A quotation from John Keats's "Isabella and the Pot of Basil" (stanza 16), referring to the exploitive practices of the heroine's brothers.

14. A failed capitalist and would-be insurance swindler—not an anarchist revolutionary—seems to have been the first mass murderer by dynamite. Keith Alexander, alias William Keith Thomas, an American merchant burdened by gambling debts, consigned a heavily insured barrel of dynamite labelled "caviar" for shipment on the Norddeutscher Lloyd steamer *Mosel* in December 1875. A prematurely tripped trigger-mechanism killed 81 people and gravely injured 200 more as the ship lay in the Bremerhaven docks, but Thomas's apparent intention had been to kill its full complement of 800 passengers and 200 crew members without a trace in the North Atlantic. He attempted suicide before his "perfect crime" was exposed, but survived four days of intermittent interrogation before he muttered "Pech gehabt" ("Bad luck") and died (Susanne Wiborg, *Die Zeit*, 52 [2002]).

countries, it came home more to every man: every man then might have to catch up his weapons and run down to the battle[,] offering at least his own body to be hacked and mangled: that is past now, & well passed; for doubtless such scenes recurring often made men callous to the evils they lived amongst: but we who live amidst happier days[,] how base it is of us if we let the carelessness of ignorant contentment take the place of that callousness of habit; and by no other way can we avoid that baseness but by every man getting to feel himself responsible for any war that the country wages: I say men are not generally malicious or ill-natured or even hard-hearted, and once let a man know what war is and feel that he himself must share the shame of every war his country wages unjustly, and then see if he will cry out for glory, or want to make a deadly quarrel of every chance wind of ill-feeling that may drift from nation to nation.

If we do not see to this, we are thoughtless fools with all that that word means, and amongst other things it means cowards: but if we get to live with our minds really enlightened on the certain loss of even necessary war, and our consciences clear from the craving after *glory*; then if the day should ever come when irrepressible *justice*, or the hard need of self defence drives us into this portentous and monstrous plague of mankind, we should then cleave our way through it with the well-assured hope of coming to better days beyond it; of its leaving no revenge behind to fall upon us at some indefinite time: perhaps in the very days when we should be going fairly and smoothly on the path of progress, and were conscientiously trying to do our best.

Let me put the matter before you once again thus:

All wars that are not merely wanton take place when matters are so bad, when the strain has become so unbearable, that the patience of patient men is exhausted; when even wise men are brought to such a pass, that they can see no remedy save in destruction: they who have been hitherto laboriously heaping up good things for the use of men, are now driven to devote themselves to destroy the health[,] the wealth and the lives of men: instead of spending their lives in striving to make their neighbours live happier and more reasonably, they must now spend them in ruining & killing the[ir] next-door neighbours. That is just and necessary war.

Surely, Sirs, it must have been but seldom in the world's history that things have been so bad as positively to drive worthy and thoughtful people into such straits as this.

In good sober truth not often: just and necessary wars are not so common as that. In how many wars I wonder has the right been clear on either side—to standers by, or even to the combatants two years after the war is over. And in how many[,] when at first there did seem to be clear right on one side[,] has not the right been sorely obscured before the end of it.

Stupid prejudice and greed have been at the bottom of most of those that have been fought by the will of the people even[.] As to those set on foot wholly in the interests of the kings and potentates of the world, I don't think we common people can enter enough into the feelings of such august persons as to be able to understand them: so we will e'en leave them alone for a while.

But apart from the necessities and family quarrels of Potentates—which are not our business—I say that the wars of civilization have mostly been set on foot by two powers, greed and National Vain-glory: you see it [is] chiefly the latter most mischievous and stupid vice which I have been combatting. As to the first, greed of gain, it is certainly not a very amiable passion, or one that we would wish to see pandered to, since we understand clearly that national morality both springs up from and reacts upon individual morality, and is in fact the very bond of decent society; yet I know that as that society is at present constituted it would be unreasonable to scold over much at either individuals or nations for pushing their fortunes to the utmost, so long as they do it without too much lying or too much overbearing, so long as they show a little respect for the rights of the weak as well as those of the strong; the question is rather, does the greed of gain lead to real gain?

It is not uncommon, and is a very instructive spectacle to see a man growing richer and richer day by day, and unhappier and unhappier therewith: and we know the reason why when we come to think of it: it is because he has not advanced all parts of himself together: some parts of his mind and his soul are left long behind in their earlier poverty: nay, worse off than then, because they have lost hope, while the advancing parts of him go on toiling with huge apparent energy and mechanical excitement, that they may come at last to—nowhere—Yes, Sirs, and as it is with greedy men, so shall it be with greedy nations: for, look you, that lust of gain by external violence cannot carry a whole people with it; for it would be too transparent a lie to pretend that the whole people could really share in the gains, and nobody intends that they shall, and people in general cannot fail to understand *that*: so that when some opium-selling, or Turkish bond holder sowing war, or some piece of land-filching is planned, the pill of greed must of necessity be gilded with flimsy stuff about the advancement of civilization, the spread of the beneficent influence of the Anglo-Saxon Race, and the like, before it will go down the throat of the nation.

National Vain-glory, in fact, must be appealed to, before any set of men in this country can get us to start them off in the quest of gain by foreign conquest or foreign embroilment: people at large do instinctively feel that a war in which one side at all events cannot appeal to the highest principles of truth and justice, is a scandal to the world, a ruinous blow to the hopes of humanity. I know that it is unhappily true, that over and over again we have allowed ourselves to be satisfied, to be gulled, by wretched travesties of justice, and, I am ashamed as I say it, seldom more grossly than in the luckless year we have just passed through: and yet, since I do not believe it altogether or chiefly hypocrisy that has made our nation so gullible, but rather want of interest in the subject, want of thought—ignorance in fact—there seems to me no lack of hope that this may be greatly changed, nay is changing now, and that in [the] future it will be very difficult for any class or set of men in the country to jockey us either into a big unjust disastrous war, or a little unjust disgraceful war.

I say this because I cannot hide from myself or you, that whatever slips there may be in our constitution, that might lead under possible circumstances to dead-lock and confusion between the people and the executive, it is really, and always must be, the people that makes war: even a thoroughly despotic prince must screw some enthusiasm or appearance of it out of his people before he can venture to face a serious struggle: and with us the sov[e]reign power and its advisers could no more dare to go to war except under certain conditions than a man who couldn't swim would dare to jump into 12 ft water. If we and they are so unlucky or so thoughtless that they have a whim for an unnecessary war (think what unnecessary war means!) they must venture to carry their whim through either because they think the war they aim at will be so small and easy that we shall not notice it, or because they think that with the help of the noisiest part of the population of all classes they can just push us into one so big that we must join in heartily when the first gun has been fired.

Now I say that if the nation, if we, if any of us are contented to accept those conditions from carelessness on the one hand, or from dread of being considered unpatriotic on the other, we shall have little wars leading to big wars, and big wars leaving us their legacy of little wars, lies and revenge breeding lies and revenge in endless succession, till we shall become the paupers and slaves we shall richly deserve to be because of our sloth and cowardice[.]

There is no escaping from the inference; the last 6 years have taught us the lesson too well: the theory has been that we put Lord Beaconsfield and his tail into office in '74 because we wanted to 'rest and be thankful':[15] I can only say that if [we] are thankful for that rest we are thankful for small mercies indeed: and I for one do not agree with that theory, but believe rather that a vague desire for military glory had bitten us about that time: even from the first, I think, the shadow of that desire lay cold over the parliament then chosen, and paralyzed[16] all usefulness in it: the parliament we then chose felt quite sure of our approbation so long as they neglected our business to attend to our—pleasure, I suppose I must call it.

Well even for this six years of such 'pleasure' in prospect and in fact we have surely paid quite dear enough: enough of pressing questions have been left to take care of themselves, and grow awkwarder and awkwarder to answer: enough of vague fears have been let loose upon industry & commerce: enough of vague threats of undoing the work of our fathers have been scattered about, to take root in the hearts of narrow-minded men, & bear fruit bitter enough both now and in the future: enough of all this has been done to show us how speedy reaction might become, if we could be got for a really long time (six years is not long luckily) to withdraw our attention from what some people call 'parish affairs': that is[,] from our own affairs.

Luckily however, those who took us at our word when we bade them get us into trouble, saw their advantage even too clearly, and, being over eager to find us in a serious reaction, have hurried the matter, and frightened many of us awake, who might otherwise have slept till the noise was well over all our heads; so that we may hope we have indeed learned our lesson, and that before long we shall set the clock agoing which has been stopped for the past 6 years.

I say us and we, and shall continue to use those words: it is unfair to lay the blame of the dreadful deeds of the past year, of the anxious toil of two years ago on the Tory House of Commons or on Lord Beaconsfield, and his ardent friend, admirer, & follower Lord Salisbury.[17] Lord Beaconsfield and his tail rule England at present? Too true—but why? Who made the House of Commons a Tory one? Who made the Tory brain, that sham shifty Ulysses, king over us? Who made that queer whimsical

15. Morris wryly alludes to the title of William Wordsworth's 1831 poem "Rest and Be Thankful! At the Head of Glencoe."

16. MS., paralized

17. Robert Gascoyne-Cecil (1830–1903), 3rd Marquess of Salisbury, served as Disraeli's foreign secretary and Britain's chief negotiator at the Congress of Berlin in 1878, and the Queen awarded him the Order of the Garter for his public and secret undertakings before and during the Congress. During three subsequent terms of office as Conservative prime minister, Salisbury's advocacy of Disraelian "peace with honour" led him to block Irish Home Rule, co-broker the partition of Africa, and preside in his last tenure over British entrance into the Boer War.

fancy a terrible reality to Greek, Bulgarian & Servian[,] to Zulu and Affghan: – and to English widows and orphans too for that matter?

It was ourselves, Sirs, Ourselves.

No, we cannot even plead that we didn't know any better than our government that Sir Bartle Frere[18] was about the land-filching business in S. Africa till it had become a war of which the very soldiers are heartily ashamed: we cannot plead that we could not guess that any man who was trusted by us with the tremendous office of Governor General of India would slily shame us through lies and treachery in the hapless city of Cabul,[19] that we might at last have the honour and glory of performing a great act of generosity, the *pardoning* of men who have fought against us in open battle in defence of their native country—and their own necks: All that has happened is but the natural & necessary consequence of our own folly, our own forgetfulness.

Well, you at least will not forget the state of feeling that was abroad at and about the time of the general election of '74: and I beg you never to forget it, but to remind our party and the great mass of the electors of it and what came of it, facing the disgraceful facts with courage, so that we may at least learn from misfortune.

We had a great statesman leading us then: he had led us through a time of unexampled progress: I defy anyone to state that the nation generally did not heartily approve the important measures that were passed in that parliament under Mr. Gladstone[']s leadership—these things were not done in a corner—Has anyone pretended that after those measures were passed, Mr. Gladstone changed his principles, the principles on which those measures were based, the principles that were professed in '68. Did we pretend to think that we were going to be governed in a different way[,] to be led in another direction to that in which we had declared by our votes in '68 we wished to be governed & led[?]

You know we pretended no such thing, yet in '74 Mr. Gladstone would no longer suit us, nor would his principles[.] And why? apparently because we were wearied with prosperity, and wanted to see what the other thing would be like.

18. Governor of Bombay, member of the India Council and later governor of the Cape Colony in southern Africa, Sir Henry Bartle Edward Frere (1815–84) may have been best known for a war he precipitated when he tried to seize Zulu territory in 1879. Waves of Zulu warriors armed only with spears charged into British gunfire and overwhelmed their opponents at the Battle of Isandlwana; the striking nature of this charge stunned British public opinion long after British troops defeated their enemies later that year. See note below on "Cetewayo."

19. Kabul in Afghanistan. See note below on the origins of the "Second Anglo-Afghanistan War."

Just think of a crew of mariners sailing happily with a fair wind under a captain & officers whom they trust and with whom nothing has gone wrong hitherto; think of them saying: nothing is going on, it is dull, and then turning to, pitching captain and officers overboard, and choosing instead of them some country-bumpkin passengers headed by a stock jobber to sail their ship for them; and then down they sit all hands, get drunk, and whistle for a gale—the gale they'll get without much whistling I imagine. That's what we were like in '74.

We are a great nation, and sometimes think ourselves even greater than we are perhaps: but that was the petty folly we played off on ourselves.

We were wearied of doing right, wearied of prudence, wearied of setting our house in order, and so we fell to fooling for our pastime: there was the disgrace, believe me; what has happened since has been but the visible token of our treachery to ourselves—a pity only that when a great nation goes astray others are involved in its punishment!

Peace, Retrenchment, Reform, modest words indeed and unromantic, but we know well, we had proved it, that these were necessary to us if we were to lead the van of civilization, if we were to fulfill the promise of our country's youth to

> —Rise on stepping stones
> Of our dead selves to higher things;[20]

Yet I say such bewilderment had come over us that we found Reform dull, retrenchment mean, and peace inglorious: we had ready to hand men and a man who could easily mend all this for us, and give us amusement: we put him in his present place to do it: has he given us less than we bargained for? How do you like the merriment, the generosity, the glory for which we craved?

Now mind if I dwell at all upon this past disgrace, it is because I want to stir up hope in you and myself for the future: it is true that we cannot get rid of the consequences of past folly, nay who can say what we shall yet have to pay for it: but the folly itself[,] we may get rid of that.

In the mood in which we were weary of prudence we made for our amusement a strange sort of monsters out of some commonplace, and, I daresay, rather decent men, and called them our rulers; we made them ridiculous to the world and ruinous to ourselves too if it should last: but it need not last; we can unmake their monstership, and restore them to themselves: let us do it, though it will be hard work; and let us when it is

20. Morris quotes this well-known passage from Tennyson's *In Memoriam* (section 1.3–4).

done not forget our former folly lest we repeat it, and thereby ruin many a hope & break many a heart.

Do not above all let the change of rulers come about by the mere swing of the pendulum, and because we have now in turn grown tired of them, but let thoughtfulness and principle make the change: let them be our leaders henceforward.

Meanwhile our respectable, but misled & misleading Tory government will with the help of adversity have taught us something. They have given us a glimpse of the terrible abyss into which we might, if we went quite mad, cast all our gains of the last 3 centuries: they have gone so far even as to show us that we might once more bring artificial starvation on the great mass of our population for the benefit of this, that or the other class: they have taught us that we must watch carefully as our fathers did, lest the letter of our constitution should be strained till our sov[e]reign power becomes a danger to us and to itself: and in short they have showed us the machinery of a trap baited with the wretched carrion called National Vain-glory: a trap for catching us and holding us fast in one place; lest we should go on too fast and do to them and to ourselves all sorts of dreadful things, I know not what – live happily great and small perhaps.

It is indeed a hopeful sign of things bettering since '74 that we have been only partly caught – a bit of our tails, as it were[,] still fast in the teeth: if they had had their machinery ready sooner I believe in good earnest we should have gone headlong into the midst of it: for once more (excuse me for singing that burden again) I can't forget what a thrill of exultation went through the country when the mountains were in labour, and produced that wretched little mouse of the Suez Canal shares:[21] after that, you know England was to take her place again amidst the Councils of Europe.

England[']s place—what is England[']s place? To carry civilization through the world? Yes indeed the world must be civilized, and I doubt not that England will have a large share in bringing about that civilization.

And yet, since I have heard of wine with no grape-juice in it, and cotton-cloth that is mostly barytes;[22] and silk that is two thirds sumach, and knives whose edges break or turn up if you try to cut anything harder than butter with them[,] and many another triumph of Commerce in these days, I begin to doubt if civilization itself may not be sometimes so much adulterated as scarcely to be worth the carrying –

21. Disraeli had heavily invested British currency in such shares.
22. Barium sulfate, a low-grade ore, was often sold as a powder.

anyhow it cannot be worth much, when it is necessary to kill a man in order to make him accept it.

Doubtless our once dreaded foe, poor Cetewayo,[23] has learned so much of the blessings of civilization within the last year, that it is hardly worthwhile to bring him over here to complete the lesson; otherwise we might show him in London some strange things: might he not say: 'poor devils! They treated me ill enough certainly, but I can forgive them since I have seen what a dog[']s life so many of their people lead at home! no wonder it maddens them.'

In short civilization has this in common with charity, (from which apparently it otherwise differs much) that it begins, or should begin at home: our first duty is to our own people, who to my mind are (all classes of them) by no means so well civilized as they should be: for instance it was common to hear apparently educated people the other day gravely insisting on the necessity for the utter destruction of Cabul as a matter of revenge: if I am not mistaken one of those not very edifying publications called Society Journals was busy over this; probably the only serious thing it had printed for months. [P]ray is such senseless stupidity aping wickedness a product of civilization, or a relic of barbarism?

Nay that is a little thing[,] for it has to do only with a few comparatively: this is neither the time nor the place to go into the matters that one cannot choose but think of when one touches on such a subject, but well you know how the heart faints when we think of all the evils of the complicated society of this huge city, this densely peopled country, nor dare anyone deny that England's place is above all things to show the world her people one and all free[,] thoughtful[,] just & happy. That is her duty and her glory.

And how have our representative government helped her to perform that duty, to earn that glory? it is no slander to say that their help has been scarcely worth having. I don't say that it is their fault but it is much their misfortune—and ours: I do not say that the gentlemen who make up the government don't wish prosperity to all classes of the community; only they do not understand, and with their principles cannot understand what the great mass of the people really need, what a great number of them are constantly crying out for: they very likely, who actually deal with affairs, would if they could, do more: but remember

23. Cetewayo, the absolute Zulu monarch whose warriors had annihilated their British opponents at the Battle of Isandlwana in 1879 pled the cause of his people in person as a captive before Queen Victoria. He led them against the British one more time after Her Majesty failed to keep her promises, and he died in 1884.

the mass of Stupidity that they represent, and that will not let them move if they would: stupidity, and the selfish fear of democracy that is bred of it is, I say, what they represent: they have to be afraid of us, and being afraid of us, they cannot understand us, and failing to understand us, they must necessarily fail in their duty; which is bad: But what is worse is that in order to keep office[,] which is necessary for their conception of our welfare, so that they may stave off democracy, they are obliged to make a pretence of fulfilling their duty.

What are they to do? The world is moving: that is hateful to them, and yet if they do not make a show of moving with it, out they go, and it will move a deal faster then: they can't do what they would, and they won't do what they should, and yet they must do something, or else – out they go: so heavy are abuses to the nation that has once begun to move on the path of progress; so intolerable are our wrongs when we have once found out that they can be righted[.]

What must they do? Again I say[,] they must find a foreign enemy a rival; if in fact the enemy is not so much an enemy as a customer, so much the worse for the facts: some country must be made an enemy of which people in general can know nothing; they themselves (our rulers) get almost to believe in the humbug; well enough at all events to be able to speak fiercely on the subject: National Vain-glory is kindled, and millions are made to believe, or to pretend to believe that, for instance, a country with crippled finances, a discontented population, amongst whom wild changes are brewing, a huge unwieldy thinly populated territory, and an enormous corrupt official body is a serious and increasing danger to the richest and most settled country in the world. I think it will seem almost incredible in time to come that such an attempt could have been made on the credulity of a great nation: at all events I believe that history will put down the matter to its right cause, an attempt to amuse the people with dramatic events abroad, while the drag is being put on democracy at home.[24]

I repeat that I do not accuse all or most members of the Tory government of consciously meaning this; but sure I am that unconsciously at least the idea has ever been stirring in their minds: it must have been; for practically it is the policy of the great Tory party since that party has in these latter days been driven to its shifts; and it always will be its policy till that party is extinguished by the general enlightenment of the people of all classes.

24. Parliament had recently passed a series of "coercion acts" ostensibly designed to repress Irish radicalism, then sharpened them as Morris anticipated it would in the 1880s.

Well[,] enlightenment even as far as it has gone did this for us, that the greater attempt failed, owing to the good sense, and I will add the morality of what was at least the better part of the nation, though it may not have been the larger: having failed, still something had to be done, and where was there a shadow of excuse for doing anything: India would do it seemed: people at home don't bother their heads what becomes of the rights and wrongs of a set of barbarians: and if an attack were made on Affghanistan it would look like an attack on Russia, without being so dangerous or costly[,] even if it really rather furthered her ambition than not: it could be slipped into without notice almost, and would be sure to be successful—*brilliantly* successful it might be called without any extra expense:—

So to work we went at making a scientific frontier, which it seems is the modern name for carrying fire and the sword (say murder and fire-raising) among a people who have done us no shadow of a wrong. On my word I cannot explain the Affghan war[25] otherwise than thus: if ever war was waged for war['s] sake that has been—that democracy might be checked in England: I can only say of it further, that the end proposed was ruinous folly, and the means employed villainous injustice.

But meantime, and setting aside the shame and disgrace of our present little wars, how have we been faring at home? As people must fare who irresolutely chase the phantom of military glory about the world; only lucky if we can give up the chase in time to look to our own house before it catches fire.

At our own doors is a curious specimen of the blessings of conquest: when I hear people scolding at those who should be our fellow citizens of Ireland as monsters of ingratitude and the very fools of anarchy, I feel inclined to wish that some man of accurate knowledge and acknowledged rectitude and impartiality would draw up a plain account of all our dealings with Ireland from Strongbow's[26] time to Beaconsfield['s]—for the use of Englishmen: it would not be either

25. In response to the Afghan ruler Amir Sher Ali Khan's denial of entry to Britain's envoy General Sir Neville Chamberlain in 1879, Her Majesty's government attacked Afghanistan in force, and an army commanded by Ayub Khan defeated British troops at Maiwand and besieged the British garrison at Kandahar. Ten thousand British soldiers marched from Kabul to break the siege and end the "Second Anglo-Afghan War" in 1880.

26. Richard FitzGilbert de Clare, 2nd Earl of Pembroke and Lord of Leinster (1130–76), was a twelfth-century warrior and warlord noted for his skill with the longbow. He harrowed Ireland with the Lord of Leinster, Diarmait Mac Murchada, and seized Dublin as well as much of southeastern Ireland in 1170. Henry II later appointed him the king's personal representative in Ireland in reward for these and other military services.

short or pleasant reading I fear; but it might teach us that it is not very wonderful if they find it hard to forget, though we forget, and that we may well try to give them further opportunities to forgive us, and they at the very least may well claim a patient hearing of, and just dealing with their grievances.

Is our own country-side[,] in spite of its beauties and pleasures[,] too pleasant a place for an intelligent man to live in, if he be neither a game preserver or a game keeper: pheasants are beautiful creatures and good to eat; but I wish there wasn't a head of them left in the country.[27]

Five years ago, nay a year ago when the election was further off, and we were still rejoicing in Peace with Honour,[28] what do you think a Tory M.P. would have said to a bill that struck a blow at entail and land-hunger?[29] And now (if the ministry lasts as long) he will have to vote for it it seems, comforting himself, I suppose, with hoping that it is so drawn that it will not work: well I must say I didn't think that we were as strong as that.

But I think we, and not the Tory tail to which he belongs[,] had better educate him on the subject of the anomalies in our Parliamentary representation: and then perhaps he will one day see that the state need not patronize religion in the form of a heavily endowed body of majestic status which it is a mere farce to call any longer the Church of England, but whose existence in that form, and under that patronage casts a slur upon all who belong to other religious bodies, bidding them and their members consider themselves outside of the pale of respectability. But while he and his are in power do we not still tremble for the small modicum of national education that has been granted us,[30] while every man of us who respects himself has to fight tooth and nail against the grossest stupidity and injustice in the district in which he lives to keep it uninjured.

I have named really but a few of the questions that our government ought to help us with; as to most of them and many more the clock has stopped for six years; when will the hands move forward again[?]

The government must make them move, but what government I won't say, for I don't believe in the miracle of sudden conversions in

27. Morris refers to nineteenth-century destruction of farmland to create game preserves.
28. Disraeli's government employed this slogan to characterize its gains at the Congress of Berlin.
29. An 1880 bill severely weakened "entail" ("life-t*en*ancy" with "fee-*tail*"), a law which had permitted testators to will "contingent remainders" of large landed estates to unborn descendants (usually grandsons).
30. For the first time in Great Britain's history, the Education Acts of 1870 (England) and 1872 (Scotland) provided for basic instruction of children up to the age of thirteen.

the seventh year of existence: and as I said before I think those who are now in have done all we asked them to do, and can do no more; and I hope that we have got our wits back and shall keep them and shall no longer need a conjuror to swallow swords and to jump backward over his chair for us[.]

For the rest, if we can't have the absolutely best man at our head, let us at least have the best we can get; and he and his fellows must be such men as look forward with hope not backward with regret; that at least, and yet that will be enough if they understand withal that they need not manufacture enemies of England's glory on the banks of the Neva,[31] or the highlands of Affghanistan, when there are plenty of them between the narrow seas.[32]

But what England's glory is, and what all political action should tend towards in the long run, if politics are not to be a mere game to be played at, I will tell you my idea of that, and see if it square with yours: [I]f it does not, and you think me a crochetter (as the phrase goes)[,][33] well I understand clearly that my crochett has no chance of being heard till Peace, retrenchment, and reform are abroad, and that I intend at the coming election to vote for any good man and true who will help me to those, and to let my crochett bide its time; and to any others of you who are, like me, crochetters,[34] I give the advice to do the same.

I think of a country where every man has work enough to do, and no one has too much: where no man has to work himself stupid in order to be just able to live: where on the contrary it will be easy for a man to live if he will but work, impossible if he will not (that is a necessary corollary): where every man's work would be pleasant to himself and helpful to his neighbour; and then his leisure from bread-earning work (of which he ought to have plenty) would be thoughtful and rational: for you understand he would be thoroughly educated, whatever his condition might be: such a man as this, (and there should be but very few else among us) would never fail in self-respect; he would live honourably, and as happily as national external circumstances would allow him, and would help others to do likewise: you may be sure he would take good care to have his due share in the government of his country and would know all about its dealings with other countries: justice to himself and all others would be no mere name to him, but the rule of all his actions, the passionate desire of his life—What King,

31. River which traverses St. Petersburg
32. Here at home; literally, between the English Channel and the southern North Sea
33. malcontent
34. MS., crochetteers

what potentate, what power could prevent such a man from both taking and giving his due?

Well, some people today would think that dull, would prefer more gambling in life so to say; more contrast of condition, of thought[,] of aspiration: it seems to them right, nay a law of nature, that many people should be boiled down as it were body and soul for the sake of one glorious one: in short they cannot do without slaves: nay they would themselves rather be slaves than free men without them—it would save so much trouble.

Would it? Well, I don't know: in the long run I think not: but then, you see, such men don't trouble themselves about the long run; or they would understand that ignorant and unhappy people are dangerous people; that they desire ignorantly, hate ignorantly, revenge themselves ignorantly, and not unseldom confuse in one ruin those who have wronged them with those who indolently refused to right them, and those that could not right them though they strove sorely.

For my part, Sirs, so that we may have no strife in the land save what may be carried on with the printing-press and the ballot-box, I say let us take the trouble—any trouble to live like free men. And now, look you, it is some 6 years that I have scarcely felt like a free man,[35] and that lies heavily upon me; and in spite of all my good wishes for your welfare I hope it does upon you also, and upon all those whose principles bind them to Peace, Retrenchment, and Reform.

For in that case I know it will not be long before we shall all be free again, and shall see the England that we love once more moving on the forward path, and with a clear conscience shall be able to cry, May the Right prevail!

W.M. Jan 30th 1880
2:30 a. m.
Kelmscott House Upper Mall Hammersmith

35. The Liberal Party had lost the election of 1874. Morris's attachment to a living and organic history shapes his ideals—we should "look[] backward with gratitude and forward with hope."

4

A Lecture Delivered to the College for Men and Women ["Art and Inequality"], 1880

Editor's introduction

In *William Morris: Artist, Writer Socialist* (2.63–72) May Morris reproduces portions of an early lecture which she describes as "one, written in 1880, which is specially full of the doubts and questionings of pre-Socialist days," and notes that Morris has written on the manuscript, "Queen Sq.: to Men and Women's College." This was the College for Men and Women at 29 Queen Square, the descendent of the Working Women's College founded in 1864 by Elizabeth Malleson and renamed the College for Men and Women when it became coeducational in 1874. An adult education college would have been an appropriate venue for Morris, who some years earlier had helped found the 1856 *Oxford and Cambridge Magazine*, which manifested a strong interest in the women's and worker education movements of its time. Throughout his speaking career Morris lectured to several such institutions, among them the West Bromwich Institute, the University Settlements Association, and the Ancoats Brotherhood, formed to provide cultural experiences for Manchester-era workers. The manuscript of the lecture is housed in the British Library as Add. MS. 45,331(1), and the catalogue description notes that it had been entitled "Of the Popular or Decorative Arts" by Ronald Briggs. I have suggested the title "Art and Inequality" as more fully conveying its contents. The selections in *Artist, Writer, Socialist* omit about 40 percent of the original text as reproduced here.

Morris's lecture shows the influence of John Ruskin in its cadences, its assumption that a nation's art expresses its social morality, and further, that the aim of art should be direct social betterment: "that the residuum of modern civilization[,] the terror of radical politicians, and the tool of reactionists, will become the great mass of orderly thinking people, sweet and fair in its manners, and noble in its aspirations . . . is the sole hope of worthy, living, enduring art."

Morris employs frequent metaphors—"fighting a shadow," "civilization is murdering her own children," "before I cast my thimbleful of advice into the ocean of fateful necessity"—as well as allusions to his own art: "if you weave a pattern on a piece of cloth, and then turn it over and look at the back of it, you will see the back of the pattern, and not another pattern: material riches bred by material poverty and slavery produces vulgarity. . . and hardness of heart." As an active speaker for the Eastern Question Association, Morris had criticized Britain's ongoing imperialist wars (see No. 3), and he notes that increased material prosperity has also prompted the destruction of other ways of life, as "masterful races of the world . . . blinded by the hurry of their fate, are too apt to give a stone for bread or a scorpion for a fish to their somewhat unwilling children."

He pays careful tribute to influential cultural figures—"Mr. Thomas Carlyle, who still lives to be the glory of England,"[1] and Matthew Arnold, whose 1878 essay on "Equality" he recommends to his audience. Arnold's essay is concerned less with income equality per se than the effect of social inequality on manners and culture—"it is by the humanity of their manners that men are made equal"[2]—an interest reflected in Morris's dismay at the gulf in tastes and social habits between the members of different social classes: "a difference not of title, position, or the like, but of manners, habits of thought and aspirations: that this should be the case after the gain of so much liberty, after so much of aspiration toward knowledge[,] is an evil sign."

Like the claims of his predecessors Ruskin and Arnold, Morris's argument for the degradation of the contemporary arts is expressed through interpretive history. In this case, he makes a revisionist return to such canonical sources as Tacitus's *Germania* and Edward Gibbon's *Decline and Fall of the Roman Empire.*[3] Both have dismissed as "uncivilized" the true bearers of freedom: "we, wise after the event, see behind all the ruin [of the fall of Rome] the image of the vigorous life of the barbarians, which was once more to lead the world onwards—and whither?" Fresh from co-translating Icelandic sagas such as *The Story of Grettir* (1869), *The Story of the Volsungs and Niblungs* (1870), and *Three Northern Love Stories* (1875), Morris presents an idealized view of the inhabitants of a society of strife and plunder: "rough men if you please but not brutal; with some sort of art among them, genuine at least and spontaneous men who could be moved by poetry and story, . . . quarrelling sometimes, even to dry blows. . . .

in short, men, free and equal." His basic point, however, is that the great inequalities of present-day society now cancel out its claims to progress and culture.

As in most of his historical writings, Morris both accepts and rejects the Hegelian view of history as a progression upward—though the "barbarian" ages were on balance an advance over the earlier classical ones, yet his present age represents a decline: "knowledge, freedom, peace—is our attainment of these so triumphant to-day that we no longer need the solace that the arts of beauty bring to those that love them? . . . what is to fill up the void where the love and knowledge of beauty once had place[?]" On the other hand, degeneration cannot be permanent: "that void [of the arts] *must* according to the laws of nature and life be filled somehow . . . therefore I must believe in its new birth by some means or other." One possible result of society's descent into inequality is violence—and here Morris shares the concern of many of his social peers who fear revolution: "history has taught us . . . [of] the terrible vengeance that time stores up for [unequal societies]." In contrast to his later views, in this early lecture he assumes "the great nations of modern Europe, are not likely to be overtaken by this last and most fearful revenge; yet the prospect must remain dark and doubtful before us, both for the arts and for that daily life of men from which they spring. . . ."

But though social equality is the only remedy for the decline of cooperative art, we cannot yet see the means for redress: "Are we not one and all blind to the relief that the future may bring us, though we cannot help feeling the oppressions of the present[?]" Honesty is necessary, however, not complacence, and none are absolved from the obligation to search for remedies: "we are surely therefore bound by our knowledge to put ourselves, each as we can, in the position of reformers: to seek out the seeds of life, to thrust aside the weeds that choke them. . . ." Morris warns against the temptations of escapism—fleeing the "confusion of civilization"—and the selfishness of striving for an improved status only for oneself. He calls his audience to action, both to preserve the democratic nature of the decorative arts and to combat social distinctions: "we are chained to London life by desires, by duties, by necessity: well, if London is no very good place for the pleasure of repose, it is not so ill for the joy of strife. . . ." Although ["Art and Inequality"] is arguably less specific and concise in organization than many of Morris's later political writings, it thus remains interesting both for its mode of argument and its testimony that as early as 1880 Morris dedicated himself to an equality that to the end of his life he promoted as the basis for "true socialism."

Notes

1. Carlyle died February 5, 1881, at the age of eighty-five.
2. *Selections from the Prose Works of Matthew Arnold*, ed. W. S. Johnson (New York: Houghton Mifflin, 1913), 463. Arnold continues: "on the one side, inequality harms by pampering, on the other by vulgarizing and depressing. A system founded on it is against nature, and in the long run, breaks down."
3. Publius Cornelius Tacitus, *De Origine et Situ Germanorum; The Agricola and Germania of Tacitus*, trans. Alfred John Church and William Jackson Brodribb (London: Macmillan and Co., 1869); Edward Gibbon, *The Decline and Fall of the Roman Empire* (London: Strahan & Cadell, 1776–89).

Before I go any further in speaking to you of the popular or decorative arts I will ask you to consider if you are quite sure that you care about them. I do not mean to say whether you care about having them talked of, or about pondering over them as a curious part of the history of the thought and action of the human race; for everybody who cares about knowledge in general must have some interest in them from that point of view, at all events up to the present time, and until much is forgotten that men of our own day are strenuously trying to bring to light for future memory and thought to exercise itself upon: what I ask rather is whether you care enough about these matters to desire earnestly that they shall live now and in the future, guiding and being guided by the thoughts and hopes of men, as they lived in the past. I believe that to be a serious question and worthy to take its place among other serious questions of the present time; and that those who are at all dealing with those arts whether as users or makers of them, who do not in some way or other put to themselves to answer this question will neither be getting nor giving any help from the practice of them[.]

Now mind you, I must for truth[']s sake make an apparently discouraging statement of my belief: I say discouraging because it is the belief tacit or expressed, of many and many intelligent people who think over such matters, and why I say apparently discouraging you will presently see: this is the statement: that the popular arts, the arts in which the whole people shares, have in these latter days fallen all over the world into a state of degradation: I find that whenever I think or speak of the arts, I cannot escape admitting that to be true. I can well understand how many of you may be pained, and as I said, discouraged, by such a statement: but if I had time I could only too easily prove it to be [true,] and if it be true we must needs face it, and see what is to come out of it: for as life can have no pleasure without *memory*, so it [can] have no honour and no use without *foresight*.

To qualify the discouragement just spoken of put the case in this way, that there are two issues from that degradation[,] that sickness of the popular arts, either complete recovery, new life, or death; one or other of these is natural and necessary, there is no third way, no possibility of compromise; now, till modern civilization was not merely astir in the world, but till it was in a sense paramount, these popular arts were fresh, and vigorously alive, were cultivated eagerly and practiced without thought of shame or fear of failure: nay it comes to this, they [may] well even be looked to [as] that that great portion of the arts, that portion with which I have most to do, the architecture, or if you will, upholstery arts were almost the gift of *modern* civilization to the world; that civilization which sprung from the meeting and clashing of the remains of old exclusive civilization, struggling to be exclusive, with young and eager barbarism come forth from savagery and struggling into civilization: the remains of the art of old Rome carried to new Rome met there, as on native ground and no longer banned, the remains of Greek art mingled with the memories and aspirations of the East; and something new came forth[,] a gift that barbarism struggling to be civilized seized upon and dealt with, using it as an expression for thoughts and desires that seemed new perhaps to the men of the Byzantine Empire, but had their roots and beginnings doubtless as far back as the beginnings of that state of society of which Empire was the slowly dying remnant; thus sprang what for want of a better word I must call Gothic art, by which term I mean that art that filled all the world that had any dealings with organized Society from the time of the Emperor Justinian till the time of the Emperor Charles the Vth. This was [the] natural birth and outcome of modern civilization, even as the art from the living though sick remains of which it sprung was the natural birth of that much slower-grown ancient civilization: you all know something of the history of it, and how its life in Europe, so vigorous and eager, as soon as it had made conquest of that great wave of the new life of the world that was once called barbarism, that it went from change to change, from hope to hope, so speedily that it never gained the perfection of the older art, though its aspirations were at once wider and higher: and if, as I hold, it has been scarcely alive for the last 300 years its fate is in strong contrast with the fate of its foregoer: for that sprung from the earliest civilization of the world faded as that civilization died out into something new; but this, sprung from that very same new civilization is, it seems, to be killed by the progress, by the perfection it may be, of the thing that gave it birth.

That is so much the case I think that if there are none in this room, there are in the world at large many serious and cultivated people who would answer my first question in the negative without the least shame or embarrassment; they would say, no, that they do not care at all for the popular arts, or for any of the arts, except as a curious study teaching us something of what was once stirring in people's minds: if you pressed them home, and they were to think quite clearly on the subject and to answer quite truthfully and without prejudice or conventionality[,] they would have to say that they did not care about beauty at all; and you would find that practically they denied its very existence: I shall be saying now in another form what I said before about the degradation of the arts, when I say, that in my belief, that is the real condition of the greater part of the civilized world at present: they have lost the love and knowledge of beauty. I am prepared to find people defending that [state] of things as an advance that the world [has] made, a casting aside of old encumbrances and follies: nor should I be shocked or scandalized at such a defence: I cannot help knowing that in those days when beauty was so beloved and followed, it could not utterly fill the hearts of men; other things they strove for and hoped for, nay or scarcely dared to hope for, other things they failed of, which we have in part gained since then: knowledge, peace, freedom: amid the confused struggle for these things, often amidst the apparent defeat of the hope for them, were the arts I love, loved and followed and brought somewhere near to perfection: knowledge, freedom, peace—is our attainment of these so triumphant to-day that we no longer need the solace that the arts of beauty bring to those that love them? Or do we perhaps work so much more strenuously on those foundations of all good life than did the "famous men and the fathers that begat us" that we have less time for noting the beauty of the world than they? Or lastly, I would ask those who think the loss of the knowledge of beauty a gain to the world, how it will be when our triumph over its ancient evil is more manifest: how that triumph will be decorated and honoured, and what is to fill up the void where the love and knowledge of beauty once had place.

I must needs say that even when I feel most hopeless about the future of the arts this last question somewhat comforts me; because that void *must* according to the laws of nature and life be filled somehow, and no man can frame in his mind even the faintest conception of anything that will do so, except that love of beauty that has now grown so faint; therefore I must believe in its new birth by some means or other.

So that the conclusion I must ask you to come to in answer to the question with which I began is this: that those who do not care for the arts: i.e. who deny the existence of beauty, which is beauty whatever people may think of it; these, I say, are lacking their share of one of the natural gifts of mankind; or at least their capacity for the development of it is smothered and hidden by disease: they are, to be short something less than men, not something more. To come nearer still to our special subject of tonight[,] the incapacity for appreciating the use and delight of architecture or popular arts among those who do not wholly remain careless of the arts in general is just a milder form of this disease; a sign, moreover, of that languor, carelessness and ignorance of all art which has almost extinguished the lesser arts amongst us, and even grievously oppresses the few great men who yet carry on the practice of the higher arts in the face of all discouragement.

So then we, who have come to know that art, the birth of civilization, is sickening, and who believe that the love and culture of it is a necessary part of the life of man, unless he is to sink lower instead of rising higher in the scale of civilization: we who know all this must needs think that civilization has gone astray somehow in the matter, and we are surely therefore bound by our knowledge to put ourselves, each as we can, in the position of reformers: to seek out the seeds of life, to thrust aside the weeds that choke them, to cherish them and let them have fair play from nature, this is surely our duty: it cannot content us if we are rich to buy a few pictures here and there; to gather up and shut up in our houses the rags and tatters that greediness has filched from the carelessness of Italy, the confusion of Constantinople, or the famine of Persia: it cannot content us if we are unrich to wander hopelessly through our museums discouraged by sight of the mastery that we cannot approach, learning little by it, beyond the fact that our hearts are gown cold, and our hands feeble. I repeat we must surely be reformers if we accept, as we cannot evade the responsibility of our civilization, the civilization of Europe I mean, not England only. The so-called changeless East has long been changed and changing it seems as far as its own civilization is concerned, in our direction—towards decay.

As far as I can make out it is about a hundred years ago that sudden degradation seemed to fall upon its arts, which really until then had not changed much for the worst since the fourteenth century: I do not know enough of history to give any distinct reason for this sudden seeming change; but I cannot doubt that it was feeling the touch of our civilization: and how fast will it change now? Who can measure the greatness of the change that is going on now under our eyes in these wonderful and doubtful days? I suppose the East must go through the same mill as we have done: I can scarcely doubt but that Europe will in some way cast her cloak over the East: great blessings it will bring her—in time: security for goods and body at least, I suppose: but is it not at once melancholy and ridiculous that these blessings must needs be weighted with the curse of ugliness in all that concerns daily life: that in those countries to dress decently, to keep any liking for the art that has been practiced and understood in an unbroken time for a thousand years should be considered the mark of slavery or failure? In this thing also I cannot help thinking that the responsibility is great of those masterful races of the world whom ambition or destiny drives on to rule over peoples of alien race and different ideas of life, and who, blinded by the hurry of their fate, are too apt to give a stone for bread or a scorpion for a fish to their somewhat unwilling children.

But on another side this responsibility touches us perhaps even closer: for these same masterful and restless nations not only bring on to the ruling of alien and faraway peoples; but in their own progress and hurry gather round their own doors, nay in their own houses[,] a set of people of whom they know little or nothing, their restlessness and masterful qualities make the cleverest, the luckiest or the most unscrupulous among them very rich; and rich men as you very well know, must have poor people to fetch and carry for them, and do their dirty work while they sit above and cultivate their tastes and intellect, or in a lordly and dignified manner refrain from cultivating them: the responsibility that lies on these, and on the people that has bred them seems to me heavy—nay too heavy: I know that many of them feel this responsibility, and strive with the overwhelming duties that it lays on them, for there are of course many good men among them; nay their position gives them opportunity of being better as well as worse than other men: but I repeat that while those inequalities exist, those duties above mentioned are to my mind overwhelming, and cannot be striven with successfully: all that those good rich people can do is to free their own souls from the burden of willfulness and malice: all that the nation that breeds them can do is to be anxious and troubled about its own unequal miseries and burdens, and to be of goodwill to palliate and, if only it were not blind, to cure them: history has taught us what happens to nations that do less and worse than this: and the terrible vengeance that time stores up for them: it is a sign of the world's progress and a token of hope that we, I mean the great nations of modern Europe, are not likely to be overtaken by this last and most fearful revenge; yet the prospect must remain dark and doubtful before us, both for the arts and for that daily life of men from which they spring, so long as those strange inequalities are considered a necessary part of that daily life; so long as we are not troubled at the thing itself but only at the miseries and crimes that arise from it. I know there have been and are many men of cultivation, some perhaps very highly gifted men, who contended and contend that this state of inequality is both necessary and beneficent; nay, as to our immediate subject, the arts, it will be the commonest opinion that you cannot have them without rich men for patrons: this doctrine of the blessings of aristocracy, which once concerned itself only with the material side of things, being much clipped and pruned on that side, has of late sprung out on another side, and developed a strong belief in the necessity and beneficence of an aristocracy of the intellect: it is good, says this doctrine, that the many should be kept in ignorance, unrest, and brutality so that the chosen few may be wise, restful and perfect: I protest that it is not fighting a shadow to speak of this opinion, which is spreading very largely among us now.

To some of us such a doctrine, no doubt, seems a wicked one; but to me I confess that plan seems rather ridiculously impossible: like people, like priest, is forever a true proverb, and a people's rulers do really represent it, and not only formally: a state of things that produces vices among low people, will produce, not opposing virtues among high people, but corresponding vices; if you weave a pattern on a piece of cloth, and then turn it over and look at the back of it, you will see the back of the pattern, and not another pattern: material riches bred by material poverty and slavery produces vulgarity of mind and life, and hardness of heart; for we must shut our eyes to troubles that we cannot help; intellectual riches bred of intellectual poverty and slavery produce scorn, cynicism and despair.

Lest you should say that I have been wandering too long from my subject: though I have not been wandering; for it cannot be too often said that all art is the necessary blossom of a fair and good life: to keep strictly to my subject, I say, I beg all people who know what beauty is to consider an ordinary rich man's house in this monstrous and hideous town, and say in what respect as a matter of art it has the better of a poor man's house: it is bigger, it is cleaner, perhaps: and if it is I admit that is one advantage even as a matter of art: if you go inside it the only signs of extra refinement you will see in it will be a few feeble copies from an art whose practice the world has long forgotten, or perhaps of late some pieces of the manufactures of the barbarous East[,] an art now rapidly falling into mere degradation under the inroads of European civilization: as a rule he cannot help this: at the best unless he is rich enough to build the whole quarter in which he lives he must have ugliness all about him out-a-doors: the Capitalists who take in hand the housing of our rich people presuppose a desire for the utmost amount of luxury joined with a content at least in sheer cynical vulgarity: nor will it be any better commonly if you note the external life of those who are intellectually wealthy: a few more signs of their historical interest in the great art of Greece: a few more signs in them perhaps of a liking for the fading popular art of the East; and that is all that they will, or *can* rather, do to help us.

The truth is they and all of us are oppressed by the mass of brutality that the carelessness and injustice of ages has stocked the civilized world withal: they are oppressed I say, they lack help, few as they are: what can they do? And indeed this at least is good, that they cannot lose themselves up in a palace of art, and be cheerful and wise and serene, while handicraftsmen get day by day more unskillful more untrustworthy in their work; while men of commerce get shiftier and more grasping in their cheating; while the amusements of young men rich and poor in great part consist of drinking and low gambling; while the rich and poor of London, Leeds, Sheffield, Manchester and Liverpool clamour on their rulers to let loose death wounds and pestilence against a people who live they scarce know where and how, that their own days might have a little more excitement in them.

If I speak too earnestly or seemingly with an over-gloomy mind about this matter of the inequality of the lives of men, it is because whatever I do my subject will lead me back to that. I have said that that civilization out of which our art first sprung, and which for long cherished these arts, seems now to be slaying them, and in so doing to be inflicting a grievous wound upon itself: now if we seek for a remedy for that[,] we cannot help looking at what has happened before and noting what took place when the ancient classic art seemed failing, when its civilization from which ours has grown seemed to have gone the wrong road, and to be about to be stopped, to come to a slow ignominious end: long and long before people began to think that it was possible for such an end to befall the Roman Empire, the great historian in telling of some deadly quarrel and mortal slaughter of two tribes beyond the Rhine wrote somewhat like this: "We have now attained the uttermost verge of prosperity, and have nothing left to demand of Fortune except the discord of the *barbarians*." There is the word; the symbol of the scorn, the pride and the exclusiveness characteristic of the old civilization. Now it is strange but these words of Tacitus I have just quoted I came across the other day, not in Tacitus' Germany itself[1] but in Gibbon, and a very few pages before I read Gibbon's own words, thus: "In a civilized state every faculty of man is expanded and exercised; . . . the most numerous portion of it (society) is employed in constant and useful labour. The select few, placed by fortune above that necessity, can, however, still fill

1. *The Agricola and Germania of Tacitus*, trans. Alfred John Church and William Jackson Brodribb (London: Macmillan and Co., 1869).

up their time by the pursuits of interest or glory, by the improvement of their estate or of their understanding, by the duties, the pleasures, and even the follies of social life."[2] You see Tacitus with all his wisdom thought silently that the Roman Empire such as it had grown to be was eternal whatever troubles might vex it; still less I imagine had Gibbon any doubt that society, such as it existed before the French Revolution, was eternal, or as long-lived rather, I should say, as the world.

Those *barbarians* whom Tacitus looked upon as chiefly of use for destroying each other, so that the civilized world might live on untroubled, it was they who had the fate decreed them of catching up the torch of progress from the dying hands of Rome, it was through them that art and hope lived again, through them that the very memory of Rome was kept alive: it is with no great feeling of despondency that we read of the latter days of that ancient civilization, wearing and terrible as the time was to the people of those days; the story can scarcely impress us with its due dramatic significance, since we, wise after the event, see behind all the ruin, the image of the vigorous life of the barbarians, which was once more to lead the world onwards—and whither?

As for Gibbon's *barbarians*, the numerous portion of Society that is employed in constant and useful labour, for the use, namely, of the select few that are placed by fortune above the necessity of labour, things are certainly changed since his time, and the select few above all are not so few nor so select; and yet to many his image of civilized society will seem pretty much what we look on now: liberty it is true has spread wider and is better understood, and the class of people who are practically equal has also, as above hinted, grown wider; and yet—below that class comes a great change: there comes the difference, a difference stronger in reality than in appearance; a difference not of title, position, or the like, but of manners, habits of thought and aspirations: that this should be the case after the gain of so much liberty, after so much of aspiration toward knowledge, is an evil sign; a sign that somehow civilization has taken a wrong road: again I say that I am not wandering from my subject which has to do with the fine arts; on the contrary whatever conclusions I have come to as to the state of modern society today, and the necessity and hope of change in it, have been forced upon me by what I have noted in my pursuit of the fine arts: by what I know as a practical man to be true of their present condition: my devotion, if I may use so strong a word, to the work of my own life has driven me to cast about for some remedy for that condition of the arts,

2. Edward Gibbon, *The History of the Decline and Fall of the Roman Empire* (London: Strahan and Cadell, 1776–89), chap. 9, 1001.

and I have seen, as I think many others have seen, that if civilization is murdering her own children, the arts, it is because they and she have gone astray into confusion together, where if they strike they do not recognize each other.

Now of old when the Barbarians who once were looked upon but as accidental troublers of the serenity of the Roman world, when these Barbarians after centuries of sore strife and confusion became the states of modern Europe, then arose the new art, that at its culmination set all the world glittering with its brightness, and quivering with its energy: so we may surely hope that the residuum of modern civilization[,] the terror of radical politicians, and the tool of reactionists, will become the great mass of orderly thinking people, sweet and fair in its manners, and noble in its aspirations, and that, we cannot too often repeat, is the sole hope of worthy, living, enduring art: nothing else, I say, will help the arts; Royal, noble, wealthy patronage, whatever burning enthusiasm may be in it, will only shoot over our heads: to say that popular art can only exist at the will of the people may seem a very flat truism, but it may as well be said and asserted, for like many other truisms it is often looked upon as a dangerous and difficult paradox: without that will being exercised art must remain as it is: on the one hand a pursuit to be practiced in its higher branches by a very few men of the greatest gifts and the most iron determination, whose works will not be either cared about or understood out of a very small circle indeed: on the other hand, a senseless mechanical production of misunderstood forms that so carried out have long been nothing but a mask for bad workmanship and a nuisance to good, a trouble and a weariness to the eyes.

Now these last words bring me to the point where I must face the fact, that as a practical man in a practical country you will expect me to point out to you some direct way of trying to carry out what you and I and so many others so earnestly desire, a radical reformation of the arts springing out of a radical reformation in the manners and aspirations of all people: and when I think of this, in spite of the pleasure and honour of meeting you, I almost wish I were somewhere else tonight, for in sober truth I can do nothing [more] than say once more what has been said over and over again by men so much wiser and better than myself: and they—you (the public I mean) have honoured them for their wisdom and high-mindedness, you have enjoyed and praised their eloquence, as how could you help,—and have persistently neglected their advice. Mr Thomas Carlyle, who still lives to be the glory of England,[3] has warned you off shams and poured his scorn on cant

3. Carlyle died February 5, 1881.

many a time: Professor John Ruskin, a name I must mention at present with grief as well as with affection, and now at last with hope again:[4] without him I and so many others would be now both dumb and blind about these matters: many of you I do hope have taken to heart the great principles that lie at the bottom of that wonderful eloquence that does so often delight us: and if not how can I help you? You have Moses and the prophets, how shall you be persuaded though one rose from the dead.[5] Pray do not ask for miracles of foresight, for mechanical guidance that shall rid you of responsibility; look into the face of nature and the course of history yourselves.

Well, before I go on to cast my thimblefull of advice into the ocean of fateful necessity I should like to speak to you of another name, that of Mr Matthew Arnold: all the more because if I had not read his article on Equality in the *F[ortnightly] R[eview]* I doubt if I should have had the courage to say a good deal of what I have already said to you:[6] I hope you will all read that admirable paper of his . . . I am sure that you will be impressed by the fact that you cannot in the least read between the lines; that he has given you his whole mind on the subject-matter. Under his name and example also I will shelter myself against the accusation of impracticability and generalization; that I speak of existing evils without suggesting remedies: after all how can we do otherwise? Are we not one and all blind to the relief that the future may bring us, though we cannot help feeling the oppressions of the present: only do not let us pretend that we are comfortable under these oppressions, and I think we shall find that they are neither eternal nor divine.

Now to cast forth the aforesaid thimbleful of advice into the stream that carries off advices: you may remember that I spoke before of what was left of art in our days as twofold: of the intellectual side of it that still labours to connect us with the past and the future, I spoke with respect: of the sham-popular side of it which does indeed in the dreary way of failure connect us with the past, but which can never by any possibility connect with the future, I spoke with contempt: if you do not share

4. In 1877 Ruskin had published a highly critical review of the paintings of James Abbott McNeill Whistler, who sued for libel; Ruskin was unable to attend the trial due to illness, and in 1878 he resigned his Slade Professorship at Oxford. In 1880–1 his health was sufficiently restored for him to compose essays for the *Nineteenth Century*, later collected as *Fiction, Fair and Foul.*
5. Luke 16:31, from the Parable of the Rich Man and Lazarus: after his death the rich man descends to hell, from which he begs Abraham to send a messenger to warn his brothers from their evil ways, but Abraham responds: "If they hear not Moses and the prophets, neither will they be persuaded, though one come from the dead."
6. *Fortnightly Review*, March 2, 1878.

that contempt we can go no further: look you, four bare walls, with (by some luck) an engraving on them; a timber table with a book upon it[,] a shelf of the same on the wall: and four or five three-legged stools. I say that is better upholstery for a reasonable man than the upholstery of a modern drawing room; and if you gainsay it, you must answer my first question of this evening in the negative: in that case, I say, you do not care about art and you cannot produce it. Popular art has fallen so low, that we must be humble: it is a difficult thing to play the part of God and Nature, and to fill the eye with beauty: it is not so difficult to get rid of encumbrances that will not allow us to think on and remember the works of God and Nature and the deeds of past times: and yet perhaps it is not so easy: not easy I mean to resist the slavery of fashion: and yet I say it is necessary before you can claim to care about the arts at all.

Let us think how we can begin it, this resistance, in some practical way: since it is obviously too early days to think about heroic measures yet: public opinion is not sufficiently roused yet for a popular movement to pull down Mr. Albert Grant's house at Kensington:[7] nor would this parliament or the next even I fear vote six millions towards pulling down the new houses that spread W[est] and South of the S[outh] K[ensington] M[useum] as if to show us that all our studying of ancient lore [?] would not mend the matter. Well contemptibly dull and discouraging, I confess seems the advice upon which we could all begin to act upon tomorrow, and so, perhaps, each of us in a small way do something to further the arts—here goes that thimbleful I promised: If we were one and all determined to have nothing about our houses which we didn't either know to be necessary, or believe to be beautiful, we should clear away an immense lot of rubbish, and be much freer; nay if this were widely done we should surely set free a great deal of the impulse to make beautiful things which is the cause of all art: to eschew luxury and seek beauty, and be ready to make some sacrifices to that pursuit would surely be good for us both in body and mind:

so also are we best preparing the arts for that greater equality of Society to which I am sure the world must come at last, and which as I firmly believe, will once more awake art with many other good things.

The practical advice is soon given you see: a very few words have disposed of it, and as I said before, it is dull enough: I confess I don't care

7. Mr. Albert Grant's home, described in the July 12, 1880 *New York Times* as a "luxurious home" built in an Italianate and Renaissance style, was begun in 1872 and opened for a large fete of 1500–2000 persons with the Prince and Princess of Wales attending in January 1880. The house had never been inhabited and was said to afford space for twenty simultaneous gatherings.

if it is, and if it tends to make you despair of modern London: indeed I want to bring you to that, so that some effort might come out of your discomfort. Besides suppose perhaps that there is nothing else we can do: Suppose it is the only advice about the popular arts that anybody can give you which is at once practical and founded on principle. There are some of us no doubt, who, oppressed by all the confusion of civilization, may be excused for wishing to be quit of it at times: but you know they cannot be: if they flee from it, it will still pursue them: Yet this much I will say: if our civilization is to carry us no further, to nothing better, I for one wish we had never gone so far; and there must be many of the same mind: rather than we should never be other than we are, I would we had all together been shepherds or whatnot among the hills and valleys; men with little knowledge, but desiring much: rough men if you please but not brutal; with some sort of art among them, genuine at least and spontaneous; men who could be moved by poetry and story; working hard yet not without leisure; getting drunk sometimes, quarrelling sometimes, even to dry blows; nay if the times were heroic enough sometimes with point and edge:[8] neither malicious nor over soft-hearted; well pleased to live and ready to die—in short, men, free and equal.

No, it cannot be: it has long passed[9] over, and civilization goes forward, swiftly, if unsteadily: and for us, we are here chained to London life by desires, by duties, by necessity: well, if London is no very good place for the pleasure of repose, it is not so ill for the joy of strife: and let us once be sure of what we want that we are determined seriously to strive for it, and then also we may be sure that victory will come at last, whether we see with our eyes, or our sons win it or our sons['] sons still have to strive for it.

For nature will not be turned aside from her way, as we are sometimes timidly inclined to fear: neither injustices will thwart her, or folly discourage her, nor ingratitude offend her: still she will go on. And surely this is good to think of now: now in this hour when so much is darkening about us that once seemed bright enough: now when we are like to be disappointed[10] for a while of hope that once seemed assured and present. So let us think that if we have set our hearts on social freedom and equality with all the good that will spring from them, they will surely come about, and bring with them either that art for which I long, or else—there is no else—it will come.

8. Morris's views of a previous era seem influenced by his Icelandic translations from 1869 onward (e.g., *The Story of Grettir*, *The Story of the Volsungs and Niblungs*, *Three Northern Love Stories*) and the ethos of his previous long poetic epic, the 1876 *Sigurd the Volsung*.
9. MS., past
10. MS., dissapointed

Part II

Socialism: The Middle Phase, 1883–1889

5

"An Invitation to Join the Democratic Federation," 1883

Editor's introduction

Directly after the manuscript of "Misery and the Way Out" preserved in British Library Additional Manuscript 45,334 are three folios (ff. 145–7) taken from the conclusion of a lecture. The mention of the Democratic Federation rather than Social Democratic Federation dates these pages from 1883, since Morris joined the Democratic Federation on January 13 of that year, and its name was changed to Social Democratic Federation the year following. By its content this conclusion could have been added to any of his lectures during the year that consider the degradation of popular art under the economic system he termed "commercial war."

Morris's appeals call upon his hearers to take direct action in the cause of socialism: "I ask them not to be superfine or closet socialists, but to take any opportunity that offers to further any socialist propaganda . . . . this opportunity the Democratic Federation now offers them . . . ." As often his remarks have an eloquent personal resonance: "I cannot promise you that in joining a Socialist Propaganda you will escape the loss of reputation, or the ridicule of those whose ridicule and hatred should be a badge of honour to all honest and serious men: no[,] nor that you will escape moments of depression or sense of failure: but one thing I surely can promise you, 'escape' from the reproach of your consciences; escape of the loath word [coward] being given you by that being [who] knows most about you—yourselves."

I feel that I have one duty to perform before we part: I have been complaining and bewailing and maybe I have somewhat damped hopes in some of you, which would surely be reasonable, if we didn't know all, of the speedy and certain bettering of ornamental arts; which I admit does from the outside from the skin outward seem to be mending: I am too deep in the secrets of it to believe in that smooth and speedy recovery; or indeed to wish for it on the present terms, of having it like other goods at the expense of the cultivation of one class and the degradation of another: therefore I have felt myself bound to speak out my griefs even if it damped the hopes of some of you as I have said: to atone for which I also feel bound to suggest to you something that will raise those hopes again by showing you that something practical may be done towards helping matters.

Some of you I daresay though agreeing with a good deal of what I have been saying, do not go all lengths with me, but think that palliatives may bring on a better state of things; that there [are] remedies existing in the present state of society which may be developed[,] and if developed will be enough: I have said already that I cannot agree with such people; but they have my best wishes in trying their schemes: let the fire of tribulation prove them, and what is genuine in them will live and mingle with bolder schemes if they on their side prove to be worth anything.

But there may also be here present some few, who have long thought like myself that the system of capital and labour which has governed the world since it extinguished feudalism has built up a society rotten at the core, which cannot be patched up, but must turn into something else, as rotten and putrid things do in the world of external nature: and that that which must take the place of the capital and labour or devil take the hindmost system must of necessity be some form of socialism: It is to these I now address myself, and beg them to do what lies ready to hand so as to give some kind of action to their opinions: I ask them not to be superfine or closet socialists, but to take any opportunity that offers to further any socialist propaganda which may be ready to accept their services: this opportunity the Democratic Federation now offers them, not in the form indeed of a externally splendid organization with grand offices and shining names but rather as a band of men of the middle-and[-]working classes who have real relations with working men, and no interest of any kind to further save the good of the Cause: men who have looked the thing[1] in the face and are in earnest in their work of spreading fruitful discontent among those whose numbers and griefs should make them powerful, and if[2] they are persistently treated with injustice will one day make them dreadful.

1. MS., things
2. MS., "if" repeated

I ask you therefore who agree with me, and with the paper which you have had a chance of reading here to join us and help us, with your names if they carry weight with them, with your spoken opinions in public and private if you have that gift of expression, with your written expressions of opinion when you can compass that; or lastly with the easiest thing there is to bestow, your money.

I cannot promise you that in joining a Socialist Propaganda you will escape the loss of reputation, or the ridicule of those whose ridicule and hatred should be a badge of honour to all honest and serious men: no nor that you will escape moments of depression or sense of failure: but one thing I surely can promise you, 'escape' from the reproach of your consciences; escape of the loath word being given you by that being [who] knows most about you—yourselves: if we are convinced of the necessity of certain things being done, and do not strive to do them, what are we but cowards: a truism? Well with a heavy heart I say it that even such a truism wounds us with its truth, since I believe that cowardice is the worst and widest spread vice of those that weigh upon our modern middle-classes:—let us strive for the abolishment both of the vice and the class that breeds it—of all distinctions of class. So and so only may popular art once again rise from the dead.

6

"The Relations of Art to Labour," April 1884, 1890

Editor's introduction

Morris lectured on "The Relations of Art to Labour" to the Leeds Philosophical and Literary Society on April 1, 1884. He then delivered this talk or a variant nine additional times under the title "Art and Labour," and a revised version presented in Glasgow on December 14, 1884 was included in Eugene LeMire's *The Unpublished Lectures of William Morris* (94–118). Alan Bacon has further edited a version of the original Leeds lecture later prepared by Morris for publication in the *Co-operative Wholesale Societies' Annual for 1890* (371–82) under the title of "The Relations of Art to Labour" (William Morris Society, 2004), and for this new text Bacon used the original manuscript in Yale University Library Tinker MS 1598 and an initial section omitted from the *Annual* but preserved in British Library Add. MS. 45,334, ff. 47–9. The Tinker manuscript also contains an ending which was crossed out and omitted from the *Annual* version, and so it is now possible to reconstruct the April 1884 version from beginning to end. As Bacon notes, "in the case of lectures, different versions have a particular fascination, because they can show how the lecturer tried to relate to his different audiences, what he saw as being important to stress or alternatively to play down or omit at different venues, as well as changes in the lecturer's own thinking over time" (Bacon, 9). We can see in this reconstituted early version, delivered to a middle-class audience, Morris's direct appeals to his social peers to renounce the conventional attitudes of their class and join him in embracing a new egalitarian socialism.

The lecture's introductory pages provide an eloquent defense of the importance of Morris's topic, thus preparing for the expository historical account which follows. He interprets "art" broadly to include all that adds emotional significance to our lives: this includes not only paintings, sculpture and architecture,

> but I mean all these things and a great many more, music, the drama, poetry, imaginative fiction, and above all and especially the kind of feeling which enables us to see beauty in the world and stimulates us to reproduce it, to increase it, to understand it and to sympathise with those who specially deal with it.

Yet by definition the existence of art requires labor: "art depends on the labour of the mass of men." Morris also makes what to his Leeds Philosophical Society auditors must have seemed a bold leap into his subject, for he not only claims that art has irreversibly decayed from its earlier importance but prophecies that this "decrepitude" will be succeeded by revolution: the present enslavement of workers has sickened the arts, "and would but for the coming inevitable revolution entirely destroy them in the course of time."

As Bacon notes, this early version is both more learned and more Ruskinian in its rhetoric, and indeed Morris refers to John Ruskin as an important predecessor: "Furthermore of late years some of us who most love art (and I will name my friend and master J Ruskin as the most eminent among them) have awakened to a sense of a terrible lack in the life of today." Morris also satirizes contemporary political views in ways his elite audience would recognize, as he places in the mouth of a "cultivated free citizen of the time of Pericles" rationalizations for chattel slavery which resemble Victorian defenses of class hierarchy: "a society founded on the equality of freedom would be poor in all the elements of change and interest which make life worth living; such a change would injure art and destroy individuality of character by taking away due stimulus to exertion."

Morris's account of the historical progression of labor is indebted to Ruskin's *The Stones of Venice*, Edward Gibbon's *Decline and Fall of the Roman Empire*, and his recent readings in Marxist texts such as Henry Hyndman's 1883 *The Historical Basis of Socialism*. Morris first considers the classical period, likely of special interest to his educated audience, who presumably had been taught to respect Greek and Roman culture, reminding them at length that these cultural achievements had been founded on widespread slavery. He notes that even the wisest of the ancients could not envision an egalitarian world, and he quotes with irony Aristotle's observation that slavery could only be abolished if the shuttle could be made to fly through the shed of itself as an anticipation of his own time, "as if he had a glimmer of foresight of modern machinery." The implication is clear: although to Morris's contemporaries an unequal society based on industrial wage-slaves might seem eternal, it too must give way to a higher form of economic organization. Moreover, although the Romans nominally worshipped gods of various sorts, Morris asserts that their real allegiance was to a "religion of city worship," suggesting an analogy with contemporary Britain's focus on the prosperity of metropolitan centers such as London.

As in other early lectures such as his "Address at the Cambridge School of Art Prizegiving" (no. 2), Morris presents a romanticized if attractive view of the early medieval period: "during the middle ages nothing that was made was otherwise than beautiful; that beauty formed as essential a part of man's handiwork then as it does of nature's handiwork always." Raphael Hythloday, the spokesperson of Thomas More's 1516 *Utopia*, had complained that "sheep . . . may be said now to devour men,"[1] and Morris similarly identifies the breakup of the medieval feudal order with the rise of enclosures: "Force and fraud, applied without scruple, soon did their work, and England . . . became a great grazing country, raising sheep for sale of wool to the foreign market." As England became a land of monopolies the resultant "independent" laborers became "free—to starve," and unchecked greed resulted in ugliness, both visual and moral: "popular art . . . under the grip of profit sank lower and lower decade by decade, and was employed in making mere toys and upholstery." At this point Morris cannot resist a dig at seventeenth-century neoclassicism (as in chapter 5 of *News from Nowhere*, where Dick describes St. Paul's Cathedral as one of a class of older "poorish buildings"): "it was, in general, only when men intended to show their pride of learning and riches that they made quite ugly things."

Characteristically Morris evokes two heroic forerunners, Thomas More and Hugh Latimer, who, though martyrs to opposing causes, had voiced similar warnings: "Both say the same thing, and in words which no one who has read them can ever forget[,] give us a terrible picture of the results of commercial greed in their days. It is no idle word to say that such men never die. . . ." A similar greed precludes any present progress, so that Britain is now "the most powerful nation in the world . . . but with a most miserable population, oppressed, past the power of words to tell of." As in his earlier essays "The Lesser Arts," "The Beauty of Life," and "The Beauty of the Earth," Morris indicts the ecological disaster caused by unchecked commercial rapacity:

> it has been thought a little thing to turn the rivers into filth, and put out the sun, and make the earth squalid with the bricken encampments—we will not call them houses—in which those who make our wealth live such lives as they can live.

It should be noted that there are some internal tensions in Morris's historical account, predicated as it is on an assumption of economic progression: although according to his trajectory the labor relations of the classical period, naked chattel slavery, had given way to a somewhat more advanced feudal system of reciprocal if unequal rights and duties, yet the third stage, commercial commerce, represents a regression from even these limited rights of labor, and the necessary fourth term, socialism, would therefore seem a sudden leap.

The only solution to these problems lies in reconstituted social relations; though Morris has been criticized for rejecting all gradualism, he here lays out quite concrete suggestions: every worker must live in a decent house; be educated according to his capacity, not according to his parents' wealth; and be protected by legislation from overwork and granted leisure. The catch, however, is that under a profit-driven system these reforms can never be implemented, and he again advocates "Socialism, or universal cooperation" as the sole remedy. Moreover, this change to socialism is inevitable, he warns, and he enjoins his audience: "This . . . next move in the great game of progress . . . will be made whether we like it or not, whether we help it or not. But since it is for the good of the human race, and since day by day its advent is becoming more obviously inevitable, let us learn to like it and learn to help it."

The now restored conclusion of this essay, omitted from the *Co-operative Wholesale Societies Annual* version, adds force and personal references to Morris's appeals. He warns his prosperous manufacturing-city audience of the potential upheavals they will face if they refuse to act:

> Be warned in time I beg of you. . . . I say in the interests of peace and order, I beg you to keep your eyes open to the signs of the times; so that the change may be brought about as little mechanically as may be, . . . leaving as little heart-burning and injustice behind it as may be.

And finally, Morris presents his own choices as a model for his fellow middle-class listeners:

> I am the bolder in begging this of you since I myself belong to the middle class, and I think represent an increasing number of men of that class who, whatever happens must throw in our lot with the workers at every stage of this struggle: to us the name Socialism does not represent a political party but a religion rather, to which we are bound to devote our lives. . . .

As in his poetry, Morris is a master of evocative cadence: "Rich and poor are the words which divide the world, and I earnestly beg you to join yourselves to the cause of the poor, in the hope that those two names so long expressive of the curse of the world shall one day have no meaning to us. . . ." This final section of this lecture may have been omitted as unsuited for Morris's later working-class audiences, and, as Bacon notes, it may also have seemed inappropriate for insertion in the publication of a gradualist cooperative society (19–20). These final paragraphs provide a fitting complement to the essay's opening evocation of socialism, however, and they also witness Morris's ability to mix deep emotion, even self-revelation, with appeals to principle and rational action.

Note

1. Thomas More, *Utopia* (Leuven, 1516), Book I.

Opening passage

I must ask you to understand that by the word art, I mean something wider than is usually meant by it: I do not mean only pretty ornament though that is a part of it: I don't mean only pictures and sculpture, though they are the highest manifestations of it; I don't mean only splendid or beautiful architecture, though that includes a very great deal of all that most deserves to be called art: but I mean all these things and a great many more, music, the drama, poetry, imaginative fiction, and above all and especially the kind of feeling which enables us to see beauty in the world and stimulates us to reproduce it, to increase it, to understand it and to sympathise with those who specially deal with it. In short by art I mean the intellectual and therefore specially human pleasure of life, distinguished from the animal pleasure, and yet partaking of its nature in many ways, and which pleasure is produced by the labour of men either manual or mental or both.

Now this pleasure I am clear the world cannot do without: nothing can take its place: if we lose that we lose civilisation; nay all life that is worth living: for surely whatever degradation men may undergo they can never live the innocent life of the beasts, or be happy in such pleasures only.

Furthermore of late years some of us who most love art (and I will name my friend and master J Ruskin as the most eminent among them) have awakened to a sense of a terrible lack in the life of today: they have felt as if this pleasure of life were slipping away from the world, as if something or other were robbing us of it.

Many of us still, all of us, perhaps, some time ago were blind as to the meaning or causes of this loss, plainly and bitterly as we could feel the loss itself: but as the years have grown and link by link the great chain of necessary circumstance that is drawing forward the cause of the people has become plainer to us, we are beginning to understand what it all means: that decrepitude of art which once only filled us with dismay and hopelessness shows with another face now, and we recognize in it one of the tokens of the coming change in the basis of society which we so ardently desire: all along we have dimly seen that what is called modern Commerce or the reckless war of the market has been the foe of art or the pleasure of life, and now at last we are beginning to see that the very sickness and confusion of that pleasure is a sign of commercial war wearing itself out, fretting itself away; that the foe itself will at last kill itself and give place to something better, nothing less than that which you and I call Socialism.

So with our eyes thus cleared we can face modern ugliness and unrest with hope, and accept it and our own discontent with it, as signs of encouragement, nay as signals for action.

Well, what we as lovers of art and defenders of the pleasure of life have learned is really this: that art depends on the labour of the mass of men, and that the Commerce of modern times is destructive to art because it is the oppressor of labour: and by the Commerce of modern times, you understand I mean the system of exchange which lives on the exploitation of labour, that system of profit-grinding of which we all form a part either as the grinders or the ground: and the practical inference we have drawn from all this is that we will do our best to overthrow this system, with good hope in spite of its apparent strength and coherence.

Now as it was by the teaching of history that we have learned this lesson, I will ask your patience while I run briefly over the relations of art to labour in past times, that we may have some kind of idea how it was that the comparatively modern monster of profit-grinding gradually sucked art or the pleasure of life into its relentless mill, to be ground up fine with many other things some of which I hope will come out of this mill in a very different condition from that which the grinders hope for: to drop metaphor what I want to show you is how the enslavement of the whole mass of workers at the hands of the capital and labour system has necessarily involved the gradual sickness of the arts, and would but for the coming inevitable revolution entirely destroy them in the course of time.

Text as published in *The Co-operative Wholesale Societies Annual for 1890*

In considering this important subject it is necessary to look into the past history of the world, and, however summarily, glance at the tale of the twins, Art and Labour, which tale, indeed, means nothing less than the history of the world.

To pass over the conditions of men as mere savages, one comes across civilised men in history served by labour under three conditions—chattel slavery, serfdom, and wage-earning.

Under the classical peoples society was founded on chattel slavery; agriculture and the industrial arts were carried on for the most part by men who could be bought and sold like beasts; and as a consequence the industrial arts, at least in the heyday of Greek intelligence, were looked down on with contempt, and what of art went with them was kept in the strictest subjection to the intellectual arts, which were the work of free citizens. Art was, indeed, kept from corruption partly by the simplicity of life, which, in a climate not exacting either of elaborate shelter or elaborate living, was the rule amidst Greek refinement, where luxury, in our sense of the word, was unknown; and partly, also, by the fact that owing to that simplicity, and the transcendent genius of a race, which you must remember was divided from still simpler conditions of life by no very long lapse of time—owing to the simplicity of life among a vigorous and uncorrupted people, full of natural cleverness and skill of hand, the love for and knowledge of the more intellectual forms of art was common, was rather the rule than the exception. The result was, as to the arts, that while there was abundance of their higher manifestation, in the lesser branches, there was rather, as far as we can judge, an absence of revolting ugliness than a presence of entrancing beauty. Meantime, to the cultivated Greek citizen, there seemed nothing wrong or burdensome in chattel slavery. It was part of the natural order of things, and the greatest minds of the day could see no possibility of its extinction, if one excepts the remarkable passage of Aristotle, where he says, that if the shuttle, for instance, could be made to fly through the shed of itself, one might then be able to do without slaves; as if he had a glimmer of foresight of modern machinery, concerning which and its dealings with art and labour I shall have a word to say presently. Apart from this, I suppose a cultivated free citizen of the time of Pericles, if the question of keeping his fellow-men in subjection to the supposed necessities of a few had been pressed on him, would have found ready answer enough to extinguish any revolutionary ideas, and to strengthen his conviction that the order of things under which he lived was eternal. "Apart from the impossibility of doing away with chattel slavery," he would say, "which is obviously founded on the moral nature of man—apart from that, a society founded on the equality of freedom would be poor in all the elements of change and interest which make life worth living; such a change would injure art and destroy individuality of character by taking away due stimulus to exertion. At best, in a world where all were free before the law, there would he nothing but a dull level of mediocrity." So he would have argued, and, I imagine, would have obtained the suffrages of most cultivated men of the present day; who, it appears, do verily think, and not unnaturally, that the cultivated gentleman of Attica or England is such a precious and finished fruit of civilisation that he is worth any amount of suffering, injustice, and brutality in the mass of mankind below him; but, also, our Greek gentleman might go on with his argument in favour of chattel slavery in a manner rather embarrassing to us of these days of progress and widespread political rights. "Besides," he might say, "are you sure that you will better the condition of the slave by freeing him? At present it is the interest of his owner to feed him and keep him in health—nay, in many cases, if the owner be a good-tempered fellow, he will even exert himself to do his best to make his slaves happy for his own pleasure. But I can conceive a state of things under which the greater part of the free citizens may be free indeed, *free* to starve, and in which the sour faces of overworked and underfed wretches would have no chance of impressing a sense of discomfort on men who, so far from feeling any responsibility for their livelihood, did not even realise their existence. Nay, believe me, you had better trust to the humanising influence of the philosophical simplicity of the noble and free citizens of our glorious City, which, as you well know, in spite of all the tales of the poets, is the real god that we worship, and which indeed is, in some form or other, immortal."

So he might have argued, elevating the conventional rules of successful tyranny into natural and irrevocable laws; but what followed? The worship of the city found its due expression at last in the growth and domination of Rome, the greatest of cities, whose iron hand crushed out the ceaseless bickerings of ambitious clans and individuals, and cast over the world of civilisation the chains of enforced federation under the rule of tax gatherers, dominated at last by the strange superstition of idealised authority under the symbol of the master of the world enthroned in an Italian city. And chattel slavery had still made good its claim to be considered the effect of natural and eternal laws for some time to come, although the condition of the slaves, now mostly working for the profit of the great Roman landowners, was more dangerous to the State than it had been under Greek civilisation. The hideous greed of these capitalist landowners, whose slaves were in a worse condition than even the agricultural labourers of England to-day, discounted the fertility of Italy, and at last the change came again, this time a tremendous one. The huge crowd of starving slaves, in whose minds a revolutionary eastern creed was now fast implanting ideas quite foreign to classical civilisation, were by no means touched by the religion of city worship, which once had put such irresistible might into the hands of the Roman legionaries. In all directions the slaves recruited the bands of brigands and pirates, whose exploits are the groundwork of the plots of the late classical novels,[1] and formed an element of disorder ready to the hand of any external invader. Thus hunger, the child of monopolist greed, did her work within the empire, while without it another force, probably hunger produced by other causes, was at work, and allied itself to the stir caused by corruption within. For the tribes of the north fell upon the empire, where, as a matter of course, they met with no really organised force to resist them, since the corruption of a gross form of individualism had sapped all public spirit; and so, attacked by slaves, Christians, and barbarians, classicalism fell, and, to the eyes of most historians then and since, chaos took its place, a chaos from which, as people used to think, there grew accidentally the collection of independent states which we call modern Europe; used to think, I say, for it is now clear to thinking people that the change, dreadful as it seemed to the cultivated of that time, bore with it the seeds of order which at once began to germinate.

Now, it is worth while noting for our present purpose of looking into the relations of art to labour, that one of the chief signs of that nascent order, which sprang up at the time of the breakup of the Roman Empire, is to be found in the art produced at the period.

The times which followed the complete supremacy of the Roman name, and during which chattel slavery was in full swing, saw only so much change in the condition of art as was involved in increasing luxury and corruption. The more intellectual arts became chiefly imitative of bygone ideas, or at least academical and stationary. The soul of them was feeble, and lacked faith and life, although their body was still fair enough; as to the lesser arts, in them, there was, as far as we can tell

1. Since late Roman literature seems to have been comprised of treatises rather than novels, Morris may possibly refer to more recent novels set in the late classical period, such as Wilkie Collins's *Antonina, or The Fall of Rome: A Romance of the Fifth Century* (1850) or Felix Dahn's *A Struggle for Rome*, trans. from the German (1878). Morris's *The House of the Wolfings* (1889) and *The Roots of the Mountains* (1890) are further examples of this genre.

from what scanty knowledge we have of them, more tendency to their being occupied with making mere elaborate toys, and for the rest it is inconceivable that they turned out ugly things any more than under the period of Greek art. But the exterior of art changed under the Roman rule, in one respect at least, very much, for under influences whose origin it is very difficult to discover, but which were certainly absent from the art of Greece, they invented architecture, by inventing and habitually using the arch. On the other hand, the ornamental side of their art was so entirely academical and artificial that they failed, as long as the classical period lasted, to produce a style of architecture, properly so-called, which was really harmonious with this great invention. On this side of things they were completely under the domination of the forms of Greek art, which they used merely superstitiously, as one may call it. What is really admirable in the architecture of classical Rome lies in the qualities of its building—in its majestic solidity and massiveness—to gain which no amount of material, care, or labour has been spared. It stands before us to-day, even when we come across it in this out-of-the-way corner of the empire, as the very embodiment of that worship of the city which I have spoken of, and which, without all doubt, was its animating spirit. Here, then, at any rate, was a body for any new art to creep into, and a body which, unlike Greek temple-architecture, could adapt itself to its new soul with ease.

This new soul of art did not fail to take its advantage amidst all the disasters and miseries of the birth-throes of feudal Europe, and found expression in a new art, which we call, and accurately call, Byzantine art. The creed which it served came from the East; the city which was its centre, standing between Europe and Asia, dealing in peace and war with the great kingdom of Persia, had plentiful communication with the East; therefore it is not wonderful that Eastern influence is obvious in this body of art; but as my purpose is social, somewhat more than historical or artistic, I must not linger over the entrancing subject of the origins of Gothic art, but will rather beg you to note that this Byzantine art was very far from being a clumsy blending of the misunderstood elements of the art of classical times—a rude and barbarous resetting of the *disjecta membra* of Romano-Greek art; a conception of it which may still, perhaps, linger in some people's minds—but rather that it was a genuine historical development, born indeed, out of the corruption of Romano-Greek art, but a vigorous style, orderly, beautiful, and, above all, alive and growing—not a dead toy, but a living organism working in men's minds, and by them unconsciously furthered. Now, you see as the dead waste period of the corrupt Roman tax-gathering produced a dead art, so was this living art produced by a social growth in the midst of what seemed to be chaos and ruin.

Under[2] the break up of the old Roman society, wrought upon as it was by nations who were called barbarous, but who bore with them real ethical ideas, however rude, and real social laws, however different from those which it was their mission to destroy, under this break-up, or new birth, chattel slavery fell and yielded to a new condition of labour; and I assert that the Byzantine art, whose tendency, considering the state of things at that time, was certainly towards freedom, was the token and the effect of that new condition of labour, which may be briefly described as serfdom struggling towards freedom by means of co-operation for protection of trade and handicraft. Serfdom is the condition of labour in the early middle ages, as chattel slavery was in classical times. The slave was fed by his master, and kept in just such a condition of comfort as was convenient to his master or owner, who, in very bad periods indeed, as sometimes in the days of the Roman *latifundia*, was driven by hopes of exorbitant profit to allow him to supplement his short commons by the industry of brigandage, but who in general would find it more profitable to keep him in pretty good condition. The serf, on the contrary, had to perform certain definite services for his feudal lord, so many days' work in the year generally, and for the rest of the time worked for himself, and fed himself on the portion of land allotted to him. Thus doing, he was living in harmony with the general arrangement of society in the early middle ages, a time in which every man had legal, definite, personal duties to perform to his superior, and could claim certain degrees of help and protection from him.

So was formed the hierarchical feudal system, which was founded on *a priori* ideas of divine government, and under which every man had his due place, which (theoretically) he could not alter or step out of. Personal duties for all, personal rights for all, according to their divinely-appointed stations—that was the theory of the middle ages as opposed to that of classical times, where the supreme city was lord and ruler, exacting rigid obedience from her children, the citizens, who were served by chattel slaves entirely unrecognised by the State, except as beasts of burden might have been.

Well, it seems natural enough that this hierarchical system of the middle ages should have been looked upon as still more reasonable, necessary, and eternal than that which preceded it. But revolution was in store for it no less than for the other system; for, as the half-starved chattel slave of the Roman *latifundia* was driven to better himself by

2. Paragraph break added

brigandage first and then by rebellion, and service with the invaders, so the mediaeval serf was driven by the compulsion of labour in feeding himself after his *corvée* was done, into trying to better himself altogether, and to slip his neck out of his lord's collar and become a free man; which struggle, as is said above, took the form of co-operation in various ways.

Apart from the religious houses—which afforded protection to labour, and even offered it a chance of rising out of its caste on the conditions of definite acceptance of hierarchical government in its fulness—apart from the monasteries, there were other bodies which grew to be powerful and far-reaching; these bodies are called the Guilds.

The tendency of the Germanic tribes towards co-operation and community of life showed itself quite early in the middle ages. In England, even before the Norman conquest, this tendency began to draw the workmen and traders into definite association. The guilds, which were the outcome of this association, were at first mostly of the nature of benefit societies; from that they changed gradually into the Merchant-guilds—associations, that is, for mutual protection in trading; and lastly into the Craft-guilds, or associations for the protection and regulation of handicrafts.

In all these guilds the real object was for the individual to shake off the domination and protection of the feudal lord, and to substitute for that the authority and mutual protection of the members of the guild; to free labour from the power of individual members of the feudal hierarchy, and to supplant their authority by that of corporations, which should be themselves recognised as portions of that hicrarchy, out of which the mediaeval mind could scarcely step. Of course, all this took a long time, and was by no means carried out without some very rough work; the Merchant-guilds, in particular, resisting the changes which brought the Craft-guilds into power tooth and nail, especially in Germany. In the process of the struggle the Merchant-guilds for the most part became the corporations of the towns, and the Craft-guilds took their place fully as to the organisation of labour, and also at last shared largely in municipal government. By the beginning of the fourteenth century these latter were fully established, and were the masters of all handicrafts. All craftsmen were forced to belong to the guild of the craft they followed. For a time, only too short a time, their constitution was thoroughly democratic; every man apprenticed to a craft was bound, if he could satisfy the due standard of excellence, to become a master in his turn. There were no mere journeymen. This condition of things, however, did not last long, for as the towns grew, and the serf field-labourers became free, they began to crowd into the Craft-guilds, and the masters, who at first were simple complete workmen helped by their apprentices, or incomplete workmen, began to be small capitalists and employers of labour, to the extent of being privileged members of the guild; and besides, their privileged apprentices employed journeymen, who, though forced to affiliation to the guild, were unprivileged, and would not in the ordinary course of events become masters. This must be looked upon as the first appearance of the so-called free workman, the wage-earner, in modern Europe. And this beginning of the proletariat was at the time felt as a trouble, and some attempt was made by the journeymen to form guilds of their own beneath the Craft-guilds, as those latter had done beneath the Merchant-guilds. In this revolt against privilege they were unsuccessful, and the Craft-guilds went on getting more and more aristocratic, although the power of their privileged members over the journeymen was checked by laws made in favour of the latter.

The labour of the Middle-ages, therefore, was carried on amidst a struggle—partly conscious, partly unconscious—for freedom from the arbitrary rule of aristocratic privilege, which at first crushed almost all workers down into the condition of serfs. Before glancing at the results of that struggle, let us consider the relations of art to labour during this period of the fully-developed Middle-ages.

Examination of such facts as are within our reach, which have to do with the economic condition of England during that period, show us that, however rude the general conditions of life were, the struggle for livelihood among the workers was far less hard and eager than it is under our present system of capital and wages. The earnings, both of common labourers and artisans, were, in regard to the price of necessaries at the time, much higher than they are now. Life for the working classes was easier, though general life was rougher than in these days—that is to say, there was more approach to equality of condition, in spite of the arbitrary distinctions of noble, gentle, churl, and villein. Well, as the distribution of wealth in general was more equal than it is now, so was that of art in particular.

It has been noted by those who have studied the history of labour in the middle ages that the remuneration of those who superintended labour—builders, architects, and so forth—was very little higher than that of the men who were under them. Nor were those who were doing what is considered more intellectual work—artists, in short—paid higher than ordinary craftsmen. Moreover, there was very little competition in the market, and next to no middleman's work. The workman had but one master—the public. He had full control over his time, his material, and his tools—of his work, in short—that is, he was a free workman, an artist. It was this condition of labour which produced the art of the middle ages, and nothing else could have produced it. The theories of religious enthusiasm, and the like, as the motive power for that art, are, I suppose, pretty much extinct by this time; indeed, such a theory could hardly stand before the first glance at the hideous splendour of some foreign Jesuit church, where religious enthusiasm was at its height, with artistic results that make a sensitive man shudder even to think of. In fact, the more the question is studied, both through the existing remains of mediaeval art and through the records left us of the condition of the people at the time, the clearer it is seen that it is no exaggeration to say that during the middle ages nothing that was made was otherwise than beautiful; that beauty formed as essential a part of man's handiwork then as it does of nature's handiwork always. And further, that this essential beauty of handiwork was, amongst a vigorous and healthy people, the inevitable result of the workman working freely, and for no master; having, as I have said before, full control over his material, tools, and time.

On these terms art, or the pleasure of life, was shared by the whole people. No one could be ignorant of the simple arts of life, and general interest was taken in their production; so that the standard of excellence in wares was kept up and pushed forward at once by the intellectual and the material interests of the people at large. The distinction between artist and non-artist did not exist; it was only a question of the difference of mental gifts between one man and another. Such as those gifts were, no one was debarred from the means of expressing them in art by some means or another.

This was the position of art in the feudal period, brought about by a life of labour which was a struggle for freedom from the restraint of privilege. That struggle ended in victory. How and with what results to labour and art?

We have seen that in the fifteenth century the distinctively free wage-earning class, or proletariat, was coming into existence in the form of the journeymen of the crafts-masters; but their position was, of course, by no means that of the present factory hand. Their wages were high, and indeed wages rose in the fifteenth century; and as to their work, they were on an equality with their masters—organisers of labour, as we quaintly call people who do nothing but stand and look on at labour, being unknown in that time, and division of labour in the workshop having scarcely begun. But in the first half of the sixteenth century the body of men available for journeymen grew greatly and suddenly. Commerce was spreading all over Europe, and tending ever westwards. In this country the bonds of feudal personal service had been much shaken by the wholesale slaughter of gentlemen in the Wars of the Roses, and the impoverished landlords saw before them a chance of recovering a position by throwing themselves into the market of new-born commerce. Then began in England the great change, and whereas, hitherto, men had produced wares for a livelihood, and for the supply of the wants of their neighbours, they now began to produce them for profit, and for a gambling-market. The first step in this change was taken towards the land. The landowners, as I have said, saw their advantage, and turned all their energies to the raising of wool as a marketable commodity. The impulse towards commerce was irresistible, although, under Henry VII, legislation tried to check the expropriation of the yeomen from the land. Force and fraud, applied without scruple, soon did their work, and England from being a country of tillage, interspersed with common land for the pasturage of the people's live-stock, became a great grazing country, raising sheep for sale of wool to the foreign market.

Two representative men have left in their writings full tokens of how bitterly this spoliation was felt. Sir Thomas More, one of the most high-minded and cultivated gentlemen of his period, an enthusiastic Catholic, a martyr for his honesty to that cause, was one. Hugh Latimer, a yeoman's son, the very type of rough English honesty, an enthusiastic Protestant, and a martyr to his honesty in that cause, was the other. Both say the same thing, and in words which no one who has read them can ever forget[,] give us a terrible picture of the results of commercial greed in their days. It is no idle word to say that such men never die; and now, once more in our days, it seems as though the axe of More and the faggot of Latimer were still at work producing fruit which [not] even they—no, not even More himself—had conceived in their minds.

But meantime commerce went merrily on her destructive way. The direct spoliation of the people above mentioned was followed by their indirect spoliation in the form of the seizure of the lands of the religious houses, under the pretext that they no longer performed the public function for which they were held, and *therefore* should no longer perform any public function at all. This fresh robbery of the people, apart from the hideous brutality with which it was carried out, had immediate results, woeful enough; but the point on which it touches our subject is that it added to the army of lackalls cast loose on the world (and of whom More and Latimer speak), in consequence of the discovery of the landlords that they could farm for a profit, and that men were less profitable animals to keep than sheep.

So you see, between one thing and another, there was created a vast body of people who had no property except their own bodies, which, in consequence, they were bound to sell to anyone who would buy them on the terms of keeping them alive to work. Thus was established the class of *free* labourers of whom our Athenian friend was afraid, not without reason; men who were free—to starve. This was the material ready for the use of the plague of profit-mongering (politely called commerce), then newly let loose on the world. At first the market was hard to adjust, and the "material" somewhat intractable—so much so that by Mr. Froude's pious hero, Henry VIII[3] (whom we may call one of the greatest scoundrels that ever disgraced the name of Englishman), and by others, it was hanged out of the way by the thousand.

However, things shook down again at last. A poor-law, which, unlike the existing one, was humane and reasonable, was enacted to fill the place of the almsgiving of the monasteries; and things grew a little easier in relation to labour, and so was established the new order of things founded on commerce, and its dawning gospel of supply and demand.

Thus had the struggles of labour, to set itself free from feudal arbitrariness, succeeded in a sense; feudalism had got its death blow, and commerce was taking the empty place in its old throne. The workman had entered into his kingdom, then? All was straightforward justice and good life for him henceforward? Strange to say, not at all. On the contrary, he had been shoved down a step or two, and was, in fact, worse off than his predecessor, the serf, had been. He had laboured, and other men had entered into his labour. For out of all those elements of freed villein, corporate trader, privileged guild-craftsman, yeoman, et cetera, had gradually grown up a middle class, who increased speedily in wealth and power, being fed by that very misery first created by the expropriation of the peasants, who, as I have said, became the due material for the profit-mongering of new-born commerce.

This new middle class made a stout and rigorous set of men, rough-handed and unscrupulous enough, and pushed on against privilege, with all the old traditions behind them of men who were struggling under very different circumstances, and with aims, at least partially different, and towards the middle of the seventeenth century they began to aim at supremacy in the State instead of freedom for

3. J. A. Froude, *History of England*, 11 vols. (London: Longmans, Green, and Co., 1893). Henry VIII's reign dominates volumes 1–4. After an account of incessant quarrels, machinations, and cruelties on all sides at the onset of the Reformation, Froude offers a qualified assessment of his subject: "His personal faults were great, and he shared, besides them, in the errors of his age; but far deeper blemishes would be but as scars upon the features of a sovereign who in trying times sustained nobly the honour of the English name, and carried the commonwealth securely through the hardest crisis in its history."

commerce. As to the condition of labour under them, it was poor enough. Although some of the crafts were carried on in a domestic manner without division of labour and untroubled by the middlemen, in most competition and the rule of master over man was fairly established. As to the arts, it fared in likewise. The craftsmen were now divided into artists who were not workmen, and workmen who were not artists. Popular art, which was once universal art, and in which the changes from the highest intellectual to the lowest ornamental art were gradual and imperceptible—popular art lingered in a rude form where it was allied to the domestic labour aforesaid, but elsewhere, under the grip of profit sank lower and lower decade by decade, and was employed in making mere toys and upholstery. Architecture, or ornamental building, retained some of its charm and beauty where life was rude and simple, but elsewhere had lost all life and hope, and sank into a dull, pedantic exposition of the misunderstood rules of bygone ages. Yet a tradition of the better days still lingered, and it was, in general, only when men intended to show their pride of learning and riches that they made quite ugly things.

Such was the art of the seventeenth century; but there was a growing tendency to change in the organisation of labour necessitated by its growing commercialism. The workmen were collected into workshops, their simple machines—the loom, the lathe, the wheel–though not for the most part altered in principle, were lightened and improved; division of labour was introduced; and an intelligent man, who once would have schemed and carried out a piece of work from the first to the last, was now forced to concentrate all his mental power on a small portion of such work, speed and precision being the qualities now sought for in a workman, instead of thought and artistic finish.

This system of work was carried to perfection during the next century (the eighteenth), with the result of the entire destruction of popular art except in places so remote from the centres of civilisation that they scarcely felt the influence of commerce; while as to the intellectual arts, painting, sculpture, et cetera—they sank as low as possible, given a certain amount of flippant cleverness as to invention, and low manual dexterity in execution. To what extent they have recovered from this living death at this day it is not easy for us contemporaries to settle. Doubtless men of genius exist, and that genius will, with terrible effort, break through unfavourable surroundings, and produce something; but, as to popular art, it is as a tale that is told, and the people is dissociated from the pleasure of life.

Even in the eighteenth century it was commoner for people to make things ugly than beautiful; and no wonder, for the worker had, as a rule, no longer to think of what he was making, and so could take no pleasure in it—no satisfaction, for instance, in taming a troublesome material to his will, and so producing beauty and interest from roughness and risk. He worked at the bidding of some designer outside his craft, who himself was hurried and harassed by working for the profit-grinder, and cared nought for the material his hands were not to deal with, or the finished wares he might never see.

Here, then, at the end of the seventeenth century, as far as history goes, is an end of art, properly speaking; but for labour there was still another change in store. The division-of-labour system had, indeed, made a great change in the manufacture of goods, and produced enormous quantities of them for the markets; but those markets were growing every year in their demands, for obvious causes too long to speak of here; and, though England had had her share in the growth of commerce, she still remained, on the whole, a quiet agricultural country, even in the first half of the eighteenth century, and was then, as to her working population, more prosperous than she had been for centuries. Then came the tremendous change which has made us what we are now, the revolution of the great machine industries. The real history of the fifty years that effected this revolution has yet to be written, if, indeed, it can ever be written truly; but, at all events, we all know its outlines, and how the terrible war which we undertook, nominally in defence of monarchical principle, but really to preserve our foreign and colonial markets, landed us early in this century in a strange position—the most powerful nation in the world, with the monopoly of trade in the great industries, but with a most miserable population, oppressed, past the power of words to tell of, by the recklessness of the pursuit of commercial gains, which, so long as a profit could be made, heeded not the sufferings produced by some new change in machinery, nor attempted to regulate that change so as to save us from its worst consequences.

Where are we now, after all this? is surely the question we must ask ourselves. As to the relation of art to labour, I can only say that labour in the mass has no longer anything to do with art. Even under the division-of-labour system of the eighteenth century there was left some poor remains of attractiveness in the fact that it was still thought creditable to turn out good work, "well and truly made," as our forefathers phrased it. Well, we have got a step beyond that now, and understand clearly that profit is the one sole aim of all manufacture; therefore, as far as the work of the worker is concerned, there is no attractiveness—that is, art—in it, whereas once, as we have seen, his work was almost always attractive.

But, if his work is no longer pleasant, surely there is some compensatory pleasure otherwise in his life. Where is it, then? His home? Alas, in the manufacturing districts, or London, or any great town, not even a rich man can have a decent home, much less a poor man, since it has been thought a little thing to turn the rivers into filth, and put out the sun, and make the earth squalid with the bricken encampments—we will not call them houses—in which those who make our wealth live such lives as they can live.

Does leisure compensate our workman, then? We need not go into that question, I think. Or do high wages, if they could be any good to him, compelled to live in the toiling hell from which, as long as he is a worker, he cannot escape? Nay, we now know that, under the present system, his wages must be limited to the amount which will keep him from day to day in the condition he is used to, or profits will come to an end. Or education—shall that be his recompense? Why, there are still people who are wishful to deprive him—or his children, rather—of the pitiful modicum of education which has but lately been doled out to him,[4] and in this country of compromise (cowardice is another name for that word), I can pretty well guess how that is likely to end, for the present.

The question—What are the present relations of art to labour? is soon answered. The relations are simple enough, for labour is wholly divorced from art. As to his work, the workman is either himself a machine or is the slave of a machine. There is no art in his work; and as to his life outside his work, he has neither money, leisure, [n]or education—that is, refinement—sufficient to obtain art.

It is to be feared that some of our readers[5] will think that this does not matter at all. The workman is fed, clothed, and lodged in such a way that he makes a good workman—for making a profit for other people—and is contented with his lot, as yet. Those who think thus will not care to read an answer to another question—What *should be* the relations between art and labour?

Let us take the surroundings of the workman's life first, because his work can never be set right unless the surroundings of his life are, which, indeed, will include the surroundings of all our lives. Let us see what these surroundings should be.

1. The workman must live in a pleasant house in a pleasant place. That is a claim for labour which I know most people will be inclined to

4. Morris may refer to the Education Acts of 1870, 1872 (Scotland), and 1880. See Florence S. Boos, "The Education Act of 1870: Before and After," *BRANCH*, Spring 2015, available at http://www.branchcollective.org (last accessed February 22, 2023).

5. MS., I greatly fear, that some of my readers

agree with until they consider how impossible it is to satisfy it under our present profit-grinding system; for please to think what time, money, and trouble it would take to turn London into a pleasant place, and also that a pleasant house is, and must be, a costly house.

2. The workman must be well educated. This, again, most people will agree to till they know what it means—namely, that all children shall be educated, not according to the money their parents happen to possess, but according to their capacity. Less than this means class-education, which is a monstrous oppression of the poor by the rich.
3. The workman must have due leisure. Once more this is agreed to till the meaning of the word is clear. Overwork for profit must be prevented at any cost. The necessary maximum of a day's work must be found out, and made legal and compulsory. It follows, as a corollary to this claim, that everybody must labour.

So much for the necessary surroundings of life under which art for the whole people would be possible. I think my readers[6] must see that what these three things really mean is refinement of life, or, as we call it now, the life of a gentleman; and we must clearly understand that if the workers have no hope of becoming refined, or gentlemen, they will in the long run become brutes, and the well-to-do classes will be no better. Let us think of that, and what it means. The lives of some of us may see its terrible meaning explained unless we grow wise in time.

Now as to the manner of work, if we are to have art among us once more.

1. There must be no useless work done. This, indeed, follows, as a matter of course, on the limitation of the daily hours of labour; but also, of course, I know many of my readers[7] do not agree with me at all in this, as we mostly live, we of the well-to-do classes, on useless labour—the turning of the wheel of the profit-grinder.
2. Whatever necessarily irksome work must be done should be done by machines, which should be used to save labour really, and not, as now, to grind out profit. I know that this involves what some will think the monstrous proposition that machines should be our servants, not our masters, but I make the claim without blushing.
3. No useless work being done, and all irksome labour saved as much as possible by machines being made our servants instead of our masters, it would follow, as a matter of course, that what other

6. MS., You will, I think see
7. MS., ~~you~~ crossed out, and "many of my readers" added

work was done (which in truth would be by far the most important part of work) would be accompanied by pleasure in the doing, and would receive praise when done; and most true it is that the product of all work done with pleasure and worthy of praise is art—that is to say, an essential part of the pleasure of life. Beauty is the necessary expression and token of such work.

Now, of course, it will be said this kind of work is desirable doubtless, but impossible to realise. But let me remind my readers[8] that to a certain extent it was realised in the Middle-ages, when the workman was master of his material, tools, and time. In order to realise the kind of work I have been speaking of, he must once again be master of these things; and this must be brought about not by reverting to the system of the Middle-ages, which is obviously impossible, but by making the workman the master of his time, tools, and material collectively or socially—that is to say, that the labourers must regulate labour in the interests of the labourers. Of course, it is clear that this involves the altering of the basis of society, since it means nothing less than supplanting[9] the present system of competition, or—the devil take the hindmost—by Socialism, or universal co-operation, whichever you like to call it. And some will think such a change a heavy price indeed to pay for art, even if it he true (and I still assert that it is) that you cannot have art without that change.

Yet I must ask you to remember that I have called art the pleasure of life, which, indeed, means nothing short of happiness. Tell me, then, what is too high a price to buy general happiness with?

Remember, also, that I have said it was necessary for the new birth of art that the workman should be well housed, well educated, and have due leisure in his life. I know that this cannot happen to him under the present competitive system; if you do not know it you may find it true some day, when you begin to try that the workman shall be well housed, well educated, and be in possession of due leisure. And if the present system will not do this for him, what will? That is an important question, which he will one day ask and answer for himself without our help if we do not look to it. My answer to the question once more is—the supremacy of labour used in a social sense for the benefit of the community. That is, I feel quite sure, the next move in the great game of progress, and will be made whether we like it or not, whether we help it or not. But since it is for the good of the human race, and since day

8. MS., you
9. MS., end of word written over; Bacon has "supplying," but "supplanting" is more likely.

by day its advent is becoming more obviously inevitable, let us learn to like it and learn to help it.

Conclusion in original manuscript, omitted from the *Wholesale Cooperative Societies Annual* version

[To me indeed all things seem moving that way; it was partly my intention when I gave you just now that hurried glimpse of the history of labour to show how practically all history has been the history of the antagonism of classes, that all change and progress has come about by that antagonism, the oppressed class striving to raise itself constantly in opposition to the dominant one, which in its turn resists as blindly as vainly. I told you how the rise of the middle-class took place from the struggles of the enfranchised serf of the middle ages for freedom of competition; that struggle was not fully triumphant till the French Revolution, which is commonly but erroneously supposed to have been a struggle for the freedom of the lower classes, but which was really the last attack of the middle-classes on feudal privilege which it practically abolished. This triumph of the middle classes or commercial classes was sealed finally by the tremendous economical revolution of the great machine industries, and the middle classes, long struggling with the classes above them, at first for existence and latterly for supremacy, had now entered into a new phase, and are arming themselves to resist the class which has formed below them during that struggle, and which has now taken their place in the march of progress.][10]

I cannot doubt that you have noted some of the tokens of this new struggle: the success of the trades unions in England, though they themselves hurriedly founded at a time when the principles of Socialism were not well understood in one of the darker periods of our history have grown to be conservative bodies looking only to the interests of the aristocracy of labour; the sudden collapse of the *laissez faire* doctrines so confidently proclaimed as eternal natural laws of the universe, and now discovered not to be possible to be carried on in a small corner of it; the re-awakening of Socialism supposed to have been dead, in a new and scientific form, even in England the stronghold of middle-class supremacy; its rapid spread over the continent of Europe, and especially in Germany, the land of education, all these things point to the coming of the great change when the time shall be ripe for it.

10. Paragraph from "To me indeed . . ." to "march of progress" crossed out in Yale MS., and not necessary for sequence of ideas.

Nor on the other hand are there lacking signs of that ripeness—that rottenness: England the great commercial country is not losing, but has lost her monopoly of trade which she had after the great French War: competition is eating its own heart out: everywhere I hear the manufacturers telling the same story: wages are high they say though business is bad; it is we the hapless profit-grinders who are suffering: we are making no profits: that is their version of the state of things to which periodical inflation, gluts and slackness have brought us, and I can't think a triumphant outcome of the reckless gambling called Commerce. Meantime let them ask themselves, I say this to the trades unions also,[11] what will happen when wages do begin to fall widely; when the working classes having brought their standard of life up to a certain pitch find that under the present system that standard cannot be maintained, that it is slipping away from them; it seems to me that when that pitch comes the conservative instincts of the British working man, on which you gentlemen of the commercial classes so much depend will fail you,—and then—[12]

Be warned in time I beg of you. I beg it not in the interests of our class, which I hope to see melt away into the general community founded on the equality of labour, but in the interests of the individuals of it who may be alive at the time; nay, in the interests of that peace and order of which, excuse me, you are apt to make a fetish of, or treat as the Portuguese sailors do their saints, sometimes worshipping them, sometimes thrashing them soundly when they think more is to be got out of them by that process. I say in the interest of peace and order, I beg you to keep your eyes open to the signs of the times; so that the change may be brought about as little mechanically as may be, as completely as may be, leaving as little heart-burning and injustice behind it as may be.

And I am the bolder in begging this of you since I myself belong to the middle class, and I think represent an increasing number of men of that class who, whatever happens must throw in our lot with the workers at every stage of the struggle: to us the name Socialism does not represent a political party but a religion rather, to which we are bound to devote our lives: that religion I preach to you now in what feeble words I can, of which the last are these: there are even now but two camps, one of the people and one of their masters; between these

11. MS., "I say this to the trades unions also" an interpolation above line
12. Morris is responding to contemporary conditions, including a trade depression that intensified during 1884–6. Not coincidentally, the Social Democratic Federation was founded in 1881 and the Socialist League in 1885. Not until the National Insurance act of 1911 would unemployed workers be granted economic relief.

two you must make your choice. Rich and poor are the words which divide the world, and I earnestly beg you to join yourselves to the cause of the poor, in the hope that those two names so long expressive of the curse of the world shall one day have no meaning to us but that we shall all be friends and good fellows united in the communion of hopeful and pleasurable labour which alone can produce art, the Pleasure of Life.

THE MANIFESTO

OF

SIGNED BY THE PROVISIONAL COUNCIL AT THE FOUNDATION OF THE LEAGUE ON 30th DEC. 1884, AND ADOPTED AT

THE GENERAL CONFERENCE

Held at FARRINGDON HALL, LONDON, on JULY 5th, 1885.

—o—

A New Edition, Annotated by

WILLIAM MORRIS AND E. BELFORT BAX.

LONDON:

Socialist League Office,

13 FARRINGDON ROAD, HOLBORN VIADUCT, E.C

1885.

PRICE ONE PENNY.

Figure 7.1 *Manifesto* of the Socialist League. Courtesy of the William Morris Gallery

7

Address at the Opening of the Fourth Annual Loan Exhibition, Whitechapel, April 1884

Editor's introduction

This innocuously titled, carefully developed speech was delivered only once by Morris, on April 8, 1884, at the opening of the Fourth Annual Loan Exhibition, sponsored by the Rev. Samuel Augustus Barnett at St. Jude's Church, Commercial Street, Whitechapel. The Rev. Barnett (1844–1913) was a social reformer who had moved to the East End parish St. Jude's in order to work among the London poor. He and his wife, fellow philanthropist Harriet Rowland (1851–1936), founded the University Settlements Association, leading to a university extension program and the establishment of Toynbee Hall in 1884. Morris was perhaps invited as an extension lecturer on art with sympathetic interests.

Morris's remarks may have startled even this well-intended audience. He deals only briefly with the art objects on which he has been invited to speak, instead emphasizing the cultural deprivation which attends poverty. He begins by attempting a broad definition of art relevant to persons of all social classes, "reverence for the life of man past and present and to come which is the foundation of all art, which gives an interest [to] the representation of common landscape . . . even to the . . . decoration of houses and so forth with which we strive to bring our lives into harmony with the beauty of the universe." He then pointedly asserts the incongruity of juxtaposing high art and extreme poverty, an early expression of his lifelong skepticism toward palliative reforms. Such remarks may also reveal discomfort with his own position as a middle-class reformer speaking to an audience of philanthropists and workers, as he comments that "I am told that various people of good will amongst the cultivated classes have been used to attend here of evenings to explain these works of art to the uncultivated who come to see them: a sad business, a wo[e]ful admission that seems to me . . . ." Instead the whole system of classes must be dismantled: "only I must ask what must be done before we can meet before a wall covered with pictures on an equality . . . ."

Morris then explains in detail what he sees as the inherent nature of this systemic divide: "this specially sharp distinction of classes is really bred by that competition I have already mentioned, and the motive of which is: what you win, I lose. That in few words expresses what commerce is, what the relations are between employer and employed . . . ." The result is nothing less than war: "war between the employers and employed, war between the capitalists, war between the trading countries. Defend the system if you wish, but you must defend it as war; it is idle to talk of the blessings of peace while this terrible struggle is going on implacably, ceaselessly." Nor does this war spare even the more fortunate such as Morris himself: "You see, the capitalists are driven too, like the workmen; only their ruin does not commonly mean what it means with the workmen." Even the motivated will find resistance difficult: "Try it and see how easy it is for us surrounded with competition, hampered by the condition of family life, to strike each for himself against the system which has bred us and by which we earn our livelihood." Morris's description of the conditions of Merton Abbey skilled textile workers, "reduced to working as ordinary day-labourers . . . by no fault whatever of their own," also likely reflects his personal conversations with employees, perhaps including members of the Merton Abbey branch of the Social Democratic Federation he had initiated in 1883.

In modified religious rhetoric Morris enjoins his settlement-house audience to consider a better way: "now as ever the choice lies before us between light and darkness; between heaven and hell as the theologians say, I had rather say between Earth and Hell—that is, between Life and Death." Lest his hearers draw back because of the depressing nature of his analysis, Morris makes the rather ingenious argument that it is better to blame a system than individuals, and that this insight has enabled him to cope with the refusals of others:

> I can assure you from experience that to recognize and strive against the evils of our present system as a system does tend to allay our bitterness against individuals, since we [see] that they are bound by the same chain as we are; at worst, it makes us think of them as our friends, [not] the enemy?

In concluding his lecture Morris calls for a radical shift in class allegiance: "What we middle-class and rich people have to do, I feel sure, is to renounce our class, and at every stage of the struggle throw in our lot with workers . . . . fostering discontent with the miserable system which makes slaves both of them and [of] us." As an alternative he asserts the necessary conditions for what he bluntly calls Social Revolution: "the uncompromising building up of a society founded on the equal rights of labor and the gradual but uncompromising destruction of the present state of society which is founded on the supposed right of property or the strongest individual to enslave labour at its will." These are strong words for a property owner and employer, embodying a significant shift from the tone of Morris's pre-socialist essays. Combining reasoned argument and direct, personal appeal to his social peers, "At a Picture Show" deserves to be recognized as one of Morris's better early essays.

This essay is preserved in British Library Add. MS. 45,334(8), ff. 151–67. May Morris included extracts amounting to about a quarter of the essay in MM2, 164–9.

[A]s our life in general depends on the condition of labour, so it is clear that which we call art does more particularly depend on it: this fact makes it impossible for us to consider the objects for which this exhibition of pictures has been got together without looking at the condition of labour amongst us: the object of this free exhibition of pictures is I take it to show to a set of people much in need of such instruction that there are such things in the world as beauty, imagination, fancy, and that a serious man may well devote the whole of his life in expressing these qualities for the benefit of his fellows: we are not wanting to show the workers of the East of London a collection of mere ingenious toys, but to ask them to note that there are men amongst us living under the same laws, swayed by the same prejudices as themselves who are intensely interested in gaining insight into the wonders and beauties[,] nay the sorrows even of the earth on which we dwell, and more especially in the life of man thereon; which we still call by the name which our forefathers gave it, the World: giving it that name, I think, in religious reverence for the mystery of their existence.

It is this manly reverence for the life of man past and present and to come which is the foundation of all art, which gives an interest to the representation of common landscape which surrounds our life, the corner of a field, a bit of wayside waste, the beasts and the birds with whom we have to do, nay even [otherwise] trivial things, decoration of houses and so forth with which we strive to bring our lives into harmony with the beauty of the universe: nay it is only by means of art, using the word in its widest application[,] that this reverence can be shown: therefore I say once more that those who look upon art as merely a handmaid to the luxury of rich and idle people, do not understand what it means; most often I fear because they have had no chance of understanding it, what of art they have come across being in truth not art but the pretense, the sham of it.

So you see it comes to this that in these days there is something which pretends to art and is not, and that a great proportion of our citizens have to put [up] with this[1] poison instead of getting the real food which they should do: and the result of this is that they have forgotten the reverence for the life of man, or if they have in their own minds any glimmer remaining they have lost all hope of expressing their sense of it themselves or seeing [it] expressed by others.

That loss seems to me a most grievous one, for it means in few words that a large part of our own citizens are so far brutalised: and I must say in passing that if there are any here who think that those who are cultivated can escape the contagion of the brutality which oppresses their fellows, they will find themselves deceived: in other words if there is to be a larger class amongst us condemned by the accident of their birth to an existence knowing nothing of art[,] the reflection of that miserable injustice will so overshadow all art that in the long run it will destroy it: it is no question whether we are to have art for the few or the many, but whether we are to have art for the many, or not at all.

We admitted, as I am sure we must all admit, that the loss of the sense of beauty and the hope of expressing it is grievous, what is the remedy for that loss, what shall bring us back to the Reverence for the Life of Man?

Or do any of you think that there is no need for asking that question, for seeking that remedy: alas if you think so in that very doubt lies full proof of how far we have gone on the path of degradation. We in this richest of all Countries of the world, this richest of all Cities, do we not find that here where we are now, where men dwell thickest together, sordid ugliness and squalor is the rule in our dwellings? Weak words indeed to express the horror and wretchedness of this foul blot on the surface of the beautiful Earth! Nor only so, but still wherever the town spreads, spreads this revolting ugliness. How many beautiful spots do we not remember which have been destroyed (I will not say forever) by the spreading of our bricken encampments? It is not a question now of

1. MS., put with with this poison

the wisdom of letting London grow without limit, much as might be said on that question, but on our being unable to limit its hideousness and vileness. Now of course I know that there are many who think the same of this evil as they do of all existing evils, that they are natural and fore-ordained and cannot be dealt with or changed, just as they think that Man must always live a life of competition for existence[,] or in other words by ruining his fellow, so they think that it is impossible for him to think seriously of anything save the mere material struggle for existence, that for the sake of livelihood he must of necessity destroy the reasons for living: such men are ignorant of the past and therefore are dully content with the present and hopeless for the future: otherwise, they would know that time has been when so far from the dwellings of men disgracing the Earth they added fresh beauty to it, and so we may hope they may do once again, when they have looked to it and, taking advantage of the rottenness of the system under which we now live, shall make up their minds that they will make that very rottenness fruitful to us of new conditions which will not endure that men should be heaped together like stinking fish to produce ugliness, disease, and brutality for the sake of they know not what.

Now we may be sure both that we have lost our sense of beauty and power of expressing it, our Reverence for the Life of Man, and also that it is worth enquiring what remedy there is for the disease, since it is not essential to our nature that we should live contented under this loss produced not by the necessity of nature, but by the perversity of Man.

Once again, then, what is the remedy? Let us first ask what is the cause of it? The hurry of modern life you will say[,] that will allow us no rest or leisure to consider how best to live: the necessity of struggling for material advancement which drives us all on[,] both rich and poor[,] to think of nothing save money.

Yes, indeed, that is it: we do not essentially like ugly things; we do not like the country to be defiled with smoke and squalid litter, the sun to be hidden and the rivers to run mere pollution: we do not like a great part of the population to be shamefully fed, clothed and housed, to be ignorant of all history and art, to be poor in short, but we have no time, no rest, to set it right: at best we can apply but some poor palliatives to the worst symptoms of the disease, which, to speak plainly, have as much influence over stopping the disease itself, the race to destruction on which we are bent, as a peacock's feather has of stopping a big waterwheel: well, if we are so hurried and driven by the race for money that we have no time to live, what is it that hurries us and drives us?

I say it is the system under which we live, which has grown up to enslave us through a long series of events, which by many people in spite of its having been the growth of centuries, is supposed to be the one natural and eternal system under which all civilisation must be carried on, but which is as much doomed to pass away and give place to something else as those systems which it has supplanted. This system is the system of commercial competition, which in its complete form has not existed for more than two [centuries] and which already shows symptoms of decay: it oppresses us all in reality but to some of us only it shows in its real form of a curse and a tyranny; to the rest of us[2] it is apt to put on other guise; to some of [us] seeming to [grant a][3] dignified dominion of leadership over other men; to others the opportunity for displaying our special energy or talent; to others the happy chance of living a secluded and beautiful life due to our superior merits as the pick of the universe, a life where we dwell above the tumult like the worshipped but unheeding, like the Gods of Epicurus:[4] yet to all, if they did but know it, it is an oppression and a slavery: to the slaves, to the slave-holders, and to their hangers-on.

For the special characteristic of modern society is that there are two sets of men, what we call classes: one of these is cultivated or refined; the other uncultivated and unrefined; that I say is the foundation of it, real and not arbitrary distinction between the classes: in this it differs from the society of the classical periods when, though people were divided into freeman and slaves, the slaves were not necessarily men of lower cultivation than the freemen; still more it differs from the society of the middle ages in which there was a regular hierarchy of castes but in which also the distinction was arbitrary and not real: the serf was theoretically a different animal from the lord almost, but he thought the thoughts and spoke the same language; he did not drop his h's: if we were to meet him in our present society we should think him a gentleman, not a cad as we used to say at school and college.

I want you to note this matter of the gentleman and non-gentleman very decidedly and not to be led astray by the fact that here in England we have still got a semblance of the old hierarchical distinction in the form of titles of nobility; but they really mean now little more than that the nobility is richer than the rest of the well-to-do; a very rich man is quite as much worshipped as a Lord; and in fact when a man becomes

2. MS., to the rest of us some the rest it is apt to ~~show~~ put on
3. MS., seeming to be dignified dominion
4. The Greek philosopher Epicurus (341–270 BCE) advocated the cultivation of *ataraxia*, or equanimity and peace of mind. He believed humans had no need to fear the gods, since the latter took no interest in human affairs and therefore did not mete out punishments.

rich enough, he is made a Lord almost by force; so fond we are in England of keeping up appearances. Meantime in America where there are no titles there is still the difference between the two classes who are really distinct from one another.

Now, this specially sharp distinction of classes is really bred by that competition I have already mentioned, and the motive of which is: what you win, I lose. That in few words expresses what commerce is, what the relations are between employer and employed; [we shall see][5] that clearer if we look into the two great divisions of the classes, setting aside the minor division of professional men who are but incidental to the great capitalist class, their hangers-on. Between these two the capitalist and the workman there is, and must be, an eternal war going on. The capitalist comes into the labour market spurred to exertion in the fight by the other fight which he is carrying on with his capitalist competitors; he finds there: men who cannot wait, and must strike their bargain (that is, contend with him) at once; they have nothing but their bodies to trade for their food, clothing, and housing, which their bodies clamorously call out for: in dealing together it is clear that he *must* give them as much as will from day to day recruit their power of labour, and enable them to reproduce their kind: however, maybe sharp may be the spur of the competition of their fellows for livelihood, [but] they cannot take less than that: less than that would mean not employing them but killing them; and I may say in passing that it has not seldom come perilously near to that, even in our own times: more than that they do generally get because by combination among themselves and by acting variously on public opinion they manage[6] to establish a standard of livelihood which is thought due and proper for them after their kind; the higher they can raise that standard of life the more they take from the capitalists' profits; the lower standard he can drive them to (and remember—competition with other capitalists drives him to seek to lower it) the more profit he makes out of their labour: you must remember also as to this standard of livelihood that, though combination among the wage-earners may force up the standard of life to a certain extent, yet it is obvious that it cannot go higher than would allow the employer to make a profit out of his hiring of labour—higher than that would mean the extinguishing of the capitalist. Well, so goes on the seesaw: "what I win, you lose".

Meantime not only does the capitalist carry on war with his brethren of the same country and so keep down the standard of life, but also

5. MS., ~~we shall see~~ crossed out
6. MS., "they manage" repeated

the nation carries on the war against nation: the workmen in France or Germany or wherever[7] can live cheaper than they can here, they can make the good[s] and the profit at a lower price, and in course of time our workmen in spite of trades-unions must lower their standard of life to that of the cheaper country: there is no getting out of that.

Here then you have a system of labour and distribution of the fruits of labour wherein labour and its fruits[8] are mere adjuncts to war: there is no other name for it: war between[9] the workmen for employment, war between the employers and employed, war between the capitalists, war between the trading countries. Defend the system if you wish, but you must defend it as war; it is idle to talk of the blessings of peace while this terrible struggle is going on implacably, ceaselessly. And tell me—how it fares in war—who are those who suffer by it most? The warring kings risk vexation and humiliation; the warring generals loss of fame and place; but 'tis the common soldier who really suffers, he and his widow and orphans: so in no other wise it fares with the soldier of War Commercial: in speaking of the contention between capitalist and workman, I have been thinking rather of the skilled workman than of the labourer, the unskilled of whom you in these east parts of the great City know so much—too much—of: it is on this latter that the whole structure of our present society rests, nor can I easily forget the eloquent and moving description of his hard life which our friend Mr. S. Barnett gave in an article of his in the *19th Century* a year ago:[10] that subdivision of the class of workingman ever tends to increase, partly because the whole tendency of the great machine industries is to get rid of the skilled workingman and to supply his place with the machine-tender, and partly because other things feed the class and will feed it more and more as trade worsens, as it must worsen in this country.

Of the first cause of the recruiting of the class of labourers [i.e. of the tendency of the machine industries to get rid of the skilled workman] I have myself some personal experience, since in the neighborhood where my works are situated the once flourishing craft of textile block-printing has been nearly extinguished by the development of the machine printing in the North of England: it is common with us to meet with men who having been brought up to a craft requiring much skill and in which large earnings could be made, are now reduced to working as ordinary day-labourers at 18s. 3d. a week by no fault whatever of their own. Such

7. Orig., or wherever one can [not can]
8. Orig., which is made ~~barren and wasteful~~ wherein
9. Orig., "between" repeated
10. Samuel Barnett, "University Settlements in Great Towns," *Oxford Magazine*, November 1882, reprinted in the February 1883 issue of *Nineteenth Century*.

men are now working for me, skillful intelligent and steady workmen who otherwise would be in that plight; and this kind of thing is common all over the country. The other cause which drives skilled labour into the mere laboring class is the regularly recurring crises in trade, which are an absolute necessity to it as things go now, even when trade on the whole is flourishing: inflation, a glut of goods, and stagnation, these come I say quite certainly from time to time, and of late at shorter intervals and are of longer duration; for the workers they mean anxiety and hope deferred at the best, and at the worst ruin and the workhouse: pray think of them when you hear rich men praise the workman's lot, and talk of the higher wages he earns in rapt admiration not unmixed with indignation, which to tell you the truth it is natural for him to feel, since his class is at war with the workman's class.

And these bad times for even the skilled craftsman [who] are quite essential as said to the present system of war Commercial, since without the reserve army of labour the war could not be carried on at all: the warring capitalists must have ready to hand for the periods of inflation more men than they can use, not only in periods of stagnation, but in ordering quiet business; that capitalist or that country which lacked this terrible advantage would be sure to fall out of the race and be ruined. You see, the capitalists are driven too, like the workmen; only their ruin does not commonly[11] mean what it means with the workmen.

So then I have arranged in these few hasty words (though the thoughts are not hasty) the squalor and misery of our civilisation which forbids art to the worker, and is killing it for the cultivated men of leisure; I have said that that misery is caused not by our malice but our misfortune; that we are so driven that we cannot heed it; I have told you that it is war that drives us and makes us blind and reckless; let us now, before we finish by striving to see how that war may be quenched with peace[,] try to have a glimpse of what that peace may mean to us and especially in the matter of the arts, which I say are the pleasure of life.

And in striving for that glimpse of the happy future, we will be modest indeed, but yet not too modest, we will not at least be craven: let us pitch our keynote high enough: let us have faith as a grain of mustard-seed. And to begin with, do not let us minimise the evil: don't let us say, after all, things are not so bad. Bad they are—as bad as may be? I don't know and don't care; I do know that they must be either better or worse: nay more than that they must either be worst or best: now as ever the choice lies before us between light and darkness; between heaven and

11. MS., comonly

hell as the theologians say, I had rather say between Earth and Hell – that is, between Life and Death.

Come then, and let us look at it: [H]ere we have a collection of pictures together expressly for the benefit of people who can't usually see such things (the galleries and museums being shut on Sundays) and I am told that various people of good will amongst the cultivated classes have been used to attend here of evenings to explain these works of art to the uncultivated who come to see them: a sad business, a woeful[12] admission that seems to me; but don't think I mean a word of blame to those who face this grievous fact in this way: only I must ask what must be done before we can meet before a wall covered with pictures on an equality; in other words what is necessary to bring back to these poor people, the workmen of civilization and the masters who are compelled to enthrall them, that Reverence for the Life of Man which, as I have said, is the foundation of all art?

1st. The surroundings of their life must be decent; that is they must live in pleasant houses in a pleasant place; words soon said about a thing which sad to say must seem but a wild dream to those who know what they really mean; houses well-built, rationally and naturally beautiful because of their fulfilling their purpose duly without stint of thought, labour, or materials in them, not without such ornament as men naturally bestow on their dwellings when they are living a healthy reasonable life: such are decent houses. The place the houses stand in clear from foul disgraces of all kinds, clear sky above them, trees, grass, and ample space around them; this is the least which will make a pleasant place.

2nd. The people who dwell in them must be well educated: How wild a dream once more, that must seem to those who know the gulf which separates the knowledge of a cultivated man, however unsatisfactory it may seem to others of his own class, from that of an uncultivated: for the least which that cultivation can mean is the habit of reading books of various kinds and picking up their meaning speedily and certainly, understanding the allusions to other books in them, or at least being able to think about such allusions, and to seek for the originals of them: I think few of the cultivated understand how narrow the range of subjects is which comes within the scope of the uncultivated: how terrible the distance is between the rich and the poor.

12. MS., woful

3rd. These educated people living among these pleasant surroundings must have due leisure; else in good sooth they will not be educated: they must have leisure to think and even to dream: leisure to make holiday travels, pilgrimages one must call it to the wonders and beauties of the world; leisure to choose the craft or employment which suits them best; leisure lastly to be fastidious about cleanliness and order and a pleasant life inside the pleasant houses. Indeed I am not mocking you in saying this—I mean it, that this is the thing we must look to; nothing grand about it all, a modest decent life—nothing more with these simple blessings attained for all men can we meet as equals before works of art; no ideal short of this is worth thinking of a moment; something short of it is [no] more than a stepping stone towards it: those of the rich and well-to-do who aim at less than this may call themselves radicals, men of progress, philanthropists, or what not, but whether they know it or not, they are partakers in the iniquity of their fathers—they are propping up injustice and stupidity—they are tyrants—yes, and slaves, also.

And how are we to do it all? How are we to bring about this social revolution and make all men gentlemen, without which art will perish and civilisation with it?

[T]he word impossible must be written across all those fine things which you think desirable if they could but be attained, and which I think necessary and to be striven for, at any risk and any price.

How then are we to get rid of this competition or war commercial? By attacking each for himself you will say perhaps, the evils in our own lives which we know bolster it up; each for himself to give up making profits, living luxuriously, making distinctions between classes and the like: well, if we could [do] it, a great many of us, something might come of it: but can we? Try it and see how easy it is for us surrounded with competition, hampered by the condition of family life, to strike each for himself against the system which has bred us and by which we earn our livelihood. For my part I think we of the middle-classes will be able to do very little till we are compelled by matters outside our wills to do that which we long to do, viz., to live simple reasonable untyrannical lives.

Rather I think the first thing we have to do is to face the facts as they are; and then we shall have to admit that there is already a class-war going on, as I have shown you before, that the material gain of one class is and must be the loss of the other: and when we have admitted that we shall know that it is our duty, if we are in earnest in wishing to live a simple life, to put[13] forward that class which, since it is struggling upward, alone has the power of abolishing all classes, of making all men working men and all men gentlemen at once: what we middle-class and rich people have to do, I feel sure, is to renounce our class, and at every stage of the struggle throw in our lot with workers at every stage of it, fostering discontent with the miserable system which makes slaves both of them and [of] us. All this may sound very dreadful to some of you, may sound implacable, unfriendly, and what not: for my part, I look at it from another point of view. Thus: if the terrible evils acknowledged to be such by all people of goodwill are not caused by the class system born of [the] commercial system, they must be caused by the faults of individuals, which faults we—if we think that—can scarcely help also thinking come of malice; and how then can we restrain our bitterness, our hatred against those whose malice makes the world unhappy: so then if we think that individual freedom or individual selfishness can mar or make our hopes of reform, we shall rage against those individuals in helpless bitterness.

But I say [as for] the malice of individuals—I don't believe it is a common thing to meet with, so also I do not admit that it could hurt us much if it was: it seems to me that I can assure you from experience that to recognise and strive against the evils of our present system as a system does tend to allay our bitterness against individuals, since we [see] that they are bound by the same chain as we are; at worst[,] it makes us think of them as our friends, [not] the enemy?[14]

No, believe me, it is not brutalising but harmonising to face those terrible facts I have been speaking of—to do your best to try to stir up discontent with the system that breeds, fearful of no consequences[,] meanwhile since you feel that as your one obvious duty: ready [to] take all that comes as part of the day's work, and if you should have the happiness to see and dare the first days of the new order of things, to be ready—and more—to accept your position in a society founded on the equal rights of all labour, in which society alone[,] I once more say[,] has art any chance of a healthy existence.

A word of warning before I finish: I press on you the renunciation of your class and your furtherance of the emancipation of labour: but do not suppose that I think you can, if you will, put back the advance of the great change from Competition to Cooperation. You cannot choose whether you will have revolution or not, for the revolution is already amongst you: but your resistance, even if it be passive, may give a terrible character to that revolution: and I say this because though I know

13. MS., ~~put~~ crossed out
14. MS., friends the enemy?

you are of good will to the well-being of the people, there may be some of you who need this warning more than you may be willing to admit, even to yourselves. It is natural when we have gone a certain way on the path of progress, and can seem to see no further[,] to resist swiftly those who do see further and cannot accept our gifts to the cause as the clearance of all scores with it: I say this is so natural that I must needs beg even those of you who think yourselves the most advanced in opinion, to remember that no step is really final on the road of progress; that there is always something ahead if we can but see it: and I will quite plainly say that to my mind what is ahead of us now, is Social Revolution, that is to say, the gradual but uncompromising building up of a society founded on the equal rights of labour and the gradual but uncompromising destruction of the present state of society which is founded on the supposed right of property or the strongest individual to enslave labour at its will.

Now this, what I have come to say, I ask the pardon of those who are offended[,] not at the thing itself but at my clumsy way of putting it.

Figure 8.1 Henry Hyndman (1842–1921), Joe Burgess, *John Burns: The Rise and Progress of a Right Honorable* (Glasgow: Reformers' Bookstall, 1911)

Figure 8.2 "A Summary of the Principles of Socialism," 1884, by Henry Hyndman and William Morris

8

Misery and the Way Out

Editor's introduction

The manuscript of Morris's lecture "Misery and the Way Out" is preserved in British Library Add. MS. 45,334(6), and May Morris included sections in MM2, 150–64. The lecture was one of a rotation of speeches Morris delivered during late 1883 to 1884 to Socialist Democratic Federation branches and other progressive groups, along with "Art Under Plutocracy," "Useful Work versus Useful Toil," "Art and Socialism," "Art and Labour," and "How We Live and How We Might Live." It must have received a favorable reception, for LeMire notes nine instances of scheduled delivery in fall 1884, on September 8, 27, and 28, October 19, November 9 and 17, and December 5, 7, and 19, and a tenth more than three years later on 1 July 1888. Interestingly it was also chosen for oral reading by others at branch meetings in Bradford and Leeds three times in 1886, February 23, March 7, and May 18. Of these twelve deliveries or readings, eight were to SDF or Socialist League audiences or their confederated ally, the Scottish Land and Labour League (Morris's November 17, 1884 talk in Edinburgh drew an audience of 3000 persons). The remaining four were to trades union or radical groups: the Tower Hamlets Radical Club, the Working Men's Club in Croydon, the National Secular Society, and the Progressive Association (later to become the Fabian Society[1]). "Misery"'s detailed anatomization of the gradations of labor was carefully designed to interest these working-class and radical audiences.

Morris's account of the oppression of workers by capitalists emphasizes the systematic nature of class division: "any amelioration of that misery [the perpetual servitude and misery of the wage-earning classes] shakes society, and the destruction of that misery would mean the destruction of Society." His view of social evils as structural, mutually reinforcing, and all-encompassing had been sharpened by recent reading in works of socialist theory and history; on January 8, 1884 he recommended Henry Hyndman's 1883 *The Historical Basis of Socialism in England* to an unidentified recipient, "It is well worth reading & very easy to read" (Kelvin, 2.254), and the next month he ordered from his publisher Ellis and White Richard Ely's 1883 *French and German Socialism in Modern Times* and Thorold Rogers's *History of Agriculture and Prices* (vols. 3 and 4, 1882); the latter may partly account for "Misery"'s relatively careful description of the lives of agricultural laborers. In April 1883 he was described by a friend as "bubbling over with Karl Marx, whom he had just begun to read in French." He paid T. J. Cobden-Sanderson to bind his copy, and enthusiastically recommended Marx's works, writing to an unknown enquirer on February 28, 1885, "If you read German or French, you should tackle Karl Marx *Das Capital* at once" (Kelvin, 2.393).

Morris's account of England's hierarchy of workers is more personal than these treatises, however, as he encourages his working-class audience to acknowledge and then act on their discontent. He appeals in concrete terms to his listeners as he categorizes the different varieties of hardship and precarity experienced by each class of laborers. However, he takes care to note that a segment of workers have already achieved somewhat better living conditions through their own efforts at unionization: "Remember too how hard he and his [i.e., skilled artisans] have fought to bring the wages up to the point at which they are . . . Remember that he has done that for himself by combining with his fellows. . . ."

His description of the class with which he identifies, that of "hangers-on," recalls his reported exclamation of self-reproach circa 1877 when decorating a house for Sir Lothian Bell, ". . . I spend my life ministering to the swinish luxury of the rich!"[2] In any case, his comments on his own situation are perhaps the most personal of any in his political essays, as they certainly are the most agonized. Presumably the most fortunate class, those granted the advantages of education and chosen employment, should be contented, but no:

> Yet here I stand before you, one of the most fortunate of this happy class, so steeped in discontent, that I have no words which will express it: no words, nothing but deeds, wherever they may lead me to, even [if] it be ruin, prison, or a violent death. . . . The truth is we discontented ones of the intellectual or hanger-on group are conscious that the whole thing is a desperate battle, and we are not contented to oppress those below us as we must do under the present system, not only for the sake of keeping ourselves in our position but also for the sake of piling up the monstrous fortunes of the rich men whose hangers-on we are. . . .

Morris's parody of the attitudes of the wealthy members of his own class is a masterpiece of sarcasm, as he considers what he might do if he agreed with those who found social evils irremediable: among other stratagems he would seek to render the poor illiterate, preach to them of the advantages of poverty, promise a heavenly reward for hell on earth, claim that members of his class were necessary "wealth creators"—in short, all the practices of the Tories and other members of the establishment of his day. Yet such selfish deception will in the long run lead to violence, in which the defenders of the present system will find themselves "surrounded by a crowd of terrible beings fierce-eyed and careless of anything but rapine, deaf to [their] prayers for mercy. . . ."

Repeatedly Morris urges concerted action as the only means of overthrowing the monopoly that reduces workers to abjection: "they do not call you their slaves, but they claim it indirectly. . . . I say you cannot resist except by combination of some kind or other. . . ." Instead workers must become their own masters: "you the workers should have in your own hands those things which are necessary to make labour fruitful; the land, the machines and the power of distribution." Yet he warns that unity, effort, and determination will be needed to gain this end:

> If we are to shorten the period of strife, the rough and it may be terrible period of transition from the old to the new, it must be by that complete combination which at present I know seems also so unattainable to the workman, . . . therefore hard as it will be to bring about, needing the most strenuous efforts of many serious men, I do above all things urge on you to do your very utmost to combine to shake of[f] the economical slavery of today. . . .

Nonetheless Morris's concluding appeal to his working-class audiences remains optimistic, if sketchy in addressing the problems to be faced in the self-organization of uneducated workers. He warns of the trap of ever-lessening expectations—"you will not get the little if you are contented with it," but enjoins a personal but shared vision: "try to think of the life you might live and would naturally live if you were not forced into misery by your masters, and then I do not think you can help coming together . . . ." If Morris's lecture is more detailed in its critique of the present ("misery") than in suggestions for concrete remedies ("the way out"), it nonetheless lays out clearly the need for a worker-driven, unified resistance to economic injustice, a view which would motivate much of the content of his essays and lectures in succeeding years.

Notes

1. The Fabian Society had adopted its present name in January 1884, so the use of the name "Progressive Association" for a group sponsoring a talk at Ye Old Mansion House, Essex Road, London on November 27, 1884 seems a holdover.
2. W. R. Lethaby, *Philip Webb and His Work* (Oxford: Oxford University Press, 1935), 95–6.

What is the condition of Society under which we live? Is it satisfactory, is it quite as we should all like it to be? Does it quite please you who are listening to me, so that there is nothing you want to alter in it?

If that is the case, then none of my hearers are poor, and none have any fear of becoming poor; I am speaking to a crowd of rich men who are quite sure that they will always be rich. Well I see that is not quite the case; some of us are poor, some of us are afraid of becoming poor; some of us have to do very unpleasant work; all of us know of people who are worse off in all these matters than we are: So we do want to alter things if we could: we are not quite contented: if we say we are, we are not speaking truly but say so because we don't want to argue, or because we want to get something out of rich people whose interest it is that we should or be contented.

Well I should wonder if we were contented; for when we look at the present state of Society we find that the majority of people have every reason to wish to be better off than they are, that in point of fact they are living in misery. Let us look at the various conditions of life and see what proportion of the whole people has good reason to be pleased with their share of wealth, ease, good living, in a word, the happiness of this most highly civilized country.

Now first, the greatest part of us have to work, all those who are not very rich that is; it is true that what is usually thought the lowest stratum of Society is generally supposed not to, the criminal population, the vagabonds, loafers, and so forth, some of them do work very hard, undergoing all kinds of hardships, plenteous weariness, and as far as I know don't earn very high wages for all that: they at least I should think have a good right to be discontented: perhaps you will say that they have their bed and must lie in it, that 'tis their own faults; I am not sure whether 'tis worth while arguing on the matter, but I think I shall be able to show later on that it is not their own faults as a class, that their lives with all their horrible sufferings and still more horrible degradation are made by the present society, and are an essential part of it.

But let us leave them and go a step higher; let us look at the condition of the lower order of labourers: those who live most from hand to mouth, those who are themselves conscious of being sweated and oppressed and who cannot help being conscious of it, including a vast number of poor women who have no protectors or bread-earners to help them and are obliged to work for themselves without help, to earn themselves such livelihood as they do earn. In London at least we all know of this class, and that it is not such a very small one because it is always being recruited [for] by those who have been unsuccessful in various trades and livelihoods. Well have these any reason to be discontented? I confess I have never dared myself[1] to visit the homes of these poor people though I have seen them in the streets and have heard plenty about them: I know of them that they work hard and very hard, that they live in daily fear of being deprived of that hard work miserably paid as it is: I know that their houses, their clothes, their food, all are foul, wretched, unhuman, a shame even to think of.

Well, is it[2] their faults that have brought them to this? Friends, there are not wanting people who will say, Yes it is their faults, that if these poor wretches had been (at what period of their poverty) thrifty, provident, sober, courageous, they would not have been in this condition: I say these people are liars: I use the word in the fullest significance and say they are liars. Granted that this class of miserably poor is recruited by people who have made mistakes in life, or who are vicious or whatever it may be called, we all know well enough that as a class they have never had the chance offered to them of being thrifty and provident: if a man of the well-to-do classes is a drunkard or otherwise vicious does it necessarily follow from this that he will be poorer than he otherwise would be? A very small acquaintance with the modern scandalous chronicle will answer that question. No, be sure that this class of poor wretches who have such very good reason for being discontented with the present conditions of Society is a necessary product of that society and will only cease to exist when it does.

And now let us go a little higher yet, one step—not a great one; and consider the condition of the ordinary labourers, the unskilled, including in that class the ordinary agricultural labourer. Shall we ask him to be contented? We all know what his lot is; daily toil without hope: insufficient coarse food: bad housing, no amusement, no pleasure scarcely even of the most animal kind, no education; a short life: if you think the

1. MS., to myself
2. MS., it is

last thing a blessing rather under his circumstances, well and good, only remember it means general ill-health while he does live: also I forgot, he has one place of refuge before he reaches the last haven of rest, and that refuge the workhouse, where he is looked on by everybody including himself as sort of criminal. Nay I won[']t ask him to be contented. Well, and is it his fault also that he is in that position? I believe you will find people to assert that also, and I will waste no words in saying what I think of *them*. Again, I assert that his life, his misery and anxiety and overwork rather, scarce worth calling a life, are absolutely necessary to the existence of the present state of Society: I tell you that, let him raise his class even but a little out of its present horrible condition, and the foundations of Society will be shaken.

Again a step; this time a bigger one: we have got to the skilled artisan. Surely he might almost be contented with his lot: at any rate if he is not, it is not for want of being preached at, and having it pointed out to him in one way or other that he is really quite a rich man; there he is with a vote, happy fellow![3] Able to pay subscriptions to societies and Trade unions, money in the savings-bank, money in building-societies; and in short able to [do] a great deal more with (a precarious) say 38s. a week than I could do—even if I were a conjurer: that's the view of him through rose-colour glass: I can conceive an evil-disposed man, an agitator, say, looking at him through a medium less sweetly pretty, and seeing him to be overworked and not overpaid, wretchedly housed, without intellectual amusement, his work mere drudgery, unhonoured, unrewarded: at best a workman not a man, a machine that is, fed and housed and tended as a machine is, that is to say, enough to enable [him] to go on working for ever—No, not for ever: for please to remember whatever his wages may be, they are and must be precarious, as too many of our countrymen are feeling at the present moment: a change in machinery, a glut in the market, and out into the streets he goes with plenty of leisure to study the average of wages: and what becomes of his money in the savings-bank, in the building-society?[4] Nay what becomes of his bits of sticks at home? Remember too how hard he and his have fought to bring the wages up to the point at which they are, to raise the standard of life with him to what it is—such as it is. Remember that he has done that for himself by combining with his fellows: think how

3. The Representation of the People Act of 1884 extended the franchise to all males paying a rent of ten pounds annually or owning land valued at ten pounds. An estimated 60 percent of males were enabled to vote, though this varied by region.
4. As part of a European–United States economic downturn 1873–96, the 1884–6 UK recession brought widespread unemployment.

pleased his employers would have been if they could have kept that standard down!

Why, they would have made England the first country in the world—for ever—if only those foolish working men had been contented to live upon less, to run a race with their French and German brethren in pinching themselves for the glory of England: alas my friends for your lack of thrift and your want of knowledge of the true principles of political economy, which would have taught you the beauty of starving yourselves to-day that your sons might be worse starved years hence! Well, well, such as you are[,] you have become by your discontent [the] aristocracy of labour: but even if you are pleased with your present condition, and see nothing left to strive for but the abolition of the house of Lords, I warn you you will not keep it without fresh discontent, and ever fresh discontent. Friends, you must battle to keep your present condition, I say, and in the course of that battle you will begin to see that there are ever fresh things ahead for you to struggle for and at last that it is all or nothing: believe me it will very soon be all then.

So far I have been going on one line and speaking of those who earn their living by manual labour, by labour which tries the bodily strength chiefly; but I cannot go further without mentioning another class of workers, whose work however it may enfeeble their bodies, does not strain their muscles: the clerks and shop-assistants I mean; and I think you will all agree with me in thinking that they at least have some reasons for the discontent: of course I am speaking of the rank and file of them, and of them I will say that they seem to me far worse off than the artisans: nominally they belong to the middle-class, but their earnings are lower than those of artisans, and they are compelled to make a show of gentility, save the mark,[5] and moreover have less hope of rising out of their misery, for indeed it is no less, than an ordinary skilled workman at any rate; and their position such as it is, is I should say even more precarious than that of the artisans: it is strange however that with such very solid reasons for discontent, the clerks as a body are reactionary in their politics: I suppose it is their very hopelessness which forces them to follow the politics of their bosses: well, we cannot ask any individual of their class to run the risk of instant dismissal by overt acts of what the said bosses would call rebellion; yet I do call on them to think about the matter, to cherish their discontent, to make up their minds to the fact that they are in a wretched and slavish condition from no fault of their own, and to do all they can to help us short

5. "[God] save the mark": an exclamation of humorous astonishment, irony, or contempt.

of incurring the pain of dismissal: we cannot do without them; taking the widest definition of their class, they are a huge mass of men, unfitted by their present slavery for most useful occupations, but not without education: the very conditions, I say straightforwardly, for turning men into revolutionists.

What other classes or groups are there which have reason for discontent with the present state of things? We are not very far up the social ladder yet, I think there must be one or two more: or what do [you] think of the pleasures of the life of a small shop-keeper? His freedom from sordid anxiety, his leisure; his plentiful opportunities for exercising his body and improving his mind? You see he belongs to a body of men whose occupation is undoubtedly doomed to extinction: the great store, Whiteley's or such like on the one side,[6] the Co-operative Store on the other, are drawing nearer and nearer to the wretched small tradesman like the two claws of a nutcracker, and day by day he is forced into the ranks of the manual labourers or the servile army of clerks. Once again I call on the small shopkeepers also, although they may consider themselves to belong to the middle-class, to join their most righteous discontent to the discontent of the lower classes, in the full certainty that nothing else will help them.

Higher yet: shall we speak of the farmers, whom also the present system bears hardly enough on: I don't sympathise with their troubles quite so much as I should indeed if I could [put] out of my head the thought of the lives their labourers lead; if I could forget the contrast between the jolly, well-fed burly farmer between 50 and 60 years old and his labourer, the miserable worn-out bow-backed crawling old man 50 or 60 who has helped him to his burliness and jollity: still it is not to be denied that here also the present system has done no marvels of prosperity: here also among the farmers is plentiful cause for discontent: perhaps even among them we might win a few recruits.

Once more, how is it with the professional classes? The noble class of hangers-on to which I myself belong? Here at any rate I am at home, and I think I can tell you something about them. Well, perhaps we ought to be contented: we are all clothed, well fed, well housed: we at least have reaped the advantages of the progress of civilization: for us perhaps education is more than a name: for us the standard of intelligence has really been raised since the middle-ages: it is we who in a sense rule our rulers, tell them what to think, what to admire, how to express their thoughts, and arrange their mandates into words

6. A London retail chain, later department store, founded in 1863 and closed in 1961.

which their slaves or masters will listen to. For us the history of the world, the memory of man, lies open; for us the course of nature, her operations, and the hopes and fears to be deduced from them, have been unveiled. Yes, our bodies and our minds are both well cared for; there need be no limit to our aspirations for the good opinion of our fellow-men while we live and after we are dead: neither our anxieties nor our responsibilities should be crushing: even if our business ties us to the filth and hubbub of a great town for the greatest part of the year, we are almost all of us rich enough to be able to rest ourselves by change of scene and the contemplation of the beauties of nature and art during some time of the year: and when we are at work there is mostly with us some interest in the work we have to do: not infrequently indeed we have chosen our careers on those very grounds: easy in our lives then, our minds expanded by education so that we never lack amusement, and with more or less congenial employment, we at least are bound to be contented whoever else above or below us are discontented.

Is it so indeed? Yet here I stand before you, one of the most fortunate of this happy class, so steeped in discontent, that I have no words which will express it: no words, nothing but deeds, wherever they may lead me to, even [if] it be ruin, prison, or a violent death. And I think you will believe me when I say that my case is not so uncommon among men of my class: nay the members of the S.D.F. who address you are by no means all of them working-men, there are plenty of whom are in the same position as myself, and who work harder for the extinction of their class than I do. Well and why is this, what are our causes for discontent? It may well be that as a class we have none, but as individuals you must remember that our position also is precarious: for as some men may by dint of good luck, tireless industry and hardness of heart climb up out of their class into ours: so it is by no means uncommon for some of our class through it may be some softness or unfitness or maybe through sheer ill luck to fall from our class into the lower; which is then the very lowest class: I say straight out that to my certain knowledge this is not uncommon. The truth is we discontented ones of the intellectual or hanger-on group are conscious that the whole thing is a desperate battle, and we are not contented to oppress those below us as we must do under the present system, not only for the sake of keeping ourselves in our position but also for the sake of piling up the monstrous fortunes of the rich men whose hangers-on we are: whatever advantages we possess over others we are willing and anxious to give up if by so doing we can win a decent life for ourselves and for others; a life from which the terrible elements of precariousness should be absent: that is one thing but we may take higher ground and say that all that civilization has cultivated our sensibility only to disappoint it, and that we suffer (merely selfishly if you will) from the consciousness of the mass of suffering and brutality which lies below our lucky class–ugliness all about us, the world made for naught.

In short we see that that system which involves a desperate struggle for bare life in the lower classes, which condemns the greater part of men to live a life unhappier than that of the brutes, and little less brutal, and which forces us even to live a life of fear and risk, can only lead the world towards civilization by destroying itself; and I must tell you that some of us have been driven to see this, and to take note of the fact that our present systems is eating its own heart out by the visible ugliness and lack of dignity of all life under it: we know enough of history to see that the dawn and progress of our present system has gone hand in hand with the sickness and continued sickness of all beauty, all pleasure in life: we see before us a great gulf gaping for the extinction of all the hopes of civilization, and into which many excellent things have already been swept; we see that nothing can fill it up save a complete change in our system—nothing save revolution; therefore we are discontented and revolutionists!

If these reasons are not enough for our discontent, I can give you none other: I can only say we are driven by discontent and unhappiness into a longing for revolution: that we are oppressed by the consciousness of the class of toiling slaves below us, whose hangers-on we are: if you distrust us because we are their hangers-on, at least make use of us for the furtherance of the cause.

Now whether there are any discontented people above this class of hangers-on to which I belong, doesn't much matter, because in number they do not amount to much: let us call all such classes the contented classes; and indeed, as a class I fear you must add my own hanger-on class, who are only discontented so far as their position as guardians of the morals and intellect of their richer masters forces them to be more intellectually active than they are.

But for others of those classes I have named I say that they have a full call to be discontented, that in few words they live in misery; yes even the better-off of them, so dull their lives are, though they may scare know it or feel it, so empty of all pleasure though they live in a world which is beautiful and might be full of pleasure.

And now comes the question, what hope of salvation from this misery is there? For here at least if there is but a glimmer of hope will be pleasure, great enough sometimes I think. Now the misery I have been speaking of is to a great extent admitted by most people who give themselves the trouble of such matters, but much diversity of opinion there is as to the nature of the hope which may cast a ray of sunlight on it: those who do not feel the misery in their proper persons, and who venture to solace their not very accurate sorrow about other men's troubles indulging in hope, have some of them a vague sort of idea that general progress, the spread of liberal ideas, the growth of education and the rest will little by little raise the condition of the lower classes as they too truly call them: nor can I say that they are wrong otherwise than in being vague; only if they could but see into the matter and have a vision that was not vague, of how that progress will work, I fear they would be startled and cry out, No no, we didn't mean that! Then there are others of a sterner mould who have got involved in those lies about thrift and industry which I have spoken of before, who will tell you that it is possible if not easy for any working-man by practice of the said thrift and industry to raise himself out of his class. Well of course that is no answer to the question as to how miserable *classes* can escape from their misery; for 'tis quite clear that if those beautifully thrifty and industrious individuals can get out of their class-wretchedness they must leave their class behind them; that in fact they rise at the cost of the mass of their fellows whose average of thrift and industry they exceed.

Again I say that our friends the thrift-mongers when they are not liars more or less unconsciously, are very vague and cannot realize in the least in the world, at what point the bettering of a class by the giving up of its more energetic members, is to stop: the fact is that under the system which rules us the general thrift of a class will not in the least better it as a class: exactly to the degree of its thrift, that is to say, its capacity to live on less, its wages will be lowered; and the misery will still be there; clean misery, undrunken misery, maybe, but misery all the same; an empty cupboard and an anxious bed.

In other words, under the present system there is no hope of the working-class bettering their condition as a class: whatever partial amelioration they have gained has been in spite of the system, in its teeth; they have torn those advantages from the richer classes at their expense. Why, the words are still ringing in my ears that our class, the middle class, cast at the Trades Unions twenty years ago; some of the younger of you perhaps scarcely remember the virulence of the expressions of hatred that even would-be Liberals allowed themselves to use against them—why? Because we felt they were bettering their class at the expense of ours: we are civil enough to them now; again why? Because of the progress of more liberal opinion among the middle-class?—no no no: because we feel that they have gone the length of their tether and can gain nothing more for their class at the expense of ours; their teeth are drawn, we are no longer afraid of them.

I so much want you to understand this point clearly that I repeat it at the risk of wearying you: It is *of the essence* of society as at present constituted, of society based on the system of capital and wages that the wage-earners shall earn no more than is necessary for them to sustain their power of labour and reproduce their kind. It is true that the standard of this subsistence varies somewhat: in times when commerce is brisk it will have a tendency to rise, in times when things are slack it will fall; but up to a certain point, that of independence of daily precarious, compulsory labour, it cannot rise, and below the point of keeping men in tolerable animal strength it cannot fall, although it has not seldom come perilously near to that point. Our present society therefore is based on the perpetual servitude and misery of the wage-earning classes; any amelioration of that misery (as we have seen with reference to the Trades Unions) shakes society, and the destruction of the misery would mean the destruction of Society.

Now when you have fully got to comprehend this you must as a matter of course see the futility of those vague dreams of improvement held by the ordinary middle-class Liberals: I mean the kind of thing represented by those who say very gravely that people are much better off than they were; that the progress of education will show the poor how they can live better than they know how to at present; and that, as aforesaid, it is only the worthless among them that need remain poor; as all the rest may if they will only try hard enough rise into the condition of comfort and refinement.

To those who are poor I know that this must sound like a cruel jest; but 'tis commonly said in so much good faith as a person can have who half consciously deceives himself so that he may dull the feeling of responsibility which would otherwise trouble him: at best, you see, and supposing it true, those who console themselves with this vague comfort must make up their minds to wait generation after generation, thousands of years I should say, before they can expect to see even the beginning of the end of poverty. Well, such consolation as that joined to the comfortable assurance that at any rate it can't be helped, that these things simply come in the order of nature: all this I say may be enough for smothering the pain which the rich suffer from the poor themselves: if I thought it true I should be very careful to do all I could to keep a fine army and police made up of people practically belonging to the middle-classes: I should if I could do my best to prevent the poor from learning so much even as to read and write: I think also I should get people to preach to the poor and tell them that if they only knew it they are better off than I am: that theirs is the real condition of happiness since they have nothing to lose; that there is something holy and glorious in being weary, dirty, ignorant and hungry, and that when they die they will go to heaven and be happy ever after with absolutely nothing to do, whereas I when I die expect to go to—'tother place, and be eternally tormented.

I think I should feel also that this would be accepted as such a very likely thing on the assumption that there is anything like justice in the universe, that it would be hardly necessary to preach any more morality to them: but perhaps sometimes when I was in a very cowardly mood and at the same time despised the intellect of the poor especially, I should set people to telling them that I (the rich man) was very useful to them, and provided them with work, and consequently victuals by the simple process of doing nothing and living luxuriously. Of course I could not pretend to believe any of this myself, but I repeat that if I were only careful enough about my army and police and in withholding education from them, I might be moderately comfortable a-nights and not dream too much of being surrounded by a crowd of terrible beings fierce-eyed and careless of anything but rapine, deaf to my prayers for mercy, nay though they were called my countrymen they would not talk the same tongue as a gentleman.

Well, you know this kind of solace to the rich for the grief of the poor has been tried long enough, nay still is, and even more than we middle-class people often think; because in truth that other solace drawn from the figures of Mr Giffen and such-like men that things are after all improving,[7] is but an adjunct to the first solace; a kind of luxury of conscience-stifling; perhaps resorted to because a dim consciousness is creeping over the rich that after all the condition of the poor may be a matter partly in their own hands.

Yes friends, that is the comfort, and the only one that I can venture to offer to the poor for their share of the discontent of modern Society; I say again their welfare lies in their own hands if they only knew it. If you think of it, you must see that on no other grounds could I venture to stand here and remind you of how hardly the world uses you: if it were indeed true that all those groups of people I have spoken of were living

7. Robert Giffen (1837–1910), statistician, Scottish financial journalist, and economic advisor to the British government, published *The Progress of the Working Classes* in 1884. He is best known for the concept of the "Giffen good," the notion that people consume more of certain necessities as prices rise, creating an upward-sloping demand curve.

in those varied degrees of misery, because the eternal order of things must needs have it so, what could I say save to bid you bear it as well as you could, and to hope that there might be a heaven hereafter as there is full certainly hell here?

Friends, this earthly hell is not the ordinance of nature but the manufacture of man; made I will believe not by their malice but their stupidity; and it is your business to destroy it: to destroy it, I say, not each man to try to climb up out of it, as your thrift-teachers tell you, but to make an end of it so that no one henceforth can ever fall into it. I say again[,] that is your business: and if you understood the matter rightly, you have no other business than that until you have accomplished it.

What is it then that you want to do in order to extinguish this Hell of misery? You of the working-classes are at present what is called free workmen: that is[,] you are so free that you are not encumbered with any property, and are free to choose between the market wages of your labour and the workhouse. I have said you have no property: yet oddly enough you are possessors of a strange commodity called "labour,"[8] that has this double peculiarity in it; that it alone of all commodities has the power of creating goods, while on the other hand you free workmen cannot as things go use this wonderful commodity for yourselves and of yourselves, but must truck it away at a sorry bargain for you to certain persons who have inherited, or acquired by force or fraud the privilege of owning it, or to speak plainly of owning you, on their own terms: those terms are that they shall exercise their privilege at your expense: that privilege of owning you they do not venture to claim its set terms; they do not call you their slaves, but they claim it indirectly, by claiming the ownership of the means whereby your commodity, labour, can breed and make goods: therefore since they own the means whereby alone you can live they can I repeat force you to sell your commodity labour, your sole possession on their terms; your force and skill is useless to you unless they choose to allow you to exercise it.

Now it is true that they are forced to allow you to exercise it because otherwise they in their turn could not live: you are necessary to their existence, although they are your masters: but the bargain which they (though the weaker party) force upon you is simply this, that they shall feed[,] clothe and house you at the lowest rate that you can live and breed upon without rebelling against them, and the rest they will take for themselves: this bargain I say you cannot resist except by rebellion of some kind or other, because competition among yourselves drives you to accept it; nor can they the masters even if they would offer you any

8. Cf., e.g., Karl Marx, *Capital*, vol. 1, chap. 6.

better terms however compassionate and pious they may be, because competition among themselves drives them to insist on it.

Now I say that this privilege claimed by a few to own the means whereby labour becomes fruitful and through that ownership, to own the very lives of the labourers is the cause of all that misery I began by speaking of: I will turn round on those thrift preachers I have mentioned, and will say, yes by all means let us be thrifty, not a few of us but all of us: for look you, this wretched system of privileged and unprivileged produces that which must produce misery, waste to wit: for understand this clearly, not only do the rich by having more than their share of the world[']s wealth prevent others from having their share; but they distinctly lessen the whole stock of wealth by their riches, for they are egged on to crave for mere luxuries, which even they themselves do not really care for, partly I suppose because of the folly bred of their false position; by want of serious occupation, the pride of power, the undue softening of their bodies; and partly also because the insatiate lust of the profit mongers for new markets in which to use up the lives of the free workmen whom they sweat, is always stimulating the abovesaid pride and folly to foolish and false desires: so that a great part of the work done by the workers is done in pure waste, and I hope you can see without long talking over it that this waste is a tax upon those workers who produce the really useful things, that they have to work longer spells in consequence of it. That is of course only a part of the waste which goes on under the present system, though I fully believe it to be a very great part; besides that waste of luxury there is the waste of commercial war; the army of people employed not in genuine distribution of goods which would of course always be necessary, but in the multifarious occupations which have to do with the shifting of money from pocket to pocket, and guarding against the various accidents to which gambling on a large scale is liable; nor can I quite pass over those who are employed in doing nothing, or in helping others in that elegant occupation: a very little consideration of all these ways of wasting wealth and the means of wealth will show you how huge the waste is, and how obvious it is that misery must come of such waste: and I want you to consider it not a little but much, and once more to look at it as being a wrong done to you, a wrong in which you yourselves will be accomplices if you submit to it when once you have learned that this misery imposed on you the workers is not an irremediable necessity of nature, but has been built up by a kind of half conscious plotting of those that have to keep those that have not perpetually in subjection, and which plot must needs at last grow and now is growing too complex and difficult to sustain. Surely when you look at the facts of that hard bargain as I have stated them you must admit, that it is not necessary that the world[']s work should be done in such an iniquitous manner; for who really that ever thinks doubts the iniquity of rich and poor?

I say[,] is this iniquity necessary? It is for you to answer the question: it is necessary now just so long as the workers fail to see the iniquity. Come then[:] I have told you how your masters treat you, how they are bound to treat you so long as they are your masters: is it not at least conceivable that you might be your own masters, your own employers? That you the workers should have in your own hands those things which are necessary to make labour fruitful; the land, the machines and the power of distribution. In that case you yourselves would bargain with yourselves, and the bargain would be that all should work and every man should have the fruits of his work, that is to say his share of the product of the collective labour of the community, each for all and all for each. And remember again that no approach to this obvious justice can be gained as long as you are ruled by the monopoly of capital, as long as certain privileged individuals by the possession of the instruments of labour can dictate their own terms to the labourer: I tell you that in this matter the first and the last step are one, everything will follow after the one determination of the workers to be their own masters, and things which now seem difficult, impossible almost[,] will be done easily.

It is for that reason, that though it is futile to cast blame on any individual of the richer classes, though we may see in those of them that we know all possible virtues, I yet want to impress the fact upon you that as classes you and they are and must be opposed to each other: whatever gain you add to your standard of life you must do at their expense, and they will and must resist it to the utmost of their power. I have said that it was men[']s stupidity and not their malice which had built up the present system; and yet though conscious malice need not be imputed to the members of a class, nevertheless the whole of the domination of the upper classes is founded on deliberate injustice; and that injustice I want you to feel, because when you once feel that you are slaves, not each one by some accident or other, but because you belong to the classes of labour[,] then the emancipation of labour is at hand: I know indeed that in a country and time like our own, people do not readily feel that slavery: if you were treated with obvious personal violence, were liable to be tied up and whipped, or to have your ears cut off at the bidding of your masters; nay if you had to go to the Police Office for a passport to go from Southwark to Hammersmith, it would be a different thing; you would soon be in the streets[,] I hope[,] expressing your feelings in something stronger than words.

Yet put another case: you are well fed we will suppose, are living in a roomy pretty house, are educating your children well, are treated by everybody as an equal, have leisure to read and amuse yourself[,] to travel even if you wish; are not tied to work and live within certain narrow limits on the one hand, and on the other are not in risk of being driven from city to city for your livelihood; and moreover that livelihood is assured you so long as you behave decently and do your share of work which is not disgusting or repulsive. Now that's what I call being free: but suppose one fine morning some one no better than yourself and for no particular reason takes your wholesome food from you and feeds you on garbage; has you stripped of your decent clothes and rigs you out in shoddy; drives you out of your pretty roomy house into a close stifling room where you haven't room to swing a cat in; cuts off your children's[9] education from a liberal into a class education; makes you work every day till you get so weary in the evening that you want bed and not books; treats your wish for a decently long holiday as a crime; chains you for years to some abominable spot because your work is there: or sends you wandering over the country from one wretched set of hovels to another in search of work, speaks to you in such a way as only thinly hides a perpetual insult, sets you to work which is nothing but a dreary task deadening to mind and body, makes even that miserable toil and the wages that depend on it precarious [and] dependent on matters over which you have no control, and so takes care that in any case in spite of all your efforts you may at last be fed and housed at the public expense indeed, but with shame well mixed with your workhouse bread and drink.

I say suppose you have all that done to you[,] you who might have led the decent life I spoke of first: have it done to you, I say by a man who calls himself your master, and you take it as a matter of course; shall I in the teeth of all reason call you a free man—not I. You are a slave. And except that it was done to you when you were born, and not in the middle of your life all that has been done to you—and alas! You have got used to it; you are contented.

Will it go on thus generation after generation; will the English workman be much the same as he is now, a hundred years hence; at the best a decent intelligent man living the dreariest and most limited of lives with little pleasure and no beauty in it, and no hope worth calling a hope? Will that be the case[,] friends? No it cannot be; he will be either much worse than he is now, or so much better, that his place as a class workman will no more be found. In all honesty I believe that the

9. Orig., childrens'

latter thing will happen: I believe that the class struggle which has gone on all through history being now based on the widest all-embracing class, and looking forward to the equality of labour will be the last of the class struggles, and that a life will be offered to men very much higher and more desirable than that humble one I sketched just now[,] which at present seems unattainable to the workman: let us cease then to think that unattainable, and we shall attain it maybe before so very long: only remembering that if we are to shorten the period of strife, the rough and it may be terrible period of transition from the old to the new, it must be by that complete combination which at present I know seems also so unattainable to the workman, since every day he is driven to compete against his fellow and not to combine with him: therefore hard as it will be to bring about, needing the most strenuous efforts of many serious men I do above all things urge on you to do your very utmost to combine to shake of[f] the economical slavery of today, which believe me doesn't differ so much as many might think form the slavery of the older world: if we live to see the day when that slavery receives its death wound we shall regret no labour or pain that we have spent in the cause: no men that have ever lived will have been so happy as we shall be.

Big words, do you think? I cannot help it, the cause is great too. Indeed sometimes I have heard it said, "the change you strive for is so prodigious, so far transcending any revolution that has yet happened, that we dare not think about it, it seems such an idle hope." Well, one might say, Don't think about it, then, but act for it, and he who lives will see. But further is it not natural that the revolution we are looking for should be the greatest of all? In these days when man's knowledge and mastery over material nature has so increased, it might be well expected that not only the change in Society will be tremendous when it is ripe for the change, but also that the prize of the change should be proportionally great; I can only say if that were not so, if in these days there were no great ideal ahead of us, no hope for a life on earth better than the world has yet seen, if the present condition of war hypocritically veiled with a sham of peace is to go on forever, then all the promises and hopes of progress are mere delusions and lies: then have we gained knowledge and mastered the forces of nature that we might be more unhappy than ever, and the future of the world is like to be universal melancholy madness.

All which I know can't be true, I know that we are moving onward: everywhere we see the apathy of the last 25 years breaking up into hopeful discontent, and if it be true, as Mr. Giffen says it is, that the condition of the workers is improving, then so much the more hopeful is that discontent, because it proves that men are preparing to claim a higher standard of life: and we call on them to raise that standard even higher, until they at last claim freedom with no doubtful voice and are determined to be contented with nothing less. It is to stir you up not to be contented with a little that I am here to-night: you will not get the little if you are contented with it: you *must* be either slaves or free: you are slaves at present: bear that always in mind, think of what it means: try to think of the life you might live and would naturally live if you were not forced into misery by your masters, and then I do not think you can help combining together to tell the world that you must be free and happy: and then all will soon be won.

Member's Name Emery Walker *Date* January 1888

JAN.	Amount Paid. / Sig.						JULY	Amount Paid. / Sig.				
FEB.	Amount Paid. / Sig.						AUG.	Amount Paid. / Sig.				
MAR.	Amount Paid. / Sig.						SEPT.	Amount Paid. / Sig.				
APRIL	Amount Paid. / Sig.						OCT.	Amount Paid. / Sig.				

Figure 9.1 Socialist League Membership cards, front and back. Walter Crane. Courtesy of Special Collections, University of Maryland

9

"Introduction to *A Review of European Society* by John Sketchley," September 29, 1884

Editor's introduction

John Sketchley (1823–1913) was a lifelong activist on behalf of working-class and socialist causes.[1] Originally a stocking maker and later an impecunious salesman, Sketchley became a Chartist organizer, radical journalist, and member of the 1860s Labour Reform League. In 1875 he founded the Birmingham Republican Association and in 1884 became a member of the Social Democratic Federation (SDF), where he met William Morris. In 1885 he joined Morris and others in forming the Socialist League, affiliating with the Birmingham Branch, delivering socialist lectures, and contributing frequently to *Commonweal*; and throughout the 1890s he continued to advocate for his version of libertarian revolutionary, antimonarchist socialism. Before publishing his 241-page *A Review of European Society: with an Exposition and Vindication of the Principles of Social Democracy* (London: William Reeves; Birmingham: John Sketchley, 1885) he had issued several shorter works, including *The Crimes of Government* (Hull: Sketchley's People's Book Store, n.d.), *Principles of Social Democracy* (Social Democratic Party, 1879), and *Land Common Property* (London, 1881?).

A Review of European Society offers more than its title promises: section one provides an account of economic and labor conditions throughout Europe during the past century; section two examines revolutionary and progressive movements since the French Revolution; and section three lays out a detailed scheme for the nationalization of the land, currency, and machinery needed for labor. Sketchley anticipates an immediate and successful revolution throughout Europe: "While the re-action is everywhere triumphant, the revolution is everywhere present . . . . No power on earth can stay its onward march." Since in his view socialist principles are now embraced by the greatest thinkers of both Europe and the United States, "Who can doubt the future of humanity?" (236, 238). It seems pointed that, although in his introduction Morris praises Sketchley's character and the detailed nature of his projections, he comments neither on their accuracy nor likelihood.

Morris's remarks instead emphasize the continuity of working people's history. The gathering to present the Great Charter at Kennington Common in 1848 had been followed by post-Crimean War prosperity, "from which sprang some of the most dishonourable deeds which have ever disgraced our history . . . ." It is not certain which "dishonourable deeds" of the past thirty years Morris had uppermost in mind, but in his 1880 "Our Country Right or Wrong" he had expressed disgust at the Anglo-Zulu War (1879), the Second Anglo-Afghan War (1880–1), Britain's support for the repressive Ottoman Empire directly before the Berlin Congress (1875–8), and its gradual invasion of Egypt (the Mahdist War, beginning 1882). However, there were other candidates for opprobrium, including (in a selective list), the Anglo-Persian War (1856–7), the Second Opium War (1856–60), the suppression of the Indian Rebellion (1857–8), the Second and Third Ashanti Wars (1863–4 and 1873–4), the Bhutan (Indian) War (1864–5), the Second Anglo-Marri (Pakistan) War (1880), and the First Boer War (1879–81).

Morris uses his introduction to commend Sketchley's courage in championing a dangerous cause "when to be a Chartist was . . . a weight not to be borne by a coward or a shuffler," and his steadfastness as an advocate of advanced causes even when these were unpopular: "when Chartism was dead, [he] yet associated himself with the forward movement, and was a pronounced Republican." Sketchley's political career embodies the historical continuity between Chartism and socialism as avant-garde working-class movements, for he "went forward with the progress of events, . . . and has grasped the principles of Scientific Socialism which were developed on the Continent." Since the issue of British nationalism evoked discord among members of the SDF, at least at a practical level, it is noticeable that Morris also praises Sketchley for his understanding "that no social agitation which is not international has any real chance of success." In commending Sketchley's antiparliamentarian beliefs—"the suffrage will be but little—nay, no use in the hands of those who look upon a vote as an end and not as a means"—Morris is, of course, also expressing his own views. Even trade unionists will not be able to protect a "worker aristocracy" from oppression but must join with the broader movement to grant power to all workers.

Morris's introduction is dated September 29, 1884, a time when he was still a member of the SDF. It is notable that he uses the Marxist term "Scientific Socialism" to refer to the present political movement, perhaps to distinguish the SDF from earlier Owenite or Fourierist socialism, or to differentiate their shared views from those of the newly formed Fabian Society (founded January 1884). "Scientific socialism" is a term Morris seldom uses later, however, perhaps because it suggested the deterministic claims he found ahistorical and unconvincing (see his 1889 speech to the Second International, No. 15, and his final essay in *Justice*, "The Promise of May," No. 27). Another indication that these remarks are from an early period of Morris's socialism is his challenge to "our enemies," that is, his fellow employers and members of his own class. He still hopes these may "feel their false position while it is yet time for them to become our comrades also," a targeted appeal less prominent in his later lectures as he accepted the atypicality of his own position and also addressed more exclusively working-class audiences.

Note

1. Christopher Draper, "The Talented Mr. Sketchley (1823–1913)," *Northern Voices*, December 5, 2016; https://northernvoicesmag.blogspot.com/2016/12/the-talented-mr-sketchley-1823-1913.html (accessed April 5, 2022).

The following pages form a book giving information concerning that Social Revolution which may be said rather to be in progress than to be at hand; information to those who stand outside it, either as curious spectators, or as declared enemies, but encouragement to those who are within it, and are doing their best in their generation to hasten its progress, or to light the way for its footsteps in the earliest hours of the new day.

The literature of Scientific Socialism in the English tongue is yet but scanty, and a book planned as this, and carried out with so much care as to figures—to speak of nothing else—will doubtless be heartily welcomed by all our comrades in the cause; but the book, besides its intrinsic worth, has another and special claim on our attention in being the work of an old Chartist.

The agitation towards Socialism, which is now once more afoot in England, cannot be dissociated from the expression of discontent which flickered over England so long, and in the opinion of many, nay most, of the contented classes, died out at Kennington Common in 1848.

This expression of most righteous discontent was indeed smothered for a while by the wave of material middle-class prosperity which rolled over England after 1854, and from which sprung some of the most dishonourable deeds which have ever disgraced our history; and if it could have been possible for this prosperity to last and spread downward, the tale of the Chartists might have been forgotten, or become a faint and distorted shadow on the page of history; but such a prosperity, founded on class domination and the rule of the sweaters or capitalists cannot be long-lived, as we are now on all sides beginning to find out; the discontent of the mass of the people oppressed under *communal slavery*, which, if it were to be everlasting, would be the worst of slaveries—this discontent which, as I have said, seemed to most to have died with Chartism in 1848, has risen from the dead in the more formidable shape of Scientific Socialism.

One of the few living men who form the visible links between the past hope and the present hopes of the workers of this country, is Mr. John Sketchley, the author of this book, who from his boyhood was attracted to the cause of the people, who worked steadily and faithfully through the years during which Chartism was alive and dreaded, and when to be a Chartist was no light matter, and was a weight not to be born[e] by a coward or a shuffler; who, when Chartism was dead, yet associated himself with the forward movement, and was a pronounced Republican; who finally (and this it is which makes his career so important and instructive for us) went forward with the progress of events, and instead of folding his hands and looking back complacently on his old work as on a pleasant story, as many have done, has grasped the principles of Scientific Socialism which were developed on the Continent. Since the days of Chartism he has been associated with the movement abroad, and sees clearly that no social agitation which is not international has any real chance of success.

So that Mr. Sketchley has many special qualifications for writing this book, and I repeat that the mere fact of his doing so with the care and completeness he has exercised ought to be an encouragement to us, since he represents a sleeping cause (I will not say a dead one, it would not be true) awakened again.

To many waverers also, who are inclined to pin their faith to the political promises of to-day, he can speak convincingly and with authority, showing them, for instance, that the suffrage will be but little—nay, no use in the hands of those who look upon a vote as an end and not as a means, that the slaves of capital must needs elect *masters* and not delegates; and that it is but little use our having got rid of feudalism if the greed of commercialism is to rule over us: and also that the time is coming, and speedily too, when those who have won a kind of position as an aristocracy of labour by means of the trades unions, will find that position slipping away from them, and will be driven to feel their solidarity with those hitherto more unfortunate workers who have been oppressed by the present system of capital and labour without licence or limit.

Both to our comrades, therefore, and our enemies I commend this book, with some sort of a hope that the latter may feel their false position while it is yet time for them to become our comrades also, and with a certain and assured hope that no resistance on their part will in the long run avail them, or prevent them from losing their position of masters of slaves.

Figure 10.1 Andreas Scheu (1844–1927). Courtesy of the National Trust

Figure 10.2 Philip Webb (1831–1915). Courtesy of the National Portrait Gallery

Figure 10.3 James Tochatti (1852–1928). Courtesy of Stephen Williams

Figure 10.4 John Carruthers (1836–1914). Courtesy of Economic Studies

Figure 10.5 Frederic Harrison (1831–1923). Courtesy of the National Portrait Gallery

10

"Commercial War," 1885

Editor's introduction

William Morris drafted "Commercial War" in 1885, as part of a series of critiques of capitalism written shortly before and after the period of his break with the Social Democratic Federation (SDF) and the formation of the Socialist League. Other lectures of the year included "Slaves and Slave-Holders," "The Depression of Trade," "The Dawn of a New Epoch," and "Socialism" (no. 11). He delivered it only three times, on March 27 and April 12 and 19, 1885, all to sympathetic and partly working-class audiences: the Croydon Branch of the SDF, the Labour Emancipation League at the Academy Schools in Hoxton, and the Hammersmith Branch of the Socialist League at Kelmscott House. He did not include the text in *Signs of Change* (1886), however, and May Morris reproduced only one of its more powerful paragraphs in the second volume of *Artist Writer Socialist* (2.311). The lecture therefore remained in British Library Additional Manuscript 45,333, ff. 109–31, a clear ink draft in Morris's characteristic manuscript layout, with relatively few paragraph breaks and the use of elongated spaces to mark pauses and shifts in tone.

"Commercial War" remains a powerful analysis of the interrelated effects of "competitive commerce," synthesizing Morris's critique of the social attitudes which drive inequality, imperialism, and the mass production of inferior wares. To these he adds a commentary on the power of newspapers and other establishment media to propagandize and distort—an increasing concern to Morris himself in his capacity as editor of the newly initiated Socialist League periodical, *Commonweal.* As in "Misery and the Way Out," his comments are often personal, condemning the attitudes of those in his own social circle ("I have talked with people who . . . believed that it was . . . good and right . . . for the mass of mankind to be overworked and underpaid, to dread starvation daily, to be forced to have neither education or leisure or pleasure or hope"), and expressing his frustrations with the socially destructive constraints of the marketplace ("however grand we may think ourselves; men of science, literary men, artists, we all wear the chain").

The mid-1880s were a period in which crofters rose up against Highland clearances in sporadic armed conflicts such as "The Battle of the Braes" (1882), mass meetings of angry workers accelerated passage of a Voting Rights Act in 1884; and the imperialist campaign in the Sudan reached its height (General Gordon and other British soldiers were killed in the siege of Khartoum on January 25, 1885). It was also a period during which, as an advocate for socialism, Morris participated in manifestos and demonstrations which demanded wider voting rights (October 26, 1884); condemned British invasion of the Sudan (Socialist League resolution, *Pall Mall Gazette*, February 11, 1885); protested unemployment (February 16 and April 12, 1885); commemorated the anniversary of the Paris Commune (March 22, 1885); and composed a long narrative poem, "The Pilgrims of Hope" (1885), as well as several "Chants for Socialists" (1884–5).

The striking title of "Commercial War" reflects Morris's stringent view that capitalism is a self-justifying form of armed theft, a mercantile variant of Hobbes' "ceaseless war of man against man." It follows that only a complete change in the social order of this Leviathan will bring lasting respite from its internecine extension of armed conflict by other means.

As the proprietor of Morris & Co. Morris was himself a midscale capitalist, and as the heir of shares in a major copper mine, Devonshire Great Consols, Morris had viewed the inner workings of a major commercial enterprise first hand.[1] These experiences confer autobiographical resonance on his pained confession that, within the commercial system, all, even the apparently successful, are forced to conform to its values:

> While this commercial war lasts we are all the slaves of it, not the working-classes only, but all of us. . . . I know it by sad experience, that intelligence[,] enthusiasm, knowledge of history, patience, years of hard work can contrive or accomplish nothing outside the charmed circle of that slavery: here is your one hope of success, to tack yourself on to the skirts of Commercialism, do its bidding, accept its morality and – despise yourself and the whole human race.

In his everyday and familial life, Morris would also have met many whose self-satisfied views he parodied in his first paragraph:

> [W]e find that the rich and well-to-do, the usurpers of property, try to wiggle out of acknowledging this fact by all kinds of ways, and mostly protest loudly that they are friends of the workers

> and wish them well. . . . I have been almost forced to believe in the genuineness of such professions as far as individuals are concerned: I have talked with people who, at least for the moment, believed that it was not only good and right in the abstract for the mass of mankind to be overworked and underpaid, to dread starvation daily, to be forced to have neither education or leisure or pleasure or hope, that it was not only good for the universe, but good for the slavelings themselves, and that the wise among them see it to be good, the ignorant among them feel it to be so, and that they have nothing to gain and everything to lose by any possible change in the basis of society.

More generically, Morris identified several great taints of corporate capitalism: its enormous waste; the widespread destitution which follows in its wake; and its role as a willing engine of imperial wars. Five years later, *News from Nowhere*'s "Old Hammond" would succinctly characterize the economic motivations of the latter: "the countries within the ring of 'civilization' (that is, organised misery) were glutted with the abortions of the market, and force and fraud were used unsparingly to 'open up' countries OUTSIDE that pale."[2] All of these ill effects of capitalism were intimately linked with an enabling propaganda ministry, the advertisement-driven commercial press:

> [O]ur newspapers and periodical press are little more than puffing sheets . . . sugared with a little news, a little politics and sometimes a little literature.
>
> [E]verything must be puffed; not only the rotten wares, or the low medium, as manufacturers phrase it, but even the reasonably good ones. . . .

As an artist, he also observed the great power capitalist 'taste-makers' have over people whose freedom to think and design for themselves has been blunted or traduced:

> [W]hen I see the kind of thing which does duty among [poor people and even shabby genteel people] for art and ornament, I confess I feel an indignation I have no power to express that people should have had such things thrust upon them for money . . . . such travesties of beauty[,] such wretched twaddling folly as they are.

And these consumers, he reminds his audience, are the *lucky* ones. Somewhere—preferably out of sight—a factory floor exists where these commodities are made by people who "lead a life that offers them no interest or variety save the interest which is inspired by doubts about next week[']s food," and who are "overworked[,] made to fear starvation, live in hovels, . . . herded and jammed in foul places called towns, while the houses in the countryside fall into ruins, and once fertile fields go uncultivated . . . ."

The "once fertile fields" Morris had in mind lay mostly in southern England. As Karl Marx had noted in the *Communist Manifesto*, however, the abuses of capitalism are also exported as the search for markets leads inevitably to ruthless competition between competing "empires," even as Morris notes presciently that "England, once the undoubted head of that system, is losing her leadership." These observations naturally led Morris to consider a current example of Britain's imperial dominion, and to offer a then rare expression of sympathy with the Mahdists who were resisting the extension of British domination in Khartoum and the Sudan:

> Nobody I think finds it very difficult to understand why those Arab men and boys threw their lives away so resolutely: we may give the feeling different names, and call it fanaticism, patriotism, love of liberty: for my part it seems to me much the same spirit as that which held the long-haired Greeks at Thermopolae, or the Swiss at [Morgarten,][3] and if we praise them for the manner of their death, and the cause they died for, I cannot see how we can withhold praise from the desert warriors whom we have been slaughtering lately. . . .

In February 1885 the Socialist League had passed a resolution condemning the invasion of the Sudan, and circulated a proclamation expressing pleasure at the fall of Khartoum. (For a twenty-first-century comparison, imagine a hypothetical resolution which expressed pleasure at the failure of a "coalition" attempt to "secure" Marjam in Afghanistan.) As for Britons' "patriotic duty," ". . . it is for [the capitalists] that we let our money, our name, our power, be used to drag off poor wretches from our pinched fields & our dreadful slums, to kill and be killed in a cause they know nothing of."[4]

At this point Morris shifts registers, pausing to honor pioneers of socialism such as the co-operator Robert Owen—"the most generous and best of men"—and to criticize Positivists and other liberal humanists such as Frederic Harrison[5] (characterized somewhat sarcastically as the "distinguished Priest of the Religion of Humanity," who opposed imperialism but not capitalism. For Morris at least, such liberal reformists offered little or nothing to ordinary workers, who must above all "see . . . how far we are bound by mere folly and superstition which we can shake off . . ., and first of all by the means of knowing it for what it is."

Morris had concluded "Misery and the Way Out" by assuring his listeners that after grasping their oppressed condition, "I do not think you can help combining together . . . and then all will soon be won." The "combining together" could be a difficult process, however, and Morris here acknowledges that no single form of organization or mass movement can effect such an outcome, much less render it inevitable: "I suppose nobody, however rash he may be, can suppose that such a change can be brought about suddenly, or by the conscious efforts of a few or even a great many people." Like Marx Morris conjectured that such a change would inevitably be caused by the collapse of the current system beneath the weight of its internecine enormities: "It is the commercial system itself which will kill the commercial system . . . ." Although he cherishes hopes for the results of such a cataclysm, even these are somewhat qualified:

> . . . if by chance the great capitalist and despotic communities are to meet in a huge all[-]embracing conflict, I don't believe for one that the new heavens and the new earth that will arise from that Ragnarók or Twilight of the Gods will turn out to be the paradise of exploitation which the Imperialist liberals have figured to themselves.

But what if the weaponry and technology of the "commercial war" were to destroy "us" as the "system" destroyed itself? Morris concludes with a prophecy of the imminent crisis and need for resistance: ". . . though slaves suffer pain because they feel their degradation, and machines do not: yet there is hope in that; because slaves can at least rebel when the opportunity serves: and now the opportunity draws near." Morris's identification of economic competition with pervasive war is both an appeal to rebellion and a first step in that resistance, quickened by a sense of what Walter Benjamin would call *Jetztzeit*, the possibility for major historical change within one's own time.[6]

Notes

1. See Charles Harvey and Jon Press, "The City and Mining Enterprise: The Making of the Morris Family Fortune," *JWMS* 9.1 (1990): 3–14, and Florence Boos and Patrick O'Sullivan, "Morris's Socialism and Devon Great Consols," *JWMS* 19.4 (2012): 11–39. Morris sold his shares in Devon Great Consols gradually, disposing of the final ones in 1877.
2. *News from Nowhere*, *Collected Works*, vol. 16, 94.
3. MS., "Morgarten" inserted in pencil in margin by editorial hand, possibly by May Morris.
4. Joseph Arch, head of the National Agricultural Labourers' Union, also opposed an Anglo-Russian war, warning Disraeli that "he must not count on being able to take the

agricultural labourers of England to be shot at for thirteen pence a day." Patrick Laity, *The British Peace Movement, 1870–1914* (Oxford: Oxford University Press, 2002), 70.

5. Martha Vogeler, *Frederic Harrison: The Vocations of a Positivist* (Oxford: Clarendon Press, 1984). Among other things, Harrison designed and promoted a set of Positivist rituals for worship designed to serve as a secular humanist alternate to organized religion.
6. "Theses on the Philosophy of History," *Gesammelten Schriften* I:2 (Frankfurt am Main: Suhrkamp, 1974); trans. Dennis Redmond, 2005.

When we Socialists point out to people that under our present system of capital and wages the workers are and must be defrauded of their due, that they are robbed of their property in fact, we find that the rich and well-to-do, the usurpers of property[,] try to wiggle out of acknowledging this fact by all kinds of ways, and mostly protest loudly that they are friends of the workers and wish them well, and that they dread a change in the basis of society quite as much in the interest of the workers as in their own interests: some of them will even tell you that they feel keenly their duty of being mere trustees of the wealth which law and custom gives to *them* and takes away from those who have produced it: I have been almost forced to believe in the genuineness of such professions as far as individuals are concerned: I have talked with people who, at least for the moment, believed that it was not only good and right in the abstract for the mass of mankind to be overworked and underpaid[,] to dread starvation daily, to be forced to have neither education or leisure or pleasure or hope, that it was not only good for the universe, but good for the slavelings themselves, and that the wise among them see it to be good, the ignorant among them feel it to be so, and that they have nothing to gain and everything to lose by any possible change in the basis of society.

That's a strange story certainly[,] but as they talk, it is the apparent position taken up of the well disposed of the possessing non-producing classes at the present day, and I really think that the individuals among them believe that the poor like being poor and wouldn't be otherwise if they could. In fact they have made, some of them at least, an article of faith[,] a religion indeed of this queer story and call it the Moralization of Capital.[1]

1. Promoted by the Positivist Frederic Harrison (1831–1923), the doctrine of the "moralization of capital" had been originally espoused in Adam Smith's *Theory of Moral Sentiments* (1759), which argued that commercial activity encouraged moral as well as economic development; Smith's *The Wealth of Nations* (1776) further claimed that individual economic effort would maximize social good, since "the invisible hand" of competitive markets naturally restrains selfishness in favor of the common welfare.

But though the individuals believe in this astonishing theory, I must needs say a hard word, that after all the whole thing is hypocrisy, not individual hypocrisy but class hypocrisy. Just as in past times the wealthy classes fortified their position with haughty priggish superciliousness, or with aristocratic insolence and superstition, so do they at present with hypocrisy, which as a matter of course in a commercial age is at once the great instrument and the great vice of the time. In its heart of hearts the modern wealthery[?], the possessing[,] non-producing class[,] holds the same opinion of the necessity and beauty of the contrast between rich and poor, which the slave owners of Greece and Rome and the serf masters of Medieval Europe held: this namely[,] that it [is] a beautiful arrangement of God or nature that the great mass of men should be poor and toilers in order that their labour may produce that fine flower of civilization[,] the well to do man with superfluous money[,] which will by ever fresh and fresh acquisition of unpaid labour produce more money; that it is orderly and right that the masses should be overworked, in order that a certain class may obtain immunity from productive toil: this has always, and very naturally been, the view of the dominant class; only in older days they stated it plainly and without hypocrisy, they now have to veil it with hypocrisy enough in public at any rate, though of course you will find the rougher members of the class stating it with perfectly natural brutality in private, and the whole class acting it always and steadily whatever their words may be.

The maxim therefore of the dominant class is now no less than of old, it is expedient that the many should toil and suffer for the few; nor does the maxim which I have heard in the mouth of a distinguished Priest[2] of the Religion of Humanity (the Positive Religion) really differ from it:[3] quoth he[,] a great man has said 'Everything for the people, nothing by them.'[4] The idea that runs through all this tyranny now so decently veiled, is that it is possible and expedient to train a few men up to be Gods or heroes by putting them above the lot of the common herd; that thus a standard of superexcellent humanity is held up to the world which furthers the progress of the race. Well, it may be there once was something in the idea, though for my part I hope I should always have borne in me the heart of a grimy hard[-]handed rebel against this hierarchy: the Athenian citizen did something worth remembrance with the leisure which the unpaid labour of his chattel slave gave him (prig):

2. MS., ~~Pos.~~ crossed out [for Positivist]
3. I.e. Frederic Harrison, leader of the Positivists, who promoted a rationalist "Religion of Humanity." An "advanced radical in politics," he nonetheless opposed socialism (see note 1 above).
4. This saying is attributed to the Holy Roman Emperor Joseph II (1741–90).

the medieval baron appears to us at this distance of time to have lived a romantic life on the unpaid labour of his serf (school bully): and surely one might think that the capitalist of today could do something with the life free from labour which he wins from the unpaid labour of his slave—the wage earner. Something he does do certainly, but the question is whether that something is of any great use to the world; does he waste the free noble life he has—stolen? That is a serious question I think: I remember another saying of my friend the positivist priest in which he formally stated the question: said he: "A great man has said, It is of no importance how a man has acquired his wealth, so long as he uses it properly." Perilous morality[,] you may think[,] for even a capitalist society! but never mind that; how does the capitalist use his wealth which he has acquired–never mind how? that I say is the question.

Well[,] of course he spends some of it in real leisure which is good for him at all events; idleness if you enjoy it and don't hurt your neighbor by it is always a good thing; but you know the capitalist is always telling us that he is a busy man, and truly he is; though he sometimes overdoes his account of his laborious sufferings. What does he do with all that business? Well, what did the Greek citizen do, what did the Medieval baron do? They made *war* and so does our modern capitalist: I am not now thinking of his occasional spurts of vicarious war, his collecting bands of hard[-]pressed labouring men, putting muskets in their hands and the ghost of a worn out superstition, called patriotism, in their hearts and setting them to kill people with whom they have no quarrel for the sake of winning fresh markets for him: that is only an incident in his life of continuous warfare. For indeed that is his life: if he is busy, as he is, and he does not produce, as he doesn't; what can he do but spend his life in fighting[?] His business is to contend with the other individuals of his class for the amount of the share of the product of unpaid labour which he shall individually possess: this war is technically called competition, and of course you will hear it spoken of as a beautiful and providential thing[:] the stimulus to exertion, the friend of liberty, nay the very bond of Society itself: but don't be deceived by the mere words; for this Commercial war has all the essential elements of the gunpowder war in it.

And first of all comes its waste, which indeed has no limits, and is carried on with immense variety. [B]ecause it goes with this as with other kinds of war that everything must be subordinated to it; a victory won in it is a real success, no other kind of success is thought anything of: so as all the most powerful part of society is engaged in this war[,] nothing else is, as I said, considered worthy to be thought of: the convenience, the happiness of society at large may go hang, so as only commerce may be brisk, and money turned over quickly: and you may take it as a curious familiar illustration of the waste of Commercial war that poor countries are by far the most comfortable to live in for all except the distinctly rich; that is[,] they are on the outskirts of the war and don't feel it so much: people in the rich countries don't live better, or healthier[, or] don't have better goods; they simply have the advantage of seeing greater contrast between their own moderate lives, or their own poverty and the rich people above them.

Now as to the forms of waste which Commercial war drives us into; I think they may chiefly be classed under three heads: 1st[,] the waste involved in the mere conduct of the war. 2nd[,] the forcing useless wares on the public, and 3rd[,] downright cheating, if indeed it is worth while making a separate heading of this last.

[A]s to the first: there is all the work that goes to watching lest the interests of each individual should be injured by the other combatants; safeguards against risk: book-keeping, insurance, checks against fraud in commercial houses and the like; not an inconsiderable waste, I should say: and there is also the waste incurred by competitive salesmanship: not a little one that: I have given it one name, I will now give it another and call it puffery: just consider what that means. You must all of you know that there are many articles in these days of machinery which cost a great deal more to sell than they do to make; for we have got to be so stupid, or so overworked, that everything must be puffed; not only the rotten wares, or the low medium, as manufacturers phrase it, but even the reasonably good ones still have to be puffed. I say again consider what all this means; amongst other things it means that our newspaper and periodical press are little more than puffing sheets, when they are successful, sugared with a little news[,] a little politics and sometimes a little literature.

Take these for types of this kind of waste, I dare say many of you can call to mind more such things; but they may all be classed I think under these two subdivisions of precautions against fraud and risk, and puffery of wares; all this waste would disappear at once with Commercial war: and I hope you understand that this is no light matter: I can't give you the statistics of either of these subdivisions of waste, and of the latter one[,] the puffery[,] I suppose it would be hard to do so; but at any rate 'tis quite clear that its discontinuance would set free a vast number of people from absolutely useless work, that is[,] would enable them to keep themselves instead of being kept perforce by the labour of others.

The second form of waste that competition imposes upon us is the production of useless wares made simply to sell, that is[,] forced on the public owing to their poverty, want of leisure[,] ignorance or folly[.] I know this is a wide subject, and also that in treating it I lay myself open to attack from economists of all schools unless I tread lighter on eggs than I am likely to; that at least I may [not] be accused of sentimentalism: I can only say that in treating of it I don't want to be unreasonable or over sentimental or superfine. One thing you must remember[,] that though the 'captains of industry' do depend on us the public as their customers and *seem* to be in our hands, they really are our masters in the matter, because I say again they can expend all their energy[,] set free for that purpose by their monopoly of unpaid labour, in working on our poverty[,] our want of leisure, our ignorance, and our folly; using these as their instruments they can force on us such goods as they please, and they use them unsparingly without any other aim than the monopolising as much of the product of unpaid labour as they can.

Our poverty is the vice which serves their turn best because so many of us are poor: here I think I can't be accused of being sentimental: it['] s quite clear that we cannot desire cheap wares on their own merits, or demerits; we have to take them[,] as Marx says[,] not because they serve our needs best as men but as workmen, as poor people in short: and here clearly we are wholly in the power of the capitalists; these cheap wares are just the bones thrown to the dog: nay by means of cheapening our necessaries they get our labour cheaper, and thereby are able to carry on their war with the greater vigour, and roll up capital into greater heaps and keep it in fewer hands: because there being more workers than there is work for them to do, more mouths than meat under our present system of war, the ordinary wages of the worker[,] as you probably know[,] is kept down by competition among *them* to[5] something not much more than will enable them to work tomorrow as they have worked today, and to breed fresh machines for the turning out the product of unpaid labour; so that the very cheapening of the things considered as necessaries by the workers, which is hailed as a blessing in some quarters[,] does nothing in the long run but keep the wages down, and the mills a-going, and makes the war of money against money the brisker, and as I said tends to accumulate capital in fewer and fewer hands, since cheap wares can only be made on a large scale and [with] improved organization of production of all kinds: moreover the necessity of using the weapon of cheapness against competing manufacturers as against the public forces the capitalists to ever fresh improvements in machinery, thereby making them ever more and more independent of skilled labour, and allowing them to avail themselves of the competition of women's and children's against adult male labour, and so still more surely keeping down wages, and making their system stronger till at last[,] but for causes of disruption of which more presently[,] it looks as if it might last forever, and the worker be like a ball thrown from hand to hand of the capitalists in their ceaseless game of commercial war.

5. MS., "to" repeated

Beautiful thrift of the 'captains of industry'[,] this forcing the worker by cheap wares to forge his own chain; no wonder they should exalt that skinny virtue to [a] seat beside the old fashioned ones of fair-dealing and trustiness, and kindness.

After this stupendous waste of forcing poor wares on poor people in order to perpetuate their poverty[,] the exploiting of the other vices I named seem[s] colourless and feeble: it seems a little thing that they should take advantage of the ignorance of real life, of the conventional stupidity of their own class; or of the vacant desire to spend money somehow which is bred of their idleness and fullness of bread: besides one of the things one seems to see clearest in the coming change is the manly simplicity which must come of people living in equality of condition, and facing daily the reality of work for the benefit of the community, for the developing of the fullness and abundance of life: and yet though I could easily pass over with silent contempt the ugly inanities of the drawing-room of civilization as a mere passing phase of idiocy like bag-wigs or crinoline[s] or high-heeled shoes, I cannot help remembering that poor people and even shabby genteel ones are furthermore exploited by a kind of reflection of these gentilities: when I see the kind of thing which does duty among them for art and ornament, I confess I feel an indignation I have no power to express that people should have had such things thrust upon them for money and that 'captains of industry' should make their fortunes by them, such travesties of beauty[,] such wretched twaddling folly as they are.

And all the while with decent leisure and decent surroundings the workman[']s own brain and hands might have served his turn and expressed his desire for beauty[,] however small it might have been: how different such things are from these drivellings of commerce those only know who like myself have followed the hand of the English workman from the Cathedral and palace to the little village church and the yeoman's house, and learned his ways of work and thought in the days when his work was free and his exploitation was the obvious tyranny of the strong hand which happily he did not always submit to tamely. [R]emember they have these trumperies thrust on them and cannot have elbow room [and] good housing.[6] However all I know full surely will right itself when we no longer work for the profit of the monopolist, but for the livelihood of ourselves and each other: if we might but live to see the day: how many days of folly[,] corruption and misery are to pass between this day and that, it is for you working men to decide.

6. In the MS. this sentence was a pencil interpolation.

A few words about the direct cheating which is part of the war material and the drill of Commercial War: 'tis got to be an old story now though it[']s growing every day[,] so I need not say much about it; only this[,] it is mere delusion for any one, I won[']t say, to get rid of it, but to lighten the load it lays upon us to any considerable extent: meantime the waste in this kind of *industry* is not hard to note even for the dullest, although on the grounds of the mistake that the cheapening of wares by itself makes life easier for the workers you won[']t lack people to defend it; of course it is inextricably interwoven with the forcing of useless wares both on the poor and the rich, but 'tis followed with such cool scientific energy that one can hardly help looking upon it as a distinct kind of the waste caused by Commercial War: and mind you when Mr. Frederic Harrison sets about moralizing capital in good earnest he will find his captains of industry pull rather long faces when he bids them leave off the industry of adulteration: 'tis really an invention like the invention of machinery: you might theoretically have had competition without it, but once started it would be like going back to the middle ages to give it up: the first few who try [to] be moralized on this point will certainly and swiftly be ruined and in short–it can't be done while competition lasts.

Besides I have sometimes almost thought that our morality has been forced down to such a low point by commercialism that the public as a rule, at all events the well-to-do part of it[,] rather likes to be cheated: you see that is one of the worst sides to this Commercial War: the captains of industry fairly conquer a population native or foreign, and having done so, treat the conquered people as other conquering Lords do; make them their slaves, [and] force them to live the kind of lives their masters may be pleased to allot them. While this commercial war lasts we are all the slaves of it, not the working-classes only, but all of us[,] however grand we may think ourselves; men of science, literary men, artists, we all wear the chain. I know it by sad experience, that intelligence[,] enthusiasm, knowledge of history, patience, years of hard work can contrive or accomplish nothing outside the charmed circle of that slavery: here is your one hope of success[,] to tack yourself on to the skirts of Commercialism, do its bidding, accept its morality and—despise yourself and the whole human race.

Well if you think of it, it must be so; now as always industrial production *must* settle what kind of lives we are to live: our struggles to feed[,] clothe and shelter ourselves, from those struggles with nature who gives us nothing gratis, must come everything that orders our daily life: this it is which creates our desires, shapes our hope, directs our energies, imposes our morality upon us, and as it were paints our religion for us as a man paints a picture of past events—or future ones, using the material which lies all about him familiar and well known[,] to express scenes and characters of which he knows nothing.

Well since it is so[,] let us briefly before we go further sum up the present condition into which our struggle with nature for livelihood has drifted, so that we may see how far it is necessity which compels us to accept our sad slavery, a necessity which we cannot fight against; and how far we are bound by mere folly and superstition which we can shake off by some means or another, and first of all by the means of knowing it for what it is.

Our present manner of wresting our livelihood from nature, then, is that we should waste two thirds of all the advantages which we have won from her in a ceaseless struggle with each other: it is a necessity of this contention carried on in one form or another for so many centuries that the strong should form themselves into a strong class, and that the weak should be crushed together into a weak or servile class, and that there should be constant war between these two classes, since while the strong class would throw all the burden of the waste of commercial war on the workers if they could, the workers are unable altogether to submit to that, and in one way or other strive to better themselves at the expense of their masters.

I have been trying to show how the masters wage war against each other since they can use for that end their energies as they are set free from the necessity of producing what they consume, and compel the weaker or servile class to produce whatever is produced, a great part of which product of labour is only useful to people living in a degraded and falsely artificial society: but, as I have hinted, the workers themselves, are not only set on by the masters to contend mass against mass for their benefit, as in the rivalry of national trade competition, and the wars of nation against nation; but are also driven by the fact that they have no property of their own except their labour-power to contend with each other for their livelihood, for their position as privates in the great industrial army; especially since the captains of industry[,] like other captains[,] cannot always keep their armies on the highest war footing, and at times are obliged to disband a great many of their men, as too many people know practically at the present moment.

This then is the constitution of industrial society at present[,] that is to say of the society in which we live; and I think there can be no question if this is admitted that it is a state of society which should be changed from its basis if that be possible: if it be not possible it is no use trying to do anything toward the progress of humanity, and perhaps we had better hunt up some delusion, new or old, and try to believe in it, and so wear away our days toward the grave.

But if it be possible to turn this ceaseless war of man against man, I will not say into peace, but at least into a condition of things in which war should be spasmodic and incidental–if this be possible, how or by what means can the change be brought about?

Now first I suppose nobody, however rash he may be, can suppose that such a change can be brought about suddenly, or by the conscious efforts of a few or even a great many people: It is true that in times past there have been great men who have noted the wo[e]ful way in which the mass of people live, and who from the depths of their own insight and benevolence have imagined schemes for a better life, and in some of them enthusiasm and energy have been so strong that they have tried to realize those ideals, and for a time have seemed as if they might succeed; but the relentless march of the Commercial Army has crushed those schemes, and the ordinary shrewd bourgeois intelligence that can see no further than a limited part of its own time has cried out mockery against Socialism over their ruins.

Robert Owen thought that if the advantages of a communal or cooperative life were only shown to people clearly enough, they would embrace it as people take to a new form of theology; forgetting that the chain which binds them is real enough and that mere hope and example of the success of such a life on a small scale will not break that chain which it has taken so many centuries to forge. That on the one hand, but on the other the bourgeois rejoicing over the ruins of New Lanark and the failure of the schemes of the most generous and best of men has had no eye for the cloud as big as a man[']s hand which has been gathering and growing while he has been hugging himself over the cleared heavens of his commercial 'do or you will [be] done brown'[7] paradise: It is the commercial system itself which will kill the commercial system, and we Socialists[,] hard as we shall have to work[,] shall only have to assist nature in that operation.

But as the change from commercial war to comparative peace cannot come artificially or with real suddenness (though the last act of the change may be sudden) so also it will be no easy thing to bring about; it will die hard. Now I will make a kind of confession, and say that whereas I in common with others of our persuasion have spoken of our present society as being a mere state of confusion, I have used the word inaccurately; perhaps rather as expressing a horror at the external results of it, than qualifying the system at all: it is not an anarchy; it is unjust, burdensome, wasteful, a tyranny, but not properly speaking an anarchy. I have been calling it an army; that implies strict organization, though it

7. "done brown": thoroughly deceived, cheated, or fooled

be only organization for destruction, which is unconsciously to itself the end it aims at; to create wealth and distribute it according to the needs of the community one would think should be the aim of organized industrialism; to create wealth and waste it, that is to destroy it as [if] it never existed[,] would seem to be the end of our organized Commercialism.

But its destructive tendency is now at last beginning to react upon itself, and therein really lies our hope: no man can respect more than I do the ideal of a better state of things which is now beginning to form itself in the brains of many men of good will, or the obvious budding of a new morality all the more obvious when seen against the dark shade of the ever increasing corruption of bourgeois society: but I do not think this is the cause but rather the effect of the change which commercialism is preparing for itself; the hope is growing, and we can dream with some chance of our dream coming true: nay with a certainty of its general features being realized[,] though it may be not after the full manner of our dream.

For what after [all][8] is happening? What has become of the confident tone in the perpetual commercial prosperity of this country[,] for instance[,] in which there was scarcely a break some twenty years ago? As far as outward appearances go there is not so very much to account for the feeling now abroad that our commercial prosperity is on the wane: true there is depression in trade at present, but so there has been before and it has recovered [from] that depression: as far as mere mechanical signs go I do not see any reason why we should not recover from it: but I venture to say that few people really believe that we shall do so, or see any way out of [the] blind alley that our commerce has gotten into.

It seems to me that the truth is that the new society is forming underneath the old; as has been often said the workers are being forced into recognizing the fact that they are a class of themselves, not a mere appendage to capital, but a class from which a true society can be developed: capital has treated them as labour, as a mere commodity, to be bought and sold in the market under the laws of supply and demand: it is forcing them to see that that labour power which is a part of themselves and their sole possession need not be bought and sold by hucksters at all but be used for their welfare, that is to say[,] for the welfare of society; for it is easy to understand that when once commercial war has exhausted itself the classes which consume without producing will have nothing to exercise their energy upon and must come to an end, so that society becomes a society of workers producing what they consume.

8. MS., "all" added in pencil by an editorial hand, possibly that of May Morris.

All this the workers are beginning to see, or at least are ready to see: though they are collectively the great machine which grinds out profit for the monopolists of capital, yet they are not machines themselves, but men with men's desires which will force them one day to claim to live not on the footing of workmen, that is[, as] parts of a machine, but on the footing of men: you know well how by a kind of instinct the masters have resisted the first signs of this claim being put forward; how the thrift cry for instance has been raised, so that people feeling less anxious about their livelihood might be more contented, and be more ready to acquiesce in such a standard of life as would leave a margin for profits to the employer.

But while the workmen on their side are being driven into a position which will enable them to take their due place when change comes, their masters, or their master['s] capital, are gravitating towards the certain end. And still I must speak about the outlook as regards England, for as modern commercialism first culminated here it is only reasonable to suppose that here it would show its first signs of disintegration: but though I am speaking of our national affairs, I will take you out of England for a moment or two, to the scene of those desperate skirmishes which have been going on on the shores of the Red Sea: Nobody I think finds it very difficult to understand why those Arab men—and boys[—]threw their lives away so resolutely: we may give the feeling different names, and call it fanaticism, patriotism, love of liberty: for my part it seems to me much the same spirit as that which held the long-haired Greeks at Thermopylae[9] or the Swiss at [Morgarten,][10] and if we praise these for the manner of their death, and the cause they died for, I cannot see how we can withhold praise from the desert warriors whom we have been slaughtering lately: it is no paradox to say that they died for the life they knew and loved, the only life which they could bear[,] for the life that made them a real living part of humanity and not drilled and ordered machines.

But if they died for this, and so must ever be accounted as champions of the people, for what did our soldiers die, men once fellow workmen with us? I don't say they do not deserve the name of brave men, though the risk of death to them is nothing as compared to that of their enemies[,] but one would like to be clear as to what they are fighting for: you can easily run over in your minds some of the causes of the quarrel, all of which do certainly seem at first sight utterly disproportionate to that spirit of fanaticism[,] patriotism or liberty which drives their Arab foes to death. However we will pass by various explanations of why our people are fighting over there, and admit if you please the cause which

9. MS., Thermopolae
10. MS., space left in text; Morgarten inserted in pencil in margin by editorial hand, possibly that of May Morris.

people give when they are hard driven; we are fighting in the cause of civilization; add to it our particular form of civilization and I quite agree to it that that is what we are fighting and slaughtering for, and quite plainly say that I think the other cause the better one.

For this cause of civilization simply means spreading to countries which are developing on their own lines, and which as long as they do so offer some refuge from the tyranny of commercialism, of spreading into barbarous countries the curse of exploitation which we ourselves are suffering from. This kind of Commercial War it is true is by no means a new manipulation of this decade in itself; but there is something new in the way in which it is set about, which to my mind shows among other things that the great commercial system is shaken, or at least that England[,] once the undoubted head of that system[,] is losing her leadership.

For first you cannot fail to have noted the frequency[,] persistency and bare-faced cynicism of these wars of exploitation of barbarous countries amongst all European nations these last few years; and next as far as we are concerned we are not merely contented with safe little wars against savage tribes with whom no one but ourselves wanted to meddle, but will even risk wars which may or indeed must in the long run embroil us with nations who have huge armies[,] who no more lack the resources of civilization than ourselves: Still more noteworthy it is that the Commercial liberals[,] 'the Manchester School' as it has been nicknamed[,] which once at least looked coldly on all war[,] is aiding and abetting this war, and crying out for annexation of whatever is annexable, and is not ashamed to take up one after another all the old jingo cries, finishing up with a grand scheme for creating a new fanaticism[,] a new religion, the foundation of a holy race, mongrel indeed in fact, but in theory and name Anglo-Saxon, which should be prepared to contend for the mastery of the whole world against all comers.

Now I can understand your being inclined to laugh at this as merely a magnificent piece of nonsense concocted in the addled brains of a few newspaper writers; but there is more in it than that: it is simply the agony of capitalism driven by a force it cannot resist to seek for new and ever new markets at any price[,] at any risk. Time was when however fierce the competition was between rival manufacturers at home, they had as a nation of manufacturers no rival abroad, and they went on recklessly and blindly expecting it to last for ever: I well remember when any one suggesting the possibility of that slackness of trade happening which every one now admits is happening was simply laughed at as a fool. But now all the great nations are England[']s rivals in trade, and are growing every day more successful rivals: and what are our capitalists to do? They have created a huge industrial army for the manufacturing of profits, and it is failing them in that aim, it is ceasing under the present conditions of civilized nations to produce profit for them: what is to be done? Change the conditions; conquer new markets from day to day; flatter and cajole the men of our colonies to consider themselves what they are not, Englishmen responsible for every quarrel England may lead them into: conquer valiant barbarians all over the world; rifle them[,] rum them[,] missionary them into subjection; then train them into soldiers of civilization, sepoys of a new honourable company, the company for forcing everybody to buy everything English; and what for? That we may be slaves for ever to the profit-grinders[,] the monopolists.

Don't be afraid! It can't be done: even if we at home were to be for ever the sheep which some of our shearers think we are, and indeed I fear that we give them some cause to think us so, even then all European nations are engaged in the same enterprise, and a holy all-conquering race has now become impossible. And if by chance the great capitalist and despotic communities are to meet in a huge all embracing conflict, I don't believe for one that the new heavens and the new earth that will arise from that Ragnarók or Twilight of the Gods will turn out to be the paradise of exploitation which the Imperialist liberals have figured to themselves.

Here then you have the two sides of the tokens which show the approaching change: on the one hand the workers, the machine created by the capitalist middle class beginning to feel their community of interest[,] beginning to feel that society[,] which can do without everything else[,] cannot do without them, growing in intelligence[,] education and political power: and also now growing poorer or soon to do so: in E[ngland] at least[,] on the other hand[,] the capitalists who hitherto have been triumphant conquerors checked in their course and turning desperate. It has been said of the Turks, that as soon as they cease to be conquerors their decline begins: and the same thing is true of a capitalist community that has once gained ascendency: its prosperity depends on its keeping the machine going at high pressure: Nay it is worse than that, the old fable is wholly applicable to capitalist England: a magician raised a devil who consented to be exploited on the terms that he should never lack work an instant: all went well for a while and the happy magician grew richer and richer; till at last came 'overproduction,' the magician's wits failed him and he gave no orders; whereon the devil wrung his master's neck and went his ways grinning at the folly of mankind.

Fable apart[,] here are two classes face to face with each other: [a] working class driven into cohesion, growing in education and political power, and depending as things now go, on employment from the other class, who are beginning to fail in employing, and are rushing about hither and thither to see what can be done before it is too late. Don[']t you think that under these circumstances some change must take place? [B]e assured it will, and that no man or body of men can prevent the change.

That however is no reason why we should sit with our hands before us: in the first place we cannot do so: no man can exist in society and be neutral, nobody can be a mere looker on; one camp or another you have got to join: you must either be a reactionary and be crushed by the progress of the race, and help it in that way; or you must join in the march of progress[,] trample down all opposition and help it in that way.

What is there then to do? I have told you what the position of the workers is: the one thing they need besides the pressure which is most surely coming on them, is to know their position, and to understand that they are no mere appendages to capital, but the living germ of the new society which is forming while men wrangle and devise means to prevent the seed of it being sown. When they understand that they can employ themselves and live in comfort and hope, each one free to choose the life that suits him[,] do you think that they will submit to be drilled into machines for the conquering capitalist and lead a life that offers them no interest or variety save the interest which is inspired by doubts about next week[']s food, and the variety of living for a month or two on the pawn-shop instead of the mill?

For once again I tell you that our present system is not so much a confusion in spite of its inequality and injustice, as a tyranny: one and all of us in some way or other we are drilled to the service of Commercial War; if our individual aspirations or capacities do not fit in with it, so much the worse for them; the iron service of the capitalist will not bear the loss, the individual must: everything must give way to this; nothing can be done if a profit cannot be made of it: it is for this that we are overworked[,] are made to fear starvation, live in hovels, are herded and jammed up into foul places called towns, while the houses in the countryside fall into ruins, and once fertile fields go uncultivated 20 miles from London:[11] it is for this that we let our money, our name, our power, be used to drag off poor wretches from our pinched fields and our dreadful slums, to kill and be killed in a cause they know nothing of.

Can it be that we like all this, that it is our ideal of life? Happily not so: Capital has tried to turn us into the machines of Commercial War but it has failed; we cannot sink lower than its slaves, and though slaves suffer pain because they feel their degradation, and machines do not: yet there is hope in that; because slaves can at least rebel when the opportunity serves: and now the opportunity draws near.

11. *Morris's original note*: It is for this that we let half Scotland be depopulated and produce a few pounds of venison and [*sic*] instead of tons of beef and mutton, and still worse that we turn its stout peasants and herdsmen into mere flunkies of idle fools.

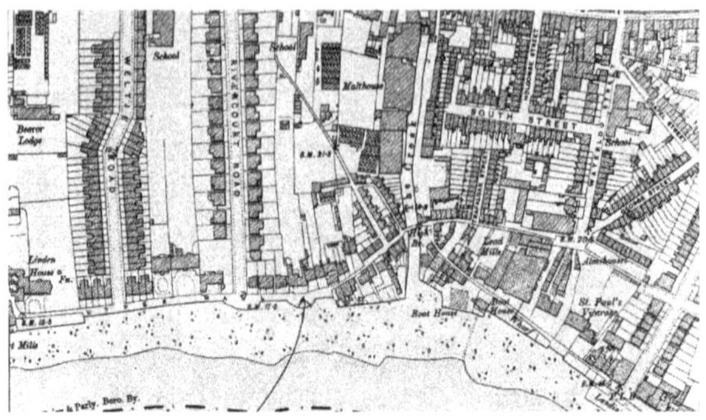

Figure 11.1 London Survey Hammersmith Map, 1896.
The Morris house is marked by an arrow.

Figure 11.2 Kelmscott House, Upper Mall, Hammersmith (WA1941.171.6). © Ashmolean Museum, University of Oxford

Figure 11.3 The Coach House of Kelmscott House, site of Hammersmith Branch Social Democratic Federation, Hammersmith Branch Socialist League, and Hammersmith Socialist Society meetings.
Courtesy of William Morris Gallery

11

"Socialism," 1885

Editor's introduction

William Morris designed his 1885 lecture "Socialism" as a full exposition for working-class audiences of the need for a new social order, laying out first principles clearly and methodically: "it will be convenient to look upon our wide[,] nay stupendous[,] subject from an elementary point of view. . . ." He delivered the lecture twelve times between June 9, 1885 and November 8, 1887, in eight instances to branches of the Socialist League or other socialist audiences, as well as to the Northampton National Secular Society, the Bloomsbury Working Men's College, the Peckham and Dulwich Radical Club, and the London Patriotic Club (LeMire, 66).

The manuscript of "Socialism" is now housed in the British Library as Add. MS. 45,333, ff. 13–38. May Morris printed selections interspersed with paraphrases as a five-page segment of *Artist, Writer, Socialist* (MM2, 192–7), noting that "The lecture is a good elementary one, describing the modern position of labour, employer, and middleman, . . . and the claims of Socialism. He balances with simple directness the claims of the poor and the denials of the wealthy and comments on the conflicting of moral precept and self-interest of class" (192). As in his other relatively early lectures such as "Misery and the Way Out" and "Commercial War," Morris's tone is familiar and personal without condescension. He offers insights from his own situation and exposes the smug attitudes preached to his own class, balancing earnestness with mordant sarcasm.

Morris had begun to study Marx's writings in 1883 and publicly included the word "socialism" in a lecture title for the first time in "Art and Socialism" on January 23, 1884. Though respectful of Marx—he wrote in 1887 that Marx seemed to be "the only completely scientific Economist on our side"[1]—he also held to the conviction that socialism is fundamentally an ethic, not a deterministic science, and he largely avoided specialist terms such as "surplus value," "commodity fetishism," and "exchange value" in his attempts to convey this ethic in jargon-free language to radical, reformist, and working-class audiences.

Morris began "Socialism" with a stark description of the chasm between a small propertied class and a kind of corporate-feudal underclass of workers who could not "be said to have more than a subsistence wage," and who were protected from penury only until "their time, of industrial death so to say, comes on them." Members of this underclass were "free," of course, to sleep under one of Anatole France's notorious bridges. But their "masters"—a medieval expression Morris often employed—were also free to exploit them without let or hindrance, keeping down their livelihood "to as low a point as they will bear"; to force displacements of populations, cruelly undermining familial solidarity; and to let hunger and exhaustion demoralize them and force them to compete with one another for employment.

Another pattern also remained from Roman slavery and medieval villeinage: "the class which lacks wealth is the class which produces it." Production would cease, therefore, if all the world's oppressed workers could manage to withhold their labor (the great dream of a "general strike");[2] but, by contrast, if all the worlds' managers, shareholders, and board members withheld their labor, the "production of wealth would go on pretty much as before, though we might reasonably hope that its method of distribution would be altered." Some members of the propertied class, Morris readily acknowledged, made useful contributions to society, "chiefly [in] physic, education, and the fine arts"—the latter a nod to his belief in the necessity of artistic surroundings for happiness. Others in the learned professions, lawyers and clergymen among them, would in his view be harmless enough if they didn't draft repressive laws and bless the cannons of the real ruling class: those who "engaged in gambling or fighting for their individual shares of the tribute [they have] compelled the working class to yield . . . ."

Morris next makes the striking claim that a consequence of this intraclass conflict is the defrauding of ordinary workers of "about two thirds of all they produce." His argument for this assertion is compelling and worked out in detail, "besides the profit or unpaid labour that [the worker] yields to his immediate master, he has to give back to the employing class . . . a great part of the wages which he receives from his immediate master." Capitalists' direct profits might appear to be 10 percent or less. But workers' indirect losses—like the widow's mite—included everything they possessed. For they had no choice but to pay exorbitant prices for rent, basic needs, a workhouse system, dues for self-protection to trades unions, and the services of other exploiters who "form[ed] a system of wheels within wheels" that left them with little or nothing. The propertied class, moreover, also profited from the labor which created and improved their properties, even though such improvements might make take destructive forms—for example, "not seldom when a piece of barren ground or bog becomes a source of huge fortune to [the landowner] from the growth and development of a town or district, and he pockets the results of the labours of thousands of men and calls it *his* property." No matter: the tip might be exhausted and the land poisoned for generations, but the masters could "begin the game over again, and carry it on forever, [they] and [their] heirs . . . ."

In this instance Morris spoke from direct personal experience. Most of his original family's wealth had derived from extraction of copper and arsenic from a 142-acre patch of land in Devonshire, which his father and others had leased from the Duke of Bedford, vastly enriching the value of the latter's land. A brief stint on the board of directors of Devon Great Consols would have acquainted Morris with the exploitive practices of management, and one of his uncles continued to serve as the mine's resident director.[3] When, therefore, he described someone who

> *seem*[s] to be doing something and receives his pompous title of an "organizer of labour," but what he does even then is nothing but organizing the battles with his enemies[,] the other capitalists who happen to be in the same way of business as himself . . .

Morris knew whereof he spoke.

At this point Morris asks if there is no way we can hope to eliminate the gross inequities "written into the constitution of our present society." Must we resign ourselves to limited mitigations of evil, hoping that "the good nature and kindliness of individuals may more or less palliate the evils the source of which can never be dried up?" If so, it might seem natural to cry out from the depths for a "new religion . . . [which] will take such a hold of the hearts of men that those who have the opportunity will forgo the excitement of gambling with other people[']s property . . . ." Socialism, then, is a matter of spirit as well as economics, a doctrine of fellowship: "equality of fellowship is necessary for developing the instincts of good and restraining the instincts of evil which exist in every one." It is the realization of this egalitarian ideal which embodies a "religion of humanity," as later described in *News from Nowhere*.[4] In the language of a young Marxist in Julian Mitchell's *Another Country*,[5] the elusive object of Morris's "religion of socialism" might be called "earth on earth": a regulative ideal of fellowship and solidarity which would offer "a chance of happiness to every one [so that] . . . an injury to one will be an injury to all," and free us from the "abiding fear . . . and all the self[-]inflicted misery of our civilization [which] form a terrible burden, the sense of which is deeply impressed on the art[,] the literature[, and] the religion of mankind."

Morris's argument encounters a paradox, however; although class differences have intensified over time, yet the process of historical change itself must bring redress: "to suppose that when the former systems [of slavery, for example] have passed away this latter one must necessarily outlast the world is manifestly absurd"; indeed, "whenever [egalitarian ideals have] appeared, [they have] always done so with renewed force and wider scope." Morris also takes comfort in recent signs of a new consciousness: he finds that workers are more "conscious of the antagonism between the classes," as well as more aware that "the real question . . . is whether the masters have any claim to profit at all; that is[,] in other words[,] whether the masters are necessary . . ."; trades union leaders who affirm the rights of employers to control workers do not, therefore, represent the whole class of wage-slaves, but rather are "charged [by employers] with the office of keeping the human part of the capitalist machinery [free] from any grit of discontent."[6]

Morris also found hopeful signs of awareness in the political sphere, for even the Radical members of the Liberal Party had become hard-pressed to define issues which distinguished them from the Conservatives, and "the boundaries between the old [political] parties are now thrown down." The "great class of workers," by contrast, were a force which Morris hoped was "slowly but surely developing into a new society, and only needing complete organization of their scattered elements to become that society." He does not label this new society a "party," however, since its aims are more encompassing—nothing short of the transformation of consciousness and human relationships. People would then find themselves "face to face with revolution, that is to say the New Birth of Society."

This hope came with a caveat, however: what if the desired revolution were violent or failed to achieve its purposes? Morris earnestly hoped that that this "birth" would not be an agony, and warns his audience that ". . . the waste and misery of civil war may be avoided: but remember that it can only be avoided by the combination and organization of all that is most energetic, most orderly, most kindly, most aspiring among the working classes." Only through peaceable means, including solidarity with their fellows in other countries, can this inevitable change become true socialism: "the change in the basis of society must come, and [we must] cho[o]se whether there shall be . . . violence[,] confusion and chaos, or whether we shall glide into the future peaceably. . ." Morris's optimism thus coexists with a potentially darker message; the longed-for revolution could fail, or fail to bring true equality. And although "nothing but mere brute force of armed men or abject poverty now prevents that outbreak of the last stage of struggle"—both brute force and poverty remained powerful forces.

To overcome these obstacles requires what Miguel Abensour has called "the education of desire,"[7] and Morris turns to envisioning what the abolition of classes would mean in the broadest sense. First, "We want to make people leave off saying this is mine and that is thine, to say this is ours"—the message of Morris's "Mine and Thine," a poem he published in *Commonweal* on March 2, 1889.[8] Yet collective ownership would (or should) not mean that the state would hold all property, merely that it should ensure that "there is none left out, or it has no right to call itself a community, a Commonwealth . . . ."

All must work, for wealth comes from labor, but this work cannot be rewarded hierarchically: "[workers'] needs will not be estimated conventionally by the supposed value or dignity of the work which they do." Anticipating the objection that nursing a child (say) is not as significant as designing a steam engine, or that higher gifts must be rewarded, Morris appeals to the justice of the formula "from each what he can do; to each what he needs." He argues that "the man who can do the higher work does it as easily as he who does the lower." The proper analogy is that of a family, which cares for all its members including the sick and the old, and so "why it is that in the bigger family called society[,] the rule should be for each to do his best to snatch the meal out of his fellow[']s mouth as starving wolves are used to do?"

Moreover, socialism will remove any need for the sheer wastefulness of capitalism, with its mantra of chronic overproduction. In one of the essay's most eloquent passages, he links this capitalist waste with overt war:

> You cannot give away the overplus; nay you cannot even carry it out into the fields and burn it there and go back again merrily to make some more of what you don't want; but you must actually pick a sham quarrel with other people and slay 100,000 to get rid of wares which rid of you are still intent on producing with as much ardour as heretofore: O lame and impotent conclusion of that Manchester school[9] which has filled the world with the praises of its inventiveness and its energy[,] its love of peace!

But if, as he hopes, individual ownership will be abolished, the producers will have all the means of labor at their disposal: "when this takes place, the land, capital, the machinery, the plant and stock in short, will naturally fall into the possession of the producers, since it would be useless to anyone else[, and] our class society would cease to exist."

In what constitutes a slight shift from his earlier appeals to workers, Morris acknowledges that the process of change will be lengthy: "I do not say that this would at once bring us to that condition of collective or communal holding of property which I have already put before you." Admittedly "much would have to be done first, troublous times, partial failures even would have to be met before we could quite shake off that old fear of starvation." But if workers came together to demand their "final freedom; freedom to work and live and enjoy," then "the mask [would] fall . . . from the face of this huge tyranny of the modern world . . . [and] the risks of destruction [would] seem light compared with the degradation of championing an injustice." If, finally, (Morris wrote "when"),

> the intelligent of the working classes and the honourable and generous of the employing class could learn to see the system under which we live as it really is, all the dangers of change would seem nothing to them[,] and our capitalistic society would not be worth 6 months purchase.

Morris here retains an early ideal of a cross-class alliance which would guide society to its next stage, with "the honourable and generous of the employing class" joining with the workers to achieve socialism, a hope noticeably absent from his later lectures.

Like his other early lectures, Morris's "Socialism" attacks the belief in the inevitability of social inequality and mounts a blistering critique of capitalist short-sightedness and waste. It also lays out Morris's criterion for any society which can properly claim to be "socialist": absolute equality despite human differences and an underlying ethic of solidarity, a "religion of socialism." "Socialism" further anticipates Morris's later writings in warning of the difficulties which would be faced by those striving to bring society to its "new birth." If, like Immanuel Kant's "realm of ends," a completely egalitarian society has remained "nur ein Ideal" ("only an ideal"), Morris enunciates the attitudes necessary for creating a fully realized and authentic socialism.

Notes

1. Kelvin, 2.393–4. He would also have been acquainted with the outlines of Marx's ideas through H. M. Hyndman, whose 1881 *England for All* borrowed heavily from *Das Kapital.* On April 23, 1883 Cormell Price recorded in his unpublished diary that "Top . . . was full of Karl Marx, whom he had begun to read in tr." (Nicholas Salmon and Derek Baker, *A William Morris Chronology* [Bristol: Thoemmes Press, 1996], 126).

On November 26, 1884 Morris described Marx's theory of surplus value to William Allingham (Kelvin, 2.340), and on February 28, 1885 he advised an unknown recipient, "On the whole tough as the job is you ought to read Marx if you can; up to date he is the only completely scientific Economist on our side." But he essentially saw Marx's system as one of many arguable rationales for socialism, and remarked to a correspondent whom Kelvin has identified as possibly E. J. Collings on December 30, 1887 that "Socialism does not rest on the Marxian theory" (Kelvin, 2.729).

2. Robert Owen's Grand National Consolidated Trades Union had advocated a "General Strike," an idea later taken up by anarchists.
3. Charles Harvey and John Press, "The City and Mining Enterprise: The Making of the Morris Family Fortune," *JWMS* 9.1 (1990): 12, and Florence Boos and Patrick O'Sullivan, "Morris's Socialism and 'Devon Great Consols,'" *JWMS* 19.4 (2012): 11–39.
4. In chap. 8 of *News from Nowhere*, Old Hammond describes the faith of the new society: "But now, where is the difficulty in accepting the religion of humanity, when the men and women who go to make up humanity are free, happy, and energetic . . . . This is what this age of the world has reserved for us." Similarly, in their "Socialism from the Root Up," Morris and E. B. Bax take up the issue of religion in the new society: "As regards the future form of the moral consciousness, we may safely predict that it will be in a sense a return on a higher level to the ethics of the older society, . . . and the identification of individual with social interests will be so complete that any divorce between the two will be inconceivable to the average man" (*Commonweal*, May 13, 1888, chap. 23, p. 155).
5. *Another Country: A Drama* (New York: French, 1982).
6. Before the Trades Union Act of 1871 gave legal status to trades unions, their leaders could do little more than request higher wages in periods of expansion. And throughout the 1870s and 80s the worker representatives of Devon Great Consols had been repeatedly forced to accept lowered conditions under threat of police intervention.
7. Miguel Abensour, *Utopies et dialectique du socialism* (Paris: Pavot, 1977); see Thompson, 786–92, 798–9.
8. Florence Boos, "Poems Published after 1875," no. 21. http://morrisarchive.lib.uiowa.edu/listpoemslatertext.html#21. May Morris told her readers that he had composed this poem—which included translations of two strophes of "Wapene Martijn" by the Flemish poet Jacob van Maerlant (ca. 1230–after 1291)—after the discussion which followed a talk about "The Fourteenth Century" he had given at Kelmscott House (*CW*, 9, xxvii).
9. The Manchester School was associated with political leaders Richard Cobden (1804–65) and John Bright (1811–89), laissez-faire Liberals who promoted free trade and an end to tariffs and other restrictions, arguing that unrestricted commerce would bring greater prosperity to all. Both were instrumental in the 1846 repeal of the Corn Laws, and Bright, a Quaker, opposed British military campaigns in the Crimea and elsewhere.

I think I may without offense assume that a large part of my audience know no more of Socialism than the name, and that it will be convenient to look upon our wide[,] nay stupendous[,] subject from an elementary point of view; and this all the more as I shall be liable to the same criticism so treating it, as I should be if I attempted something more elaborate: for this is a subject where the admission of the principle is the one important matter, nor ought it [to] be so difficult for me to lay these principles before you; while at the same time if I can do so with any amount of clearness, there is nothing so abstruse in them[,] nothing so technical[,] but that any intelligent person could at once understand them.

Indeed it were strange if it were not so since Socialism has to do with all that is practical in our daily life[.]

But again even those of you who know that they know nothing of the principles of Socialism may think that they understand pretty well those on which our present society is based, and that they have nothing to learn here: but this assumption I beg leave to deny: it is only by learning something of Socialism that we can understand what the present society is, what it aims at doing, and what are the means whereby it carries out its aims.

Most of you I fancy never put to yourselves the question[,] why am I in the position in which I am? Why is the workman[,] the beggar, the pauper, the criminal in his position; and why is the great capitalist[,] the landowner, in a word[,] the rich man in his position: few of you have ever doubted the necessity for the existence of classes into which society is divided, or suspected that the arrangement might not go on for ever. Even when you have felt most discontented with your own lot or that of your fellow men, you have supposed that it is[,] has been and will be necessary for the existence of society that there should be a rich class and a poor one; therefore you have never troubled your heads as to what makes some men belong to the poor, some to the rich class, but have supposed that it was a piece of accident, or say a provision of nature so deeply rooted and abstruse in its origin that it is no use enquiring into it.

We Socialists on the contrary believe that we know why these classes exist and how they have grown into what they are, a growth inevitable indeed, but so far from being eternal that it will itself destroy itself and give place to something else, a society in which there will be no rich and no poor.

Therefore before we look specially into the matter of what Socialism is[,] let us consider how our present society is composed; since by the light of that contrast we shall see things that might otherwise be obscure.

The society of the present day[,] like all others[,] is founded on the necessity of the human race for constant labour, for a ceaseless contest with nature who without labour gives us nothing: when you hear people talking about the possibility of things being free; education, libraries and what not, you must understand that some person or persons have to pay for them, we don't and can't mean to say that they are given to us; we have made them and won them before we can use them.

There is no question then as to whether man must labour in order to live, but there has always been a question as to how that labour shall be apportioned amongst the members of society, and also how its results shall be shared amongst them. I have no time to go into the history of the answer to these questions; I will only remind you that for ages both the work and the wealth won by it from nature have been unequally divided: there has always since the dawn of history in communities called civilized been a class which has had much work and little wealth living beside another class which has had much wealth and little work. Also during all this time those civilized communities have professed various religions which have inculcated justice and fair dealing, and have even sometimes bidden men to bear each other[']s burdens,[1] the strong to work for the weak, the wise for the foolish, the provident for the thriftless; and yet these precepts of morality have always been thrust aside and evaded by class by-laws so-to-say, and today it is still a rule of our society amidst all our refinement[,] all our shrinking from violence and rudeness[,] that those who work most shall fare the hardest, and that the reward of idleness shall be abundant wealth. Clearly then[,] either those precepts of morality are mere foolish dreams and bid us to do what we recognize now to be impossible; or else those class by-laws which bid us evade them with a clear conscience are ruinously misleading, the foundation of continuous unhappiness and of future degradation and the downfall of civilization.

That to my mind is the alternative.[2] Yet I admit that at the present day people do try [to] evade the horns of the dilemma; the inequality and undeserved misery of our class society they say are inevitable, nor can we apply the precepts of justice and love to them except that within those classes we can palliate the poverty on one side[,] the luxury on the other by our individual efforts toward kindliness and manliness: hapless and futile compromise! to fight feebly against the results of the very machine that we have made and uphold, conscious all the time of certain defeat: thus do we the well to do and prosperous dull the sting of conscience, and yield ourselves to the stream of class violence, our best hope being that joy may oppose itself to grief, health to disease, right to wrong[,] life to death—for a little while, but that the sum of all is and must be irresistible evil.

1. Galatians 6:2 KJV: "Bear ye one another's burdens, and so fulfil the law of Christ."
2. MS., comma

With this modern pessimism which has taken the place of the stern hope of mediæval pietism wherein the wretched slaves of this world were to be joyous masters of the next; with the pessimism of the well[-]to[-]do of a luxurious age we socialists have nothing to do: we say those precepts of morality were not and are not mere 'Counsels of perfection[,]' the birth of dreamy fanaticism, but rather the principles of reasonable action, rules of mutual defence against the tyranny of nature, and that the society which acts on them will be far wealthier and infinitely happier than our present one; that the sum of its wealth will be so great, that even the rich men of the present day would find in it ample compensation for the loss of the riches which they cannot use now for their own happiness but which, whether they will it or not, must be used for the unhappiness of their fellows.

For what is the composition of society at present, the society founded on so called freedom of contract, on labour and capital, cash payments, and the supply and demand of the markets?

It is simple; far simpler than that of past ages and especially of the last age, the feudal period, which was based on a hierarchy wherein each from the highest to the lowest had (in theory at least) his rights and his duties to those above and below him: all these elaborate groups have since the full development of the commercial period been resolved into two great classes, those who possess all the means of the production of wealth save one, and those who possess nothing except that one, *the power of labour.* The first class[,] the rich[,] therefore can compel the latter, or the poor, to sell that power of labour to them on terms which ensure the continuance of the rich class, and therefore properly speaking *own* the poor class and indeed are called their masters: only as the latter are very numerous and the former but few, the masters dare not drive them into a corner for fear they should rebel against them: indeed in one way or another they have rebelled even in our own times, and are organized, for rebellion (though but badly and loosely) into trades unions, at least in England.[3] If it were not for this fear of revolt, this constant struggle on the part of the workmen to get more out of the employers[,] all workmen would only get as much as would supply them with bare necessaries, that is[,] would enable them to live[,] work and breed; but as it is[,] a proportion of the workmen do get more than this bare subsistence wage: these are the skilled workmen, especially in those crafts where women and children cannot be employed to reduce the wages of adult males, and those protected by trades unions; of the rest[,] few of them can be said to have more than a bare subsistence

3. MS., colon

wage, and when they grow sick and old would die if it were not for the refuge afforded them by the workhouse, which is purposely made as prison-like and wretched as possible for fear that the lower paid workers should in their despair take refuge there before their time, of industrial death so to say, comes on them.

This then[,] is the first distinction between the two classes, that the one possesses nothing but the power of labour inherent in their own bodies, and the other possesses everything necessary to make that labour fruitful; so that the labourers cannot work until they have obtained leave from their masters to do so, which the latter will only grant on the condition that the workers will yield up to them all they produce over and above their livelihood, which as I have said above[,] is mostly only just enough to live on and seldom or ever rises much above that. Unless they rebel the workers must accept these terms, since they must live from day to day: moreover owing to the ever increasing productivity of labour[,] helped by the wonderful machines of our epoch, and organized for production with so much skill, and owing also to the long hours of labour, and the employment in most trades of women and children to whom it is not even pretended that a subsistence wage is given, there are, taking one year with another, more workers than there is work for them to do, so that they compete with each other for employment, or in other words[,] sell their labour-power in the market at Dutch Auction[4] to their masters: so that the latter are able now-a-days to dispense with the exercise of visible force in compelling them to work which in earlier days of the world masters used towards their slaves.

Besides this distinction between the classes of one possessing wealth, and the other lacking it, there is another to which I will now draw your attention: the class which lacks wealth is the class which produces it, the wealth owners only consume it. If by any chance the whole of the wage-earners or 'lower classes' were to perish or leave the community, production of wealth would come to a standstill unless the masters were to descend to the level of their former slaves and learn to work for their livelihood: if on the contrary the masters were to disappear[,] production of wealth would go on pretty much as before, though we might reasonably hope that its method of distribution would be altered.

I will here meet an objection which will probably occur to most of you: you will say[,] do not the masters[,] or what you call the possessing class[,] work? Undoubtedly a large part of them do work, but for the most part their work is unfruitful or sometimes directly harmful.

4. In a Dutch Auction, a high price for the object on sale is initially set; in this case, employment, or the right to labor, is offered at the highest possible price.

There are some useful occupations[,] chiefly physic, education, and the fine arts[,] which are exercised by members of the privileged classes: of whom one can say nothing worse than that they are paid too high in proportion to their workmen; so that they partly earn their livelihood and partly fleece it from the workers: but these are but a small part of the possessing classes, as to number, and as to the wealth they hold it is insignificant compared with that held by those who do nothing useful. As to these last, some of them do not pretend to do anything but amuse themselves, and these probably do the least harm; of the rest[,] some are engaged in work which only our complicated system of compulsion and inequality, of injustices in short, makes necessary, they, as lawyers and clergymen[,] for instance[,] are the parasites of the system: but the rest are engaged in gambling or fighting for their individual shares of the tribute which their class has compelled the working class to yield to it; they are never producing wealth[,] hard as they may work.

Again to answer another possible objection: the tribute taken from the workers is no trifle, but amounts in all to about two thirds of all they produce: but you may say such profits as that are seldom made by the employer[,] who has to be content with 10 percent perhaps, or perhaps even less in bad times. Well I have just said that it was the rich *class* that took this tribute[,] not the individual employer only; besides *his* tribute, which in all cases is as much as he can get amidst the competition or war with other employers, the worker has to pay *taxes* for payment[,] amidst other things[,] of the interest of the national debt which the privileged classes take to themselves: and remember that all taxes are in the long run paid by labour, since labour only can produce wealth: *rent* also he has to pay, and much heavier rent in proportion to his income than rich people[, as well as] the *commissions of middle-men*, who distribute the goods he has made, and who instead of doing this distribution simply and for a moderate payment, form a system of wheels within wheels, and make monstrous profits from their busy idleness: lastly if he is fairly well to do he has to pay to a *benefit society or a trade unions* a tax for the precariousness of his employment brought about by the gambling of his masters, he has to help them to pay their poor rates and thus actually enables the master to shut his factory gates on him when there is an open trades dispute between employers and employed; since otherwise the master would be taxed for his subsistence in the workhouse. In short[,] besides the profit or unpaid labour that he yields to his immediate master, he has to give back to the employing class to which his master belongs a great part of the wages which he receives from his immediate master.

Now it is clear from this that there is a class struggle always going on between the employers and employed, though neither party may be conscious of it: the interests of the two classes are opposed to each other: it is the object of the employing class to get as much as it can out of its privilege, the possession of the means of production, and all it makes can only be made at the expense of the workers, any increase in the fertility of the possessions of the rich must come from the labour of the poor: on the other hand if the workers succeeded in raising their standard of life they can only do at the expense of the rich; what one gains the other loses; there is therefore constant war between them, and yet it is a war in which the capitalist must always win until the workers resolve to be an inferior class no longer.

Meantime observe that the privilege of the possessing class consists in their power of living on the unpaid labour of others: if the capital of the rich man consists of land, he forces his tenant to improve his land for him[,] exacts tribute from him in the form of rent[,] and still has his land improved generally when the transaction has come to an end, so that he can begin the game over again, and carry it on for ever, he and his heirs: If he has homes on his land, he has rent for them also[,] often receiving the value of the buildings many times over, and at the end house and land once more: not seldom a piece of barren ground or bog becomes a source of huge fortune to him from the growth and development of a town or district, and he pockets the results of the labours of thousands of men and calls it *his* property. Or the earth beneath the surface is found out to be rich in mineral, and he is paid enormous sums for leave and license to labour them into marketable wares. And all the while in each case he has been sitting still doing nothing, or it may be worse than nothing; devising means perhaps in parliament for strengthening and continuing his pernicious domination. Or again if his capital consist[s] in cash, he goes into the labour-market, and directly or indirectly buys the labour-power of men[,] women and children and uses it for the production of wares which shall bring him a profit, keeping down their livelihood to as low a point as they will bear in order that the profit may be greater, which indeed the competition or war with his fellow capitalists compels him to do. Nor does he do anything to earn this profit, nothing useful in any case, and he need do absolutely nothing; since he can buy the brain power of managers and foremen on terms a little higher than he buys the hand-power of the ordinary workmen; mostly he does *seem* to be doing something and receives the pompous title of an "organiser of labour," but what he does even then is nothing but organizing the battles with his enemies[,] the other capitalists who happen to be in the same way of business as himself, and so both his idleness and his industry do but serve to make [life] hard and anxious for all of us.

Thus then[,] I have told you briefly what the composition of our society is in this age of Commerce. Let me recapitulate before I go further: There are two classes, a useful and a useless class: the useless class is called the upper, the useful the lower class: the one class having the monopoly of all the means of production except the power of labour can and does compel the other to work for its advantage so that no man of the workers receives more than a portion, the lesser portion too[,] of the wealth he creates; nor will the upper class allow the lower to work on any other terms: I must add that as a necessary consequence the rich class[,] having great superfluity of riches[,] withdraws many of the workmen from the production of wealth and forces them to minister to its idleness[,] luxury or folly, and so by waste makes the lot of the labourer harder yet.

This I say [is] the constitution of our present society; and surely you will not deny that if I have stated the matter truly, it is but a sorry result of all the struggles of man toward civilization. You may admit that, yet think the misery of it inevitable and eternal, and that nothing can be done but to hope that the good nature and kindliness of individuals may more or less palliate the evils the source of which can never be dried up. Or you may perhaps hope that some new religion will arise which will take such hold of the hearts of men that those who have the opportunity will forgo the excitement of gambling with other people[']s property and the pleasure of living luxuriously at other people[']s expense, and will live justly and austerely[,] considering themselves as nothing more than trustees of the wealth which the people have made and entrusted to their care. I will not say that this will not happen[,] but I am sure that when it does these leaders of humanity will at once manifest their newly gained moral sense by begging their fellow men to relieve them from their position of dignity and authority which will for ever tempt them[,] or rather compel them[,] to live in that very way which they have found out to be degrading to themselves and oppressive to their fellows. In sober earnest I say that no man is good enough to be master over others; whatever the result to them, it at least ruins him: equality of fellowship is necessary for developing the innate good and restraining the innate evil which exists in every one.

But indeed I do hope for the rise of a new religion, nay with all earnestness I preach to you now, for it is called *socialism*. It proclaims the necessity of association among men if the progress of the race is to be anything more than a name; Society it says must be the condition of man[']s existence as man: and the aim of that society is something higher than the greatest happiness of the greatest number: it is to offer a chance of happiness to every one; that is to say[,] an opportunity for the full development of each human life: it denies the title of society to any system which degrade[s] one class to exalt another; nay more[,] it asserts that if we injure any one member for the benefit of all the rest,[5] we have poisoned and corrupted our society: an injury to one will be an injury to all, and will so be felt in the long run.

Instead of that system now existing which exacts a tribute from one class in order that another may be freed from the necessity of labour, it asserts that each should pay his tribute of labour to nature, and each in turn receive his share of the wealth which each has done his best to create: so only[,] it says[,] shall we avoid the waste of the few and the want of the many: so only can we rise above that perpetual condition of war in which indeed the beasts live not unhappily, since their memory is so limited that they are not conscious of abiding fear, of anxiety, or of aspirations; whereas with us anxiety and hope deferred and all the self[-]inflicted miseries of our civilization form a terrible burden[,] the sense of which is deeply impressed on the art[,] the literature[, and] the religion of mankind.

Combination for livelihood[,] therefore[,] and the assurance of equal chance[6] for every one are what we socialists want to bring about, and probably most of those here present will agree in thinking such an aim is good: but I suppose some will say the thing is impossible; a little knot of people preaching certain utopian doctrines cannot bring about such a stupendous revolution as this. Well, no set of people know that better than socialists: at no time can a part of a society existing change the basis of that society unhelped by those of past ages: but we socialists claim that the progress of mankind has really been steadily in this direction, and that all we have to do is to help [in] developing the obvious and conscious outcome of this progress.

I have not time now to go into the historical side of the question: I prefer to lay before [you] the aims of socialism in as much detail as possible: but I am obliged to remind you that there have been since the beginning of definite history three conditions under which industrial production has gone on: mere slavery under the classical peoples; serfdom in the Middle Ages, and wage labour and capital today: to suppose that when the former systems have passed away this latter one must necessarily outlast the world is manifestly absurd, and there are abundant signs of the approaching change for those who can read them. There has always been a double thread running through the history of mankind; contention for individual gain has been visible always[,]

5. MS., "the" repeated
6. MS., comma

but so also has the tendency towards combination for common gain, the two have been always visibly contending with one another, and whenever the latter has appeared, it has always done so with renewed force and wider scope: and in these later times combination for the production of wealth has progressed immensely with the result that the productive powers of labour have so increased, as to become at last an absolute evil under the present system; of that more presently.

It was discovered ages ago that one man working with tools could produce more than was necessary for his own subsistence, and on this discovery class society was built; tribes when they went to war took prisoners and made them slaves instead of killing them, because the slave could live on less than he produced: but to jump over a long interval of various transition[s,] the change from mere tools to machines as auxiliaries of man[']s own powers has quite enormously increased the margin between the necessary livelihood of a man and his capacity of production, especially since an elaborate system of cooperative organization has gone along with the invention of the machines: the increased wealth so produced has notoriously not gone to the labourer but has enriched the classes who live upon his labour, and especially has almost made a rich middle class whose life is not distinguishably less easy or luxurious than that of the territorial nobility: so that though there was theoretically more difference between the slave of ancient Greece and Rome and his master[,] the gentleman citizen, or between the serf and the baron of the feudal period than there is now between the workman and the capitalist, there is really more difference in the manner of life and the refinements attainable between these two classes than between the employer and employed of earlier times: in fact there is so much real difference that there is now no necessity for making those arbitrary and legal distinctions which once drew [a] line of demarcation between rich and poor: the upper classes can now with a cheap generosity afford to declare all classes equal before the law; since they well know that they cannot avail themselves of that sham equality; a sham equality I say, so long as men have not economical equality, so long as they are not on equal terms in disposing of their labour-power: for we have seen that the whole of the working class is compelled to give an hour[']s work for less than an hour[']s just pay[,] that is[,] for less than the amount of wealth produced by that work.

Now the upshot of all this [is] that the contest of classes which has always gone on is now limited to a narrow issue and simplified by being cleared of all by-issues. It was necessary for the supremacy of the commercial classes, the capitalists, that political and legal freedom should be established, since they on the one hand needed the working class as allies against the aristocracy of hereditary privilege, and on the other needed the workman free from all bondage and all support which would hinder his labour power from being a mere commodity saleable in the market like other wares. Therefore two classes[,] the employers and employed, that is[,] the sweaters and the sweated[,] are now face to face; and though it is true that the ashes of the old struggle are not quite burned out, and in England the working classes are not fully conscious of the antagonism between the classes, yet the consciousness of that struggle which has so long been going on cannot be much longer delayed.

On the defeat of Chartism[,] itself a political movement on the surface, though at bottom it meant revolution, the Trades Unions became the visible token of the class struggle in this country: they gained during a period of great commercial prosperity all the success they were capable of gaining, to wit an improved position for the better off of the workmen engaged in the more consolidated industries: but they can no longer be considered as fighting bodies, partly perhaps because they have been lulled asleep by their very success, but chiefly I believe because the issue has been changed since the time when they were most vigorously at strife with the masters: the Trades Unions claimed a mere rise of wages when the selling price of the article they made rose, admitting the necessity of their accepting lower wages when it fell: only in their palmy days the general tendency of the market was to rise as it now is to fall, so that they appeared to sustain the class conflict much more than they did, as their strikes were then often successful[,] and of course were so at the immediate expense of the capitalists: in any case a rate of wages roughly proportioned to the rate of profit made by the masters was what they strove for: all classes are now feeling that that point is won so far as it goes, though there may be a little bickering in individual cases, and that the real question now is whether the masters have any claim to profits at all; that is[,] in other words[,] whether the masters are necessary, and accordingly the Trades Unionists and their leaders who were once the butt of the most virulent abuse from the whole of the Upper and Middle Classes are now praised and petted by them because they do tacitly or openly acknowledge the necessity for the masters['] existence; it is felt that they are no longer the enemy; the class struggle in England is entering into a new phase, which may even make the once dreaded Trades Unions allies of capital, since they in their turn form a kind of privileged group among the workmen: in fact they now no longer represent the whole class of workers as working *men* but rather are charged with the office of keeping the human part of the capitalists' machinery in good working order and freeing it from any grit of discontent.

Again look at the change which has come over the world of politics: the boundaries between the old parties are thrown down; the difference between the programme of the Tories and the Liberals is so small that no one but a mere party man can take any interest in the conflict between them; nay the very radicals whose name was once used for frightening babies with, are at this moment finding it difficult to get out a programme which shall distinguish them from the Tories, and have to rely on the hope that the chapter of accidents may force their opponents into a position reactionary enough for them to attack safely: without the fear of their lending themselves to the progress of Revolution.

For you see the explanation of this is that the real movement of today is quite outside the conception of political parties: it is true that those parties are conscious of the existence of the great class of workers, but they look upon them merely as an instrument to be played on for the 'good of society,' instead of what they really are[,] a great force slowly but surely developing into a new society, and only needing completer organization of their scattered elements to become that society. Such a contingency as that our Parliamentary system does not recognize and cannot recognize: it can see nothing but the relation of master and servant repeated in various forms throughout all society: it is driven indeed into trying to make those relations bearable to a large portion of the servants, for it has to admit that on its success in so doing depends the very existence of our present society: further than this it cannot go: when it is discovered as it is beginning to be[,] that the relations of master and servant is *un*bearable and produces misery and suffering that cannot even be largely palliated[,] its function will be gone and it will find itself face to face with revolution, that is to say[,] the New Birth of Society.

When that day comes all that is progressive [in] it will melt into the Revolution, while its reactionary part will openly oppose the happiness of mankind: most vainly certainly, and one may hope so feebly, that it will have to yield to the mere threat of force, and that the waste and misery of civil war may be avoided: but remember that it can only be avoided by the combination and organization of all that is most energetic, most orderly, most kindly, most aspiring among the working classes: a moment's thought will show you that the Upper and Middle classes who are divorced from useful production could not resist the union of the useful, the Lower classes for a week. Take note then, working men, that the Revolution[,] the change in the basis of society[,] must come, and choose whether there shall be a transition period of violence[,] confusion and chaos, or whether we shall glide into the great [change] peaceably because obviously irresistibly.

It may be news[,] perhaps, as a further sign of the times, to some of you that though in England the consciousness of the necessity for revolution is only dawning, the populations of the continent are fully awake to it: nothing but mere brute force of armed men or abject poverty now prevents the outbreak of the last stage of struggle: or perhaps we may rather say that they are only waiting for one thing[,] the awakening of England, the great country of Commercialism, and consequently in spite of all appearances to the contrary, the country where the opposition of classes is most trenchant.

Now as to the claims of that socialism which is advancing upon us certainly, though possibly slowly, I have in a way stated them in putting before you a sketch of the tyranny and folly of our present conditions; but I will now try to state them positively instead of negatively, which I feel to be all the more necessary since[,] though the word of socialism is now in everybody[']s mouth[,] I believe that the ideas of most people as to what it is or aims at are very vague.

The aim of socialism is to make the best by man's effort of the chances of happiness which the life of man upon the earth offers us, using the word happiness in its widest and deepest sense, and to assure to everyone[7] born into the world his full share of that chance: and this can only be assured to him by men combining together for this benefit: if we fight with each other for it[,] it is certain that some will gain it at the expense of others and in the struggle will waste as much as they gain.

We want to make people leave off saying[,] this is mine and that is thine, and to say[,] this is ours.

In other words we look forward to a society in which all wealth would be the property of the community, would be held collectively.

But do not misunderstand this assertion as you easily may by not being clear about the use of the word property: property at present means the power of preventing other people from using wealth; as for instance a man may and often does refuse to cultivate a tract of land himself or to allow others to do so: but as we understand property[,] it means the possession of wealth which we can use ourselves: it is necessary to explain this because with present ideas of property[,] when one talks of the community possessing all property you may have the idea of a government or state having the property and only granting the use of it to people on certain arbitrary conditions, that is[,] to certain privileged persons. But a socialist community would hold wealth only to use it, and it could only use it as a community by satisfying with it the needs of all its members, since a community consists of each and all the

7. MS., every one

individuals composing it: there is none left out, or it has no right to call itself a community, a Commonwealth.

Everyone's reasonable needs must be satisfied therefore[,] first for food and shelter, and next for pleasure bodily and mental; which would include the full development of every individual according to his capacity, an aim which is rendered possible by the great variety of capacity existing in the individuals of the race, and which socialism would foster as sedulously as the present system depresses it.

I have said that no arbitrary conditions would be imposed on the members of a true Commonwealth for the satisfaction of their reasonable needs: but there is one condition which is not arbitrary and which all must accept: they must all work for the commonwealth or there will be in the long run no wealth: but their needs will not be estimated conventionally by the supposed value or dignity of the work which they do; because that would at once give rise to a fresh system of classes, that is[,] of privileged people tormenting the unprivileged: and why should labour be divided into privileged [and unprivileged]? [A]ll kinds are necessary to the common weal; nor is the difficulty and labour of exercising a specially excellent capacity at all proportioned to its excellence. The man who can do the higher work does it as easily as he who does the lower: neither again is the expensiveness of the workman[']s needs necessarily proportioned to the excellence of his work; nay the man who does the rougher work may need the more expensive livelihood, and if he does he ought to have it: In short[,] the maxim which true Socialism would carry out is[,] "From each what he can do; to each what he needs."

And if that seems to you an impossible maxim to carry out; pray consider what goes on in a well conducted family which is above the pressure of mere poverty: the sick[,] the weak, the old, the infants are not stinted of food or shelter or such pleasures as they can enjoy because they add little or nothing to[8] the wealth that the family subsists on: they do what they can and have what they need: and if it be the rule in a decent family to bear one another's burdens, tell me[,] I beg of you[,] why it is that in the bigger family called society[,] the rule should be for each to do his best to snatch the meal out of his fellow[']s mouth as starving wolves are used to do?

You may still say[,] but is it possible on this larger scale? I have alluded before to the fact that every man working with due combination of his fellows in a civilized society can produce more than is absolutely necessary to his own subsistence: this [is] the basis of all industrial society; but in these latter days man[']s productivity has increased

8. MS., "to" repeated

enormously because of the invention of machines and general improvement of organization, while his necessities remain what they always were. Now of the difference between what the workman needs to live on and the value of the wealth he produces[,] a very small portion goes to him, the main part being claimed by his masters as profit, rent, and interest; and the increase in that surplus value has in our days grown so enormous that nobody ever dreamed of the workman receiving a proportionate share of it: it seems to me that that increase has gone to create a rich middle-class whose occupation is to fight with each other for their shares of the surplus value of labour. This occupation cannot be necessary to the production of wealth, but unfortunately a large part of the working classes (whose occupation obviously is necessary to the production of wealth) is still under the influence of the superstition that the "employers of labour"[,] so called[,] are necessary to their employment: there is no wonder in that, they are ignorant, hard driven by need, and without leisure for thought, and moreover have been habitually hoodwinked by the writings of the intellectual part of the employing class, themselves probably unconscious or but half conscious of the fraud which class instinct compels them to commit.

But now at last their eyes are slowly opening to the real state of the case: the course of events is compelling them to feel[,] if not to see[,] that they must no longer depend on people to employ them who will very naturally make them pay for the fulfillment of that function: it is actually now being proved that the middle-class occupation of fighting for the share of the surplus-value wrung from the workers is useless and wasteful: trade is said to be suffering depression caused by over-production: over-production of what? Of wealth? That should mean that every person in the country has more than he needs to eat, more than he needs to wear, more and better house-room than he wants; well that would be a curse which we might soon modify into a blessing: but indeed it seems it does not mean that, and whatever it means it strikes people as a real evil to be abated at any cost: at Manchester lately I was told that it was the general opinion sustained by one of the economical lights there that the one thing needed to amend the Depression of Trade was a great European war so that some of the surplus wealth might be destroyed. One's brain whirls at the enormity of the confession of helplessness or stupidity in the present system which this involves[.] What! You have created too much wealth? You cannot give away the overplus; nay you cannot even carry it out into the fields and burn it there and go back again merrily to make some more of what you don't want; but you must actually pick a sham quarrel with other people and slay 100,000 men to get rid of wares which when got rid of you are still intent on producing with as much ardour as heretofore:

O lame and impotent conclusion of that Manchester school which has filled the world with the praises of its inventiveness[,] its energy[,] its love of peace! Strange that the new Atilla, the new Genghis[9] Khan, the modern scourge of God, should be determined to stalk through the world wrapped in the gentlemanly broadcloth of a [Q]uaker manufacturer!

In short[,] my friends[,] what this depression of trade really means, this overproduction, is that for the time at least the middle-class who live on our labour and fight among themselves for their share of what it produces are finding that their warfare does not even pay them: and if they the plunderers must teach us this[,] surely we the plundered should not be slow to learn the lesson, which is simply that they are not needed. The remedy lies in the hands of the workers; their masters as a class cannot see it, will not tell us how to get rid of them.

The way[10] to get rid of the useless classes is to abolish the profit of the individual, to let the producer have in one way or other all that he produces: when this takes place, the land, capital, the machinery, the plant and stock in short, will naturally fall into the possession of the producers, since it would be useless to anyone else: nay[,] there would soon be nobody else to possess it, for there would be no surplus value available to keep an idle class[,] a non-producing class[,] upon: our class society would cease to exist.

I do not say that this would at once bring us to that condition of collective or communal holding of property which I have already put before you: much would have to [be] done first, troublous times, partial failures even would have to be met before we could quite shake off that old fear of starvation which our present competitive or plundering system has imposed upon us: before we got to see quite plainly that the loss to one involved loss to all: before we got instinctively to consider it a disgrace unendurable to an honest man to shoulder off our burden, now grown so light, on to another man[']s back; before the ease of livelihood[,] leisure and simple refinement of life allowed us to look upon work, the useful exercise of our special energies[,] as a daily recurring pleasure and not a daily recurring curse.

Yet all these good things we should[,] I am sure[,] gain in time when we had once taken that first [step][11] of insisting that all shall produce as all consume, which means the abolition of classes.

And lastly if this revolution seems to you a prodigious one, as surely it is, I say once more it lies in the hands of the workers, of the useful classes[,] to bring it about: whatever they demand must be yielded if

9. MS., Ghengis
10. MS., way how
11. MS., [step] added in pencil, possibly by May Morris.

reason backs them. When the complaint of the poor which has ever been heard dimly or less dim amidst the excitement of life rouses people at last to definite organization[,] they gain what they claim; yes[,] even when that organization is partial and imperfect. The Chartists claimed political freedom: it is now yielded: the Trades Unions claimed some share in the increase of the profit of the capitalists; that also had to be yielded, how ungraciously accompanied with what unmanly complaints, what base slander of the workers at the hands of their masters[,] some of you may forget but I remember: and now this last claim for final freedom; freedom to work and live and enjoy[,] as it is infinitely greater and more important than the others[,] so surely will be claimed more widely with greater intelligence and if possible greater determination. With what amount of resistance it may meet none can tell, but this is certain[,] that it [will] meet with no forcible resistance unless the upper classes can delude some part of the workers [to] take their part in defense of their unjust and pernicious position: nor less certain, I believe, that when the mask falls from the face of this huge tyranny of the modern world, and it is shown as an injustice conscious of its own wrong to the honest and just of the upper classes themselves[,] the risks of destruction will seem light compared with the degradation of championing an injustice.

Yes[,] I believe that if the intelligent of the working-classes and the honourable and generous of the employing class could learn to see the system under which we live as it really is, all the dangers of change would seem nothing to them and our capitalistic society would not be worth 6 months purchase.

It is in this belief that I am here tonight preaching to you that new good tidings of Socialism.

[*notes, probably taken during discussion*]

how to carry out—
Malthusianism
details—
force
who is [to] ini[t]iate
head work
competition & emulation
people have all power when they know [it]—class-abstinence
community   individual earnings
unequal shares—
state holds the capital difference in tastes—
failure of communities
marriage   democratic politics
    education
dissolute persons in families
criminal—

Figure 12.1 May Morris, G. B. Shaw, H. H. Sparling, and Emery Walker, 1889. Courtesy of The Wilson, Cheltenham

Figure 12.2 Charles Faulkner (1834–92). Courtesy of the National Portrait Gallery

Figure 12.3 John Bruce Glasier (1859–1920), *Labour Annual*, ed. Joseph Edwards, 1895

Figure 12.4 Fred Henderson (1868–1957). Courtesy of the Norfolk Public Library

12

"The Political Outlook," 1886

Editor's introduction

Morris delivered "The Political Outlook" eight times between January 10 and May 17, 1886, first to his familiar Hammersmith Branch of the Socialist League, and then to Socialist League branches at the Socialist League Hall, Farringdon Road (January 15), Clerkenwell (January 27), Mile End (February 2), Dublin (April 10), Leeds and Bradford (April 17), and Birmingham (May 17). His only nonsocialist audience for the lecture was the Hammersmith Liberal Club (February 10), and it must have taken some courage to present his views on the Liberal Party's failures in this venue.

"The Political Outlook" differs from many of Morris's other lectures in discussing alternative approaches to politics in general rather than laying out the nature of a socialist vision, and this may account for the fact that it was not selected for inclusion in his 1888 *Signs of Change*. The text is preserved in B. L. Add. MS. 45,333(11), ff. 234–54, and May Morris reprinted portions in *William Morris: Artist, Writer, Socialist* (MM2, 77–87); the full text is reproduced in Owen Holland's *How I Became a Socialist* (Verso, 2020).

As editor of *Commonweal*, Morris followed contemporary political events carefully in order to craft an oppositional running commentary in his column "Notes on News." "The Political Outlook" synthesizes these reflections, avoiding most details of specific issues of contention, such as police repression of dissidents or unemployment relief, in order to assess the emotions and economic interests which motivate each political faction. He attempts to answer three questions. First, why should we concern ourselves with politics at all? Next, what are some ineffective approaches we should avoid? And finally, what is the current state of British political parties, and what hope is there of breaking their monopoly? Morris's ability to identify repeating ideological patterns enables him to mount an often dryly amusing critique of the obstacles to forming an alternative extra-parliamentary opposition, what he would later describe as "one socialist party." His assessment of the shifting characteristics of a faction-riven two-party system offers insights not only into the politics of his own time but those of other political systems that offer little choice beneath a veneer of democracy.

Morris begins with a fundamental question: when one considers that politics "chiefly mean a record of the crudest blunders and follies of mankind," why should persons of discrimination and goodwill concern themselves with them at all? Ultimately, however, criticism must lead to action, for "as long as there is discontent with the present state of things there will be hope of altering it." Inevitably those who wish change must combine with one another, and yet this leads to an impasse; as various factions engage in a war with their opponents, "[s]uch war, like all wars, is in itself an evil." Nonetheless to avoid action is cowardly, and moreover all spheres of life bear some relationship to politics: "strong opinions on religion, ethics, economy, science[,] nay even art and literature (as I myself have found)[,] will at last bring us face to face with the question[,] 'what is true society?'" The rest of Morris's remarks then address the question of how one can be political in the broader sense without succumbing to the narrowness of factionalism and partisanship.

Socialists should be "practical," not by "pragmatically" acceding to compromises which undercut their essential aims, but in the Aristotelian sense of *praxis*, a commitment to action. Morris notes the temptation to self-satisfied theorization: "we cannot be content to sink into a mere philosophical society enunciating opinions which some people may accept if they will without altering their daily relations with other people." In alluding to a "philosophical society" Morris may have in mind the Fabian Society, recently founded in 1884 to promote democratic socialism through gradual means, as well as likely the Positivists of his day—believers in rational progress who in 1878 had inaugurated a "Church of Humanity." By contrast Morris emphasizes (in a passage omitted from the *Artist, Writer, Socialist* version) the revolutionary nature of Socialist League commitments: "Meantime it is our business as revolutionary or political, or if you please practical, socialists to educate people out of their position as obstacles to revolution . . . and therefore we call ourselves revolutionary."

In other contexts Morris praised early utopian communities as forerunners of modern socialism (Charles Fourier, for example, is mentioned briefly in chapter 10 of *News from Nowhere*), but here he dismisses communities such as Robert Owen's New Lanark or Fourierist phalanxes as escapist—"they do not pretend to meddle with society at large." Such self-contained societies present no threat to the authorities, for "they have renounced the conflict." Worse are the educated and refined progressives who refuse to act to bring about their beliefs—Morris again waxes sarcastic against Positivists such as Frederic Harrison, who hope for reform "in a thousand years."[1] Although these profess superiority to the business class, the vulgar bourgeoisie, they are in fact contented with, and sustained by, the status quo; even the bourgeois heaven would reward only members of their own class: "most of them look forward to another Bourgeois world beyond this wherein indeed they have not allowed any part for the service of the ignored proletariat. . . ."

Despite what Morris sees as evasions of true socialist transformation, he finds hope in the increasingly widespread assumption that Britain is becoming more democratic; here he may be referring to the Representation of the People Act (the Third Reform Act) of 1884, which had extended the vote to include two-thirds of men (though not women). Some groups look with optimism toward these new possibilities, others with dread, but all agree that a fundamental change in society is underway. In the past "advanced politicians" had hoped that suffrage reforms would enable ambitious workers to rise without changing the British class structure, but under the onslaught of recent trade depressions and the paradox of poverty amid overproduction, this has been proven a mirage. Armed with fear, a powerful new party is forming from the pieces of former ones to consolidate the ongoing reaction: "the break up of old party ties and distinctions [is] joined to a retention of the old names: the ground is covered by the same troops under the same banners. . . ."

Morris then adumbrates the features of this new-old faction: it is formed of Tories pretending to be more moderate than heretofore; a Liberal party Whig element, little changed from former years; and a "radical" Liberal section upholding laissez-faire ideals of property and free contract at the expense of actual workers. Though ostensibly the Tories and Liberals are distinct, yet they form an amalgam, as both unite in refusing to implement democratic demands and abhor the thought of "revolution." Morris finds the new center of power lies among the conservative Whig Liberals, what he terms the "party of Moderation," who steadfastly refuse economic reforms even as they accede to political ones. The latter initiate targeted colonialist wars, force open new markets, and maintain an exploitive control of Ireland, even as they are willing to "give the more energetic part of the working-classes every opportunity for bettering themselves so long as that can be done at the expense of the working-classes themselves, as they neither will nor dare touch the purses of the rich." Even these limited reforms are doomed, for the distribution necessary for a widened middle class is contrary to the competitive production that favors "gathering up into bigger and bigger heaps."

Yet the dialectical foe of these reactionary parties is also present, a movement embodying "the germs of the new democratic ideal," formed in part by "the political working men," that is, those with whom Morris had collaborated in the cross-class Labour Representation League and the Eastern Question Association.[2] Employers have also been forced to offer instruction to their workers, and "instruction breeds education"; the example of European revolutionary movements has nonetheless provided a model for present-day workers (i.e., the Paris Commune), and the violent crushing of such movements by a coalition of both parties has likewise "[hastened] the education of the workers." The advent of a new socialist party will cause confusion to the old centers of power, for "Parliament, like poverty, will make strange bedfellows." Since Parliament itself is antidemocratic, "the struggle will [then] be outside it." The false progressives in Parliament will ally with their reactionary colleagues, and when "the Reactionists will not be able to resist their fear and impatience of revolutionary opinion and will try to stifle it forcibly," they will provoke "the necessary consequence of forcible resistance."

Morris closes with a striking metaphor, shaping his youthful love of medieval effigies to a new use: the workers' enemies are changed "in outward aspect . . . as I have seen their images many a time, carved by their own slaves, sitting solemnly in their high places, their half-drawn swords laid across their knees, their haughty but eager faces looking into the life of personal energy and contention which were its chief elements." By contrast, pure capitalism spawns a world denuded of desire and purpose: present rulers "rule us as if they themselves were dead," and as their own inner lives are drained of energy, they remain "only haunted by the terrible power of capital. . . ." Such leaders live for privilege and mastery: "they must live on the labour of others or the reason for their existence is gone." Morris admits the fearful nature of their power: "sometimes in moments of depression one thinks they may succeed; one fears then that the world may become nothing but Bourgeois and machines." Such a "monstrous attempt" must evoke resistance, however, if as yet somewhat unspecified. As often Morris invites his audience to join with him to "save the world from that terrible doom," and his final adjuration might be said to encapsulate his life ethic—"hope always then and work always."

Notes

1. A jurist, historian, and radical journalist, Frederic Harrison (1831–1923) was a promoter of Comtean Positivism, conceived as a rational, non-supernatural "religion of humanity." In 1886 Harrison campaigned to represent the University of London in Parliament, and so Morris may have read one of his campaign speeches. One of Harrison's interests was in trade union legislation, and he contributed to the trades union periodical *The Bee Hive*. See also the notes for No. 10, "Commercial War."

   One of Morris's lifelong friends from his Oxford days was the Positivist Vernon Lushington (1832–1912), and so the two would likely have discussed Positivism.

2. E. P. Thompson, *William Morris: Romantic to Revolutionary* (New York: Pantheon, 1976), chaps. 5 and 7.

The Political Outlook

Perhaps some of our friends may be surprised at a Socialist whom they may be disposed to look upon as a purist having anything to say about politics at all, and indeed it must be admitted from the first that politics of any kind are no very pleasant study, since they chiefly mean a record of the crudest blunders and follies of mankind, so that it is not to be wondered at if many men of good feeling, and who are deeply impressed with the evils of our daily life and would sacrifice much to do away with them, do nevertheless shrink from politics: it is not strange that such people should say, Let us teach people what to aim at, try to educate them, form opinion that is, and then stand by and see what will happen.[1] That's all very well, and I am far from saying that such men are not useful; but after all what will happen? Why when opinion becomes strong enough, that is, becomes the opinion of many people, it must strive to get itself carried out in action: as long as there is discontent with the present state of things there will be hope of altering it.

That hope can only be realized by the combined action of those who are moved by it, who as soon as they are so combined with a view to action, and are determined that they will by some means or other get people in general to accept their opinion, must become a political party whatever they may call themselves; and when they have reached this point they are and must be in spite of all disclaimers hostile to all parties who are obstacles to the furtherance of their opinions. As far as their opinions are concerned[,] the world is composed of friends of their party and enemies to it: he who is not with us is against us: they are at war in short. They may carry on the war feebly or stoutly, well-manneredly or ill-manneredly, implacably or forgivingly, but it is war no less as long as they are a party. Such war, like all wars, is in itself an evil; or at least there go with it such turmoils, miseries, disappointments, such traps for the unwary in morals and honour on all sides, that it is hard to separate its beneficent essence from its evil accidents. Yet for all that[,] those who hold strong opinions and who shrink from it must have some doubts of the value of those opinions or else are overmastered by very natural timidity or love of ease: I don't blame them for that, but I do

1. This version of Morris's essay is indebted to the careful renditions in Holland, 86–101.

rather blame them for putting forward their timidity and love of ease as standards for others to follow as they not seldom do: it is weakness not strength in them that they dare not enter into the war necessary for the realization of their hopes. Let them at least stand aside lest they become mere obstacles and enemies of the very opinions which they hold.

People therefore who hold strong and definite opinions on the relations of men to each other must either belong to some political party or be cowards: I say there are questions of the day that press so strongly on thinking men for solution that they can only be evaded by cowardice: neither can I allow that some of men's dealings can be wholly separated from others so as to escape the sweep of the net political: strong opinions on religion, ethics, economy, science[,] nay even art and literature (as I myself have found) will at last bring us face to face with the question "what is true society?" If we answer that question rightly and accept all the consequences which flow from that answer we are free in mind at least[,] whatever compulsion may do to our bodies, if we answer it wrongly we are slaves: nor less slaves if we evade it, however proud we may be of our superior education, intelligence and refinement.

Therefore it seems to me that we Socialists must be political in the sense in which I have been using the word: in point of fact it means the same thing as practical, which is a title however which I should be slow in claiming as the word has been so terribly misused in these days, and so in political language at least has come to mean pretty much the same thing as cowardly or evasive.

We of the Socialist League have fully expressed the fact that we consider ourselves political by calling ourselves Revolutionary Socialists: it is quite clear if you come to think of it that since we condemn not only the obvious evils of modern Society, but also the ethics and economy of which they are the result, we must have a practical and political aim in view: we cannot be content to sink into a mere philosophical society enunciating opinions which some people may accept if they will without altering their daily relations with other people: if our opinions are to be accepted they will alter the relations of men altogether, nobody will be able (or willing) to stand out of the society which they will form: in other words, we believe that they will be *forced* on the world, not indeed artificially or by a little body of men, but by the general march of events even by those which may seem hostile to the movement. Meantime, it is our business as revolutionary or political[,] or if you please practical[,] socialists to educate people out of their position as obstacles to Revolution until circumstances drive us into compelling them not to be obstacles to it—that is our policy; and therefore we call ourselves Revolutionary.

It is quite necessary for us to face the position and see what we really are, because there are on the one hand so-called Socialists who are not revolutionary or political at all, and on the other some who are political but with whose policy we cannot agree. The first are represented by various experiments in association, for instance communities some of which are founded on absolute conditions of equality as amongst themselves, but do not pretend to meddle with society at large: as for these it seems to me they are destined either to failure and extinction after having played their part of experiments of association more or less valuable; or else if they can live long enough to meet the active revolutionary period they will gradually melt into the general party, and in that case be of much use to it from the habits of association and of the practice of equality which their experiments will engender: in any case except as a token and offset of the general movement they are valueless because of their standing aloof from politics as I have been using the word. Apart from that function of betokening the great change[,] our enemy in the present state of things can afford to disregard them because he does not fear them, since they have renounced the contest.

On the other side are those who would be political from a false point of view: they would mix with the political parties of the day whose aim is not the destruction of our slave society, but its continuance, and would ally themselves as opportunity serves with one or the other band of those who are their direct enemies in the hope that those enemies can be cajoled or frightened into doing the Socialist's work and not the Bourgeois's: I shall have some more to say of this view further on, so at present I will only remark that this kind of policy is what is commonly but I think erroneously meant by political Socialism, and I think it is a mistake in tactics altogether. When they have got as far as they can the enemy will still be the enemy and will have to be met directly and in face, and they will have to begin again on the road which the Revolutionary Socialists have been following steadily all the time.

But though we have nothing to do to mix ourselves up in the parliamentary squabble, and though to many worthy people that degraded and degrading twaddle-shop called Parliament means nothing at all, it would be a mistake not to watch the signs of the times in all directions. We socialists must not forget how many persons there are of political instincts, to use the word in its better sense, who know nothing of socialism except the name, besides the many who have only a slight inkling[,] quite inaccurate[,] of what it means. All these look toward Parliament as the means by which some change or other has to be brought about, and their vague hopes and longings influence that strange body and bring about its queer contortions, which in turn come of the attempt to square intentions of pleasing the constituents so long as they don't ask too much[,] with ignorance of what the constituents are thinking of and may ask for. Meantime worthy people who have nothing to do with Parliament and yet are interested in watching the game played there, are beginning to feel sufficiently uncomfortable about its goings-on, since they are not so blind as those who are actually playing the game, and are conscious that it shows signs of great changes coming on. Between these two, the timid, well-to-do people who fear further change as they are disgusted with what has already taken place and the people who vaguely desire change, as they have abundant reason to do, both of which groups watch Parliament with a superstitious interest, and we may be sure that there is something to watch, not for its own sake, but for what it indicates. The sort of thing which people think is going on, is shown[,] to take one instance among many[,] by such utterances as Mr. F. Harrison's speech to his co-religionists last New Year's Day:[2] he is to be reckoned I think among those who fear the change, rather than among those who desire it; and he seems to be so much alarmed by it as to have lost all appreciation of what is behind it, though to be sure he should have had some inkling of that.

Anyhow[3] he is much put out and the other evening he no longer talked about the *coming* triumph of democracy but asserted that it had really taken place; and to him that democracy seemed very much of a tyranny, and to be dreaded accordingly. I must say no wonder, for the Positivists having a righteous dislike to the more commercial aristocracy of the time, have nothing to put in its place except the spectre of righteousness definitely drawn indeed, but quite imaginary, which may be born they hope some thousand years hence.

Well, what Mr Harrison, a disinterested man and of real goodwill towards the people, fears in a not unreasonable manner if his blindness could be taken for a standard of fact, if what he fears were all that could come between the present muddle of things and the orderly hierarchy of realized Positivism, what he fears in this way there is many a man fears in other ways, for the most part thinking that life will be rougher and harder for those who now live refined and delicate lives, that they will have to work more when the final triumph of Democracy comes.

But besides these men who may be credited with a certain amount of insight into what is going on before their eyes, there are some whose blindness is as instructive as the short-sightedness just mentioned: perhaps if I say that the *Spectator* is a representative of these folks[,] you will be rather inclined to smile at my quoting so small a manifestation

2. *Daily News*, January 2, 1886, p. 3, col. 5: "Mr. F. Harrison on Positivism and Democracy." Harrison remarks, "The last Reform Act and the events of the last few years have made this country as near an approach to a simple democracy as perhaps any in Europe." He regrets the absence of constitutional checks on popular rule, since "Government now is merely a committee of that huge democratic club, the House of Commons . . . ."
3. MS. Any how

of the signs of the times: the amount of advertisements however which accompany its weekly wisdom imply that it has a good circulation and surely among people of a superior class of intelligence. To this type of political person, Parliament is a God, no less; all is going well [—] there will always be checks enough to prevent that evil tendency towards the Triumph of Democracy. It is worthwhile noting that those who on the whole are the sturdiest worshippers of Parliamentary system are Bourgeois of the Bourgeois; in the naivest and most unconscious way the one standard of good or evil[,] of better or worse is the comfort and morals of the Middle-Class; except as a machine useful for the progress of the race (of Bourgeois) these wise-acres ignore the existence of any class below the intelligent lesser Bourgeoisie; they very naturally therefore are always fairly contented with the world as it is, especially since most of them look forward to another Bourgeois world beyond this[,] wherein indeed they have not allowed any part for the service of the ignored proletariat, which if they knew it, they could not do without here: but you see a man cannot think of everything.

Here then you have different kinds of minds all of them looking on parliamentary matters with various degrees of attention, some fearing it, some hoping from it, nay almost worshipping it.

First there is the great body of uninstructed people[,] such of them as are well enough off to have time to think about politics at all, who by hereditary habit have got to expect that "government" can do something for them, and who after all in spite of their improved political position are not conscious yet of the terror which that improvement has carried into the souls of their masters; perhaps because they are quite conscious that they are still needy and have a hard time of it, and that former political improvements have not helped them much. Yet when they get to know what real politics mean their enlightenment may be both sudden and complete.

Then comes the group of the intellectual aristocracy, pessimists mostly who fear for their position, prematurely perhaps but certainly not without reason if a *monopoly* of culture and refinement is what they wish to preserve, and I fear few of them have much wider views than that.

Lastly there is the group (a big one) who have not found out that there is any danger underlying their comfortable position of culture and superfine morality: to these optimists the world is good because they know nothing of it but their own drawing-rooms; as they get enlightened they join the ranks of the timid pessimists, and learn to fear a new foe, the people grown bold enough like Oliver Twist to ask for more.[4]

4. In chapter 2 of Charles Dickens's *Oliver Twist*, the orphaned Oliver, consigned to the parish workhouse, evokes anger and shock when he asks for more than the inadequate bowl of thin gruel he is granted for a meal.

What has happened to give these ideas to those groups of hopers, fearers, and self-complacent people? Democracy has developed, as surely every thinking person expected it to do, but it has not developed in the direction it was expected to: I don't think it is misrepresenting the views of advanced politicians of, say, twenty years ago, to say that their hope in democracy was that without levelling all distinctions of rank or talent it would turn the whole of the decent working-class into small bourgeois, leaving outside a fringe of the vicious idle incapable, or in a word the unlucky; of whom I am afraid those advanced ones took no account at all; did not even think of taking the pains to provide a sufficiency of gallows for them.

Now I should say that except among persons like the constituency of the *Spectator* that ideal has pretty much fallen through. It is not the approaching realization of *this* which frightens Mr Frederic Harrison: which makes Fitz James Stephens[5] so reasonably indignant, and so many another man of culture congratulate himself that he was not born 40 years later; and on the other hand working-men radicals do not need to be told that they have not reached this happy ideal – not yet. On the contrary, on all hands and not only in this country, but in France, Germany, and America is civilization showing us the spectacle of industrious and ingenious men, skilled artizans[,] out of employment and the hapless fringe of labour growing day by day.[6] The paradise of the little Bourgeoisie is vanishing like the desert mirage, and showing us the hard realities of depression of trade and over production, the tokens of the commercial system nearing the end which unlimited competition and the growing aggregation of capital are preparing for it.

The result of this natural and inevitable change in the economical condition of things, or rather of its due development, is the present condition of matters political: if it had been possible for everything to have gone on smoothly with the world of commerce in England, and the gains of the profit-grinders and rack-renters could have gone on increasing by leaps and bounds as was once the case, its natural fellow-traveller middle-class democracy would have gone on smoothly also on its road to – nowhere. The classes that felt themselves benefitted by the stately march of Commerce would have easily found a morality to satisfy their consciences that it was good for the poor to be poor, nay even a philosophy

5. James Fitzjames Stephen (1829–94), a lawyer, judge in India, judge of the High Court, and journalist, was the elder brother of writer and critic Leslie Stephen and the author of *The History of the Criminal Law of England* (1883). Stephen was a staunch opponent of disorder noted for his harsh sentences.
6. Economists consider the period 1873–96 one of economic contraction or recession in the UK, USA, and western Europe. A Royal Commission was established to investigate the "Depression of Trade and Industry" in 1886.

to account for that pious necessity, since they would not have been too many to be easily managed, considering the existence of the large body of artisans who would have thought themselves well-to-do, their standard of life lately so degradingly low having been raised somewhat at least. In short the music of the money dropping into the till would have drowned all qualms of conscience, and all fears. But as matters have gone and are going the dullest moneybag that ever listened in church or chapel to the gospel denunciations of the rich can grasp the idea that the poor are poor and don't like to be so; and though the spiritual 'woe unto you!' has become meaningless to him from habit and iteration, it may yet find an echo of fear in his soul when he remembers how many the poor are, and that those next above them, the skilled artisans, are not to be depended upon as formerly to keep them down. For they are also looking fearfully on the depression of trade and sinking wages: they were told that trade prosperity concerned them as much as it did their masters and that its growth would be steady and continuous, and that from that progress they would receive their due share of benefit. The last six years have given the lie to that encouragement and the way is open to showing them that they are no mere appendage to the all-producing Power[,] Capital, but are themselves all Producers. They are better instructed also: education has been provided to make them useful law-abiding workmen or capitalists' tools; but necessary as it was for the manufacturers to take that step, it was a dangerous step to take, for it will give them the nascent power of educating themselves really as men[,] not as machines.

Meantime historical intelligence has been growing, and basely as the men of culture do often use their gifts and knowledge, yet the things themselves are good and have opened the door to many a life-giving truth. History[,] which was once little more than a string of doubtful tales of the bloody wars and unaccountable follies of kings and scoundrels in which the necessary slavery of the people was taken for granted, has now been forced to confess the truth, at least in part, and to show us the ceaseless struggle of the people to be free.[7]

And all this knowledge tends to become commoner, and so between instruction and necessity, the workman is being *educated* to know what he is, the germ of the new Society in which all artificial restrictions will

7. Several late nineteenth-century progressive historians had concentrated on English social history with sympathy for popular revolts; among these was James Edwin Thorold Rogers (1823–90), several volumes of whose *Agriculture and Prices in England from 1259 to . . . 1783* Morris had read with interest in 1882. Kelvin notes, citing Paul Meier, that Rogers had been mentioned approvingly by Marx in *Capital*, and that Rogers's views of medieval society influenced Morris's interpretation of the Peasant's Revolt in *A Dream of John Ball* (Kelvin, 2.264n.). Arguably Morris and Ernest Belfort Bax's 1886–8 "Socialism from the Root Up" was another effort to narrate "the ceaseless struggle of the people to be free."

be abolished, in which there will be no more classes, and property will no longer be robbery as it is now, but will mean the satisfaction of each man's needs for each man's deeds.

Now this state of things may be only just beginning in this country, where the workman long-divorced from the land and compelled to the merest mechanical drudgery has been oppressed into special degradation; but still it is beginning; and even its beginnings have as I said changed the aims and prospects of democracy in a remarkable manner.

If it is many years since it seemed on the verge of that incomplete triumph[,] the realization of which makes Mr. Harrison so anxious, and if it had not been for the disturbing elements of fresh hope which I have been speaking of[,] that triumph would by now doubtless have been complete. I will say this of the Radicals now fast becoming Whigs, that if they are right in thinking that their mere political program pushed to the furthest is the final goal of political effort, they are also right in miscalling us Socialists for dragging a red-herring over their scent. For just as Democracy in England was advancing to the last victory, Socialism has appeared and changed its look to the enemy which it was attacking; I repeat its aim is not what it was and that has become clear to the anti-democratic party, many of whom in point of fact were and are mixed up in the democratic ranks.

The aim of Democracy till lately has been the abolition of what it considered privilege: it aimed on making a clear field for the acquirement of property (in the Bourgeois sense) by any one who for any reason was strong enough to get hold of it, and to give him every advantage to keep it and make any use of it, whether it were harmful to the public or not, which his caprice might suggest; and the property when acquired was to have its full influence unchecked by any artificial restrictions outside its own sacredness[:] the poor man who steals a loaf from hunger must go to prison; but if he can (legally) cheat his fellow, as hungry and poor as himself[,] out of two loaves, no one shall steal one from him; and if he can by a series of such transactions become a richer man than a needy Prince, his acquired riches shall bring him more influence than the prince's hereditary position. This is the doctrine of radicalism as it was. This aim called complete freedom of contract (although it is nothing of the sort) is founded on the assumption that it is possible, hereditary, feudal privilege being no more[,] for every worthy man to become rich and respected. Riches and healthy virtue are coterminous: the poor are either diseased or vicious: clearly an assumption belonging to a period of prosperity—of leaps and bounds.

Well, party feeling long outlives the realities which first founded the party; the Tories resisted this on its own grounds at first and are by some supposed to be still resisting it; the Tories also did not like losing the last rags of hereditary power and finding themselves the equals of self-made men, and there has been abundance of sentiment, prejudice, and superstition, not all of which has been quite unworthy, to support them. People could not quite believe in the clean sweep which the last 50 years of commercial prosperity has made of the [feudal system?]. So that up till lately, they have been able to keep up a decently enthusiastic resistance to the flood of democracy[,] apparently following Mr. F. Harrison in asking what D[emocracy] is becoming[.] They are now getting other allies and a different spirit to their help.

For most men who look at politics except the *Spectator* ones, have become conscious that the old ideal of Democracy has fallen through and that another one, vague enough as yet, is being forced upon it: in short the attack is now becoming an attack on that very sanctity of Property which Bourgeois Democracy was once prepared to defend with as much stiffness as the very Tories. This has changed the whole face of the battle: it is as in the tournament in Walter Scott's *Ivanhoe*, the combatants are laying aside their blunted swords and pointless lances, and are taking to real point and edge.[8]

Again the case of Ireland. What is at the bottom of all that holy horror of a country governing itself which is so widely spread? The real reason is cloaked behind various specious pretences: [we] must do our duty to the Irish, prevent them quarrelling among themselves, not allow them to relapse into savagery—that's one kind of mask. "Dismemberment of the Empire", that's another in which there is a double hypocrisy; for even when there is any real fear in it[,] it means not patriotism in any sense but market hunting: but in this Irish affair 'tis more transparently hollow. In truth what rich and respectable people really feel is that the Irish demand means a government which shall deal with the land question, and that no other government will be accepted by them. A government whose purpose is to enforce the payment of rent, which is the special Irish form of free contract (think of it the freedom of contract between an Irish peasant with no resource save the land he was bred upon and an absentee landlord, governing his property by means of thugging[?] and an agent. Here's a holy thing indeed, the very eucharist of free contract!) A government I say, whose business it is to enforce the payment of rent will be a tyranny under whatever name it exists. That this is the view of the real progressive party all party people in England know well, and that is the reason of the shrinking dread with which they look upon it. The sanctity of property is threatened again, and the ultra-Democrats at least are looking on complacently.

8. Scott's 1820 novel portrays a tournament in which Ivanhoe and his opponent defy the official rules of combat by fighting with unsheathed swords.

Meantime all kinds of schemes are afloat aiming at doing something to quiet the rising discontent; some tending to mere reaction, like the small holdings scheme; some to a crude and clumsy form of state-socialism, which ill instructed anti-socialists support to be *the* foe: and always the terms of reproach used by professed reactionaries to their more advanced opponents are Socialist *and* Communist: often good sooth used with strange infelicity against worthy people whom our mild manifesto[,] for instance, would frighten out of their skins.

Once more the idea that something more than mere political freedom, unlimited uninterfered[-]with freedom to fleece or be fleeced according as you are above or below, that more than this is wanted is the new idea that is pervading democracy and pushing out the old Bourgeois ideal. The sham of political freedom is beginning to be found out, the lack of economical freedom is beginning to be felt all round, even amongst those who have little or no conception of what that freedom means or what it will lead to.

The openly seen result of this among our political parties is the break up of old party ties and distinctions, joined to a retention of the old names: the ground is covered by the same troops under the same banners, but the cause of quarrel is different: There is a Tory party still in England which would doubtless be Tory in action if it could be, but that is quite hopeless for it, so it is obliged to clothe itself in Whig principles as the most reactionary vestments which can be worn without tumbling off in hopeless rags: there is a Liberal party also; but it includes the nominal Whigs but little changed from their old estate, and now openly the exponents of that older radical ideal which I spoke of before, the ideal of the sanctity of property and free-contract in a world turned wholly bourgeois except for a race of helots, theoretically incapable and idle people, who it is to be hoped, if the fates are good to us, will become less and less numerous as time goes on—but whom meanwhile we can by no means do without.

Besides these logical champions the Liberal party includes, especially among the political working men, the ultra-radicals, who bear with them the germs of the new democratic ideal, very vague as yet, and cumbered by crude attempts at state Socialism, which are either so insignificant or so impossible to work that they are called *practical*; and there is besides a whole host of betwixt and between people.

This [is] what has become of the old Conservative and Liberal arrangement of parties. At first sight it seems a very complicated state of things but it is really much simpler than it looks, or at least will result before long in a simple condition of matters political. As far as Parliament and the executive goes, that is to say, as power over the present goes, the real power is the Whig party: a great portion of the Tory party gravitates towards them; almost all the floating mass between the Whigs and Radicals really belongs to them: every Radical who loses faith in democracy or who is scared by the advance of Socialism, or is growing old and cynical is bound to swell their ranks. Nor are they doubtful as to their course of action in trying to realize the Bourgeois ideal. They are prepared to accept any change you please that is merely political, but resist as covertly as possible but also as stiffly, every attempt towards economical freedom: they will not involve the country in war if they can help it, unless the enemy is helpless and his purse worth having; but they must have new markets if it is possible to get them with the help of our present commercial bodyguard: but chiefly and above all it is their business to *spread the middle-class*, to give the more energetic part of the working-classes every opportunity for bettering themselves so long as that can be done at the expense of the working-classes themselves, as they neither will nor dare touch the purses of the rich. On their success in creating a new middle-class out of the present workingclass their tenure of power hangs; if they fail there is nothing for it but Revolution. For they themselves have abolished or will abolish all the old aristocratic checks and safeguards of the constitution, they have but one support, the tremendous power of organized capital and its slave: unintelligent cowardly selfishness.

This great party therefore, the party of Moderation, is our one real enemy: what are their chances of success? I have just named their supports, in other words they are, commercial success amongst the rich, ignorance and disunion among the workers. But the forces against them are amongst their own camp: their own necessities will overthrow them: capital is their master not their servant: and its very organization, so powerful against revolt while all goes well, will prevent that spreading of the middle-classes which is essential to the life of the Moderate Party, that is to say to the existence of Modern Society. The tendency of all modern production is not towards spreading abroad and dividing, but towards gathering up into bigger and bigger heaps; and the terrible King Competition will sternly forbid any artificial reaction from this tendency. Nor after all can the workers be kept quite ignorant; once more the necessities of the capitalists have forced them to instruct the workers more or less, and instruction breeds education.

Furthermore these Moderates have dangerous allies who play into the hands of progress by trying to suppress it openly: I mean the great reactionary party on the continent. You English working-men when you hear the bourgeois as you often will holding forth on the extent to which the revolutionary violence on the continent has hindered the cause of progress, throw the lie back in his teeth. What all that means is the efforts of workers not so corrupted by commercialism as we are to sustain their freedom against direct open monstrous attacks on it. And much as we sympathize with the sufferings of those individuals who have been crushed by this open brutality, most fortunate it is for us and for the world that tyranny has taken that form in countries not so commercial as ours; because it has given the cause an army of men who feel their common interests and aspirations uniting them against tyranny of all kinds, whether the tyrant be dressed in a cuirassier's uniform[9] or a philanthropist's frock-coat. I say that the Moderate Party cannot help allying themselves with the Immoderate Party and so hastening the education of the workers.

And mind you the lapse of time and the course of events may or probably must force them out of their Moderation. It is their cue at present to give nearly full license to all expression of opinion, which I think we Socialists shall be wise to avail ourselves of while we may. For suppose that opinion to be very widely spread and at the same time to have no Parliamentary outlet, no privileged place to be heard in while it is obviously subversive of the holiness of modern Society, it will be looked upon as immediately dangerous, and will be treated (only more decidedly) all over the British Islands as it has already been treated in Ireland, that is, as a police and prison matter.

People may say, Well if they do this they will be no longer a Moderate Party. That is true; they will not attempt using the high hand until their failure is obvious. It is the destiny of the Moderate Party to turn into confessed reactionaries, but of course when they do so the Revolution will not be coming, but come.

To sum up. The old parties who between them held the state in their hands and governed in the exclusive interest of the rich classes are broken up. In their place is a political muddle which is in process of resolving itself into two parties, one sustaining, the other attacking society founded on wage slavery. There will of course in Parliament be an interval during which this will be by no means clear, and Parliament[,] like poverty[,] will make strange bedfellows. When it becomes clear and the people know at last that the liberty which denies, as a monstrous demand, their right to the full reward of their labour, is a sham, when that happens it will be found that Parliament was not made for the people and that the struggle will be outside it.

The present agitation for reform by Parliamentary and constitutional means will be wholly in the hands of the Moderate or Reactionary party, which will attract to it all men who desire the stability of things as they are: even many I fear who now pose as progressive and truly liberal:

9. A cuirassier was a French cavalry soldier equipped with a cuirass, or metal body armor. Morris may here refer to the "open brutality" with which the Paris Commune was crushed, as opposed to the more subtly invidious tyranny of laissez-faire commerce.

in Parliament those who were the progressive party will partly fall off from timidity and corruption, and the rest will be hopelessly defeated and will be driven into the arms of those who have refused to meddle with Reform by Parliament from the first, and thereafter will become declared revolutionists. How that revolution will accomplish itself it would be absurd to prophesy: but it is not unreasonable to suppose that the Reactionists will not be able to resist their fear and impatience of revolutionary opinion and will try to stifle it forcibly, with the necessary consequence of forcible resistance where possible, and thus the two camps of people and masters no longer doubtful to anyone.

Thus I have tried to show you what our enemies are. Changed indeed they are in outward aspect from what the enemies and tyrants of the workers once were, as I have seen their images many a time, carved by their own slaves; sitting solemnly in their high places, their half-drawn swords laid across their knees, their haughty but eager faces looking into the life of personal energy and contention which were its chief elements. All that is changed now. In no cathedral of the future will the effigies of our present rulers make fair and fitting architectural ornaments: the sword is laid aside and the unseen compulsion of famine has taken its place. The natural mask of hypocrisy cultivated so highly that it does not know itself has supplanted the warhelm; our masters of to-day will not confess the desire of the strong man to enjoy life at anyone's expense; nay they seem almost to have lost all energy, all sense [of] pleasure in their practice of their one necessary virtue, and rule us as if they themselves were dead, their bodies only haunted by the terrible power of capital which has made them and us, which has made the hideous sham peace that is, and the stern reality of the strife which is to be.

Yet dull as they are, vacant as their lives are, changed as they are in all respects from those lords of the old violent and eager life, their aim is one with theirs: they must live on the labour of others or the reason for their existence is gone. To live like masters is their aim. Nor should our aim be other than mere contradiction to theirs, which embraces the intention of making us live like machines.

On their success herein all their political hope is founded; and sometimes in moments of depression one thinks they may succeed; one fears then that the world may become nothing but Bourgeois and machines: yet in moments of depression only: if we are determined to live like men, come what will, we shall foil that monstrous attempt and save the world from that terrible doom—hope always then and work always.

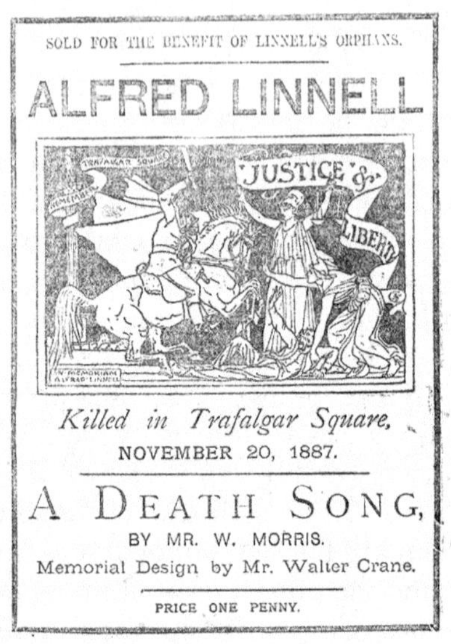

SOLD FOR THE BENEFIT OF LINNELL'S ORPHANS.

ALFRED LINNELL

Killed in Trafalgar Square,
NOVEMBER 20, 1887.

A DEATH SONG,
BY MR. W. MORRIS.
Memorial Design by Mr. Walter Crane.

PRICE ONE PENNY.

Figure 13.1 "Alfred Linnell: A Death Song," 1887

Figure 13.2 "The Riot in Trafalgar Square,"
The Illustrated London News, 1887

13

"Equality," 1888

Editor's introduction

Morris delivered his talk titled "Equality" eight times between September 30, 1888 and February 9, 1890,[1] in most cases to audiences of his fellow socialists.[2] May Morris excerpted sections in *William Morris: Artist, Writer, Socialist* (MM2, 197–293), and I prepared a fuller text for the *Journal of Pre-Raphaelite Studies* 20 (Spring 2011). The manuscript remains in British Library Add. MS. 45,333(11). Morris's message throughout was quite radical, if familiar: only near-complete equality of condition and dispersion of power would sustain the integrity of the revolutionary ideals he and his comrades professed.

Morris began the essay with an admission of the impediments to progress: "[t]here must be a long period of half formed aspirations, abortive schemes, doubtful experiments, and half measures interspersed with disappointment, reaction and apathy," a change from his more hopeful view in earlier lectures. Nonetheless he insisted that one such "aspiration" would have to be an unwavering commitment to keep an originary ideal of "fellowship" in view. For

> . . . it is not a small change in life that we advocate but a very great one. That socialism will transform our lives and habits, and leave the greater part of the political[,] social and religious controversies that we are now so hot about forgotten[,] useless and lifeless[,] like wrecks stranded on a sea shore.

Equally categorical was his claim that an egalitarian "society, a community, a commonwealth" would have to dispense with a "cast clout of feudalism[:] the creed of the superior person," a treacherous mirage which had its origins, Morris believed, in

> the assumption of the existence of a . . . God of the universe[,] the proprietor of all things and persons, to be worshipped and not questioned . . . whose irresponsible authority is reflected in the world of men by certain . . . [lesser] governors whose authority is

> delegated to them by that supreme slaveholder and employer of labour up in heaven.

As for these lesser lords, he pointed out the active harm caused by their parasitism:

> [t]he civilized workman . . . besides keeping himself almost as well as the savage, can also keep a queen[,] a landed aristocracy[,] a house of lords and commons, an army and navy, annual piratical wars against harmless people capable of being robbed, an Irish constabulary, a Parnell Commission, a great population in short of harmful or useless persons[,] a mass of corruptions[,] luxury, waste and confusion such as the world has never seen before.

(The world had, in fact . . . but no matter.) All these lesser lords, as they passed across the scene, had also left most of their fellows "to put it mildly[,] insufficiently supplied with food, clothing and house-room." Yet since man does not live by bread alone, once these minimal preconditions have been met, thoughtful human animals naturally next yearn for "leisure[,] pleasure and education." Art and creative labor, the subjects of several of Morris's most eloquent essays, he here subsumed under "pleasure": for "leisure after due work *is* both in itself pleasure and is also the parent of pleasure, which is really but the consciousness of a useful and manly [*sic*] life."

If "rights" are needs and opportunities for which a just social order would assume a collective responsibility, for Morris one such right was to education, which he defined "as the opportunity for developing our faculties pleasurably." Instead the rich have denied education to the poor and hollowed out their own more privileged forms until these lack meaning. One wonders if Morris is referring to aspects of his own formal education or intellectual milieu in his indictment:

> [T]hey have robbed others of education which their folly has turned to an instrument of mocking cynicism baser than the grossest ignorance. I am ashamed to live; I am afraid to die, is the true watch-word of the last development of tyrannous inequality. . . .

It is natural to see in this passage a brief wince of personal pain.

Even more radically, Morris compared successful capitalists and their workers to "slaves and slaveholders." He characterized such "slavery" as a form of murder (a point to which he returned in his peroration) and attempted to refute the claims of political economists that the "market" simply caters to people's needs by pointing out that such "needs" are socially constructed. Alleged "desires" for cheap goods are the by-product of poverty; anyone "forced to live in a tumble-down house" would also be "forced to desire an undue amount of . . . plumb[ing]." Moreover, other supposed "needs" are fictitious; some "men cannot keep their self respect . . . in a palace that would comfortably house a hundred families . . . ." Finally, some forms of manufacture produce Ruskinian "illth": for example, products "[which] . . . exist . . . for the sole purpose of making adulterants for various articles of consumption." (Morris may have had in mind the frequent adulteration of staples such as milk, tea, and bread.)

Worse still ("now comes the worst part of it") was and is the insidious trap of forced conscription into an interconnected system: "[W]hile the present system lasts we must go on [for] if . . . the rich leave off being luxurious, as some moralists (very naturally) bid them[,] they will by so doing throw the dependent workmen out of employment."

A deeply corrupt and corrupting social order of this sort might come to an end, he conjectured, as "happened at the time of the break up of the Roman empire[, when] civilization was being first overwhelmed and at last resuscitated by healthy barbarism." This was a transition Morris had found (or thought he had found) in the Icelandic sagas, as manifested in *The House of the Wolfings*, a historical romance also drafted in 1888. But the analogy failed to work in the present instance, for

> . . . where are the healthy barbarians to come from? From the democracy. I doubt it if things do not alter from what they have been; for . . . though the workers are more useful than the idlers, yet they too are corrupted and degraded by their position. No one can expect to find the virtues of free men in slaves. No[,] if the present state of Society merely breaks up without a conscious effort at transformation, the end[,] the fall of Europe[,] may be long in coming, but when it does come it will be far more terrible[,] far more confused and full of suffering than the period of the fall of Rome.

This was a bleak and prescient admission, then and now: revolutionary opponents of a corrupt social order can only come from those who are in one way or another corrupted by it.

Morris acknowledges that even the Victorians had managed a few advances—from him a striking admission—but only for a narrow subpopulation, and this was its betrayal:

> [W]e . . . who have created the Equality of the Educated Middle-classes, who have forced the so-called aristocracy of birth to recognize their position, & to receive as equals the deft man of

> business[,] the learned scholar, the gifted professional man . . . ? [But t]he ordinary labourer[, by contrast,] is in a worse position than a savage living in a good climate.

The lies the "Educated Middle Classes" told themselves to justify this betrayal of Enlightenment ideals—as they fondled the elitist Ring, so to speak—came in various guises. Pseudo-Darwinian "survival of the fittest" offered a scientific rationale for simple greed in its new *habillement* as an "ideal of commercial society which puts forward the acquirement of riches as the one aim of life." In the end, however, if this aim is pursued "society will explode volcanically with such a crash as the world has not yet witnessed." For as competition, overproduction and spoliation of the environment become more intense, corporations will form larger and larger cartels and compete more ruthlessly against their workers, in "an elaborate scheme for shutting down the safety-valve and sitting on the boiler."

The sole glimmer of hope Morris found lay in new forms of international solidarity. The first—which might be called "workers without borders"—would require that we take seriously Eugène Pottier's hope that "l'internationale sera le genre humain":[3] "for . . . unless we recognize the unity of the working classes through the world and cast aside our old absurd jealousy of the workmen of other countries[,], all radical improvement in the position of the workers is hopeless." He suggested that working people might accept a need for "syndicalism"—worker-controlled production and communally owned endeavor—on an international scale, and reconcile "the claim of independence for the workman with the necessary acceptance of responsibility by him."

Mindful of the contingent nature of these projections, Morris appealed to us all to "be on the side of the change so that we may look at it not with fear but with hope." Rather we should embrace its benefits, "the pleasures of fellowship[,] the joy of converse with our equals; the advantage of the give and take which ought always to be between two men good[-]tempered and useful to society, whatever the different caliber of their minds may be . . . . Can we not change our ideal[?]"

Remembering the thousands of people who had gathered at the funeral of Alfred Linnell, the victim of police violence at "Bloody Sunday," at which mounted officers charged a crowd of demonstrators in Trafalgar Square, November 13, 1887, Morris observed pointedly:

> Among those poor people were[,] I know[,] many and many who might not perhaps have been made into great men, but who certainly might have been made into happy and useful ones; and I tell you plainly that we are criminals because they have not been

> so made, and if the consequences of our crime overtakes us, who shall pity us[?]

He then posed the following question, a socialist recasting of Dostoyevsky's parable of the cynical "Grand Inquisitor":

> Or do you think, as some do, that it is not ill that a hundred thousand harmless people should be boiled down in the fire of misery to make one single glorious great man? . . . . I would rather have a hundred thousand happy persons than one genius made up of murder.

Instead, inequality breeds revenge: "[M]orality[,] her eyes cleared by the advance of necessity[,] is beginning to remember the ancient legend of the first murderer, and the terrible answer to his vile sneer. Am I my brother[']s keeper?" The answer in the "ancient legend," was "*What hast thou done? His blood cries out to me from the ground*" (Genesis 4:9).

In "Equality" Morris tried to identify dilemmas honest seekers after social justice must confront, describe some of the shape-changing capacities of political manipulation, and offer rationales for his "obstinate refusal" to embrace "the degrading game of politics."[4] These were openly utopian views, but were not naïve. He was not, for example, a "little-England" socialist. He had entered political life through an antiwar movement and understood all too well the atavistic force of nativism and chauvinism, and its power to corrode fragile ideals of social solidarity. Nor—his historical allusions strongly suggest—did he underestimate the gradients of ruthlessness, cynical brutality, and diversionary cunning which may corrupt anyone who accedes to power.

Finally, "Equality" is one of Morris's most powerful essays, in part because of the stringency of its ideals: its attack on hierarchy; its exposure of capitalist waste; and its blunt confrontation with the obstacles to a just revolution, or even revolution at all ("where are the healthy barbarians to come from?"). To avert the collapse of civilization into violence Morris proposes a true internationalism, as we cast aside "our old absurd jealousy" of other countries to offer all workers the shared satisfaction of needs and a fellowship of kinship within difference.

Notes

1. These were an open-air meeting of the Clapham Common Branch of the Social Democratic Federation (SDF) on Clapham Common, September 30, 1888; a meeting of the Nottingham Socialist Club at the Secular Hall, Beck Street, Nottingham, November 18, 1888; of the Fulham Branch of the Socialist League at the Branch Rooms, 8 Effie Road, Walham Green, November 25, 1888; of the Hammersmith Branch of

the Socialist League at Kelmscott House, Hammersmith, December 23, 1888; of the Edinburgh Branch of the Socialist Labour League at the Queen Street Hall, Edinburgh, February 13, 1889; of the Southwark and Lambeth Branches of the SDF at the Nelson Coffee Tavern, Westminster Bridge Road, London, March 31, 1889; of the Fulham Liberal Club at Walham Green, London, April 14, 1889; and of the Hammersmith Branch of the Socialist League at Kelmscott House, February 9, 1890. See LeMire, 312.

2. Less directly political essays written and delivered in this period included "Tapestry and Carpet Weaving," "Art and Its Producers," "Gothic Architecture," "The Art of Dyeing," and "On the Origins of Ornamental Art."
3. "L'Internationale," st. 1.
4. Cf. "What We Have to Look For," British Library Add. MS 45,333, f. 56 (no. 11).

It is usual when a Socialist is addressing an audience of those who wish to know what his Socialism means, to touch lightly on the aim that Socialism has in view and to dwell chiefly on the means by which that aim is to be reached. The speaker assumes (usually I am glad to think with reason) that his audience are sufficiently with him to sympathise with his wish to better the present condition of affairs, and are eager to know what process he proposes to them as the means for the bettering of the life of the great mass of the population; it is natural for people to say to an earnest reformer, tell us what it is that you wish to have done at once, and then we will look at the matter; and all the more natural perhaps when the aim of the speaker is far reaching and all inclusive, when in fact he is preaching a change in the basis of society and not a mere palliation of its worst evils: because people say, and reasonably, we cannot be expected to change that basis suddenly, to go to sleep on Saturday night in our present condition and wake up on Monday morning with the revolution accomplished and everything going smoothly with a contented population round about us.[1] There must be a long period of half[-]formed aspirations, abortive schemes and half measures interspersed with doubtful experiments, disappointment, reaction, and apathy before we get anywhere near the beginning of the obvious and dramatic change which people know as revolution, and it is a matter of course that people should ask the would-be revolutionists what the first step is to be, and that socialist lecturers generally spend a great part of their lecturing time in showing what the first step *may* be and hold keen argument about it with their audiences.

1. This conjectural fantasy forms the frame of *News from Nowhere*, written two years later.

You cannot however fail to agree with me when I say that not even the first step can be taken until the advocates of a complete change have managed to persuade a sufficient number of people that it is necessary and should be a change of a certain kind. It is true that there are some people of a timid or very opportunist mind who press on us the necessity of leading people on by little and little, concealing the object they have in view, until people are so far committed to the steps to be taken towards it that they cannot draw back again. We are told for instance not to use the word Socialism, but rather to tell people that what we want to lead them into is a kind of advanced democracy and so forth: nay one quite ingenious author has even started the curious paradox that it is possible to be a good Socialist and a good Tory at one and the same time.[2]

Now passing by the question whether or not this is quite honest[,] I do not think it is very effective strategy. If you want to convert people to a new and unpopular creed that obviously has no immediate material advantages, no loaves and fishes, to offer you must not expect at first to get hold of persons whose intelligence is not somewhat above the average; and to such extra intelligent persons your opportunism will be too transparent for deception; so I think it is always best to face the matter from the first, and to say right out that democracy or radicalism is not incipient socialism although the two things have something in common; that it is not a small change in life that we advocate, but a very great one. That socialism will transform our lives[3] and habits, and leave the greater part of the political[,] social

2. Morris reacted strongly against the position taken by some members of the Social Democratic Federation that aiding the Tories in electoral contests might help defeat Liberals and thus contribute to the rise of socialism. This sentence may be an indirect reference to Henry Hyde Champion (1859–1928), who had shocked many fellow socialists by allegedly accepting "Tory gold" to help split the Liberal vote for an 1885 election. Champion's publications to date included *The Truth about the Unemployed* (1886), *Wrongs That Require Remedies* (1887), *Co-operation vs. Socialism: being a report of a debate between Mr. H. H. Champion and Mr. Benjamin Jones . . .* (1887), and *Social-Democracy in Practice* (1887). Another candidate for this reference may have been the SDF leader Henry Mayers Hyndman (1842–1921), who before his conversion to socialism had been characterized as a "Tory radical," and whom Morris repeatedly accused of political opportunism and lack of realism. In addition to editing and writing for *Justice*, Hyndman was the author of *The Historical Basis of Socialism* (1883), *The Coming Revolution in England* (1884), *A Summary of the Principles of Socialism* (1884), *Socialism and Slavery* (1884), *Will Socialism Benefit the English People?* (1884), *Socialism versus Smithism* (1884), *The Chicago Riots and the Class War in the United States* (1886), and *A Commune for London* (1887), as well as several books denouncing British policy in India.

3. MS., lifes

and religious controversies that we are now so hot about forgotten[,] useless and lifeless like wrecks stranded on a sea shore.

Let me begin then and not end by telling you what the nature of my ideal as a Socialist is, an ideal which I believe to be really held by all socialists though some may be unconscious of it, and which the very first steps of conscious Socialism will inevitably lead to directly; it is complete equality of condition for all. That is to my mind the aim of Socialism stated in the fewest possible words: any sacrifice that is necessary for its attainment is worth making: no further mastery over the powers of nature that we may gain can be a substitute for it; without it freedom[,] education[,] happiness, in one word[,] progress is impossible; whatever we have done is done, but this lies ahead, and we *must* attain it, there is no second course open to us; whatever great change as yet undreamed of lies before the world must be reached through this: reaction is an empty word in this matter for a thing which is not and cannot be.

That is my faith: now let me try to give you some reasons for my holding it.

But remember before I go on that I have just admitted that there must be a transitional period before this ideal can be realised; a transition during which democracy or radicalism will work itself out by performing its ultimate function of getting rid of the fag end of the idea surviving from the epoch before this, the feudal epoch, of a hierarchy of divinely appointed government; which idea takes refuge now in places quite unexpected by the radicals of 50 years ago in the form of the claim of an aristocracy of intellect to govern the average man for his own good even if he suffers by it.[4] It is the flourishing of this cast clout of feudalism, the creed of the superior person, which has given rise to the delusion that there is a reaction in progress in favour of a kind of refined (but exceedingly corrupt) Toryism, and which bears the same relation to the old Toryism as a rotten moldy apple does to the unripe fruit hanging on the tree: it has more flavour in it—but ugh! it is nasty. I think one reason why we continue to be plagued with it is because radicalism has been somewhat hampered by the growth of socialistic ideas and in fact scarcely exists in a genuine and intelligent condition except in conjunction with them. However I think that the democratic idea, even as socialism grows, will gather strength until equality is ready to supersede it, and so sweep away this last feeble recrudescence of

4. Here Morris may aim at the Positivists and Fabians, as well as perhaps Henry Mayers Hyndman, known for his gentleman's manner and autocratic approach to the organizing of workmen (see note 2 above).

Toryism and clear the ground for the true Socialism of equality and the new world which it will bring about. Meantime[,] you see I have no quarrel with radicalism, so long as it is regarded as the last of the old and not the first of the new order of things: when it has fulfilled its function partly by its own strength and partly in alliance with Socialism it will quietly disappear[,] not because it has been defeated, but because it has triumphed, and in consequence been transformed into Socialism.

Having said so much I must now tell you what I mean by *equality*, so that we may not begin by a misunderstanding. I have advisedly used the phrase equality *of condition*; for of course I admit that it is [no] more possible that men should be equal in capacity or desires or temperament than that they should be equal in stature or weight: but in fact if there were not this inequality in this sense I doubt if we could have equality of condition; I think in that case we should begin again to create artificial inequalities and so get back to something like our present condition. But the variety of capacity and gifts and to a certain extent of desires is just what will enable us in the long run to live without competition, that is to say[,] without forcibly taking from others to aggrandize ourselves; since if our labour were properly organized it would be easy to produce enough of all ordinary objects of desire to satisfy the needs of all; and as for extra-ordinary objects of desire[,] the innate variety of disposition would prevent competition when life was easy enough to allow each man to sacrifice something he desired little for something he desired much without forcing someone else to forego his desire.

Now I must make the assertion, which I have made elsewhere, that it is the object of true Society to prevent any one of its members from being injured by any other or by all the others; or to put it in another way[,] to satisfy the needs of each and all so long as they do not forfeit their rights by behaving in an unsocial manner.

You will find that if on consideration you do not assent to this proposition, your dissent must be founded on the crudest Toryism, that you do in fact assert the necessity of slavery in some form or other.

For consider whether it is possible to call any collection of people working together a *society* if their efforts are not directed towards the common good: you will find that this idea is obvious even in the words by which we have to designate groups of men so working together, a society, a community, a commonwealth[,] all these imply the fact of working together for the good of each and all; and I repeat[,] the opposing idea is that of a hierarchical government. An idea founded on the assumption of the existence of an arbitrary[,] irresponsible God of the universe[,] the proprietor of all things and persons, to be worshipped and not questioned: a being whose irresponsible authority is reflected in the world of men by certain other irresponsible governors whose authority is delegated to them by that supreme Slaveholder and employer of labour up in Heaven.

As to whether Society *can* satisfy people's needs,[5] it is obvious that it can do [so] according to some standard or another: the savage running wild in the woods does at least live, although he has scarcely attained the most elementary form of cooperation: as the standard of livelihood rises the difficulty of satisfying its needs by no means rises with it, on the contrary cooperation, gradually increasing[,] as it makes new objects of desires so it makes it easier to attain them: the savage can keep himself poorly; the civilized workman working under a system of cooperation so involved and elaborate that it is a standing miracle, and aided also by miraculous machinery, besides keeping himself almost as well as the savage, can also keep a queen[,] a landed aristocracy[,] a house of Lords and Commons, an army and navy, annual piratical wars against harmless people capable of being robbed, an Irish constabulary, a Parnell Commission, a great population in short of harmful or useless persons[,] a mass of corruptions[,] luxury, waste and confusion such as the world has never seen before.

In sober earnest all these artificial wants and wastes our labour produces, and no man who has ever thought about the matter at all can doubt that a man working in civilization with cooperation and by means of machinery and workshop organization can produce more than enough to keep himself in mere necessaries, or that if his labour were properly organized toward the production of useful things there would be enough wealth produced to enable everyone to live comfortably except those who were criminally idle. If this is the case it is clearly owing to some huge blunder that our present gross inequalities exist; it is owing to the fact that our Society has missed the aim of true Society, which I must now again assert to be the satisfaction of the wants of everybody in the community in return for the exercise of their faculties for the benefit of the community. Or as the formula of us Communists has it: *To* everyone according to his needs, *from* everyone according to his capacities.

Now what are the needs of a human being living in a civilized society which like ours has gone far on the road to the subjugation of external nature to the necessities and desires of man?

Perhaps you will not quarrel with me for words used for convenience rather than for accuracy, when I say that the needs of men may be

5. MS., strikeover on "s" in "needs", although this could be either an ornamentation or a deletion.

divided into two groups, necessities for the body and necessities for the mind. Do you not think once more that a true Society ought to satisfy those two groups of needs according to the measure of its aggregate wealth? The capacities[,] dispositions and desires of men are various[,] as I have already admitted; but some desires are common to all absolutely. All men must eat and be sheltered from the weather by clothes and housing: people vary indeed as to the amount and kind of food and shelter which they require[,] but they all want not only these things but they want [them] in due quantity and of due quality, or else as a matter of fact they have not got them but only makeshifts for them: here surely the rule for Society is clear: to each according to his needs:[6] if you give him less than his needs you starve him; and why, for whose benefit? For the sake of giving someone else more than he needs: is that a benefit to him? Surely not; it is a curse, as many a rich man knows. Well[,] does our society satisfy even the most elementary wants of all its members? You know very well it does not: you know very well that now while I am speaking there are many thousands of people in this country, the richest country that ever has been, who[,] to put it mildly[,] are insufficiently supplied with food[,] clothing and house-room; and if you think that this lack[,] this misery[,] this murder can be of any benefit to anyone—well I have done with you–But of course you do not and cannot think so: there are few here of the well-to-do[,] I believe sincerely[,] who would not willingly give up at once the greater part of their superfluities if they knew that by so doing they would be able to extinguish abject poverty for others, while they themselves remained well-to-do. That you cannot thus renounce your luxuries for the benefit of the miserable is really the key to the whole mystery of iniquity which I am considering, as later on I hope to be able to show you.

Well[,] this much for the bodily needs, as I have called them[,] and I repeat that these could be fully satisfied for every person living in our community if our system of the production and the distribution of wealth were put on a proper basis; and I must say in the face of all the misery and suffering I see about me[,] the satisfaction of these elementary bodily needs is the first thing that I think of: because if the whole of our population were well fed[,] clothed and housed[,] in twenty years time the face of the country would be changed, and our people would be a new race as much superior to the present one as they are to the [digger?] Indians. Nevertheless I think you will all allow that man has other absolute needs besides the merest bodily ones which a rich society is bound to satisfy or be convicted of being an imposture. These are

6. MS., needs'

broadly speaking[,] Leisure, pleasure, and Education: the attainment of these along with the attainment of the material needs does in fact mean the attainment of the life of a man, and in some proportion they are possible of attainment by even a very poor community; a community in fact which has to struggle sorely to supply its most elementary needs may[,] and generally does[,] take care that at least it shall not lack leisure[,] pleasure and education; but this it does and can do only when inequality of condition is reduced to a minimum.

In any case I assert that these three things are absolutely necessary to the life of a free man: I need not ask if the whole population has leisure[,] pleasure and education[,] as it obviously has not; but again I ask[,] if you take them away from one man, why do you do it, and for whose benefit? Cannot every person have these necessaries also? Yes[,] certainly he can if labour is so duly organized amongst us that each and all are engaged in doing some useful work for the community and their livelihood is not precarious: for if all work at things useful no one need do more than enough work; and leisure is attained; and leisure after due work *is* both in itself pleasure and is also the parent of pleasure, which is really but the consciousness of a useful and manly life. No less do leisure and pleasure between them make education possible, for what is education but the opportunity for developing our faculties pleasurably; believe me there is no education save this which is anything else than a mockery.

But if you take away these mental necessaries from people, for whose benefit do you do it? For nobody's benefit. Look round you and note the use which the rich make of the blessings which they have filched from the poor! How does it benefit them that they have robbed others of leisure when all they can do is to turn it into vacuous idleness; that they have robbed others of pleasure that in their foolish hands has turned to mere weariness and boredom; that they have robbed others of education which their folly has turned to an instructed mocking cynicism baser than the grossest ignorance. I am ashamed to live; I am afraid to die, is the true watch-word of the last development of tyrannous inequality; a glorious result truly of the modern reaction against the somewhat mechanical materialism of the last generation of democracy.

Here is the plain truth; the results of labour employed on the gifts of nature *must* be consumed in some way: there are in fact but two ways of consuming them: the one way is to *use* them, the other is to *waste* them. If you use them[,] by their means you add to life and the joys of life; if you waste them you sicken life and destroy its joys: but they can only be used by those who need them, if you hand them over to those who do not need them they must waste them, they have no choice. And please to consider what that means; it means the waste of labour, that is of men's lives. In every community there is a certain amount of potential wealth: what is that possibility of wealth? [L]abour, and raw material to exercise it on[,] i.e. men and the earth and its gifts. How can such a community thrive? Surely by using the labour and the natural gifts to produce what is necessary and desirable for men and women–and nothing else. Is it not clear that if you employ that labour and that raw material in producing what is unnecessary and undesirable you are wasting them irremediably?

You will say no doubt that the only test for this necessity and desirability is the test of the market; that people will buy what they want. In a manner [this is] true, but only true where there [is] absolute freedom, and there can be no freedom except among equals: in our present Society people are forced into conditions which force them to desire wares not desirable in themselves. If you are forced to live in a tumble-down house you are also forced to desire an undue amount of tilers['] and plumbers['] work: but, granted reasonable conditions the tilers' and plumbers' services should not thrust aside those of the baker and the butcher; it is only misfortune[,] ill-management[,] in a word[,] the compulsion of circumstances that makes them do so: and in the great case of Society which I am considering we ourselves have made the circumstances and are ourselves responsible for their continuance.

Perhaps you will think that I am flying in the face of scientific economics when I make the assertion that what the brutal man desires is not desirable although it may be marketable, that what the fool, what the rogue desires, is not desirable: but political economy[,] remember[,] does not concern itself with what ought to be, but what is, and what will result from it, granting certain conditions of life. It says[,] suppose a certain part of the population are brutes[,] fools and rogues[,] certain goods in certain proportions must be produced; but it does not say (and if it did we should not listen to it) that the workers must be condemned for ever to slave for brutes[,] fools and rogues two thirds at least of their working hours. Once more if there were no artificial rules which forced men in whole classes into a position in which the due development of their faculties is hopeless[,] this test of the market would be near enough for practical purposes. But as a matter of fact there are such artificial regulations into vacuous life, dishonesty, and brutality, and [these] therefore force them to waste the lives of men and the resources of nature in ministering to brutality[,] folly and roguery.

For in short we are in our present Society divided sharply into slaves and slaveholders; and whatever a slave may in the abstract desire, for market purposes he can only be said to desire what he has some chance of getting[,] i.e. slave-wares[,] and these slave-wares are what the workers make for themselves; if they were free they would not make them because they would not need them. E.g. a friend of mine told me he had recently visited a great chemical works somewhere in England; these works[,] most admirably and scientifically managed[,] existed for the sole purpose of making adulterants for various articles of consumption:[7] here is an industry which must surely be forced on people by the surrounding circumstances; wares so made were certainly not needed by anybody; the labour on them is pure waste[,] to say the least of it.

On the other hand all the thousand and one luxuries of the proprietary or slave-holding class are not in themselves desirable[,] however marketable they may be; they must consume the wares made for their idle lives, if they did not the whole affair would come to an[8] end, as they would not be able to employ[,] i e to feed their slaves: but these wares are not really usable: men cannot keep their self respect and be surrounded by flunkies, and make a pretense of feasting every day, and live two or three unhappy wretches of them in a palace that would comfortably house a hundred families, all this kind of thing is only waste[,] not use[,] of the results of labour. And only think how frightful the waste of it is. As we now living indeed may perhaps live to discover when some war or other earthquake of the market has upset all our calculations as to the exchange of useless articles against useful, and we find out that a warehouse full of silk velvet or kid gloves won[']t buy us a few hundred bushels of wheat, and our fleet of gorgeously appointed steam yachts have to be turned into very inefficient fishing smacks.

But now comes the worst part of it—that while the present system lasts we must go on with it. If we are determined to sustain a society based on inequality we must use the necessary instruments for doing so. Those instruments are the continued dependence of the workers on the employers, and the competitive market for forcing wares on people who either do not or should not need them. As long as the workmen are dependent they have no chance of raising their condition as a class: the non-socialist professor Cairn[e]s[9] says this and echoes what we socialists have to say on the subject: but the dependent workmen being poor are

7. In *Plenty and Want: A Social History of Diet in England from 1815 to the Present Day* (Harmondsworth: Penguin, 1968), John Burnett notes that, after the Sale of Food and Drugs Act 1875, an 1877 sampling of food throughout the country revealed that 19.2 of the random samples analyzed were adulterated (263).

8. MS., and

9. John Elliott Cairnes (1823–1875), the author of *Some Leading Principles of Political Economy* (1874). His opinion that under capitalism free competition is limited by the class system, and that the members of each class compete with one another, resembles Morris's own view.

bad customers to the workmen; they can buy nothing [except] dependent workmen's wares. Nevertheless the competitive market must not be allowed to languish on account of their poverty; what is needed to supplement this poverty? The waste of the rich: if therefore the rich leave off being luxurious, as some moralists (very naturally) bid them[,] they will by so doing throw the dependent workmen out of employment; and what can happen then? That must mean the employers ceasing to employ, failing those who are dependent upon them; and what do you think is likely to happen then? That might happen which happened[10] at the time of the break up of the Roman empire[,] a long agony during which civilization was being first overwhelmed and at last resuscitated by healthy barbarism.

And yet I don't know; where are the healthy barbarians to come from? From the democracy. I doubt it if things do not alter from what they have been; for surely all I have [been] saying tends to show that though the workers are more useful than the idlers, yet they too are corrupted and degraded by their position. No one can expect to find the virtues of free men in slaves. No[,] if the present state of Society merely breaks up without a conscious effort at transformation, the end[,] the fall of Europe[,] may be long in coming, but when it does come it will be far more terrible[,] far more confused and full of suffering than the period of the fall of Rome.

That is the reason why I am here speaking to you about equality; I do not speak to you about it as a mere abstraction, but as a thing quite practical, and indeed the *only* practical political matter, that which lies at the root of all our politics. I can see looking back to past history that whatever has been achieved in the arts and in letters, in all those delights of life which[,] rather than arbitrary coercion, are the true bond of Society, Equality has been a necessary element. The life of the ancient Greeks with its Equality of free citizens gave us that brilliant epoch of thought[,] literature and art on which the world has lived ever since. The Equality of the ancient yeomen citizens of Ancient Rome gave us the organization of the family and the state which still abides with us.[11] The Equality of the g[u]ildsmen of Mediæval Europe has given birth to our own society with all its comfort of middle-class life and its triumphs of science and the organization of labour.

You will say; but all these equalities were in existence side by side with hideous inequalities, tyranny which now for many years we have

10. MS., comma inserted here

11. Morris would have been aware of Friedrich Engels's *The Origin of the Family, Private Property and the State*, published in German in 1884 and reviewed by Eleanor Marx for *Commonweal* in April 1885.

agreed to curse though we are not so eager to curse that amongst which we ourselves live. Yes[,] that is true, but note the lesson which that points out to us. Greek citizenship was supplemented by Greek slavery, and in consequence was unstable: the egotism of people who had their rough work done for them by mere chattel-slaves overthrew the patriotism of the city which was the real religion of the Greeks.

Roman citizenship was supplemented by an iron chattel slavery worse than that of Greece; and as it developed, and the place of the yeoman cultivating his narrow patrimony with the help of his sons and his household slaves was taken by the great capitalist landowner with his stewards and gangs of most miserable slaves, so Rome staggered on towards its final corruption and after a long period during which it was as it were the mere jail of civilization[,] fell before the onset of the free tribesmen who bore with them a rougher yet a purer form of that equality which had once made Rome great.

No less the g[u]ildsmen of the M[iddle] A[ges,] though free in their work and within their city walls, had not won political freedom, and their condition of life also was lamentably unstable, and fell before the bureaucracy which was the inevitable outcome of a feudal hierarchy which had outlived the possibility of the performance of its functions.

And we in our turn who have created the Equality of the Educated Middle-classes, who have forced the so-called aristocracy of birth to recognize their position, and to receive as equals the deft man of business[,] the learned scholar, the gifted professional man, do we think that we can escape the doom of inequality, and that our society can be stable when it is founded on the misery and discontent of the slaves whom we are gradually educating? No[,] we shall go the way of the societies turned tyrannies which were before us. And if you ask me how it will come about[,] I think I can see the logical outcome of it, although the actual historical event no man can forecast.

The inequality of our days differs chiefly in two respects from that of the ancient world: In the first place it is more real and trenchant than that of the ancient and still more of the mediæval world: the ancients lived simply, the mediævals rudely, but we live delicately and luxuriously: there is far more comfort or luxury to be shared between us all than there was in times past. But this extra wealth is not shared at all amongst the lower classes; the ordinary labourer is in a worse position than a savage living in a good climate; and consequently he is an inferior animal to that savage. On the other hand as far as material advantages go the well-to-do man has advanced enormously on his forerunners[,] the citizen of the ancient world and the noble of the mediæval world. For the well-to-do man the world has progressed; for the labourer it has not. We have exaggerated inequality: that is the first difference. The second is that the inequality of the older world was arbitrary on the surface. Ours appears at first sight to be the result of natural causes. There is no legal arbitrary obstacle to a labourer raising himself into the privileged class, and this fact is the safety-valve to our society of inequality, which without it would at once explode in mere violence. But this safety valve is the creation of the ideal of commercial society which puts forward the acquirement of riches as the one aim of life; i.e. bids every man struggle to attain a position of social uselessness as the reward of labour: which means in plain terms that our Society ignores all society but that of club-law:

> That those shall take who have the power
> And those shall keep who can.[12]

Now this safety[-]valve[,] called in the ignorant[,] illogical[,] sham scientific jargon of the day, the law of the selection of the fittest applied to society,[13] is being at present attacked by the two great forces which rule the world, Necessity and Morality.[14] And I say once more that if we pay no heed to the matter and give it all up into the hands of necessity, Society will explode volcanically with such a crash as the world has not yet witnessed. Competition is the instrument by which our society is worked, not free competition of course, but competition among the privileged on the one hand and competition among the wage-slaves on the other. But competition is only another name for war, and it is of the very nature of war to exhaust itself, which competition is now doing, to the great damage of the above-mentioned safety-valve. Competition is getting so fierce among the privileged that they are reducing profits to a minimum, and as a result they are abolishing more and more the small steps to great fortunes which once gave opportunities to the workers to rise out of[,] i e to betray[,] their own class; nay to such a pitch is this getting that as you know, the last new discovery of commercialism is an

12. The epigraph to Walter Scott's *Rob Roy* (Edinburgh: Constable, 1817): "The ancient rule, the good old plan, / That those shall take who have the power / And those shall keep who can."
13. The "survival of the fittest" was a phrase first used by Herbert Spencer (1820–1903) after reading Darwin's theory of natural selection. Its proponents argued that competition among males was necessary for human progress, that only the relatively favored should be encouraged to reproduce, and, in some cases, that attempts to improve the situation of the poor were genetically counterproductive. In other contexts there was an attempt to broaden the notion of "fittest" to include skills of social feeling and cooperation, as propounded by Peter Kropotkin in *Mutual Aid: A Factor of Evolution* (1902).
14. "Necessity and Morality" is a Morrisian variant on the Hegelian/Marxist tenet that history is dominated by the dialectical forces of "necessity" and "freedom."

elaborate scheme for shutting down the safety-valve and sitting on the boiler. The rings [?] and trusts which are now being elaborated[15] form between them an event which crowns the once despised Socialist with the wreath of triumph[;] they indicate the decrepitude of Compe[ti]tion and are a forecast of its fall, and as a Socialist I wish their promoters complete and speedy success.

Now as competition among the privileged is growing sick[,][16] so also among the workers it is being discarded. Competition for employment among the workers received its first check at the hands of trades unionism, which claims that there shall be some relation between the profits of the masters and the wages of the men. That was the first step in combination; but it was a very incomplete one, because it recognized the dependence of the men on the masters, and dependents cannot dictate to their masters the terms of their slavery. But this older form of limited trades-unionism is, I firmly believe, now in process of transformation into a new unlimited combination of the workers from which everything may be hoped. I must refer you to the International Congress just ended in London[17] as a very encouraging sign of the times: for in the

15. Morris here observes a phenomenon recorded by historians. According to Derrick Murphy et al., "Although some historians have seen 1889 as a turning point for the development of British trade unionism, the strike victories of 1888–89 were of limited success. During the 1890s the employers began to fight back. In 1890 the Shipping Federation was created to help break the hold of the Dockers' Union. In 1893 the National Free Labour Association was able to provide blackleg labour to the Federation and other employers. . . . The success of the employers in the docks was matched by similar developments in the cotton and coal mining industries. If 1889–91 was a period of rapid growth for trade unions, the 1890s proved to be a period of retreat" (Derrick Murphy, Richard Staton, Patrick Walsh-Atkins, and Neil Whiskerd, *Britain 1815–1918* [London: Collins Educational, 1998], 277). Through his familiarity with his family's investments in the Devon Great Consols, Morris would also have known of the Association of Smelters, which had organized the Devonshire and Cornwall mining companies through the mid-nineteenth century to fix wages and set prices "in restraint of trade" (J. C. Goodridge, "Tamar View, the Horn of Plenty and the Devonshire Great Consolidated Copper Mining Company," *Devonshire Association for the Advancement of Science* 140 [2008]: 238).

16. competition among the privileged is growing sick: During the fall of 1888 Morris frequently mentions the rise of employer cartels in his "Notes on News" for *Commonweal*, commenting on a Salt Trust and Coal Trust on September 22, 1888 (4, no. 141, 297, in Nicholas Salmon, *Journalism: Contributions to Commonweal 1885–1890, William Morris* [Bristol: Thoemmes Press, 1996], 462–3), the Salt Trust on October 6 (4, no. 143, 314, in Salmon, 467), and again on the Coal Trust on October 27 (4, no. 146, 338, in Salmon, 472).

17. Morris refers to the International Trades Union Congress in "Notes on News" in the November 17, 1888 *Commonweal*, stating that this "took the course which might be expected: that is to say, it was a contest between the reactionary trades unionism of the ordinary English workmen and the Socialism more or less pronounced of their Continental brethren" (4, no. 149, 361, in Salmon, 483). In "Equality" Morris stresses the positive aspects of this meeting rather than his disappointment with English trades unions.

first place unless we recognize the unity of the working classes throughout the world and cast aside our old absurd jealousy of the workmen of other countries[,] all radical improvement in the position of the workers is hopeless; and in the second place at that Congress there was a general recognition of the fact of that unhappy struggle of the classes which is the inevitable result of inequality[,] and which it is our business to bring to an end.

While therefore competition among the privileged classes is being found out not to pay, among the working-classes it is giving place to combination[,] the end of which is the claim of independence for the workman with the necessary acceptance of responsibility by him. This claim[,] joined to the failure of monopolist competition[,] will bring about practical Equality amongst us; and no price is too high to pay for this blessing; but as it is clear that it must come through Commercial ruin unless we organize ourselves for the new world of production before it comes, unless we lend ourselves consciously to bring about the change, we shall have to pay a high price.

For my part[,] unless we face the situation from a moral as well as an economical position I do not think we can do this. Our wills must be on the side of the change so that we may look at it not with fear but with hope. Even apart from the danger of it, the threat of ruin in it, are we contented to meet at every turn those savages of civilization I have spoken of? Do we not understand the pleasures of fellowship[,] the joy of converse with our equals; the advantage of the give and take which ought always to be between two men good[-]tempered and useful to society, whatever the different caliber of their minds may be? If we do not[,] we are not *men* but *workmen* or *shopmen* or *businessmen*[;] the man in us is cumbered and half destroyed. Can we not change our ideal[?] Surely to have the privilege of being no longer useful is a poor reward for past usefulness. Surely the continued development of our faculties is a better and happier ideal; nor need you think that this means a life of ceaseless unrest; for in your very work itself will be rest when once you have full opportunity for the pleasurable exercise of your faculties, and your obvious rest that the wear of life compels you to take will be fertile with thought and happy contemplation: will not this make happiness for you this combination of happy work and fruitful rest? Does it not already to some of you make happiness? To all those I would especially appeal to help to spread the happiness which they themselves have gained. And to those who have it not, who have never had the chance of having it, I appeal also, and bid them claim their birthright of happy work and fruitful rest with no doubtful voice. Remember that he who allows himself to be robbed makes the robber and must accept part of the guilt of the robbery:

a rebellious slave[,] even to his master[,] is less of an evil than an obedient one.

I should like you sometimes when you are looking at an assembly of the lower, the lowest classes, such as I saw many many thousands of them at Linnell[']s[18] funeral,[19] to ask who made all these poor people what they [are] and to consider what they might have been, and not to evade the question with some tag about selection of the fittest, but to consider what you would have been if you had been born in such a condition, among such surroundings, where would be all those clevernesses[,] gifts and virtues on which you much pride yourself. Among those poor people were[,] I know[,] many and many who might not perhaps have been made into great men, but who certainly might have been made into happy and useful ones; and I tell you plainly that we are criminals because they have not been so made, and if the consequences of our crime overtakes us, who shall pity us[?]

Or do you think, as some do, that it is not ill that a hundred thousand harmless people should be boiled down on the fire of misery to make one single glorious great man? I honestly believe that there are people who are fools enough to think that. I answer plainly[,] great men are nourished on no such soup, though prigs may be; it is the happiness of the people that produces the blossom of genius. But even if it were so I should say that I would rather have a hundred thousand happy persons than one genius made up of murder. That is the word[,] my friends; the splendid position of the well-to-do classes is based on the murder of the wage-slaves, and a useless murder too since we all of us might be wealthy if we put from us the waste of inequality. This miserable

18. MS., Linnels

19. Linnell's funeral: Alfred Linnell, a passerby, was one of three persons killed on November 13, 1887, "Bloody Sunday," by police attempting to disband a demonstration in Trafalgar Square in favor of free speech and against a further Coercion Bill for Ireland (a fourth was killed in another police action the following week). At Linnell's funeral December 18, Morris's "A Death Song for Alfred Linnell" was sung:

> We asked them for a life of toilsome earning,
> They bade us bide their leisure for our bread;
> We craved to speak to tell our woeful learning;
> We come back speechless, bearing back our dead.
> *Not one, not one, nor thousands must they slay,*
> *But one and all if they would dusk the day.*

According to E. P. Thompson, "Despite the poor weather, the people—Radicals, Irish, and Socialists—turned out in their tens of thousands, in the greatest united demonstration which London had seen." "[I]t was a victory," wrote Morris, "for it was the most enormous concourse of people I ever saw; the number incalculable; crowd sympathetic and quite orderly" (493–4; Kelvin, 2.728).

condition of things will last no longer than the time when people on both sides begin to be conscious of it; and they are beginning: necessity on the one hand is as I have said turning the competition of the privileged into combination against the interests of the public, and at the same time is turning the competition of the worker into combination for the interests of labour[,] i e all honest men: and on the other hand morality[,] her eyes cleared by the advance of necessity[,] is beginning to remember the ancient legend of the first murderer, and the terrible answer to his vile sneer. Am I my brother[']s keeper?[20]

20. the terrible answer to his vile sneer: In Genesis 4:9 KJV, the Lord answers Cain's question, "Am I my brother's keeper?" with "What hast thou done? the voice of thy brother's blood crieth unto me from the ground."

Figure 14.1 Invitation to Socialist League Meeting, 1890. Courtesy of Special Collections, University of Maryland

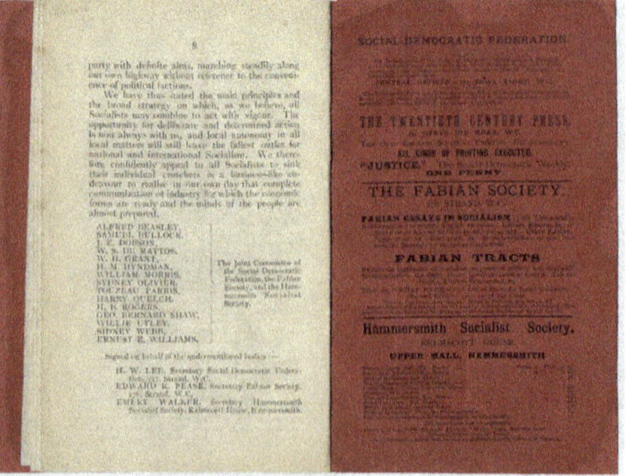

Figure 14.2 *Manifesto of English Socialists*, 1893. Signed by William Morris, G. B. Shaw, and others. Courtesy of Special Collections, University of Maryland

14

"How Shall We Live Then?" March 1889

Editor's introduction

Morris delivered this lecture five times over the course of a year, first to an audience of the Fabian Society in Bloomsbury Hall, London, March 1, 1889; then to three meetings of the Socialist League (March 3, 1889 to the Hammersmith Branch; January 22, 1890 to a meeting sponsored by the North London Branch of the League; and February 2, 1890 to the North Kensington Branch); and on February 3, 1890 to the Leicester Radical Club. The manuscript was later preserved in the collection of the International Institute for Social History in Amsterdam (hdl.handle.net/10622/ARCH 00903), and thus largely orphaned, remaining unknown until published by the Marxist scholar Paul Meier in 1971 as "An Unpublished Lecture of William Morris."[1] An alternate version with deletions and corrections marked appears on the Marxists Internet Archive.[2]

"How Shall We Live Then?" is one of Morris's more important essays, notable for its personal tone, informality, practical detail, pointed metaphors, and distinctive arguments. As a projection of some possible specifics of an egalitarian society, it forms a companion piece to his slightly earlier "The Society of the Future," first delivered in November 1887 and serialized in *Commonweal* March–April 1889, and anticipates several features of *News from Nowhere*, also serialized in *Commonweal* from January through November 1890.

Meier's introduction notes that the essay's organization was shaped by his awareness of its first audience, the London Fabian Society, whose members were gradualist socialists with whom he had long disagreed over tactics and goals. Avoiding a quarrel about strategies and immediate possibilities, Morris instead posits the qualities a society would need to possess in order to merit the label "socialist" (a position that a few years later he will come to call "communist"), emphasizing the need for an absolute, radical equality of material rewards ("For when you have satisfied the man's needs[,] what else can you do for him?"), and lists the occupations he believes such a society would require, noting that for reasons of fairness and variety these tasks must be shared.

Meier also notes that Morris was "the only Socialist of his period in England to have been the explicit exponent of the Marxist theory of the two successive stages of Socialism and Communism, the former being only a transition," a theory he suggests that Morris would have encountered through his acquaintance with Friedrich Engels and his collaborations with Ernest Belfort Bax (219–20). Indeed, such a "two-stage view" was inherent in the actual political platforms of 1880s socialists; in addition to advocating a socialist revolution, for example, the Social Democratic Federation, of which Morris was a member 1883–4, also advocated universal education and an eight-hour workday. For this 1889 Fabian audience, however, a recognition that the gradualist forms they sought could lead to something better was especially appropriate, for it validated their present efforts while suggesting that more were necessary:

> But now I must say that this decentralization with all the decent life and manly responsibility that will come of i[t], can only be got in any measure at all as a forecast of advancing equality, and can only be reached fully when we have attained to practical equality; that Equality is in fact our ideal.

Indeed, in the quite detailed account of "the Great Change" provided in chapter 17 of *News from Nowhere*, the actual transfer of power from the government to the people occurs only after a series of fairly radical reforms, including the imposition of price controls and creation of government-run factories and supply systems.[3] Nonetheless, despite his audience, Morris cannot repress some skepticism toward the gradualist faith that over time the powerful will relinquish their power: "As a transitional step I say nothing about this proceeding, as an ideal I cannot fail to see that it is incomplete and illogical."

In attempting to bridge differences with his audience, Morris also adopts a more personal tone than usual, including wry self-deprecation ("I had to set to work to read books . . . in order to become a practical Socialist—which rank I have no doubt some of you don't think I have gained yet") and a friendly allusion to the Bloomsbury Branch's most distinguished literary figure, George Bernard Shaw. He probes the psychological complexity of human desires and identity to argue that, however they may have otherwise agreed to differ, he and his audience have much in common:

> I am almost prepared to deny that there is such a thing as an individual human being: I have found out that my valuable skin

> covers say about a dozen persons, who in spite of their long alliance do occasionally astonish each other very much by their . . . profound wisdom, their extreme folly, their height of elevation, and their depth of baseness . . . . So that when I tell you of my so-called personal desires for and hopes of the future the voice is mine, but the desires and hopes are not only mine, but are those of, I really think, many others . . . .

Morris rarely commented in public on the emotions of his youth, but here he narrates his increasing unease with society's deep inequalities from boyhood onwards as an experience his audience may also share:

> [F]rom the earliest time that I can remember catching myself thinking . . . [I saw] that the greater part of people were ill-fed[,] ill-clad[,] ill-housed[,] overworked. . . . These thoughts made me uncomfortable and discouraged . . . so of course I thrust them aside as much as I could. . . . Well the time came when I found out that those unpleasant thoughts about the greater part of the population were intimately connected with the very essence of my work. . . . Now . . . I would not have said a word of all this, but that I know that what has happened to me has happened to other people though not quite in the same way.

As in many of his essays, and increasingly in his later ones, Morris speaks honestly of the difficulties that faced socialists:

> The most sanguine of us know that there will be such heaps of trouble of one kind or another before the first serious blow has got any reason at all out of the monopolists, that mere trouble is pretty certain to be part of our reward for daring to hope that society can be improved.

His tone seems more informal than usual, an effect increased by pithy expressions and metaphors: "the corporation which I call I"; "get myself into absurd messes and quarrel like a schoolboy"; "anyone who had wits enough to feed himself with a fork"; "to give up their ordinary advantages for the nourishment of this Queen Bee"; "will have to seek it of the Father of Lies"; "you must have 1200 proletarians at your back in order to produce the due element of stir and movement for those 12 treasures." Amusingly he identifies commuting as one of the evils of modern life, since we spend "a great part of [our lives] in the condition of parcels sent from one place to another."

News from Nowhere embodies Morris's reflections on the present and possible future roles of women through its representation of the characters of Annie, Philippa, and Ellen, and so it is pointed that he here points to the need for men to share in domestic labor: "Once more whoever was incapable of taking interest and a share in some parts of such [domestic arts] would have to be considered diseased; and the existence of many such diseased persons would tend to the enslavement of the weaker sex."[4] In other ways, also, "How Shall We Live Then?" anticipates motifs of *News from Nowhere*; for example, when Morris remarks that "we cannot look upon the world merely as if it were an impressionist picture, or be pleasantly satisfied with some ruinous piece of picturesque which is but the envelope for dullness and famine," he anticipates the sentiments of *News*'s Dick, who at the journey's end articulates the ethos of the new society:

> I can't look upon [nature] as if I were sitting in a theatre seeing the play going on before me, myself taking no part of it. . . . I mean that I am part of it all, and feel the pain as well as the pleasure in my own person. It is not done for me by somebody else, merely that I may eat and drink and sleep; but I myself do my share of it.

Other parallels between the society detailed in "How Shall We Live Then?" and that of *News* are found in its view of education, whereby "learning would not be gained in the technical school method, but as apprentices learn when it is anybody's business to teach them"; similarly the children of *Nowhere* attend no official school but learn a variety of skills and crafts in association with the adults who practice them. Equally central to Morris's vision of happiness is the dispersal of excessive concentrations of population: "As for the great factory districts, it seems to me that they also could disappear . . . we should come to the conclusion that it would be worth while to work a little longer in order to live in a pleasant place." This balance between town and country is attained in Nowhere after the Great Change, when, as Old Hammond explains to Guest:

> People flocked into the country villages, and, so to say, flung themselves upon the freed land like a wild beast upon his prey . . . but the invaders, like the warlike invaders of early days, yielded to the influence of their surroundings, and became country people; . . . .and it was indeed this world of the country vivified by the thought and briskness of town-bred folk which has produced that happy and leisurely but eager life of which you have had a first taste. (chap. 10, *CW*, 71–2)[5]

Likewise Morris's view in "How Shall We Live" of farm work, doubtless romanticized—"I do e.g. hope most sincerely that we shall manage not to [be] so driven for the production of food as not to allow ourselves the pleasure of getting in the harvest by hand"—finds its expression in the culminating hay harvest scenes of *Nowhere*, with their resonant overtones of organic fulfillment.

In addition, two principles advocated in "How Shall We Live Then?" are thoroughly embodied in the society of *News*—internationalism and decentralization—the latter in line with the Fabian focus on improving the services of municipal governments. In his essay Morris closely associates the two aims: "Nationalities as rival corporations would have ceased to exist and centralization in our present sense of the word would give place to Federation for definite purposes of small units of administration, so that the greatest possible number of persons might be interested in public affairs." Similarly, in *News* Hammond patiently explains to an at first skeptical Guest that past national wars have been merely quarrels between merchants over profits, and that Nowhereans now arrange their affairs through local gatherings or councils in which everyone may vote.[6] Since a consistent theme in Morris's thought is his distrust of "the degrading game of politics" ("What We Have to Look For," 1895, no. 21), that is, "parliamentarianism," it is interesting to see his alternate proposal for radical participatory democracy within a denationalized regional community.

A seldom acknowledged aspect of Morris's thought is his recurrent ambivalence about revolution, or at least about the means which an ill-guided revolution might take. Conceived as a largely nonviolent "Great Change," true revolution is an object of Morris's intense desire and hope, but when seen as a social cataclysm prompted by grievances, he fears that evil may in turn beget evil. In the present society, in which a parasitic few oppress the laboring many, one must live "in one or the other of two opposed camps of enemies, which we feel certain must one day fall upon each other ruining many a hope and many a quiet life in the process."

Still, the notion of change brings hope, for the "change from Monopoly to Freedom" will "make a new world for us, and will be far greater than any change that has yet taken place in the world." He accordingly rejects the notion that history is predetermined, for though Social Darwinists may predict decadence (we "have been told that . . . the logical sequence of the development of man's ingenuity will involve the gradual loss of his bodily faculties"), he appeals to his audience to resist such an ethical and sensory loss, "to do our best to remain men, even if in the struggle we become barbarians." What others may view as regression will contain the seeds of new birth, and Morris reminds his audience that under socialism, the "way we shall live then" would also resurrect the spirit of energy, simplicity, and egalitarianism that he ascribes to their "barbarian" forebears.

Notes

1. Paul Meier, "An Unpublished Lecture of William Morris," *International Review of Social History* 16 (1971): 217–40.
2. www.marxists.org/archive/morris/works/1889/how.htm
3. For a discussion of the two-stage hypothesis as embodied in *News from Nowhere*, see Owen Holland, "Morris and Marxist Theory," in *The Routledge Companion to William Morris*, ed. Florence S. Boos (New York: Routledge, 2020), 465–85.
4. For a discussion of Morris's views on women in relationship to Victorian socialist feminism, see Florence S. Boos, "Morris, Gender, and the Woman Question," in *The Routledge Companion to William Morris*, 58–86.
5. For the context of Morris's views on the balance of town and country, see Florence S. Boos, "News from Nowhere and Garden Cities: Morris's Utopia and Nineteenth-Century Town-Design,"" *Journal of Pre-Raphaelite Studies* 7, n. s. (Fall 1998): 4–-27.
6. For a discussion of Morris's interest in local councils in the context of the late nineteenth-century movement toward municipal government, see Michael Martel, "Romancing the Folk Mote: William Morris, the Socialist League, and Local Direct Democracy," *Useful and Beautiful* 1 (2018): 7–17.

What I have to say to you relates to matters that may be discussed amongst Socialists, mingled or not with their declared opponents, but cannot be altogether a matter of controversy amongst Socialists. I want to give you my personal view of the Promised Land of Socialism, with the hope of eliciting an account of the views of several of this audience; and I do not think the hour and a half so employed ought to be waste[d] time if we tell each other honestly and as clearly as we can what our ideals are, if we have any, or confess to our having none if that is the case. We are engaged in a common adventure for the present, the abolition of the individual ownership or monopoly of the means of production; the attainment of that immediate end will bring about such a prodigious and overwhelming change in society that those of us with a grain of imagination in them cannot help speculating as to how we shall live then: and the expression of the results of our speculations, of our hopes and fears will certainly give our friends and associates some insight into our characters, and temperaments, will make us know each other better; and that in turn will save much friction and loss of time, will in short make us better friends; to come sometimes from out of the hedge of party formulas and show each other our real desires and hopes ought to be something of a safeguard against the danger of pedantry which besets the intellectual side of the Socialist movement and the danger of machine politics which begets its practical and work-a-day side.

It is true that some of you may have anticipated my paper must necessarily under these conditions take a personal character and be somewhat egoistical. I do not offer an apology for that but I may offer an explanation. I have had some 55 years['] experience, I won't say of the world, but of myself; the result of which is that I am almost prepared to deny that there is such a thing as an individual human being: I have found out that my valuable skin covers say about a dozen persons, who in spite of their long alliance do occasionally astonish each other very much by their strange and unaccountable vagaries; by their profound wisdom, their extreme folly, their height of elevation, and their depth of baseness. So that though it may be possible that the complex animal who has now the pleasure of addressing you has not his double in the world, (though I decline to admit that also) it is impossible but that the men inside my skin who go to make up that complexity are but types of many others in the world, and probably even some of those are in this room at present. So that when I tell you of my so-called personal desires for and hopes of the future the voice is mine, but the desires and hopes are not only mine, but are those of, I really think, many others, and you as practical men, as I hope you are, cannot afford to disregard them.

Now I will ask what draws men into the Socialist ranks at this stage of the movement? I mean of course what makes them *genuine* socialists. I do not think it can be any hope of personal advancement; such hopes would be much too wild to be entertained by anyone who had wits enough to feed himself with a fork; for the most sanguine of us know that there will be such heaps of trouble of one kind or another before the first serious blow has got any reason at all out of the monopolists, that mere trouble is pretty certain to be part of our reward for daring to hope that society can be improved. Is it intellectual conviction deduced from the study of philosophy or from that of politics or economics in the abstract? I suppose that there are many people who think that this has been the means of their conversion; but on reflection they will surely find that this was only its second stage: the first stage must have been the observation that there is a great deal of suffering in the world that might be done away with. That is I think the first thing that draws a man toward the socialists, whether he feels the suffering in his own person, and becomes conscious of a wrong done to him by what we now call society; a wrong which is not accidental but can be fixed on a certain set of events; or whether he himself is unconsciously one of those who do the wrong, but has the ordinary good-natured wish which anyone[1] who is not a mere ill-conditioned blackguard will have, to see all men as happy as they can be.

Now in this respect the corporation which I call I is not at all peculiar: from the earliest time that I can remember catching myself thinking (an operation which all healthy and happy young people avoid as

1. MS., any one

much as possible) the thought was from time to time thrust upon me that the greater part of people were ill-fed[,] ill-clad[,] ill-housed[,] overworked, and as a consequence nasty and disagreeable. These thoughts made me uncomfortable and discouraged and took the flavour out of my amusements and my work (there was not much distinction between the two) so of course I thrust them aside as much as I could. Yet I was conscious that I was acting a shabby part in doing so, for I was not such a fool as not to see clearly that these degraded persons that came between me and my pleasure had not degraded themselves, and that consequently there was something or other which a strong and honest man could attack. In all this there was nothing peculiar: you would say that a natural sense of the injustice of our Society was growing up in me, as it has surely in many others of my class and condition.

But in what followed I was perhaps peculiar. I was indifferent honest, I was by no means strong; for I must tell you that one of those persons inside my skin is the peaceablest, and another the laziest of all persons — in that again I am not peculiar. So it is probable that that rising sense of injustice would have been damped down till I had grown old enough and tough enough to bear it easily: but something happened to me that prevented that. Though my work was pretty much my amusement, yet it was serious enough to me: I daresay some of you would be astonished if you could understand the pleasure it has given me; but at last it gave me perhaps as keen a pain. It was a big job that I had taken in hand; no less than the regeneration of popular art as it used to be called. I was not fully conscious how big a job it was for a long time; though I was fully conscious of the complete degradation of the arts in general.

Well the time came when I found out that those unpleasant thoughts about the greater part of the population were intimately connected with the very essence of my work, and at last that I had undertaken a job quite impossible under the present conditions of life. You may well think that I did not come to that conclusion all at once; in fact I tried to wriggle out of it for a long time till at last I was pinned, and there was the greater part gone of my pleasure in my work: which indeed was a serious matter for me, since I cared for it so much and so heartily. Well I cannot tell you whether it was about this time that I first heard of socialism as a definite movement, but I know that I had come to these conclusions a good deal through reading John Ruskin's works, and that I focussed so to say his views on the matter of my work and my rising sense of injustice, probably more than he intended,[2] and that the result of all that was that I was

2. In *Unto This Last* (1860) and other later writings such as *Fors Clavigera* (1871), John Ruskin (1819–1900) espoused a form of hierarchical socialism in which distribution would be managed by paternalist "masters."

quite ready for Socialism when I came across it in a definite form, as a political party with distinct aims for a revolution in society. My position then[,] which I am sure has been and is the position of many others, was profound discontent with the whole of modern life, a feeling of the deadly sickness of the world of civilization, which if I could have found no outlet for it would have resulted in sheer pessimism, as I think it often does.

That outlet as you know I found, and I was hindered from coming to the conclusion that the art to which I had devoted myself was a mere idle folly, that I must go on with partly because I knew no other way of earning my livelihood, partly because I must have something more or less pleasant to do on some terms or other. My Socialism began where that of some others ended, with an intense desire for complete equality of condition for all men; for I saw and am still seeing that without that equality, whatever else the human race might gain it would at all events have to relinquish art and imaginative literature, and that to my temperament did and does imply the real death of mankind—the second death. Of course with the longing for equality went the perception of the necessity for the abolition of private property; so that I became a Communist before I knew anything about the history of Socialism or its immediate aims. And I had to set to work to read books decidedly distasteful to me, and to do work which I thought myself quite unfit for, and[3] get myself into absurd messes and to quarrel like a schoolboy with people I liked in order to become a practical Socialist—which rank I have no doubt some of you don't think I have gained yet. But all that did not matter because I had once again fitted a hope to my work and could take more than all the old pleasure in it; my bitterness disappeared and—in short I was born again.

Now I repeat that I would not have said a word of all this, but that I know that what has happened to me has happened to other people though not quite in the same way. We, (I will say we now) are alive in the world and not in the least pessimists, but we are most sorely discontented with all things as they are, except the bare elements of life, and the hope for the future which we have somehow or other got into our heads.

We are alive and we can take the keenest pleasure in all those elements of life which the barbarian has in full measure but which civilization has largely deprived us of: the sensuous pleasures of life is the technical word for them; or shall I say the innocent sensuous pleasures? E.g. we keep our eyes in our heads and take in impressions through them; whereas civilization bids us put them in our pockets, and is mostly obeyed. And it must be said that there is reason in this since Civilization is such a foul slut, and wherever she can manage it gives us nothing pleasant to look at, so that we are driven to have to thank her, like my friend Shaw, for

3. MS., in

the wreaths of steam which float from the funnel of a locomotive;[4] at all events when they are not defiled by the smoke of the coal which the Company has no business to burn but which it generally does.

However from such impressions, we take our pleasure as well as our pain; but there is so much pain in them that on the whole they do but add to our discontent; for as things go whatever we see almost has some share of that sickness in it, and we long and long to better these things: we cannot look upon the world merely as if it were an impressionist picture, or be pleasantly satisfied with some ruinous piece of picturesque which is but the envelope for dullness and famine. But there again comes in our hope: for if we live in the present on such crumbs as we can pick up amidst the general waste and ruin, we live generously enough in the future; and one part of our pleasure in the ordinary life of today, the animal life I mean and the goings on in field and flood and sky and the rest of it, comes from the fact that we see in them the elements of which the life of the future will be built up far more than of the thought of today,[5] its literature, its so-called art, its so-called science.

In sum our hope is so generous that whatever there is which is distinctive of the sickness of civilization will disappear before our regained freedom: what we aim at, the purpose for which we want to use the instrument of the transition, which is what some understand by the word Socialism[,] is no mere rectification of our present society, but the construction of a new society in which we shall adore what we used to burn, and burn what we used to adore.

How shall we live then? Whatever system of production and exchange we may come to, however justly we may arrange the relations of men to one another we shall not be happy unless we live like good animals, unless we enjoy the exercise of the ordinary functions of life: eating sleeping loving walking running swimming riding sailing[,] we must be free to enjoy all these exercises of the body without any sense of shame; without any suspicion that our mental powers are so remarkable and godlike that we are rather above such common things. Also I will say in the teeth of the very natural repulsion to bodily labour that our present conditions force upon us we must be strong and healthy enough to enjoy bodily labour, a good stout wrestle with the forces of nature which will make us feel our power. I do e.g. hope most sincerely that we shall manage not to [be] so driven for the production of food as not to allow ourselves the pleasure of getting in the harvest by hand, or, a great many of us, raising our own potherbs, of course with due

4. A possible humorous reference to George Bernard Shaw's 1887 *An Unsocial Socialist*, a novel in which the characters debate the importance of steam power.

5. MS., to day

knowledge and skill. (Also I should hope that we should not find it necessary to shorten our lives as we do now by spending a great part of them in the condition of parcels sent from one place to another. I hold that going from one place to another [on the *surface* of the earth] may be made by no means a waste of time if we don't do it as parcels, especially if one can be happy enough not to think on the road. Indeed even when I am sent on as a parcel I do my best to get my eyes out of the brown paper sometimes.)

Now all this would mean that our views on the subject of education would have to change somewhat: the equipment for life on the new terms would not and could not be the same as on the old: it is true that the capacities for dealing properly with the bodily side of life would grow to be a kind of habit: still I suppose except among the South-sea islands and such like places men have to learn swimming, and except in the Pampas,[6] riding. And I cannot easily conceive a lad knowing how to dig and plough and reap and sow without learning, although that learning would not be gained in the technical school method, but as apprentices learn when it is anybody's business to teach them. Besides I think most people would want to learn two or three of the elementary crafts whether they intended to practice them as a main occupation or not, smithying[,] carpentering (not cabinet-making) and mason's or bricklayers work, I am thinking about, and that would need definite instruction, lasting some time. Various minor arts like cooking and sewing would be learned very easily by children when they are very young; and they again would mean little more than the gaining of an easily acquired habit. This[7] education set on foot[,] we should have first a great body of out-door occupations, dealing with work necessary to be done, agreeable to healthy and strong persons, and capable of being done excellently, that is of developing real pleasure in the doing, some of them perhaps to be done by individual work but most by means of cooperative [effort]; and all the parts of them in which excellence was not possible to be much developed could be done with little effort, almost as a habit: Add to these occupations a few of what for shortness I would call *indoor* work, and you will have also (an important addition) what we call art, in which I would include beside the plastic and decorative arts imaginative and measured literature and the pursual of knowledge for its own sake, and these I think will give[8] you most of the occupations *necessary* for a happy community: and for the life of me I cannot see why we should bother ourselves with occupations which are *un*necessary.

6. Vast grazing lands in central Argentina.
7. MS., The
8. MS., will give You will have

Let me try if I cannot arrange these occupations in groups a little more systematically[,] adding some few perhaps doubtful ones.

1st. The open air arts; (I had better call them arts at once, because to my mind all work which is done by a man in the course of the due exercise of his faculties and therefore pleasurably is an art.)

Agriculture and its kindred arts; gardening, fishing, butchering, ship and boat-sailing. Driving carts, trains, omnibuses and the like (a cross division here with distribution). The habits of swimming, good walking and running, and riding would be mixed up with these, and also an habitual knowledge of the ways and manners of non-human beasts.

Now as we shall live then I declare that anybody who did not take a pleasurable interest in some part of these arts and was not capable of working in them, would have to be considered as a diseased person—something less than a man, a burden on the community. If there were many such persons it would tend to the creation of a class of slaves, people doing the rougher work of the world only.[9]

2nd. The domestic arts: The arrangement of a house in all its details, marketing, cleaning, cooking[,] baking and so on; sewing with its necessary concomitant of embroidery and so forth. Once more whoever was incapable of taking interest and a share in some parts of such work would have to be considered diseased; and the existence of many such diseased persons would tend to the enslavement of the weaker sex.

3rd. The building arts: Masons, bricklayers, smiths, carpenters and the like and also the planners of buildings, engineers, and so forth. Of these arts what we now call *art*, i.e. decoration, appeals to the intellect through the eyesight, would form a necessary and integral part; therefore possibilities of excellence would here run high, and consequently only those would take a part in them who had some faculty for creation, as I believe most *free* men have; but doubtless there would be some lacking this faculty or possessing but little of it, who would prefer the rougher arts above mentioned; but as they would be doing their share of the necessary work and with pleasure, they would not be injuring any one by disease. For the rest it is clear that these arts are cooperative in the highest degree, no one necessary person's work being really separable from the whole mass of it.

4th. The workshop arts[,] weaving, pottery, dyeing, printing (textiles and book[s])[,] etc. Into most of these also art would enter and much

9. This sentence from Paul Meier's transcription is not observable in the IIHS manuscript as it appears online.

the same thing is to be said of these as of the last group. In cases where art could not be an integral part of the work[,] if it turned out to be necessary work it would have to be done by machines as nearly automatic as possible; but I should consider it a matter of course that those who tended such machines would do other work at once more pleasurable and more responsible; and whatever drudgery of this sort we could do without we should drop at once.

5th. The disagreeable arts. I will assume though I am not sure that it is so, that there would be such indispensable arts, and then proceed to divide them into:

a. The rough disagreeable arts.
b. The smooth disagreeable arts.

By the first I mean such occupations as mining, skindressing, scavengering, and so on. By the second I mean—well quill-driving of the less amusing kind, clerk[']s work, official sauntering and so on. Of both these groups I say the same thing; as above, machines where possible, and the workers to have other occupation: but also strict enquiry as to whether they are necessary; and if not, abolition.

6th. The arts concerning the distribution of goods; shipping of goods[,] shopkeeping and market-managing of all kinds. I daresay it will be possible to find people to like such work and let them do their best at it; but I am sure that they will find digging and reaping, or even perhaps leather-dressing restful to them: and such rest they ought to have.

7th. The fine or intellectual arts: i.e. picture painting, sculpture, and the lesser or reproductive fine arts, such as engraving. Also imaginative literature, and the study of history and nature. Some of these in which a good deal of actual manual labour is necessary might be followed exclusively; the others certainly not; and even in the first, or manual fine arts, rougher manual work would be desirable, unless in cases, if there be any such, (which again I doubt) where extreme finesse of hand is so necessary that it would not do to roughen the hand by harder labour. In any case I feel sure that it would not do for men to be absorbed entirely in such arts. It would tend to disease, to anti-social habits which would burden the community with a new set of idlers, and (if the others were such fools) in the long run to a new set of masters.

Before I go further I ought to say that though I don't doubt that a due amount of organization and direction would be required in the diverse branches of occupation[,] I am very far from thinking that it would be either necessary or desirable to prescribe to people what occupation they should follow; I am assuming only that opportunity will be afforded for people to do what they can do well, and that the work as far as the relations of men go will be voluntary; nature will be the compeller, in a sense the only enemy: yet an enemy that asks to be vanquished.

Now having given you my ideal as to the occupations of men in a free community, I have but to add my views as to the possibility of its being realized sometime or other: this is what might be called the political side of the question.

Decentralization and equality of condition are the necessary concomitants of my ideal of occupation: but I am not clear as to whether they should be looked on as the cause or the effect of the state of things foreshadowed by that ideal. But I think, that granted the second, the first will tend to come naturally. Difficult or if you please impossible, as it may be to conceive of such a change as will come of the abolition of the great central power of modern times[,] the world-market as we know it with all the ingenious and intricate system which profit hunting Commerce has built up about it, because of it and by means of it, yet after all it must develop into something else, and that something else can hardly be a perfecting of its perfection, but rather its contradiction, which is the conscious mutual exchange of services between equals. Nay if things now going on can be fairly understood by us who live amongst them[,] are there not signs of the coming change already visible to us? The Republic one and indivisible of 100 years ago is passing through a phase of bourgeois corruption and the only hope of France is that it will come out at the other end a Federation of Free Communes.[10] The Unity of Germany has been accomplished but a few years; yet here are we waiting for but one event, quite certain to happen sooner or later, the defeat of the German Army, to break it up again into a federation with socialism as its aim. And at home the principle of Federation is conceded in the matter of Ireland by all but the stupidest of the reactionaries; while the Tories themselves, driven on I believe by a blind fate, have given us in the County Councils the germs of revolutionary local opposition to centralised reaction.

Thus then before centralization is quite complete even, the change in the direction of its opposite seems to have begun, and once begun will surely go on till the necessary practical decentralization has been arrived at. That decentralization seems to me looking out from our present condition to be necessary in order to give all men a share in the responsibility of the administration of things which I hope will take the place of the government of persons: you will understand that I admit the possible necessity of a certain amount of mechanical centralization,

10. The Paris Commune 1871 had been an exemplar of radical localized democracy.

such as a central administration of railways in such and such a geographical district, which after all would not be centralization but the direct outcome of Federation.

I also admit that the form which the decentralization or Federation will take is bound to be a matter of experiment and growth: what the unit of administration is to be, what the groups of Federation are to be; whether or no there will be any cross Federation as e.g. Craft-guilds[11] and Cooperative Societies going side by side with the geographical division of wards, communes, and the like—all this is a matter for speculation, and I don't pretend to prophecy about it.

I may say however in parenthesis that my temperament leads me to believe that we shall be able to get rid of one outward and visible sign of commercial and official centralization; our great cities, and closely packed manufacturing districts.

As for the first, the great centres like London, Paris and Berlin, they are surely the outcome of the desperate struggle for life which competition under monopoly engenders on both sides [between] the monopolizers and their slaves. They are counting houses of commerce; the jobbing houses of officialism; the lairs for the beasts of prey big and little that prey upon the follies and necessities of a huge mass of people who have no time to find out what they want; and must have all their wares from the bread they eat down to a new novel or a play at the theatre forced upon them like a sharper forces a card: they are the sweating dens to which starvation drives up the starvelings of the rest of the country, so that they may eat a morsel of bread while they cast the dice desperately for that twenty millionth part of a chance to escape from the proletariat which is the yard of earth between modern society and the volcano it stands upon. I do not deny lastly that they are the camps to which the soldiers of revolution must flock if they are impelled to do anything to further their hope before they die.

But granted the change of conditions which we all hope for, of what use will be these monstrous aggregations of confusion? No camp will be needed, for militant socialism will be over: no man will hurry up to be sweated, for his decent livelihood will be assured to him. People will have leisure to think what they want and resources to have the reality of it; so that the parasites above-mentioned[12] will not exist, for there will be no carrion for them to feed on. Official jobbery will be dead; and profit-hunting will need no counting house or will have to seek it of the Father of Lies to whom it will have returned. There will be no use for this monstrous muck heap in which we swelter to-day. But in case

11. MS., gilds
12. MS., above mentioned

anyone should be inclined to regret what I have heard called the stir and movement of a big city, I will just say two things: first, that in those post-monopoly days, when at the very least there will be more of an approach to equality, there will relatively to men [now] be more intelligent and thoughtful men: we do everything wastefully now; so if you want a dozen highly cultivated and thoughtful persons you must have 12000 proletarians at their back in order to produce the due element of stir and movement for those 12 treasures: as a practical man I cannot approve of the plan. Again you must remember that the dullness and monotony of country-life at present, of which many complain (but not I) is the wrong side of the hubbub of town life; since the town sucks the blood of the country in all things: in post-monopolist[13] days I hope, as I have already said[,] that we should reform this.

As for the great factory districts, it seems to me that they also could disappear:[14] granted that it is possible to produce goods cheaper when you have labour and material gathered together in the closest space possible; I am sure that in post-monopolist days when the "sword of cheapness" is no longer necessary as an offensive weapon against other nations, we should come to the conclusion that we might buy cheapness too dear, that hell was altogether too high a price for it[,] and that it would be worthwhile to work a little longer in order to live in a pleasant place. Of course we must all admit that these last centres are centres of profit-bearing manufacture and huckstering, but of nothing else—save dirt. But now I must say that this decentralization with all the decent life and manly responsibility that will come of it[,] can only be got in any measure at all as a forecast of advancing equality, and can only be reached fully when we have attained to practical equality; that Equality is in fact our ideal.

Indeed I can only explain the fact that some socialists do not put this before them steadily by supposing that their eager pursuit of the means have somewhat blinded them to the end.

Surely there are but two theories of society; slavery on the one side; equality on the other. The first theory supposes that use must be made of the natural diversity of capacities in men to cultivate a class of superior beings, who are to live on the lack, the unhappiness in short, of the inferior class. The second theory says when you have got hold of the strongest and cultivated him into a stronger, you can by no means be sure that you have got hold of the best; he is only the strongest under certain artificial conditions which you yourselves have made; and you can never tell how many far better than he you have oppressed into nothingness by your masterful folly: satisfy a man's needs, and what

13. MS. postmonopolist
14. MS., dissappear

there is in him will come out of him for your benefit and his, and you can't get out of him more than he can do.

That is what communism says, and the only way I can see to traverse it is to say, I intend to have that man for my property, and all that he does is mine, whether it is little or much, only if he doesn't make more than enough to keep himself, he will be of no use to me and I will kill him as I would an old worn out horse. Any stage between these two theories I can only understand on the grounds that the antislavery man is bribing the slave owner to keep him quiet until he becomes too weak to resist having his slave taken from him and made free. As a transitional step I say nothing about this proceeding, as an ideal I cannot fail to see that it is incomplete and illogical. No other ideal on this matter of livelihood in a post-monopolist community appears to me worth considering than the satisfaction of each man's needs in return for the exercise of his faculties for the benefit of each and all; to me this seems the only rational society. And this means practical equality. For when you have satisfied the man's needs[,] what else can you do for him?

You will say doubtless what are his needs? Well of course in such an audience I need not deal with the usual quibbles of people who think that we socialists have never thought of any of the difficulties which arise in anyone[']s mind when such questions are started. But those of you, if there are any here, who think that one useful person should have (compulsorily) a different scale of livelihood than another useful person[,] I want to put a point or two to you that have occurred to me (and very likely to you also).

1st. Given a poor community which could satisfy the average elementary needs of each man for food and shelter, but could do nothing else; would you think it right (or ideal let us say) for the so called more useful man to have anything extra for his excellence? If he did so, wouldn't he starve the others, since they would then have so much less of necessaries as he had so much more? wouldn't they be his slaves then, whatever the nature of the compulsion was which he used? for they clearly wouldn't do it without compulsion. Well carry it further and suppose the community wealthier[,] even quite wealthy. There is still surely a due standard of livelihood, of leisure and pleasure which can be upheld for the citizens in general, why should they be deprived against their will of what they can and what they desire, of what they can have if they are not compelled to give it up. Either they have more than they need, in which case they had better not produce so much, or they have only as much as they need, and in that case if they are compelled to give up some of that, they are not free men.

Again I seem to see another draw-back to this new class of ability: I assume that all men's needs will be satisfied according to the measure of the general wealth: well the superior man will have his needs satisfied; and once again what more can you do for him than satisfy his genuine needs. It seems to me that even at the best what he would do with his extra pay would be to surround himself with extra luxuries, and that the result of that again would be the creation of a new parasitical and servile class which could not fail to be an injury to the Community. In short I can think of no special reward that you can give to a man of special gifts but licence to do harm to his fellow citizens, which is a strange reward for having been of special service to them. Lastly remember that when a man has special gifts the exercise of those special gifts are a pleasure to him which he will not forego if he can help it; therefore while on the one hand it is unjust and unsocial to compel the citizens to give up their ordinary advantages for the nourishment of this Queen Bee, so on the other hand nature does not compel them. Whatever is in him he will give freely if you leave him free and provide him with due opportunity for the exercise of his faculties. That is if you let him have due unprecarious livelihood with leisure and pleasure according to his desires, and the free use of raw material and the instruments of labour.

Other things I can see of the way in which we should live then, which you can also see I suppose: the splendour of public and the quiet dignity of private life, and in general all the real pleasures which would come of our being wealthy and no longer rich; of all which pleasures the greatest *now* seems to be a negative one, the relief of no longer living in one or the other of two opposed camps of enemies, which we feel certain must one day fall upon each other ruining many a hope and many a quiet life in the process; while in the meantime ethics are in hopeless confusion and pessimism increases in days when we find it hard to understand what vices and virtues mean since the collective crime of class wrong is so overshadowing and overwhelming. Of course I do not pretend to have given anything like an inclusive account in detail of what our ideal of the new world is; since I feel I have been somewhat disjointed in what I have said, I will very briefly run over the points concerning which I may differ with some here.

First the change from Monopoly to Freedom, when it is complete, will make a new world for us, and will be far greater than any change that has yet taken place in the world.

2nd. We may have in appearance to give up a great deal of what we have been used to call material progress, in order that we may be freer[,] happier and more completely equal.

3rd. This would be compensated (a) by our taking pleasurable interest in all the details of life, and (b) by our regaining the pleasure of the eyesight, much of which we have already lost, and more of which we are losing every day.

4th. Instead of toiling for some blind force, a mixture of necessity and nightmare, we should be conscious of doing useful work for our neighbours who were doing the like for us. As a result there would be no waste of labour, as useless occupations would be got rid of speedily.

5th. Work thus obviously useful, and also adapted to the capacity of the worker would mostly be a pleasant exercise of the faculties; necessary work that would otherwise be drudgery would be done by machinery or in short spells: no one being condemned to work at unpleasant work all his life.

6th. As no incentive to work would be needed save its obvious necessity and the pleasure involved in it; and as the division of labour into more or less worthy work deserving different standards of livelihood would create fresh classes, enslave the ordinary man, and give rise to parasitical groups, there would be no differentiation of the "reward of labour". (This last phrase I consider a misleading one, involving a begging of the question). I am aware that this implies the abolition of private property.

7th. Nationalities as rival corporations would have ceased to exist and centralization in our present sense of the word would give place to Federation for definite purposes of small units of administration, so that the greatest possible number of persons might be interested in public affairs.

Some such ideal as this I believe will be realized, and I earnestly hope it will be. We have been told that the logical sequence of the development of man's ingenuity will involve the gradual loss of his bodily faculties,[15] and this seems probable: but the logical sequence of events is sometimes interrupted and turned aside by the historical; and my hope is, that now we know, or have been told that we have been evolved from unintelligent germs (or whatever the word is) we shall consciously resist the reversal of the process, which to some seems inevitable, and do our best to remain men, even if in the struggle we become barbarians; which latter fate I must confess would not seem to me a very dreadful one.

15. In 1880 zoologist Edwin Ray Lankester (1847–1929) had published *Degeneration: A Chapter in Darwinism*, which argued that humans and other species could degenerate physically when inhabiting less demanding environments, a concept later embodied in H. G. Wells's *The Time Machine* (1895). A progressive, rationalist, and friend of Karl Marx, Lankester advocated social and educational reform to avoid human degeneration.

Figure 15.1 William Morris, 1884. Courtesy of the Victoria and Albert Museum

15

Address on English Socialism on Behalf of the Socialist League: Report to the First Congress of the Second International, Paris, 1889

Editor's introduction

Along with Frank Kitz, William Morris was chosen as one of two Socialist League delegates to the International Socialist Workers Congress held in Paris, July 14–19, 1889. British delegates also attended from several Socialist League branches, the Bloomsbury Socialist Society, the Electoral Labour Association, the Scottish Labour Association, the Ayrshire Miners Union, and other socialist and workingmen's groups. The conference was to be important in socialist history as the first meeting of the Second International, which continued to sponsor successive conferences until 1920.

Morris was accorded a titularly prominent role as a member of the Standing Committee in charge of setting the Congress's agenda. However, as Graham Seaman has shown in "William Morris and the Beginnings of the Second International,"[1] despite promises to the contrary, the other members of the Standing Committee blocked voting on Morris's major proposal, a motion to permit a pluralism of tactics in support of broad social transformation. The marginalized motion read in part:

> That it is absolutely necessary that the basis of society should be changed by the abolition of all class distinctions; and further, that the emancipation of labour and of mankind can only come out of the workers, acting as an organized class, that shall take hold of the political power in order to expropriate the Capitalist Class and socialize the means of production of wealth. (Seaman, 22)

Seaman summarizes his view of the outcome of Morris's involvement as follows:

> Examining the material now available it is clear that Morris was an active participant in the congress, with his own sharply differentiated politics, who intervened at numerous points. That he largely failed to achieve the results he wanted was partly due to the weakness of his political base at home, partly to the ability of the Marxist group to organize a consistent and united front against opposition of any kind, and partly to the inability of Morris and his potential collaborators in other parties to recognize the need for their own common front. The trajectory of the 2nd International was set by this failure. (Seaman, 1)

It might be argued that the respective European socialist parties were already so divided that the exclusions enforced by the Second International merely intensified existing tendencies. Nonetheless the rejection of Morris's line of thought reified a focus on national parliaments as the preferred means of reform to the exclusion of other approaches.

Morris's presence at the conference was later described by another British delegate, Edward Carpenter:

> Then there is William Morris, bluff and vigorous, in blue shirt and navy blue cloth, volcanic with suppressed irritation—his poet instincts wounded by every sight and sound of our cheap-jack civilisation. When he gets up to speak he fairly fights with his words, grows red and furious, and throws them out in lumps—lava-hot—his stormy grey hair nodding in asseveration.[2]

The Congress was further characterized by quarrels over who should be certified as delegates, the ejection of three anarchist delegates who objected to voting on motions before time was allotted for discussion, and the failure to distribute the texts of motions to delegates before the vote. All these maneuvers perhaps reinforced Morris's longstanding distaste, as expressed in 1895 in "What We Have to Look For," at "the failure and disappointment and stupidity and causeless quarrels, and in short all the miseries that go to make up the degrading game of politics."

In any case Morris himself felt that the Congress had been poorly designed for serious debate; as he reported in the July 27, 1889 *Commonweal*, "such gatherings are not favourable for the dispatch of business, and their real use is as demonstrations, and . . . it would be better to organize them as such." The social aspects of the gathering had nonetheless been pleasant, as he noted in his report: "we all met out of debate with great friendliness and goodwill. A great many of the delegates have continually found themselves sitting at the same table for the meal after the session in the pleasantest and most fraternal manner in the cheaper restaurants round about the place of meeting."

The attempt at internationalism was important in itself, as reports were translated from the speaker's original language into French, German, and English as the case required. Morris's speech was accordingly translated, though imperfectly and incompletely, into both French and German by Paul Lafargue and Wilhelm Liebknecht respectively. Morris's manuscript is preserved in torn and incomplete form in the Jules Guesde collection of the International Institute of Social History in Amsterdam (Inv. nr. 611_4, ARCH00496), and Seaman has reconstructed the content of many of the missing statements from the French and German translations for his 2019 version of Morris's report, to which the text reproduced here is indebted.[3]

The text as it remains exhibits Morris's care and skill in designing his remarks to present the contributions of English socialism as favorably as possible, avoid factionalism and overt criticism of other groups and parties, and address current debates about the means and goals of socialist parties. First, although he wished to present an accurate, balanced, and yet hopeful account of English socialism, such an effort faced factual constraints. Despite Britain's stature as a major industrial and imperial power, its socialists were few, divided, and at the time lacking national electoral victories; in the report's final metaphor, socialism's "blossom and fruit are long delayed." Morris avoids digressive details and is careful not to denigrate other socialist organizations or blame his fellow socialists for divisiveness—though he notes in passing that "the organization of the party is bad"—and he refrains from drawing undue attention to Socialist League achievements in favor of promoting English socialism in general.

These choices enable him to argue for his basic convictions: the need to spread the message of socialism in its broadest sense; for workers to seek economic autonomy rather than acceding to dependent status within a class hierarchy; for the prioritization of more winnable elections at the local level; for the rejection of imperialism and domination in all their forms; and, most important, the need to conceive of socialism as the demand for a higher quality of life: "the ideal of a beautiful and complete life, which will be realized along with Socialism, but which cannot be realized as long as the workers are in a dependent position." Trust in one's bourgeois masters to act in good faith or grant reforms is fatal; any particular grudging concession will merely lead to greater oppressions elsewhere. Moreover, a naïve faith in an inevitable, determined progress of history can lead to rigidity and blindness in responding to actual circumstances: "it is dangerous for us to rest our hope on economic fatalism, on the continued and steadily growing decrepitude of the bourgeois power." And finally, without the cultural and imaginative benefits of life such as art, literature, and the release of creativity within work itself, he warns that the socialist movement can neither convey nor embody its full message of equality and spiritual emancipation.

Morris therefore frames his report as an assessment of popular attitudes rather than party organization or achievements. He observes that the response to socialism has greatly improved even in the past six years: "Socialism is becoming a hope to workers and a fear to the middle classes." It has even become fashionable for middle-class persons to affirm their attachment to a "socialism" denuded of its basic feature of class war; immiserated agricultural workers are ready to revolt (Morris may be thinking of the National Agricultural Labourers' Union, founded in 1872 by Joseph Arch); and workers who had once heckled open-air socialist speakers now seem "generally in accord with what our speakers say." This change is, of course, partly due to the effectiveness of the Socialist League policy of presenting socialism in all possible venues—through lectures, newspapers, pamphlets, and books as well as street preaching.

Morris notes other positive signs as well. For example, a commendable feature of the English working classes is the absence of perceived competition between rural and urban laborers. He also notes with pride the strong sentiment in favor of Irish independence—perhaps a slight inconsistency since Home Rule could be viewed as yet another "palliative." The parliamentary quarrels over Home Rule have brought the added benefit of breaking up the previous clear Liberal/Tory opposition, leaving workers disillusioned with their former Liberal allies. Even the lack of electoral victories at the national level is repackaged as a blessing: "in our opinion (I speak here for the Socialist League) the workers will only waste their time and energies by trying to get their members into parliament, so that, I repeat we are far from regretting the extreme feebleness of the attempts that have been made in its direction." Instead Morris notes the possibilities opened by newly established county councils, which exhibit "a tendency towards Socialism which [was] certainly never looked for by the Tory Party who brought in the bill which created them [the 1888 Local Government Act] . . . ." His optimism fails him altogether, however, on the prospect of parliamentary reform; a national parliament is merely a cabal to defend the rights of property, and local councils are needed to "form a rallying point for the people against the Centralizing bureaucratic Parliament which in England is sure to be reactionary up to its last days." In aggregate the positive signs he brings forward are mostly prospective, however: a rural–urban working-class socialist alliance does not exist, Ireland is not yet independent, and the county councils have only recently been established.

In addition Morris warns against some misleading assumptions, including a credulous faith that industrial technology will by itself bring prosperity and progress. Without radical equality, any economic gains will be absorbed by those already positioned to demand them, leaving "that residuum which John Bright spoke of with such complacency." Here Morris refers to the Liberal politician's claim, during debates on the 1867 Voting Rights Act, that "there is a small class which it would be much better for themselves if they were not enfranchised because they have no independence whatever . . . the residuum . . . of almost hopeless poverty and dependence."[4] Full distribution of resources is needed—equality—not mechanization per se.

Without naming the more dogmatic Marxist groups that hold such views, he also warns against another form of oversimplification, the reliance on economic theory as a prophetic "science":

> Surely it is dangerous for us to rest our hope on economic fatalism, on the continued and steadily growing decrepitude of the bourgeois power; the *logical* development of production and society no doubt leads us to look for this; but then the *historical* development may interrupt it and give a new lease of life to the middle-class supremacy. England may yet go through a period of exuberant commercial prosperity . . . .

In the context of an international conference, Morris is proud that, in his view, the English socialists are not nationalistic or imperialist: "they condemn jingoism and chauvinism to the utmost extent; . . . to them the British Empire is not a thing to love or to be proud of, but a disgrace and a nuisance, as a domination compounded of fraud[,] injustice and violence . . . ." These were, of course, Morris's own convictions and those of the Socialist League, though perhaps less consistently those of the Social Democratic Federation. His chief claims for English socialism, however, are on the basis of its intellectual and aesthetic contributions, both actual and potential. He tactfully introduces its Ruskinian/Morrisian ideals of pleasurable and creative labor—"art made by the people and for the people as a joy to the maker and the user" ("The Beauty of Life," 1880)—through the lens of a European forerunner, Charles Fourier (1772–1837), who had advocated variety and choice for workers, since "in order to attain happiness, it is necessary to introduce it into the labours which engage the greater part of our lives."[5] Though Morris does not elaborate on the Arts and Crafts movement in particular nor his own major role in its widespread influence, the close association between late nineteenth-century British socialist and anarchist ideas and the revival of respect for handmade crafts, regional culture, the decorative and domestic arts, and landscape and town design corroborates his view that "the English movement . . . has done some good service to the Socialist cause if only by putting before the workers the idea of a beautiful and complete life."

Morris further observes the permeation of socialist views into literature; again he refrains from alluding to his own socialist writings (*The Pilgrims of Hope*, *A Dream of John Ball*, *The Tables Turned*, and shorter poems, fables, and dialogues) and his editorship of *Commonweal*, but he notes with satisfaction the emergence of an extensive British socialist-influenced literature in periodicals such as *Justice* and *Commonweal*, political pamphlets and leaflets, and even contemporary novels. As he notes wryly, "it may be mentioned as a sign of the times that it has become a sort of fashion amongst our modern novel writers to *spice* their books, so to say, with a certain amount of Socialism."[6] Indeed, a list of writers from the several wings of the socialist movement of the period including the Fabians would be quite lengthy; and even among Socialist League members, volumes of poetry were authored by Fred Henderson, J. L. Joynes, Tom Maguire, Edward Carpenter, Andreas Scheu, and Morris himself.[7]

Some of the previous Congress speakers had been prolix, and Morris records that as a result the last day's speakers were asked to confine their remarks to ten minutes, "which I tried to do—and I think I kept within twenty" (*Commonweal*, July 27, 1889). Within these constraints Morris offers pithy insights on a range of issues important to the future of European socialism. He recuperates the failures of the English movement—disorganization, electoral stalemate, and the failure to arouse workers generally—into partial virtues, for these limitations have focused socialist attention elsewhere. English socialists as a whole have instead contributed their theoretical insights to preaching the full meaning of socialism beyond quantifiable goals, "putting before the workers the ideal of a beautiful and complete life."

In the context of its contentious political environment, Morris's contribution to the Paris Congress was arguably an admirable distillation of important correctives. His warnings against excessive faith in the liberatory role of technology to lessen social inequities were prescient, as well as his caution against dogmatic assumptions about a unique, inevitable, and necessary path for social transformation. In its praise of idealism, egalitarianism, and the cultural and emotional aspects of any thoroughgoing socialist revolution, his speech identified a needed counterbalance to the antidemocratic forces inherent in the imposition of "party discipline." Moreover, the issues raised in Morris's responses to the debates among European socialists of his time continue to reverberate in political divisions down to the present, as different subgroups of reformers repeatedly negotiate the respective merits and obstacles to "movement" politics and the impasses endemic to more conventional electoralism.

Notes

1. Unpublished MS., 2020.
2. Edward Carpenter, *Sketches from Life in Town and Country* (London: Allen and Son, 1908).
3. www.marxists.org/archive/morris/works/1889/congress/congress.htm
4. P. J. Walker, *Town, City, and Nation: England, 1850–1914* (Oxford: Oxford University Press, 1983), 109.
5. "Attractive Labor," *Selections from the Works of Fourier*, ed. Charles Gide, trans. Julia Franklin (London: Swan Sonnenschein, 1901).
6. Although several British novels with a "spice" of socialism or anarchism were published in the 1890s, fewer had appeared before Morris's Paris speech of 1889; these would have included Margaret Harkness's *A City Girl* (1880), Oscar Wilde's play *Vera; or, The Nihilists* (1883), and G. B. Shaw's *An Unsocial Socialist* (1884).
7. See Florence S. Boos, "The Socialist League," *BRANCH*, http://www.branchcollective.org/?ps_articles=florence-boos-the-socialist-league-founded-30-december-1884.

. . . Morris a delegate of the . . .

. . . report to give nor will I dwell . . . position of the working-classes in . . . will only say something about the state [of the] socialist movement there.[1]

1. British emigration rates were high, peaking in the 1880s, and among other such efforts, a Women's Emigration Society had been formed in 1880 and several charities sent children to the new world. John Ruskin's Guild of St. George attempted to support local crafts, especially in rural Cumberland. Bismark's government in Germany had introduced unemployment insurance in 1889, the first such program in the world, though Britain did not enact a similar scheme until the National Insurance Act of 1911.

[Just six years ago] there was no socialism in England except [some remnants] of the old Chartist movement and of the [Owenite] so-called Communism blended with a reflexion from continental Socialism. The Middle classes triumphant in [their] commercial successes were ignorant of any discontent [exis]ting amidst the workers; Liberalism or Whiggery was everywhere victorious and seemed to many the furthest political goal to be aimed at.

All this is changed; Socialism is becoming a hope to the workers and a fear to the middle classes. Although indeed the latter will talk about it as much as you please, and not a few of them are prepared to declare themselves Socialists if they are not compelled to recognize the great fact of the class-war. A sort of Conscience is waking up amongst these persons, stimulated by the extreme hideousness and obviousness of poverty in England. All kinds of schemes for the amelioration of the lot of the workman are set on foot or patronized by them: state-aided emigration, to get rid of the inconveniently many; feeble attempts at turning back the hands of the clock by establishing peasant proprietorship, or village industries; insurance of workers à la Bismark; the slightly improved form of joint-stockery called cooperation, many things down to mere philanthropy and the preachment of Malthusianism and thrift are tried in turn by those bourgeois beginning to be conscious of the volcano on which their society rests.

It is true that in England up till quite lately the movement has been mainly an intellectual one though it has not been confined to those whom we call [the educated] classes, but has attracted the [thinking members of all] classes, specially I admit, those who may [be called an] intellectual proletariat. But this is now changing, [The depres] sion in trade of the last decade has made the work [of impressing the] idea of socialism on those who have most [to gain] from the change much easier, and the class struggle [in England] as in other countries is becoming clear to the [workers] and they are learning to connect the misery and [degra]dation of their lives with their position as part of the machinery of capitalistic production; they are feeling the impetus towards a change in the basis of society, and there are not wanting signs that this is the case.

E.g. from the first we have used street corner preaching as a means of propaganda, and it forms a large part of our work. A few years ago, say even 3 or 4 years ago there were [even pla]ces where our speakers were liable to interruption from working men themselves; whereas today the audiences listen quietly, and are generally in accord with what our speakers say. Again in the London radical clubs it is almost impossible to get opposition to our speakers, where once they were scarcely listened to. And I say confidently that whatever political life there is in those clubs (I am not thinking of the wire-pulling at election times) rests with those of their members who are declared socialists.

The main difficulty that meets us is the apathy of the men of the more consolidated trades; England having been the first country that fell completely under the influence of the Great Industries. The men in the great manufacturing towns have been drilled for generations into dependency; into looking upon themselves as a part of the factory, and the employer as a paymaster with whom they may wrangle at times, but who is necessary to their livelihood.

On the other hand we have none of the opposition in feeling between the peasant and the town workman which exists in France and some other Continental Countries . . . . face to face as they are with . . . most brutal form of compulsion; [the farm labourers, who are] the merest slaves of the farmers are by no [means conservative themselves] though they may be forced to vote Conservative [but remain] of inflammable material.[2]

[The evolution of] party politics has favoured our Cause [in particular the] Irish affair (in which by the way all socialists at home have taken part heartily) has quite broken [up] the old parties; so that the workers, who once trusted [blind]ly in parliament for dealing with their grievances, [are] losing confidence in it; and that the more as the new political group of the Socialist Radicals, (who may be said to be represented in the press by the London 'Star')[3] has little power in Parliament, and will have none when the Irish question is solved or shelved. This we think good because in our opinion (I speak here for the Socialist League) the workers will only waste their time and energies by trying to get their members into parliament, so that, I repeat we are far from regretting the extreme feebleness of the attempts that have been made in this direction.

On the other hand the County Councils (newly established) in the great towns and especially in London are showing signs of life and a tendency towards Socialism which were certainly never looked for by

2. The National Agricultural Workers Union (NAWU), founded by Joseph Arch (1826–1919) in 1872, attracted a wide rural membership. It championed a nine and a half hour day (the norm was twelve hours) with a minimum pay of sixteen shillings a week, and in 1878 opposed Britain's entrance into a proposed Anglo-Russian war which presumably would recruit impoverished laborers. When a farm employers' organization was formed to encourage the firing of unionized agricultural workers, the NAWU encouraged its members to continue secret union membership.

3. The London *Star*, founded by Radical MP and Irish nationalist Thomas Power O'Connor (1848–1929) in 1888, had disappointed Morris by its generally reactionary stances. See Holland, 212, n. 8.

the Tory Party who brought in the bill which created them; and it may be well hoped that they will form a rallying point for the people against the centralizing bureaucratic Parliament which in England is sure to be reactionary up to its last days. For indeed what is that parliament but a committee defending on behalf of the Capitalists those sacred rights of property which it is the business of Socialists to attack. This Committee is not sorry to have amongst it members of the exploited classes;[4] partly because their presence there acts as a safety valve for discontent, and partly [because its consequence] is that the workers [see how far the bourgeoisie] can carry their hypocrisy [given free rein].

[On the] whole the condition of the party in England [is encou]raging because the growth of public opinion is steady [even though] the organisation of the party is bad, and when . . . opinion has reached a certain point organization will [form] itself from out of it in such a way as to be irresistible.

Meantime I should mention that in Australia Socialism [is] spreading in a hopeful way and that there it is not [as might] be expected [a] reflection of American Socialism, but is of the English type.

For the rest the very fact that modern Socialism in England began on the intellectual side gives us special hope that its growth will be steady, and that the idealism which still forms so large a part of the movement there is a necessary portion of the general movement. Surely it is dangerous for us to rest our hope on economic fatalism, on the continued and steadily growing decrepitude of the bourgeois power; the *logical* development of production and society no doubt leads us to look for this; but then the *historical* development may interrupt it and give a new lease of life to the middle-class supremacy. England may yet go through a period of exuberant commercial prosperity, although it may well be that, owing to the new impetus that it will give to the invention and improvement of machinery, the workers will not profit by it in the same proportion as they did by the last one. But in any case shall we cease to be Socialists because we are better fed slaves, more prosperous parasites than of old? No, the intellectual movement will save us from that, and will not allow us to be content with anything short of the realization of our ideal. We have learned that what we have to claim is complete equality of condition for all men—and that this claim can be

4. The Socialist League Committee representatives to the Congress were William Morris and Frank Kitz, a worker employed at Morris's Merton Abbey. Individual branches also sent representatives, many of whom were workers, including watchmaker H. B. Tarleton from the Hammersmith Branch, tailor Charles Mowbray from Norwich, Louisa Tochatti, a singer and wife of merchant tailor James Tochatti from Yarmouth, and engineer and labor leader Tom Mann from the Labour Electoral Association.

made good, and we cannot unlearn the lesson once learned. We know also that however the lot of some of the [workers may be improved] there will remain that residuum [which] John Bright spoke of with such complacency,[5] until [we have obtained] complete freedom of work and life; and that [even those workers who think] themselves well off will still [be] dependent on the will of their masters, or at bottom the masters of their masters, the World market.

I believe that the claim which the English workers are learning to make will not stop short of complete independence and the responsibility which goes with it, in place of a slave's rations and ignorant irresponsibility with it. But there is a danger of our going through a period of blunders and disappointment by drifting into a more political party to be played on by political adventurers and dealers in votes for their own purposes, which party may think it necessary to feed the workers' hopes by agitating for a few palliative measures, which the Bourgeois Parliament will only grant them if it believes that they will be ineffective, and which even if effective would leave the great mass of the workers free to vote—and to starve.

Two things I wish to claim on behalf of the English Socialists; first that however they may differ in opinion they are (with a very few exceptions) thoroughly *inter*national. They condemn jingoism and chauvinism to the utmost extent; for them the word "nation" expresses a mere geographical idea; and they have so completely thrown off the old prejudices of the Englishman that to them the British Empire is not a thing to love or to be proud of, but a disgrace and a nuisance, as a domination compounded of fraud injustice and violence to be scorned by all honest men wherever possible.

Again in virtue probably of their idealism English Socialists have undertaken the guardianship of the aesthetic side of Socialism, and have become the inheritors (unconsciously for the most part) of the ideas of Charles [Fourier, proclaiming the necessity] of making labour pleasant to [the workman,] though of course they have not [adopted Fourier's elaborate] Utopian schemes for carrying out this [aim, which we] cannot think unimportant. We [Socialists are] one and all striving to get all men to share in [the fruits] of labour and the success of our

5. During the debates preceding the Second Reform Bill of 1867, Radical Liberal politician and former anti–Corn Law leader John Bright (1811–89) advocated for the enfranchisement of workingmen as opposed to the "small class which it would be much better for themselves if they were not enfranchised, because they have no independence whatsoever. . . . I call this class the residuum, which there is in almost every constituency, of almost hopeless poverty and dependence" (*Hansard Parliamentary Debates*, March 26, 1867).

endeavours will be an enormous blessing for the [world.] But shall we be content when we have reached that point? Surely not, the next step of men who have [gained] so much power that they are no longer tormented by the fear of starvation will be to abolish the pain [of lab]our, so that we may [be] as happy as we should be. I claim therefore that the English movement in spite of all its shortcomings has done some good service to the Socialist cause if only by putting before the workers the ideal of a beautiful and complete life, which will be realized along with Socialism, but which cannot be realized as long as the workers are in a dependent position.

It remains to be said that a great deal of literature has come out of the Socialist movement in England. Besides several labour sheets we have two weekly papers, *Justice* representing the Social Democratic Federation, and *Commonweal* representing the Socialist League: we also publish many pamphlets and leaflets (specimens of which are laid on the table) and larger works on Socialism are not lacking. Besides which it may be mentioned as a sign of the times that it has become a sort of fashion amongst our modern novel writers to *spice* their books, so to say, with a certain amount of Socialism.[6]

Socialism then is in England a plant healthy and of steady growth though it is young and its blossom and fruit are long delayed.

6. Morris may have had in mind such works as *An Unsocial Socialist* (1883) by George Bernard Shaw.

Part III

Some Tempered Warnings: A Final Phase, 1891–1896

Nonviolent Revolution, 1891–1894

Figure 16.1 Hammersmith Branch of the Socialist League, ca. 1888. Courtesy of the Victoria and Albert Museum

16

"Socialism Up to Date," 1891

Editor's introduction

Morris apparently delivered this talk only once, on October 4, 1891, to the Ancoats Recreation Committee at New Islington Hall in Ancoats, Manchester, at the invitation of his friend Charles Rowley (1839–1933). May Morris transcribed somewhat less than a third of this brief talk in *William Morris: Artist, Writer, Socialist* (MM2, 341–2), and the manuscript has since remained in British Library Add. MS. 45,334 (ff. 3–12, pencil).

Rowley was originally a Mancunian frame-maker, carver, and gilder, and later a Liberal Party city councilor and head of the Manchester Municipal School of Art. A tireless campaigner for improved public services, Rowley was the *spiritus rector* of the Ancoats Brotherhood, which he founded to provide recreational and cultural opportunities for the working-class citizens of his district. An admirer of Ruskin's writings and ardent lover of the arts, Rowley invited Morris to speak his Brotherhood no fewer than thirteen times between 1884 and 1894. He devoted a chapter in his 1911 memoir *Forty Years of Work Without Wages* to Morris, and when May Morris solicited his memories of her father, he responded:

> [Morris] came many times and we always had a noble audience of 900 or more mostly hard headed men. At our little social tea after these lectures we had the usual heckling. The same old questions were asked and the questioners were invariably floored good humouredly. . . . To many labouring men the gospel was welcome though I cannot say that Morris's wonderful and beautiful literary way of putting the case was clear to those not full of books or learning. The language, the method of production did not strike on their box. They required something far more obvious. But all the same that glowing personality has left an impression on all of us which nothing can efface. To some few of us it is all an abiding memory and a constant inspiration. [British Library Add. MS. 45,347, ff. 93–9]

Well aware of the need to speak in basic terms to his audience, Morris designed "Socialism Up to Date" as a straightforward, jargon-free presentation of socialist values and the outlines of a communal society. He may also have written it under time-pressure, for its last paragraph consists of a series of notes for delivery. He begins with an appeal to the immediate conditions of his hearers:

> [y]ou here present . . . mostly live by doing work of some kind; but . . . I may . . . assume that that work does not procure for you a life as full of opportunities for enjoyment, for the satisfaction of your manly and reasonable desires as the work of many others.

Moreover he observes that they have been admonished to accept their situation, a state of contentment only possible for the more fortunate:

> [T]he blessings of irresponsible poverty have been sung and said in verse and prose for many a year by rich men and their dependents, who if the said blessings had been showered on their own heads would have thought them little better than a violent death.

He amusingly parodies moralistic advice of the sort that his auditors will likely recognize:

> [workers] should have fewer children; they should spend less money on such pleasures . . . as may be within their reach; . . . they should emigrate to other countries, where (until they largely take this advice) there is more room for them; they should be more industrious; they should spend more time in educating themselves; they should furnish their houses with taste and refinement—and so on and so forth.

Morris also warns his hearers against cooptation, for mild improvements in the lives of a few—the creation of a "worker aristocracy"—will leave the present inequities unremedied:

> . . . some men of the richer classes looking at the growing discontent have an indistinct hope that it may be possible to create another class below the present middle-class, but above the mere hewers of wood and drawers of water, which shall serve as a rampart for the present society with its inequalities and injustices.

At this point he launches into an exposition of the causes of poverty: the most useful members of society are unable to protect themselves from the inroads of privilege—"the absolute ownership of a portion of the raw material and implements through which all labour can be made fruitful." Here Morris notes that manual laborers such as farmers, fishermen, and coalminers are not worse paid than craftsmen or jewelers (an example also used by Ruskin) because of their lack of skill, "but because of the accident of their not being able to combine so effectively as the town workman: because in short they are ill-armed and ill organized parts of the army which is carrying on the labour war."

A truly "beneficent and all embracing" socialist order, by contrast, would abolish the monopoly of property. Such monopolies had once been the prerogative of feudal lords, who had at least occasionally been reminded of their duties by the clergy. In nineteenth-century Britain, however,

> anyone who by skill[,] cunning or chance has acquired more wealth than he can spend on his personal necessities or pleasures [has] the absolute ownership of a portion of the raw material and implements through which all labour can be made fruitful.

Such monopolists have always built the "funeral pyre" of the societies in which they live, for they extract from workers far more value than the latter could ever "earn" (a concise description of Marxist "surplus value"). Since "competition for daily bread is the weapon which hunger has forged for the use of the privileged," the producers of wealth will remain poor unless they can find others to exploit in their turn.

Yet this is not all, for in a tragic irony inherent in the nature of extreme inequality, the excess value extracted from workers' labor is largely wasted—it "goes no good road." That which does not go into the monopolists' bank accounts is expended on "advertisements, clerks, ticket-collectors, lawyers, and the like," or is squandered in excess: "the wealth so [hoarded or] spent adds nothing to the refinement[,] to the dignity or the pleasure of life: that it is simply got rid of, because it must be got rid of somehow. Just as if it were burned on a great bonfire." Only "a band of robbers breeding artificial famine in the richest countries of the world" would attempt to justify such waste, for

> what is more precious . . . than the skill and force of the workman, the craftsman . . . . Yet this precious heritage our society of Commercial privilege wastes light[-]heartedly as if it were a part of the nature of things to make the worst of that which is the best . . . the token and reward of the world[']s progress, the hope of its future.

Morris then reiterates his basic conviction that equality of condition must be the principal aim of the new society. All persons desire the same basic circumstances: "ample and agreeable food, good clothes and good house-room, and in addition good education and innocent and uninjurious leisure." Among the preconditions of such a communal society would be imperatives shared by all socialists worthy of the name, that all resources would be owned in common, and all contributing members would benefit equally:

> the land[, for example,] the public confidence[, and] the means of transit must be unbuyable by private persons . . . . everybody would have his due share of obvious necessaries and other matters he by himself or in combination with others could procure . . . by his own extra labour.

By unpurchaseable "public confidence" Morris presumably meant that all would respect an uncoerced popular suffrage, and that no one could suborn the public trust for individual gain.

At this point "Socialism Up to Date" becomes a series of notes for Morris's peroration. Pointedly he does not enjoin his audience to any particular actions—including affiliation with a specific socialist party—but to the general project of joining together in their own cooperative ventures, by "tak[ing] their own business in hand[,] including all responsibilities." As we have seen in "How Shall We Live Then?" he suggests the possibility of electoral resistance; his hearers should support whenever possible "the new labor party-agitation" in the region and beyond. Morris may be here referring to recent calls for the formation of a new working-class identified political party; although the Independent Labour Party was not founded until 1893, two years after Morris's lecture, candidates running to the left of the Liberal Party were first elected to Parliament in 1892 (Keir Hardie, John Burns, and Havelock Wilson). Although to the end of his life Morris himself adhered to the idea of "one socialist party," conceived as an umbrella of many factions of the labor movement that itself would remain committed to the principles of full socialism, in suggesting that his worker-audience should join the activities of the local labor movements at hand, Morris's advice here is both realistic and practical.

I want to begin at the beginning, and in order to do so will ask you first if you think anything needs setting right in our modern society. You[,] living in one of the great centres of industry[,] will hardly answer the question in the negative. Let us look at it. You here present I may assume mostly live by doing work of some kind; but whatever that work may be, I may further assume that that work does not procure for you a life as full of opportunities for enjoyment, for the satisfaction of your manly and reasonable desires as the work of many others, which is not more useful than yours. Still stranger[,] the idleness of many procures them more enjoyment[,] more refinement of life[,] than your work procures for you. In short men's share of the necessities[,] comforts, luxuries of life is by no means proportioned to the share they have had in producing these good things. Those who produce nothing are often, nay most commonly, in a position of ease and comfort, while those who produce at least something most commonly lead a hard life; a life in which refinement is almost impossible, and in [which] self[-]respect can only be attained by the exercise of moral qualities above the average, by resolute and painful struggle; so that those who are not above the average must be said to live a life of degradation; and I must add that these, the average producers of wealth, are immensely more numerous than those who live pleasant and dignified lives either because of the accident of their birth or because of their special and peculiar merits.

Now this is not a state of things to be contented with, unless it can be proved to be irremediable. It is impossible for those who suffer by it to be contented, unless their natural human feelings are blunted by habit and ignorance. It is impossible again for those who look on this suffering to be contented with it, if it can be remedied[,] unless *their* feelings are blunted by habit or ignorance, or unless the fear of the consequence of a remedy makes them consciously unjust and tyrannical.

Indeed[,] though it is necessary for my argument to state all this, it is not necessary for me to dwell on it, because it is practically admitted nowadays, and remedies for it are being sought for, both by those who suffer from it, and those whose position inflicts that suffering. Nowadays it would take a bold man (and a stupid one) to assert that it is right and convenient that the average producers of wealth, the great mass of the workers[,] should live a painful and degraded life. Even the owners of mere chattel-slaves have in recent times thought it necessary to cover their monstrous position by asserting that those slaves lived lives that were happy if not dignified; and the blessings of irresponsible poverty have been sung and said in verse and prose for many a year by rich men and their dependents, who if the said blessings had been showered on their own heads would have thought them little better than a violent death. And as you well know[,] while I speak 'the amelioration of the lot of the working classes' is[,] or seems to be[,] if we may trust words[,] the main object of our statesmen, clergy and employers of labour.—If it were only the main object of the working classes themselves there would be nothing lacking to the equipment of modern society for building its own funeral pyre which shall transform it into a society of useful and happy persons unoppressed by any wrongs, and without opportunities for wronging others.

The evils then[1] (or some of them) of our present society are recognized by all classes of men more or less; surely less by the workers themselves than by any other class or they would soon cease to exist as I have just hinted. Are any remedies for these evils proposed? Are there any commonly received suggestions for putting the useful part of society in the way of gaining the due heritage of useful men, of which they are at present deprived? There are many such suggestions afloat, put forward with more or less sincerity; of which the following may serve as types; working-men should have fewer children; they should spend less money on such pleasures (poor enough I admit) as may be within their reach; they should join a certain class of joint-stock commercial undertakings technically known as cooperative societies; they should emigrate to other countries, where (until they largely take this advice) there is more room for them; they should be more industrious; they should spend more time in educating themselves; they should furnish their houses with taste and refinement–and so on and so forth.

Now of these things some are good if they could be done; some most workmen do already do perforce; and some they by no means ought to do—But good[,] bad or indifferent these kind[s] of proposed remedies have one quality in common; they all mean the expenditure of energy, none can be done without expense, and the expense of them is to fall upon the working men themselves; from their poverty is this new wealth to be drawn; from their toilsome days is the new leisure to be won; from their sordid lives is to spring up the refinement of a new world; from their degradation is to come heroism unsurpassed before—Vain dreams! the crimes of civilization cannot be atoned for on such easy terms. Or to put it in another way[,] all the remedies of this kind assume that the useful classes who are oppressed by our system of society shall still go on serving the useless classes who oppress them. They shall be thrifty, self-restrained, refined, educated[,] in a word[,] heroic,—and slaves—a preposterous contradiction. Indeed I fear that when I said these remedies are put forward with any sincerity, that sincerity is not of the hard-headed ones; they surely must know that a serious decrease in the population of this country would ruin our Capitalists whose profits are essentially the result of there being more workers than work: that a laboring man *must* be niggardly, which with a very significant misuse of the word, they call thrifty. That if the mass of working men got any benefit from so called cooperation[,] competition for employment would cause a fall in wages about proportionate to that benefit; that taste and refinement in our surroundings cost time[,] labour and thought, i.e. wealth. These things they cannot fail to know if they think of them, and knowing them must be well aware[,] if they do

1. MS., comma

not shirk the question[,] that these remedies for poverty are futile when they are not impossible for poor men to seek.

Yet I suppose some men of the richer classes looking at the growing discontent have an indistinct hope that it may be possible to create another class below the present middle-class, but above the mere hewers of wood and drawers of water, which shall serve as a rampart for the present society with its inequalities and injustices–and that this may be done mainly at the expense of the producing classes. I hope that it will turn out to be impossible; but there is a danger that it may succeed; but also if it does it will be no remedy for the vices of our society, since the burden of oppression will only be shifted, not destroyed.

Well[,] these would be remedies[2] the proposal of which is but mere evasion, consciously so on the part of some, unconsciously so on the part of more, are not real remedies; is there any other remedy proposed[?] Yes[,] a change in the basis of society which would make all people useful and all people wealthy. This change has been called[,] and well called[,] Socialism, because those who wish to bring it about understand that it means the organization of mankind into a true society[,] beneficent and all-embracing; whereas at present the greater part and more useful part are as we have seen outcasts from Society. Now as to the change in the basis; the present society is based on privilege, while true Society will be based on equality. These two words are soon said, but need some explanation of the sense in which they are used – Privilege[,] which once meant the hereditary right to a certain position of trust in the state involving certain duties to the citizens, has[,] since the complete abolition of the feudal system and the establishment of the commercial system of capitalist and wage earner on its ruins[,] a changed and extended meaning. It now means the legal right of anyone who by skill[,] cunning or chance has acquired more wealth than he can spend on his personal necessities or pleasures to the absolute ownership of a portion of the raw material and implements through which all labour can be made fruitful. And this privilege, unlike that of the feudal period which it has superseded, involves the privileged person in no responsibility whatever.

This modern privilege will be seen when looked into [to] confer on the rich classes the monopoly of the means of the production of wealth. Now no man, be he never so deft a workman[,] can produce anything without raw material, and the instruments of labour[,] or to particularize, without the land, rendered fertile by countless generations of labour, and the machinery and means of transit, the use of which our elaborate civilization forces upon us. Therefore the man whose sole wealth consists in the power of labour inherent in his own body, including the brain, and is therefore forced to labour in order to live, must

2. MS., which the proposal of which

get leave from the privileged class to use some part of the aforesaid raw material and instruments of labour before he can strike a single stroke for his livelihood. This leave the privileged will grant him, but only on certain conditions, to wit that he shall produce in his labour more than is necessary for his own livelihood; and that all that he produces beyond his livelihood, shall be the tribute of privilege. Thus the producer must always be poor: [i]t is true that he has full leave to prosper if he can[,] but not as a mere producer; in order to prosper he must become part and lot in the privilege which has oppressed him, and in some degree or other oppress others by the same process.

Now note carefully about this bargain between monopoly and labour[,] 1st[,] that it is a forcible one, that it is a bargain between irresponsible riches on one side and hunger on the other. 2nd[,] That the weight of its burden on the shoulders of the worker has been somewhat lightened in the course of time in some cases by the fact that the standard of livelihood does sometimes imply something more than mere bare necessaries. But 3rd[,] note further that this higher standard has been attained by the strenuous struggles of the useful classes against the useless; and yet 4th[,] in spite of that struggle the standard of livelihood is generally lowest in these groups of labourers who are engaged in the usefullest labour; as e.g. the field labourer and the fisherman are forced to put up with a lower standard than the cabinet-maker and the jeweler.[3] And I wish you to note this that you may the better appreciate the iron tyranny of the machine of modern commerce, which turns aside for no sense of cruel unfairness; is shaken by no monstrosity of unfitness –

Those above[-]mentioned groups are not worse paid than the producers of luxuries because they are less useful; for they are more useful; not because they are less skilled; for they are *not*—but because of the accident of their not being able to combine so effectively as the town workman: because in short they are ill-armed and ill[-]organized parts of the army which is carrying on the labour war. Let the workmen remedy this shame and see to [it] that men like these and the coal miners of these islands shall be the best organized and not the worst of the labour-army. I hope etc. Meantime note again that the reason why the workers cannot at once compel better terms from the privileged, is that since they are so poor and must at once work if they are not to become mere paupers, and since their number is so great, they *compete* for the labour[4] offered them on the terms above-stated, and this competition for daily bread, enables the privileged who employ them to carry on the commercial war with each other which is almost their only occupation. This is an explanation of what I said just now of the bargain

3. MS., jeweller
4. MS., on the offered

being between hunger and riches; this competition for daily bread is the weapon which hunger has forged for the use of the privileged.

Another point I wish especially to dwell on before I sum up the case of the socialists against the society of [the] privileged. I want you to be quite clear about this, that the extra wealth which the privileged wring from the unprivileged classes goes no good road: the capital, or wealth used for the reproduction of wealth in their hands is not only used also for the continued thralldom of the unprivileged[,] but a great part disappears in the waste caused by various forms of commercial war[,] e.g. advertisements, clerks, ticket-collectors, lawyers, and the like—But you may well ask, that part of their riches which they spend on their own personal comforts and pleasures, is not that harmlessly spent? I must needs answer no. Once more[,] the greater part of the riches so consumed is not used, but wasted. I ask any man of sense who knows the life of the wealthy middle class and upper class in civilization if it is not true that beyond a certain point all their expenditure is on things that give them no pleasure at all: that the wealth so spent adds nothing to the refinement[,] to the dignity or the pleasure of life: that it is simply got rid of, because it must be got rid of somehow. Just as if it were burned on a great bonfire. But perhaps some of you may think that this waste[,] though undoubtedly injurious to the wasters[,] is of some advantage to the producers who are 'employed' by it[.]

There is just this amount of truth in that view, that this waste of the rich is *necessary* as grist to the great profit-grinding mill, and under the system of commercial privilege the workers would not be employed unless the mill ground: The workers are too poor to employ the workers, and the rich must do that or employment will fall very short indeed. Thus we go round the vicious circle, 1st[,] employment for the production of useless things; then production of useless things in order that employment may not fall short. Is not this the very essence of waste?[5] Tell me[,] I pray you[,] what is more precious, what is more necessary to the progress of the world than the skill and force of the workman, the craftsman, which is most truly the heritage handed down to us by countless years of tradition[?] Yet this precious heritage our society of Commercial privilege wastes light[-]heartedly as if it were a part of the nature of things to make the worst of that which is the best of things, the token and reward of the world[']s progress, the hope of its future.

Now then[,] to sum up against the Society of Privilege[,] the Society of today. It divides the whole population into 2 classes, the useful and the useless: it makes the useful the slaves of the useless: as must always be the case in a society in which there are slaves. Not only that, but it has a tendency to make all people useless by wasting the labour of the workers; which once more must always be the case in a society which

5. Orig., of the very essence of

includes non[-]workers, since the treasure of labour must be taken from the production of real necessities for all and be expended on the production of luxuries for the few[,] worse than useless even for them.

And the machinery by which this system is built up and sustained is the monopoly by riches of the means of production of wealth. That is[,] the producers must pay tribute before they are allowed to produce.

I bring this indictment against the society of today; that it is no real Society but a band of robbers breeding on the wealth produced by others[,] determined to make and keep the useful as outcasts from society. A false Society which reverses the use of true Society whose aim is to make the most of the Earth[']s resources. A false society which breeds artificial famine in the richest countries in the world.

Thus far I have tried to explain to you the meaning of that word privilege, which expresses the evil[,] the terrible human blunder on which our society of inequality is founded[.] Now let us explain what that equality means which Socialism proposes as the basis of the future Society and which *will* be its basis.

Here doubtless I shall be met on the threshold by the objection that men are not and cannot be equal. True, or else I should not have to explain the word Equality as a political word the very opposite of the word privilege. Men are very various, but certain needs they all have in common. All men need food[,] clothing and shelter, all men have an instinct towards the satisfaction of a desire for pleasure and a desire for knowledge. Every man therefore who does not have ample and agreeable food, good clothes and good house-room, and in addition good education and innocent and uninjurious leisure, either wrongs himself or is wronged by others. If he wills not to have these things he wrongs himself, but unless he be sick or mad such a man is not to be found, and we may say plainly that all men in their right minds desire these things and it is only by the will [of] others that they fall short of them.

Socialists therefore declare that the will of neither one person nor many of one group or the whole of Society should be so exercised as to deprive any member of society of the satisfaction of his genuine needs so far as the resources of nature duly handled by society can give him that satisfaction. In a true Society all men[']s needs must be satisfied in return for their due labour, since their duly labouring is the necessary test of their healthy membership of Society. Equality therefore must be called Equality in Society, and means finally that every member of society shall have the opportunity of satisfying his genuine needs according to the average of the wealth produced by and for society. That this can be done I am clear because every man not diseased can be used for the general good: if diseased he must be so treated and restrained from injuring the Comm[un]ity; and I am also sure that a society of equality would gradually extinguish disease and make all life healthy.

This equality of opportunity therefore is above all things to be sought for. [H]ow is it to be obtained? The answer is clear[:] by abolishing Privilege. At present as aforesaid by means of skill[,] luck or cunning a man can buy himself into privilege: or the monopoly of the resources of nature. That must be made impossible, the land[,] the public confidence[, and] the means of transit must be unbuyable by private persons[.] They must be nationalized as the phrase goes–we shall then be on the high road to the society of Equality. Huge fortunes for one thing are impossible unless you can invest your gains in monopoly and receive by means of it the result of the labour of others which ought to go to them and not to you the private person. This would wrong no man. [E]verybody would have his due share of obvious necessaries and other matters he by himself or in combination with others could procure for his personal use by his own extra labour either by himself or in combination with others. Whereas a rich man can now cease to work and force others to satisfy his inordinate desires—

[*final paragraph a series of notes*:]

How to do this/make people want it/ get them to combine–the new labour party-agitation now in the hands of the workers—[who] must learn to understand true combination [and] aim not at mere addition to wages–capitalists will find their profits going and want to sell up[.] [T]hen workers must take their own business in hand including all responsibilities—

Figure 16.2 Eleanor Marx Aveling (1856–98), member of the Bloomsbury Branch of the Social Democratic Federation and Socialist League (Source: Wiki)

Figure 17.1 Frontispiece, *A Dream of John Ball* (Kelmscott Press, 1892)

17

"Communism—i.e. Property," 1892

Editor's introduction

The *Hammersmith Socialist Society Record* announced a talk on "Communism, i.e. Property" for August 21, 1892, to be delivered to the Hammersmith Socialist Society at Kelmscott House, and there is no record of a second delivery. This was one of only seven talks listed for 1892 in LeMire's "Calendar of William Morris's Platform Career," and one of three presented to his friendly local branch during the year. May Morris published selections in *William Morris: Artist, Writer, Socialist* (MM2, 345–52), noting that:

> It is more familiarly written and not so carefully balanced [as his essay "Communism"], but contains passages that have the intimate colour and atmosphere that . . . bring Morris and his frame of mind towards the audience clearly back to us. It contains moreover some passages which I may be permitted to consider significant both of the time and of my Father's thought. (345)

The full manuscript remained in British Library Add. MS. 45,333[12], ff. 255–62, originally numbered by him 1–15. As May Morris's remarks suggest, passages of the essay express Morris's personal responses—such as to Prime Minister Disraeli or to conventional religion—which might have been omitted from a more formal talk.

Though occasionally rough in style and toward the end lapsing into outline, "Communism, i.e. Property" provides a history of social relations from earliest times onward as judged by the communitarian features of each epoch. Morris follows recent anthropological views such as those of Friedrich Engels and Ernest Belfort Bax[1] in noting that early tribal societies were "communistic inside the narrow limits of the unit of association." The next level of organization was that of classical society, which maintained a fellowship of equals among an aristocracy of the well born, supported by the labor of slaves. Feudalism next extended this pattern of inequality, although the laboring class of serfs gained some privileges and rights to protection, and in the late medieval period a new class of artisans formed themselves into guilds, whose members "were neither masters nor served a master." As the guilds declined, however, "a much more essential change than the world had yet known" occurred, when most men were forced to became "free laborers," unattached proletarians forced to sell themselves for basic subsistence. Their employers became wealthy on the surplus profit of their workers' labor and prevented the latter from combining to procure the fruits of their efforts.

In his retrospective Morris has therefore traced a seeming paradox—as workers gained more political freedoms over the centuries, in relative terms their economic position declined. The citizens of classical times and of the Middle Ages "were all poor together," whereas now inequality is increasing, so that "the richer the country is, the poorer are the main part of its people." The result of the present society of laissez-faire "free contract" is that the distinctions between rich and poor are "both wide and deep: victual, housing, clothes, religion, justice, manners, language—in all these is the enforced inferiority of the disinherited fearfully obvious."

Although society has in some ways progressed in formal civil liberties—for example, the British prime minister is ethnically Jewish, the member of a formerly "outcast tribe scarcely tolerated in Mediæval Europe"—yet essentially a greater problem remains in that wealth now rules all. Moreover, the difficulty is structural rather than individual, for any single rich man who disenfranchises himself will fall into the same exploited position; some autobiographical resonance may perhaps underlie Morris's view that "[a rich man] is a part of the class of masters above said[,] and there he must stick."

Yet Morris finds cause for a limited optimism in that the ideal of equality is now more widely accepted: "it has become a commonplace that men ought to be equal, and in this country are supposed to be free." Material conquest of nature has also brought the recognition of limits: such progress "rather worsens than betters our life by exaggerating the contrasts between rich and poor." However there are ideological forces that resist any change; these include both orthodox religion and, ironically, its opposite: "Religious tradition also hampers us but little; or need not, save the double-faced hypocrisy has now another double face, . . . for atheism stands by its old foe orthodoxy to strike a blow . . . against true freedom and in favour of monopoly." Rather startling, too, is his bluntly expressed view of "religious tradition" in general: "Religion is gone down the wind, and will no more cumber us unless we are open fools." It is possible that Morris would have revised this passage had he prepared this essay for publication, but here it stands.

According to him, neither will the present system of two-party government further the equality of workers; the more reactionary party (the Tories) "has no real function except trying to keep in power, and annoying its enemy," while the other (the Liberal Party), though it professes faith in democracy, refuses to "recognize the citizenship of the whole of the working classes." The latter indictment reflects Morris's disillusionment in the wake of his five years as an active member of the Liberal Party's radical faction (1877–83), as well as worker frustration at the postponement of universal suffrage, which was not granted to Britons until 1928, thirty-two years after Morris's death.[2]

Faced with the inadequacy of existing political arrangements, workers should form their own party: "Now let the working-man be his own friend, and no longer the servant of either party, and he will find that he is really the friend of all the world." Morris then explains the significance of the title of his lecture; to be freed from wage slavery working people must own property as a group—private property must become communal property—and to do this they must seize control of resources through electoral means. The timing of this declaration is important, since in 1887 Morris had firmly opposed the Socialist League's sponsorship of parliamentary candidates, a position which led to the secession of the Bloomsbury Branch in 1888. By 1892, however, perhaps influenced by socialist gains in the July 1892 general election,[3] he finds a hopeful change in worker sentiment:

> [T]hey insist on some consideration, that they are to be treated not as mere necessary machines, but as citizens. . . . besides this, they are getting more and more touched by definite Socialism and large and ever increasing numbers amongst them understand that it is not wages they want . . . but the fruits of their labour themselves . . . and the self-respect which would necessarily come from their due management of the said organization, and the acceptation of that responsibility for the common good which all free men must accept, but which slaves cannot.

To the end of his life Morris continued to express ambivalence about electoral politics, but here he clearly states, first that the coming socialist revolution must come through peaceful means, and next, that "the ballot box" is likely to provide such a means:

> I confess I am no great lover of political tactics; the sordid squabble of an election is unpleasant enough for a straightforward man

> to deal in: yet I cannot fail to see that it is necessary somehow to get hold of the machine which has at its back the executive power of the country, however that may be done. And that the organization and labour which will be necessary to effect that by means of the ballot-box will[,] to say the least of it[,] be little indeed compared with what would be necessary to effect it by open revolt; besides that the change effected by peaceable means would be done more completely and with less chance, indeed with no chance of counter revolution.

Note that even here Morris's endorsement of electoral politics is somewhat tentative and conditional—the goal is not successful electoralism per se but the empowerment of workers by any efficacious method.

What is not conditional, however, is his insistence that socialism cannot be imposed by force, but must reflect an inner transformation. Morris had essentially been expelled from the Socialist League in late 1890 over his objection to expressions of revolutionary violence, and here he enunciates his position with greater urgency in the context of a recent incident that would have alarmed and saddened his audience; earlier in 1892 six Walsall anarchists had been arrested and charged with the construction of a bomb, and the current editor of *Commonweal*, David Nicholl, and a colleague were later arrested for publishing incendiary comments on the sentencing:[4]

> In short I do not believe in the possible success of revolt until the Socialist party has grown so powerful in numbers that it can gain its end by peaceful means, and that therefore what is called violence will never be needed. . . . As to the attempt of a small minority to terrify a vast majority into accepting something which they do not understand, by spasmodic acts of violence, mostly involving the death or mutilation of non-combatants, I can call that nothing else than sheer madness. And here I will say once for all, what I have often wanted to say of late, to wit that the idea of taking any human life for any reason whatsoever is horrible and abhorrent to me.

Earlier in the year he had written in the *Hammersmith Socialist Society Record* of May 1892, "It is difficult to express in words strong enough the perversity of the idea that it is possible for a minority to carry on a war of violence against an overwhelming majority without being utterly crushed." His further comments reflect deep if tempered conviction:

> There is no royal road to revolution or the change in the basis of society. To make the workers conscious of the disabilities which

> beset them; to make them conscious of the dormant power in them for the removal of these disabilities, to give them hope and an aim and organization to carry out their aspirations. Here is work enough for the most energetic; it is the work of patience, but nothing can take the place of it. And *moreover it is being done*, however slowly, however imperfectly.

In the final section of his talk Morris offers an agenda for this peaceful revolution; though largely in note form, his remarks lay out the stages of reform-to-revolution in much the same sequence as in "How the Change Came" in *News from Nowhere* (chapter 17). According to this trajectory, in stage one the workers will become much more prosperous and presumably also more influential, perhaps through gaining the right to vote; but they will still recognize that their continued relative subservience is "only endurable by them on the grounds of their aiming at very much better conditions." In a second stage, the workers themselves will control all production and distribution; such a government could be interpreted as a social democratic state, or, alternately, as one organized in smaller federations of workers. In any case, such arrangements are consistent with positions taken by both the electoral socialists (the Social Democratic Federation) and nonviolent anarcho-communists of Morris's day.

A third stage, however, would be true communism: the "abolition of the private monopoly of the raw materials and tools necessary for the production of utilities," to be gained only "after a lapse of time." However Morris defines even this as only "the first stage of Socialism," for true social equality is deeper than economics: "From that stage [to] sheer equality of condition, I believe will not be a long journey"; in fact, "we shall find ourselves insensibly lapsing into it" as people come to desire the fellowship of equality rather than "an isolated position of superiority."

Morris's final point is simply that those who fear socialism are wrong: "The threats of ruin to certain groups and moods which now frighten people so much, will turn out to have been mere turnip-lanterns." As conditions change, so will people's thoughts, and Morris wryly assures his audience that "the sun will shine for everybody." This is essentially the plot of his 1887 comic farce *The Tables Turned, or Nupkins Awakened*, which mocks the former oppressors of society such as Judge Nupkins, long the scourge of poor socialists, who when forced to enter the new society of equality weeps with vexation because he must "dig potatoes and see everybody happy."

Only in his creative futurist works such as *News from Nowhere* or even *The Tables Turned* does Morris fully elaborate on the forms of consciousness inherent in "sheer equality of condition." Nonetheless

"Communism, i.e. Property"'s trajectory for "the Great Change" is much clearer and more detailed than what he had proffered in the earliest days of his commitment to socialism. By now his views are tempered by recognition that the desired social transformation must be displaced into the future, as well as refined by ten years of exposure to the arguments of the various leftist subgroups in Britain and elsewhere.

Perhaps not in spite of, but because of, its roughness, informality, and delivery to a familiar audience of comrades and friends, "Communism, i.e. Property" provides an important condensation of many of Morris's later thoughts on practical and ideological issues, including religion, violence, socialist electoral efforts, and the stages for attaining a truly socialist, that is, "communist" society.

Notes

1. Engels's *Der Ursprung der Familie, des Privateigenthums und des Staats* was published in Zurich in 1884, and Morris would have known of its contents through his ties with fellow socialists, including Engels. An English edition first appeared in Chicago in 1902. Its description of early tribal organization influenced Morris and Ernest Belfort Bax's coauthored "Socialism from the Root Up," a series published in *Commonweal* 1886–8 and expanded and reprinted as *Socialism: Its Growth and Outcome* (London, 1893).
2. The Representation of the People Act of 1918 granted suffrage to all males over twenty-one and to women householders over thirty; women over twenty-one were granted the right to vote in local elections. The Representation of the People Act of 1928 extended voting rights to all women on the same terms as men.
3. In this election three socialist or socialist-leaning candidates, Keir Hardie, John Burns, and J. Havelock Wilson, were elected to Parliament, as well as thirteen "Lib-Lab" candidates; in Hammersmith Independent Labour candidate Frank Smith had polled more than 80 percent of the votes of the winning Conservative candidate (Thompson, 599).
4. Three of the Walsall anarchists were sentenced to ten years' imprisonment, one to five years, and two were acquitted. It was later revealed that a police spy had both prompted and reported on their actions. Nicoll served a term of eighteen months in prison (Thompson, 593).

There are but two conditions of society. One based on equality, one on inequality[.]

The latter assumes that one set of men shall serve the other. The former that men shall mutually all serve each other: the service in the one case is rendered under compulsion: in the other it is rendered willingly.

In a society of equality there is no need for any arbitrary rules for determining the manner of rendering service. [I]t is a matter of reason and easily recognized necessity; e.g. that in a society of equality every member must take some share in the production of utilities.

But in a society of inequality there must be some arbitrary rule to determine who are to give and who to accept service. Arbitrary because the mere action of the strongest on the spot and from day to day or hour to hour could not obtain in any form of society. One man saying I am bigger and stronger than you, therefore I knock you down and take your goods is far too simple a form of robbery to allow any form of associated life to go on. Accordingly as far as we know such primitive robbery has never existed.

Society of inequality has always assumed some standard of superior worth which should entitle the more worthy to be served by the less worthy, and has managed to get this standard recognized to such extent as would give the said Society some degree of stability.

[There are t]wo methods of setting up this standard of excellence [–] the one resting on the accident of birth; the other on the accident of success in winning certain advantages under arbitrary conditions. The first is now historical and has passed away except for a few survivals rather symbolical than practical. The second is in full force at present[.]

A few words of history. I have said that mere club law, the rule of the strongest temporarily and on the spot has never been a condition of things under which men lived: the earliest societies of which we know anything were communistic inside the narrow limits of the unit of association, a body of men and women who were, or assumed that they were, united by ties of kindred. But these tribes[,] though not conscious of any individual claims on or desires towards property[,] recognized no fellowship outside their own clan or tribe, or the definitely allied bodies in whom kinship existed or was feigned: from tribe to tribe mere enmity was the rule; though this was somewhat mitigated by temporary truces for purposes of markets, and though the tendency toward federation grew as time went on.

Too long to tell of transitional periods: but as men got more command over nature and produced more and more wealth over mere necessaries inequality began, though the common good was not forgotten wholly. Out of this transition emerged societies composed of a body of free men who were equals, and of slaves with no position in the community, but who were the property of the freemen. These slaves were, or were assumed to be men of conquered tribes, who had shown their lack of worth by their failure in war. The most obvious example [was] Lacedaemon,[1] where the freemen lived a life of pressing poverty, and the slaves were looked upon as enemies though conquered ones. Helot-ment.

Civilization grew and society became more complex; the inferior tribes were taken into the governing one, and in process of time became a lower aristocracy. Rich freemen manumitted their slaves and turned them into dependents whose sons in their turn became free and gained power. But all the while the basis of Society was the assumed excellence and worth of the assumed well born, and the unworthiness of the slaves who worked for them.

That was the essence of the society of the classical periods[;] however it was complicated by the element of moneymaking which so to say gilded the higher classes of that period as it does the mere sham of highbirth in our own, till there grew to be a certain kind of resemblance to modern society. By that time it was near its end, and it fell at last much more from its own corruption than from any external causes. After a period of chaos the place of this classical society was taken by inchoate Feudalism, which once more included a society of freemen, no longer indeed holding their property in common, but bound together by a social system which admitted much equality amongst themselves; and under them the herd of the less worthy, no longer mere chattel slaves as in the Classical periods, but serfs, who had certain more or less well defined duties to pay to their lords, and who were allowed to work for their own livelihood, and received a certain amount of protection from their lords. Between these serfs and their lords gradually grew up a middle-class, not of exploiters of other men[']s labour, as our present middle-class, but of artizans or craftsmen rather, who formed themselves into associations called guilds[2], which after long struggles were recognized as members of the feudal hierarchy. Inside these associations there was again much equality; the workmen in them were neither masters, nor served a master, that is an individual master[;] their master was a collective one, the association to wit which they themselves had made.

But the increase of wealth brought about by the labours of the excellent craftsmen of the middle-ages, and the stir in men[']s thoughts which followed on the dying out of the religious enthusiasm of the earlier Mediæval period—the Crusades to witness—these and lesser

1. Lacedaemon was the ancient name for Sparta, ancient Greek city-state whose well-disciplined military was supported by the labor of helots ("captives"), Messenean agricultural serfs, who formed 80 percent of Sparta's population, were forced to give much of the produce they produced to their masters, often absentee soldiers. They lived in subsistence poverty and were subject to ritual humiliation and harassment.
2. MS., gilds, passim

causes brought about another change of Society, and in truth a much more essential change than the world had yet known. The free labourer appeared, the man who had no definite place in Society, no resource but to sell himself to some one more powerful than he, and who was deft enough to use his labour in such a way that the man could live while the employer could grow rich on the surplus produce of his labour. You will say, this is the slave of antiquity over again, or at least a worse form of slavery than the serf. In truth I think so: [o]ne must say that from the disappearance of the guilds as bodies of true craftsm[e]n, till the uprising of the trade unions, the workmen of all civilized countries have been living in slavery, whatever degree of comfort might go with it—slaves are sometimes tolerably comfortable.

Well it must be said of this change of middle class that the bodies of associated craftsmen working with no individual master of them having passed[3] away, its place was taken by a new middle-class wholly composed of masters; while the place of the serfs, the lower classes of the Middle Ages, was taken by the so-called free workmen. And furthermore it must be said that the divergence of interests between these two classes was more complete and sharper than that between master and slave of [the] classical, and [the] gentleman and serf of the Middle ages. For the new master class could only thrive by keeping the inferior class poor; that was felt instinctively and always acted upon, as e.g. in the laws for preventing combination amongst the workmen; if the workmen could not combine, they, as unassociated units were utterly at the mercy of the masters. And however it may be with individuals, a master-class has no mercy, because it has no foresight.

This new Society of Contract, (contract which means as between master and man the buying a slave of himself instead of a slave merchant,) as opposed to that of status[,] developed slowly at first, and for a long time was hampered by the struggles of the survivals of feudalism to become practical realities again. It was not till the French Revolution that this society of free contract finally triumphed, and the world of civilization began to settle down into the struggle towards the next great change; that which we ourselves hope to see something of. But before we go further to talk of that great change and the chances of our seeing it[,] I will ask you to note this; that in the former societies of inequality, there was yet equality in certain circles. The citizens of a Greek City lived in practical equality amongst themselves though they were surrounded by slaves: their life was simple, and refined because of its simplicity, and really admitted of no great contrast of riches and

3. MS., past

poverty. Indeed their slaves were at least fed[,] clothed and housed, and probably not worse than the poor folk in our workhouses, or field labourers living on 10s/6 a week. Nay to judge by the works of their playwrights left us in the plays imitated from them by the Romans, the slaves were not seldom the masters of their masters. In the early age of Rome it was much the same; and in short[,] the difference between the classes was largely arbitrary rather than real.

Still more apparent are these circles of equality obvious in the M[iddle] A[ges]. The gentlemen class for as hard and fast as were the lines of the hierarchy, knew no difference in manners or life in general; and the guildsmen in their guilds were associates in equality. In both periods it is not till the society is moving fast towards dissolution, that the monstrous contrasts so familiar to us fairly show. While[4] chaotic and general inequality in all society has been from the first an essential part of the society of free contract, and its praises have been sung by numberless votaries, by those who suffer from it, as much perhaps as by those who gain[.] To some it seems so providential, to others so necessary, to some so interesting, the foundation for beautiful stories of courage and resignation and sacrifice and all the rest of it.

For my part I say I do not know if it be providential, I am sure it is not necessary, and I see no interest or beauty in it, but foulness and sordidness, and destruction of the beauty of the Earth and of man[']s works upon the Earth. For once more if it be true, as I think it is, that the inequality of the ancient and the Mediæval world was more arbitrary than real, I am sure that the converse of it is true of the modern world, and I will say especially of the country in which we live. Though there may be with us little arbitrary legal and theoretic difference between rich and poor, the real practical distinctions are, to our misery[,] both wide and deep: victual, housing, clothes[,] religion, justice, manners, language—in all these is the enforced inferiority of the disinherited fearfully obvious. How should it not be so when our actual wealth is so great, and so large a majority of us so poor; our potential wealth, i[.] e[.] what we might have if we did not waste our work[,] so much greater; [i]n the Middle Ages, in the Classical period even[,] by comparison they were all poor together. But now as you well know, the richer the country is, the poorer the main part of its people.

We have got, then, to this, that in our present society of free contract and the career open to the talents[,] we have enormously exaggerated the inequalities of former societies of inequality, nay even we have

4. Morris inserted an unnecessary "on" here as the last word before shifting to a new page.

changed their kind for the worse. Does this make the matter hopeless[?] To my mind it is far from hopeless; not merely are we nearer to equality by the development of so many hundred years; but the signs of the times give token of our attaining it; nay more[,] we are consciously on the march toward it. For as I have said the standard of worth which allows certain persons to claim service of the non-worthy, or say in short the standard of privilege, has changed: [t]he privilege of birth has waned to such a poor shadow that an outcast tribe scarcely tolerated in Mediæval Europe does now practically rule Europe; and one of these people in our country managed but a few years [ago] to persuade the extra[-]rich men who perhaps think (very mistakenly) that [they] are the lineal descendants of the baronage of our Plantagenet Kings, that he was marshalling them in triumph to the sure defence of their ancient position.

The privilege of birth has gone, and the privilege of riches has taken its place. Anyone can now be a master of men if he has gained the privilege of monopolizing a portion of the means by which labour is compelled to sell itself for less than its real worth. If he has more wealth than he needs to spend on his own necessities he can buy with the surplus, not only land and other raw materials of production, but organization, obedience and credit for the getting of more riches. Nay practically he not only *may* but *must* do this through himself or others as far as his surplus wealth goes; if he does not give it away to someone else who will do it for him; in which case he will have himself to sell his labour for less than its real worth. So that as a matter of fact he cannot even give away his privilege: he is a part of the class of masters above said, and there he must stick. Now this privilege, which in other words means forcing people who want to work usefully for their livelihood to pay a heavy tribute for doing so[,] is the cement of our modern inequality; and as long as it lasts whatsoever is 'done for the working classes,' as the phrase goes is illusory, except so far as it may help to put them into such a position as thence they may claim and obtain its abolition: whatever wealth is won by the workers as things are will go not to the improvement of their condition, but to swelling the riches of the privileged, or to speak more plainly will be idly wasted by the classes of privilege: it will, that is, be spent more and more in compelling the workers to produce toys for the few, instead of useful things for the many. Though as we shall see later on this very waste of labour in the present, lights up our hope for the future.

The long course of the centuries therefore, whatever gain they have brought us otherwise, in development of man[']s intellect, or his power over material nature[,] have brought us no improvement in our social organization; as far as our actual social condition goes we are not in a better, but in a worse state than men were in the ancient or mediæval periods. What is left us then if we are not to fall back upon mere despair of improvement[?] This, that in the present period we have become conscious that in our miserable society of inequality lie the seeds of change, and that things are tending towards a new society, the basis of which will be equality of condition. In the Ancient world, a society without slavery was inconceivable to the best and wisest of philosophers. In the Mediæval epoch, especially towards the close of it, there was indeed a rumour of communism in the air, which even now and again took form in action, and produced such demonstrations as the community of the Munster anabaptists;[5] but all this was hopeless, in the face of the political condition of affairs, the growing desire for the enfranchisement of men[']s intellect from the fetters of religious tradition, and the development of men[']s power over the mechanical side of things.

But now in the first place, a society of equality has been at least conceived of as an ideal; while it has become a commonplace that men ought to be equal, and in this country are supposed to be free. And in the second, we have so much achieved our conquest over material nature that our victory is turning sour in our hands, now that we are beginning to find out that we cannot use it to our happiness while we are hampered by the evil organization of Society[,] and that it rather worsens than betters our life by exaggerating the contrasts between rich and poor.

Religious tradition also hampers us but little; or need not, save the double-faced hypocrisy has now another double face, and can look at the same time east and west as well as north and south; for atheism stands by its old foe orthodoxy to strike a blow together with it, against true freedom and in favour of monopoly. Lastly the political conditions are so changed, and again especially in our country, that the old parties are all confused, and the confessedly reactionary party finds it has no real function except trying to keep in power, and annoying its enemy, the party which professes democracy, but which does not understand that the democracy which refuses fully to recognize the citizenship of the whole of the working classes is but toryism masquerading in the cast[-off] clothes of Oliver Cromwell.

5. The Münster Anabaptists deposed the former magistrates and established a radical theocracy or "new Zion" in Münster for sixteen months from February 1534 to June 1535, proclaiming adult baptism, community of goods, and polygamy, before they were cruelly repressed and their leaders tortured and executed by the forces of Count Franz von Waldeck.

To sum [up] the change that has come over us[, w]e know that our inequality is not a blessing but a pest. The power over nature which we have gained we now want to use for our enjoyment. Religion is gone down the wind, and will no more cumber us unless we are open fools. Middle-class democracy can go no further; the proletarians *must* form part of it, and both the old parties are crying out to them for help: each one by turn is the true "working-man's friend."

Now then let the working-man be his own friend, and no longer the servant of either party, and he will find that he is really the friend of all the world: for he it is who must realize that society of equality wherein amongst other things it is clear that every member of society must help in the production of utilities and that no man is set to labour on inutilities, as I think the most of men now are. Let me say in passing; think of it a little! What amount of wealth we should produce if we were all working cheerfully at producing the things that we all genuinely want; if all the intelligence, all the inventive power, all the inherited skill of handicraft, all the keen wit and insight, all the healthy bodily strength were engaged in doing this and nothing else, what a pile of wealth we should have! How would poverty be a word whose meaning we should have forgotten. Believe me there is nothing but the curse of inequality which forbids this.

Well, you have heard many praises of property from Aristotle to Mr Mallock;[6] and I also am now going to praise it; perhaps to your surprise: so for fear you my Socialist friends should refuse to hear me any longer[,] allow me to remind you, that William Cobbett asks this pertinent question: What is a slave? and answers it thus, A slave is a man without property.[7] In that I wholly agree. What are you to do if you have no property? You cannot get up when you will, go to bed

6. Against Plato, who had posited the value of communally held property, in his *Nichomachean Ethics* and *Politics* Aristotle argued that private property would be better administered than shared property, and that a certain degree of wealth was necessary in order for the just man to practice the virtue of magnanimity. William Hurrell Mallock (1849–1923), polemical writer whose works attacked radical, positivist, and socialist ideas, was the author of the roman à clef *The New Republic* (1878) and of the political treatises *Social Equality* (1882), *Property and Progress* (1884), and *Labor and the Popular Welfare* (1893).

7. William Cobbett (1763–1835), reformist journalist, writer on agricultural labor, and opponent of the Corn Laws, stated in his 1829 *Advice to Young Men and (Incidentally) to Young Women:* "A slave is, in the first place, a man who has *no property*; and property means something that he *has,* and that nobody can take from him without his leave, or consent . . . . A slave has *no property in his labour*; and any man who is compelled to give up the fruit of his labour to another, at the arbitrary will of that other, has no property in his labour, and is, therefore, a slave . . . . To be sure he *may* avoid eating and drinking and may go naked; but, then he must die; and on this condition, and this condition only, can he refuse to give up the fruit of his labour. . . ." (paragraph 344).

when you will, eat and drink when you will, marry as you will, amuse yourself as you will—in all that you must be at another man's beck and call—in fact you cannot so much as eat, unless you have property; in order even to live till next week, unless some benevolent person takes you by the collar and sells you, you must go out and sell yourself as Esau did;[8] who I take it was the very first example of the free labourer.

Now how are you going to get this property? No doubt your first untutored view as to that matter, with the education which you have received by the society of the present, is that you had better steal it;—that in fact there is no other way of getting it. This view is I must say the favoured one: and has been held from the A[rchbishop] of Canterbury to the late Mr Brad[laugh],[9] from the D[uke] of W[estminster] to the shiftiest of small tradesmen compelled by hard need to sell adulterated wares. But we Socialists have found out that it won't do; and really we need not crow over the discovery, for the fact lies patent before everybody's eyes. For many and many a century it has been tried, with small success indeed: as we may judge from the last results of it from the ethical side being the Liberty and Property Defence League[10] and the Positivist Society.[11]

For this process of gaining possessi[on] of property by means of stealing, and then qualifying the glorious name of property by calling it *private* property, (an ingenious but I should hope now exposed fraud) has this disadvantage, that you must find some definite and unchanging body of men who will consent or submit to be stolen from, and in these latter days that body is not so definite and is changing fast; so fast that it is beginning to state clearly its objections to its position in the creation

8. Esau sold his birthright to his brother Jacob in exchange for food, "a mess of pottage," Genesis 25:29–34.
9. Charles Bradlaugh (1833–91), founder of the National Secular Society in 1866, was a freethinker, birth control campaigner, radical working-class leader, and MP for Northampton. A "liberal individualist," he supported trade unionism, women's suffrage, and Irish Home Rule, but opposed socialism.
10. The Liberty and Property Defence League (LPDL) was founded in 1882 by Francis Wemyss-Charteris-Douglas, Lord Elcho (later 10th Earl of Wemyss) (1818–1914). As its name implied, the LPDL affirmed doctrines of laissez-faire non-interventionism and Spencerian individualism, and campaigned against trade unionism, socialism and all forms of state intervention in private affairs until its demise in the 1920s.
11. Founded in 1867 by Richard Congreve (1818–99), the London Positivist Society sought to apply the reformist secular doctrines of August Comte and other humanist ideas to public affairs. In many ways their views overlapped with those of Morris and other left-leaning Liberals and socialists; they supported Irish Home Rule, opposed British rule in India, and advocated religious tolerance. Morris would have had direct knowledge of them through Vernon Lushington (1832–1912), a friend from *Oxford and Cambridge Magazine* days onward who was a lifelong Positivist.

of *private* property, and to call aloud for a share in property. I must here turn aside, in case there are some non-socialists here, to explain that in order to steal, it is necessary to find some one who has something to steal; and that in considering social matters, it is a body or class that steal, and a body or class that is stolen from. Now in this relation therefore it is clear that you cannot steal from those who have no property of their own; that is you cannot make a livelihood from that occupation. You can indeed take from a man on Saturday evening what he may have in his pocket then, but if he does not *work* all the next week what has he to be stolen the next Saturday?[12]

So that if you take from all the screwmakers and all the Dukes what they possess[,] you have not stolen to purpose, you will have to keep them in the workhouse ever afterwards. But with the working-man it is different, because as a matter of fact he has property if he were allowed to use it; you can steal from him every Saturday evening, one after the other; if he be a golden-egged goose, as I fear he is, his owners have long ago learned that it won't do to kill him. Therefore the class of people who can be stolen from and who are stolen from is the working or useful class, simply because they produce; and doubtless if they could be kept in the goose condition for ever, the present condition of private property would last for ever. But can they be? It seems to me that the answer to that question is now before your eyes: there are hundreds of people who are speaking at this moment all over England and Scotland at least in the same way as I am[, p]eople who in one way or other are urging their hearers to consider whether property shall remain private or become common; whether all people should have property or only a few. Whether the united labour of the millions of civilization should be wasted in producing rations for slaves and toys for masters, or enjoyment and a wholesome and happy life for all men and women.

These I say are really the questions which we Socialists are asking; and unless I and the others are wholly deceiving ourselves they are being answered in the most practical way. All over the country opinion amongst the working-men is changing: and they are beginning to understand that they, the indispensable class, are being made to pay for all the waste and disorganization of our system of inequality; and they are claiming certain advantages, which, all put together, mean that they insist on some consideration, that they are to be treated not as mere necessary machines, but as citizens. I say the working men generally are making this claim. But besides this, they are getting more and more touched by definite Socialism and large and ever increasing

12. Morris here inserts a superscript, Feb: 3.

numbers amongst them understand that it is not wages they want; not the mere portion of the fruits of their labour which they can manage to wring out of the profits of their masters, but the fruits of their labour themselves; that is, the plentiful life which their unwasteful organization would insure them, and the self-respect which would necessarily come from their due management of the said organization, and the acceptation of that responsibility for the common good which all free men must accept, but which slaves cannot.

These men I say, whose numbers are growing every day and whose principles are approved of instinctively and tacitly by the great mass of working-men are determined, that our Society shall be real, the Society of citizens living in equality, and not the Society of a robber[']s cave: and they know also that they have at hand a machinery which will enable them when their opinions become general to compel their recognition at the hands of the inert mass of non-producers, who will find their life of useless work or no work will no longer earn them the position and ease that [it] has done and that their rule is slipping away from [them].

I confess I am no great lover of political tactics; the sordid squabble of an election is unpleasant enough for a straight-forward man to deal in: yet I cannot fail to see that it is necessary somehow to get hold of the machine which has at its back the executive power of the country, however that may be done. And that the organization and labour which will be necessary to effect that by means of the ballot-box will[,] to say the least of it[,] be little indeed compared with what would be necessary to effect it by open revolt; besides that the change effected by peaceable means would be done more completely and with less chance, indeed with no chance of counter revolution. On the other hand I feel sure that some action is even now demanded by the growth of Socialism, and will be more and more imperatively demanded as time goes on.

In short I do not believe in the possible success of revolt until the Socialist party has grown so powerful in numbers that it can gain its end by peaceful means, and that therefore what is called violence will never be needed; unless indeed the reactionists were to refuse the decision of the ballot-box and try the matter by arms; which after all I am pretty sure they could not attempt by the time things had gone so far as that. As to the attempt of a small minority to terrify a vast majority into accepting something which they do not understand, by spasmodic acts of violence, mostly involving the death or mutilation of non-combatants, I can call that nothing else than sheer madness. And here I will say once for all, what I have often wanted to say of late, to wit that the idea of taking any human life for any reason whatsoever is horrible and abhorrent to me.

Well, you see to-night I have only been talking round about Communism only. The subject of the organization of a communal life is too weighty a one for me to deal with at present: besides our ideas on that subject must necessarily grow clearer as we advance towards the first stages of Socialism; the steps to which seem to me briefly these: 1st. The recognition of the citizenship of the great working class, which will be betokened by their attaining to a far higher standard of livelihood than that which is now considered enough for them, but which I think means a life of degradation, only endurable by them on the grounds of their aiming at very much better conditions. 2nd. Their organization as the controllers of production and the markets: and 3rd. The abolition of the private monopoly in the raw material and tools necessary for the production of utilities.

This gained, as we may fairly hope it will be after a lapse of time, as makes it no dream to-day, we shall be in the first stage of Socialism, and the possession of property will even then be general. From that stage [to] sheer equality of condition, I believe will not be a long journey, and as I have said here we shall find ourselves insensibly lapsing into it: men[']s desires will be turned toward it, instead of being turned as they are now toward establishing each man for him[self] an isolated position of superiority; and this set of men[']s minds will make nothing of objections which now seem insurmountable to us[.] The threats of ruin to certain groups and moods which now frighten people so much, will turn out to have been mere turnip-lanterns.[13] The sun will shine for everybody, the heavens will be blue and the grass green; cakes and ale shall not be forbidden us; and though we shall have our troubles then, they will seem as the troubles in a tale compared to the grovelling anxieties that now beset us; we shall find life worth living—we shall not be afraid to die—or, worse still, ashamed to live.

13. Lanterns made from vegetables such as turnips were associated with Halloween, especially in rural areas and Ireland, and some have thought that these customs inspired the American practice of carving pumpkins. Morris may refer to the fact that their light is easily extinguished.

Figure 18.1 Kelmscott Manor, front view. Morris co-leased Kelmscott Manor in 1871 and spent much time here during the 1890s. Photo credit: Julia Griffin

18

"Town and Country," 1893

Editor's introduction

Morris is recorded as having delivered this lecture twice, on May 29, 1892, to the Hammersmith Socialist Society and on October 23 to the Ancoats Brotherhood in Manchester. It was published in the *Journal of Decorative Art* in April 1893 (no. 13, 106), a magazine devoted to household design and practical arts. A manuscript with several corrections housed in the Mark Samuels Lasner Collection in Newark, Delaware contains a final paragraph absent from the printed version. Either Morris excised this himself before publication, or the *Journal of Decorative Art* felt the final sentiments unsuitable, as Morris departs from his immediate topic to advocate a change in the labor system: "The workers have no real customers for genuine useful wares. Change all that by realizing true Society, and we shall be wealthy and able to have what we want . . . ."

In Morris's ecotopian *News from Nowhere* (1890), the inhabitants of Nowhere celebrate their freedom from the former crowded and unwholesome conditions of city life. As Old Hammond recalls, after the Great Change

> [p]eople flocked into the country villages, and, so to say, flung themselves upon the freed land like a wild beast upon his prey. . . . The town invaded the country; but the invaders, like the warlike invaders of early days, yielded to the influence of their surroundings, and became country people; . . . so that the difference between town and country grew less and less; and it was indeed this world of the country vivified by the thought and briskness of town-bred folk which has produced that happy and leisurely but eager life of which you have had a first taste. (*CW*, 16, chap. 10, 71–2)

In espousing these ideals Morris was participating in a late nineteenth-century movement to redesign cities to mitigate their worst features, for example, through the inclusion of gardens and parks. However, he was among the first to formulate carefully the need for a complementary relationship between urban and rural areas, and his projections arguably influenced Ebenezer Howard's *Garden Cities of To-morrow* (1898, 1902) and its offshoot, the Garden City movement.[1]

"Town and Country" provides a historical exposition of these social-ecological ideals. The Romans had built walled cities which the barbarians had destroyed, but medieval citizens had managed a desirable balance of dispersed houses, greenery, and communal agriculture. Their typical city was

> a place of some extent within its ancient walls, but the houses much broken by gardens and open spaces within the walls, and without them, a small estate it may be called, the communal property of the freemen. On the whole, then, the towns of the Middle Ages . . . were a part of the countrysides where they stood.

Nor was this symbiosis a happy accident, but the result of the medieval labor system: "it was not so much the houses that made the town, as the constitution, the freemen and the guilds . . . ." Morris next identifies the distorting metropole effect: by the eighteenth century "the distribution was not between the towns and the countrysides, but between London and the rest of the country. . . ." London had at least retained some advantages: "the external beastliness and sordidness of [London] is in some degree compensated by its intellectual life."

Worse, however, are the side-effects of "the Great Industries," which had created something entirely and horrifically new, the large manufacturing town. Morris's speaking tours in northern England had clearly not impressed him favorably; these industrial centers "have no such compensation [in intellectual life], and even in externals are far more horrible than London." Finally, at a third level of deterioration is the neglected agricultural countryside, doomed to depression and blight and unable to contribute to "the real life of our epoch."

Morris expands on the flaws of both city and countryside; the city is vulgar in its wealthy sections and "noisome and squalid beyond words in its poor quarters." The natural loveliness of the countryside endures—"the superabundant beauty of leaf and flower, all the wealth of meadow, and acres, and hillside"—but, as Guest and Ellen had noted during their river journey in *News from Nowhere*, it suffers from the twin predations of sporadic dilapidation and tasteless "restoration." On behalf of the Society for the Protection of Ancient Buildings Morris had often protested against ahistorical "restorations" near Kelmscott

Manor, and he notes with pain that this vulgar gentrification has rapidly intensified.

At this point Morris makes a somewhat personal observation:

> Now you may well say that all this suffering to men who are in the habit of taking in impressions through the eyes is a due reward for our living on other people's earnings; for our suffering the human live-stock of the country to live such a wretched scanty existence as they do

—a reflection which recalls Guest's painful memories of the "spindle-legged back-bowed men and haggard, hollow-eyed, ill-favoured women" who had formerly populated the countryside (chap. 30, 200). Morris refrains from developing the political implications of this observation, however, noting only that "our forefathers were involved in the same sin"—whereas by his own criteria the intensifying competitive commerce of his own century has compounded the inequities of land ownership.

Yet there remains the problem of what is to be done about so much degradation. Morris enunciates the goal clearly: "I want neither the towns to be appendages of the country, nor the country of the town; I want the town to be impregnated with the beauty of the country and the country with the intelligence and vivid life of the town," a condition surely attainable as "the heritage of the latter ages of the world." Accordingly the final paragraph of the manuscript version suggests how we might remake the landscape in accord with human needs; in a socialist society in which workers make objects for use not profit, the resultant freedom and prosperity will enable the reshaping of human environs to fuse "the beauty of the country and the brisk vivid life of the town."

Note

1. The 1898 title was *To-morrow: A Peaceful Path to Real Reform*. See Florence S. Boos, "*News from Nowhere* and Garden Cities: Morris's Utopia and Nineteenth-Century Town-Design," *Journal of Pre-Raphaelite Studies* 7 (1998): 7–27.

Town and country are generally put in a kind of contrast, but we will see what kind of a contrast there has been, is, and may be between them; how far that contrast is desirable or necessary, or whether it may not be possible in the long run to make the town a part of the country and the country a part of the towns. I think I may assume that, on the one hand, there is nobody here so abnormally made as not to take a pleasure in green fields, and trees, and rivers, and mountains, the beings, human and otherwise, that inhabit those scenes, and in a word, the general beauty and incident of nature: and that, on the other, we all of us find human intercourse necessary to us, and even the excitement of those forms of it which can only be had where large bodies of men live together.

In the Roman times of the Empire, when the lands were cultivated almost wholly by well-organized slave labour with its necessary concomitant of brigandage and piracy in out-of-the-way places, I can't think that the countrysides were very pleasant places to live in; whereas the Roman city with its handsome buildings and gardens, its public baths, and other institutions of almost complete 'municipal socialism,' must have been very pleasant to well-to-do people, and perhaps, under the Empire at least, not quite intolerable to the proletarian, whose form of pauper relief did not include the prison system of the modern workhouse. In those days the town decidedly 'scores'; all the more as manufacture was, as its name implies, wholly a matter of handicraft. But the Roman city-system was pretty much swept away by the barbarism which took the place of the Empire. In this country, and wherever the people were not completely Romanized, the town was almost always merely the development of the agricultural district; it was the aggregation of the cultivators of the soil, and its freemen were always landowners, though mostly collective ones. In fact, for a long time after the Teutonic invasion which made this country England, there were no towns at all: the English clans lived in scattered homesteads along the side of the sea, or some river, or in clearings of the wild wood, as their Anglish, Jutish, or Saxon forefathers had done, and when they took a Romano-British town they had nothing better to do with it than to burn it and let it be: though, when they got more civilized, the long extinct glories of the Roman took some revenge for this destruction, by the impression which they made on the descendants of the destroyers: *e.g.*, an Anglo-Saxon poet of about the time of Athelstan[1] wrote a poem on the ruins of an old Roman city which is as pathetic and beautiful as any lyric extant in any language,[2] and you may, if you please, look on it as a forecast of the glories of the cities that were yet to come.

1. MS., Athelstane
2. Possibly "The Ruin," a forty-nine-line poem in the Exeter Book ff. 123b–46 (I am indebted to Owen Holland for this identification). Morris might have approved its attention to the builders, "A grave-grip holds the master-crafters, decrepit and departed, in the ground's harsh grasp, until one hundred generations of human-nations have trod past. . . . The strong-purposed mind was urged to a keen-minded desire in concentric circles; the stout-hearted bound wall-roots wondrously together with wire."

Gradually, as civilization grew, the population thickened in certain places where the protection of the feudal lord – Baron, Bishop, or Abbot – made a market possible; and in short the growth of such places made our medieval towns; though, as was like to be, where an old Roman town like York or London was still in existence, it was used as such a centre. But doubtless our medieval towns were very small, smaller than our imagination of them pictures them to us; while on the other hand, the country villages were in many cases much larger than they are now. In fact in those days it was not so much the houses that made the town, as the constitution, the freemen and the guilds, which gradually grew into the Corporation. My familiarity with Oxford makes it easy to me to see a medieval town of the more important kind: a place of some extent within its ancient walls, but the houses much broken by gardens and open spaces within the walls, and without them, a small estate it may be called, the communal property of the freemen. On the whole, then, the towns of the Middle Ages, in this country at least, were a part of the countrysides where they stood.

In the Middle Ages even London was no more of a centre than Bristol or York, or indeed other places now become almost extinct. But in the eighteenth century London was become very decidedly the centre of England, and now the distinction was not between the towns and the countrysides, but between London and the rest of the country, towns and all. And here properly begins the opposition of town to country. The only further development of this was the work of the Great Industries which created the big manufacturing town, a thing so entirely modern that even London, with all its enormity, has more relation to the cities of the past than these manufacturing towns have.

On considering further the contrast between town and country we must be careful not to forget this special quality in London. For now we see that we have three things to deal with: London, the external beastliness and sordidness of which is in some degree compensated by its intellectual life; the commercial centres, which have no such compensation, and even in externals are far more horrible than London; and the country, which, instead of being the due fellow and helpmate of the towns and the Town, is a troublesome appendage, an awkward incident of town life, which, commercial or intellectual, is the real life of our epoch.

The result of all this is the usual make-shift jumble which oppresses all our life in this epoch of strange and rapid change, when we have fallen into such grievous want of reasonable organization. Even London, though far better than the commercial towns, is sordidly vulgar in its rich quarters, noisome and squalid beyond word in its poor quarters.

And the country—at this end of May I am not going to say that it is not beautiful—beautiful everywhere more or less where there are not many modern houses in sight. But I know the country well: and even for a rich man, a well-to-do one at least, it shares in the make-shift stupidity of the epoch. Amongst all the superabundant beauty of leaf and flower, all the wealth of meadow, and acre, and hillside, it is *stingy*, O so stingy! In an ordinary way not an hour's work will be spent in taking away an ugly dead tree, in mending a shattered wall, setting a tottering vane straight (even if it be pulling down the roof-beam it is fastened to), in short in mending any defacement caused by wind and weather. Not a moment's consideration will be given as to whether the sightly material should be used, if the unsightly one be a fraction cheaper for the time being. You can scarce have milk unless you keep a cow: you can't have vegetables unless you grow them yourself. I say this is the ordinary rule: it is true that when there is a rich squire, he does sometimes take some pains in beautifying his cottages, restoring his church, and so forth—with the result in *all* cases, that the village he has so dealt with has become as vulgar as Bayswater. Nor can I leave this subject of the outward aspect of the country without reminding you that through forty years of my life I have diligently and affectionately *noticed* the countryside in its smallest detail, and that the change for the worse in its aspect has been steady, and, especially within the last twenty years, startlingly rapid. Indeed, sometimes I feel selfishly glad to think that I shall not live to see the worst of it. Now you may well say that all this suffering to men who are in the habit of taking in impressions through the eyes is a due reward for our living on other people's earnings; for our suffering the human live-stock of the country to live such a wretched scanty existence as they do. True, and over true; but then why should *we* of the nineteenth century be so extra punished, when our forefathers were involved in the same sin?

I take it that after all this is the case, that we feel it because it is at last tending to change—that we at last can do something to alter it. For this is what I want done in this matter of town and country: I want neither the towns to be appendages of the country, nor the country of the town; I want the town to be impregnated with the beauty of the country, and the country with the intelligence and vivid life of the town. I want every homestead to be clean, orderly, and tidy; a lovely house surrounded by acres and acres of garden. On the other hand, I want the town to be clean, orderly, and tidy; in short, a garden with beautiful houses in it. Clearly, if I don't wish this, I must be a fool or a dullard; but I do more—I claim it as the due heritage of the latter ages of the world which have subdued nature, and can have for the asking.

[From manuscript] Some of you may say this is but an impossible ideal. But that is a mistake [–] it is impossible to a poor country but not to a wealthy one. But are we not a wealthy community? Far from it. We have rich men amongst us but they are enemies of the Community, and keep everything from it that they can; and as they are its masters they can keep most things from the Community and make it poor. Working men, as you have often been told[,] make at presently [by] their labour chiefly two kinds of wares, makeshift and rubbish (necessities) for the poor, slave wares in short, and makeshift luxuries for the rich. The workers have no real customers for genuine useful wares. Change all that by realizing true Society, and we shall be wealthy and able to have what we want; and as all sane men desire the beauty of the country and the brisk vivid life of the Town, we shall get these to interpenetrate and all will be won.

Figure 19.1 Frontispiece, *News from Nowhere* (Kelmscott Press, 1892)

19

How I Became a Socialist

Editor's introduction

Perhaps Morris's most personal testimony to his convictions, "How I Became a Socialist" was published in *Justice* in 1894 and in the Social Democratic Federation's 1896 pamphlet, *How I Became a Socialist*, issued in 1896 after his death. May Morris included this essay in volume 23 of the *Collected Works* and *Artist, Writer, Socialist*, and it has been reprinted several times since.[1] One of Morris's most beautiful essays, "How I Became a Socialist" is distinguished by its resonant poetic cadences, condensed argument, and infused emotion. Equally notable is its avoidance of the specifics of socialist tactics—for "politics as politics" is "a necessary if cumbersome and disgustful means to an end." Instead Morris probes the ethical and psychological motivation of his adherence to "the religion of socialism," the *why* rather than the *how*.

Noting that the word "socialism" has many meanings (e.g., gradualism, state socialism, anarcho-socialism, etc.), he reiterates his more exacting version:

> Socialism is a condition of society . . . in which all men would be living in equality of condition, and should manage their affairs . . . with the full consciousness that harm to one would mean harm to all—the realization at last of the meaning of the word COMMONWEALTH.

The desire for equality is the principle which has drawn all his political aspirations together; even before he had learned of the existence of England's first organized socialist political party, the Democratic Federation (founded 1881; renamed the Social Democratic Federation in 1883), he had conceived the hope of change, "what we others call Social-Revolution," a claim supported by his appeals for complete social equality as early as his 1880 lecture on "Art and Inequality." The depth of Morris's commitment is evinced by the fact that this conversion brought joy and relief rather than dread of the personal sacrifices such a choice entailed.

Morris gives careful credit to his intellectual sources, including Thomas Carlyle, John Ruskin, John Stuart Mill, and Karl Marx, as well as more recent friends. Carlyle and Ruskin had modeled discontent with the status quo, and the latter had provided artistic and social ideals. Morris had also been intrigued by John Stuart Mill's posthumously published *Fortnightly Review* articles on socialism (February–April 1879), which he (Morris) describes as an attack on socialism in its Fourierist guise. As an economist Mill's arguments centered rather narrowly on whether individual enterprise or a communal organization would likely produce greater profits, but his practice of presenting counterarguments before dismissing them prompted him to describe the principles of Continental socialism in some detail. Even he grants that socialism would appeal to a higher ethic: "The change . . . to a state in which every person would have an interest in rendering every other person as industrious, skillful, and careful as possible (which would be the case under Communism) would be a change very much for the better." Rather surprisingly Mill also sees some form of communism as the path of the future: "If Communist associations show that they can be durable and prosperous, they will multiply, and will probably be adopted by successive portions of the population of the more advanced countries as they become morally fitted for that mode of life" ("The Difficulties of Socialism," chap. 4, April). Mill's heavily hedged account of socialism's immediate prospects thus challenged Morris to prove the contrary, "that it was possible to bring [Socialism] about in our own day."

Morris also credits Marx with improving his understanding of socialism, especially in his historical account of the changing patterns of labor, a tribute born out by the many commentators who have documented Morris's increasingly Marxist views after reading *Das Kapital* in a French translation in 1885.[2] Likewise "How I Became a Socialist" was written for a *Justice* audience, and Morris is careful to credit his former associates from the early days of the Social Democratic Federation, "such friends as [Ernest Belfort] Bax and [Henry] Hyndman and [Andreas] Scheu." Morris had often been forced to choose between an imperfect alliance with state socialists or libertarian anarchists, but he here assures his socialist audience that his association with his "Anarchist friends" has taught him "quite against their intention, that Anarchism was impossible." His motivation has been service to a principle rather than any immediate personal benefit: "I might never have been drawn into the practical side of the question if an ideal had not forced me to seek towards it." For this very reason his convictions are intransigent: "Nor . . . could I ever have believed in the possibility of a *partial* setting right of those wrongs."

Morris's cadences approach metered verse as he declaims his indictment of the effects of industrial capitalism: "What shall I say concerning its mastery of and its waste of mechanical power, its commonwealth so poor; its enemies of the commonwealth so rich, its stupendous organization—for the misery of life!" Even as Dickens's Podsnap (*Our Mutual Friend*, 1864–5) had built his wealth on a dung heap, the present system, "this filth of civilization," is environmentally and humanly disastrous—"a counting-house on the top of a cinder heap." He has been saved from mere opposition—from "crystalizing into a mere railer against 'progress'"—by his recognition of "the seeds of a great change," and he summarizes with modest understatement: "all I had to do then in order to become a Socialist was to hook myself onto the practical movement, which . . . I have tried to do as well as I could."

In closing Morris attempts to set to rest the ever-resurgent view that socialism should concern itself solely with economic gains—bread not roses. He offers two alternative counterarguments: those who have been deprived cannot understand what they have lost; and further, the capacity to conceive an ideal is itself a human birthright. As abundantly testified throughout his writings, Morris's socialism was profoundly intertwined with a belief in human equality. Yet perhaps equally essential to his temperament was the conviction with which he concludes this essay, that art is the envisioning of "the true ideal of a full and reasonable life . . . in which the perception and creation of beauty, the enjoyment of real pleasure that is, shall be felt to be as necessary to man as his daily bread."

Notes

1. See Appendix, 391.
2. See, e.g., Paul Meier, *William Morris: The Marxist Dreamer* (Brighton: Harvester, 1977) and Owen Holland, "Morris and Marxist Theory," in Florence S. Boos (ed.), *The Routledge Companion to William Morris* (New York: Routledge, 2020), 465–85.

I am asked by the Editor to give some sort of a history of the above conversion, and I feel that it may be of some use to do so, if my readers will look upon me as a type of a certain group of people, but not so easy to do clearly, briefly and truly. Let me, however, try. But first, I will say what I mean by being a Socialist, since I am told that the word no longer expresses definitely and with certainty what it did ten years ago. Well, what I mean by Socialism is a condition of society in which there should be neither rich nor poor, neither master nor master's man, neither idle nor overworked, neither brain-sick brain workers, nor heart-sick hand workers, in a word, in which all men would be living in equality of condition, and would manage their affairs unwastefully, and with the full consciousness that harm to one would mean harm to all—the realization at last of the meaning of the word COMMONWEALTH.

Now this view of Socialism which I hold to-day, and hope to die holding, is what I began with; I had no transitional period, unless you may call such a brief period of political radicalism during which I saw my ideal clear enough, but had no hope of any realization of it. That came to an end some months before I joined the (then) Democratic Federation, and the meaning of my joining that body was that I had conceived a hope of the realization of my ideal. If you ask me how much of a hope, or what I thought we Socialists then living and working would accomplish towards it, or when there would be effected any change in the face of society, I must say, I do not know. I can only say that I did not measure my hope, nor the joy that it brought me at the time. For the rest, when I took that step I was blankly ignorant of economics; I had never so much as opened Adam Smith, or heard of Ricardo, or of Karl Marx. Oddly enough, I *had* read some of Mill, to wit, those posthumous papers of his (published, was it in the *Westminster Review* or the *Fortnightly*?) in which he attacks Socialism in its Fourierist guise. In those papers he put the arguments, as far as they go, clearly and honestly, and the result, so far as I was concerned, was to convince me that Socialism was a necessary change, and that it was possible to bring it about in our own days. Those papers put the finishing touch to my conversion to Socialism. Well, having joined a Socialist body (for the Federation soon became definitely Socialist), I put some conscience into trying to learn the economical side of Socialism, and even tackled Marx, though I must confess that, whereas I thoroughly enjoyed the historical part of *Capital*, I suffered agonies of confusion of the brain over reading the pure economics of that great work. Anyhow, I read what I could, and will hope that some information stuck to me from my reading; but more, I must think, from continuous conversation with such friends as Bax and Hyndman and Scheu, and the brisk course of propaganda meetings which were going on at the time, and in which I took my share. Such finish to what of education in practical Socialism as I am capable of I received afterwards from some of my Anarchist friends, from whom I learned, quite against their intention, that Anarchism was impossible, much as I learned from Mill against his intention that Socialism was necessary.

But in this telling how I fell into *practical* Socialism I have begun, as I perceive, in the middle, for in my position of a well-to-do man, not suffering from the disabilities which oppress a working man at every step, I feel that I might never have been drawn into the practical side of the question if an ideal had not forced me to seek towards it. For politics as politics, i.e., not regarded as a necessary if cumbersome and disgustful means to an end, would never have attracted me, nor when I had become conscious of the wrongs of society as it now is, and the oppression of poor people, could I have ever believed in the possibility of a *partial* setting right of those wrongs. In other words, I could never have been such a fool as to believe in the happy and "respectable" poor.

If, therefore, my ideal forced me to look for practical Socialism, what was it that forced me to conceive of an ideal? Now, here comes in what I said (in this paper)[1] of my being a type of a certain type of mind.

Before the uprising of *modern* Socialism almost all intelligent people either were, or professed themselves to be, quite contented with the civilization of this century. Again, almost all of these really were thus contented, and saw nothing to do but to perfect the said civilization by getting rid of a few ridiculous survivals of the barbarous ages. To be short, this was the *Whig* frame of mind, natural to the modern prosperous middle-class men, who, in fact, as far as mechanical progress is concerned, have nothing to ask for, if only Socialism would leave them alone to enjoy their plentiful style.

But besides these contented ones there were others who were not really contented, but had a vague sentiment of repulsion to the triumph of civilization, but were coerced into silence by the measureless power of Whiggery. Lastly, there were a few who were in open rebellion against the said Whiggery—a few, say two, Carlyle and Ruskin. The latter, before my days of practical Socialism, was my master towards the ideal aforesaid, and, looking backward, I cannot help saying, by the way, how deadly dull the world would have been twenty years ago but for Ruskin! It was through him that I learned to give form to my discontent, which I must say was not by any means vague. Apart from the desire to produce beautiful things, the leading passion of my life has been and is hatred of modern civilization. What shall I say of it now,

1. I.e., *Justice*, whose editor, Harry Quelch (1858–1913), solicited Morris's contribution to a series, "How I Became a Socialist." Other contributors included Henry Mayers Hyndman, Ernest Belfort Bax, and Walter Crane.

when the words are put into my mouth, my hope of its destruction—what shall I say of its supplanting by Socialism?

What shall I say concerning its mastery of and its waste of mechanical power, its commonwealth so poor, its enemies of the commonwealth so rich, its stupendous organization—for the misery of life! Its contempt of simple pleasures which everyone could enjoy but for its folly? Its eyeless vulgarity which has destroyed art, the one certain solace of labour? All this I felt then as now, but I did not know why it was so. The hope of the past times was gone, the struggles of mankind for many ages had produced nothing but this sordid, aimless, ugly confusion; the immediate future seemed to me likely to intensify all the present evils by sweeping away the last survivals of the days before the dull squalor of civilization had settled down on the world. This was a bad look-out indeed, and, if I may mention myself as a personality and not as a mere type, especially so to a man of my disposition, careless of metaphysics and religion, as well as of scientific analysis, but with a deep love of the earth and the life on it, and a passion for the history of the past of mankind. Think of it! Was it all to end in a counting-house on the top of a cinder-heap, with Podsnap's drawing-room in the offing, and a Whig committee dealing out champagne to the rich and margarine to the poor in such convenient proportions as would make all men contented together, though the pleasure of the eyes was gone from the world, and the place of Homer was to be taken by Huxley?[2] Yet, believe me, in my heart, when I really forced myself to look towards the future, that is what I saw in it, and, as far as I could tell, scarce anyone seemed to think it worthwhile[3] to struggle against such a consummation of civilization. So there I was in for a fine pessimistic end of life, if it had not somehow dawned on me that amidst all this filth of civilization the seeds of a great change,[4] what we others call Social-Revolution, were beginning to germinate. The whole face of things was changed to me by that discovery, and all I had to do then in order to become a Socialist was to hook myself on to the practical movement, which, as before said, I have tried to do as well as I could.

2. Thomas Henry Huxley (1825–95), a biologist, anthropologist, member of the Royal Society, polemicist, and educator, was a prominent proponent of the theory of evolution. In 1894, the same year as Morris's essay, he published a collection, *Evolution and Ethics, and Other Essays* (Macmillan). Huxley's economic views would have displeased contemporary socialists, for in one of the articles reprinted in this collection, his 1890 essay "Capital—The Mother of Labour," Huxley disputed Marx's labour theory of value.
3. Orig., worth while
4. *CW*, 23, "chance"; Morton and MIA, "change"; the latter seems closer to Morris's meaning.

To sum up, then the study of history and the love and practice of art forced me into a hatred of the civilization which, if things were to stop as they are, would turn history into inconsequent nonsense, and make art a collection of the curiosities of the past, which would have no serious relation to the life of the present.

But the consciousness of revolution stirring amidst our hateful modern society prevented me, luckier than many others of artistic perceptions, from crystallizing into a mere railer against "progress" on the one hand, and on the other from wasting time and energy in any of the numerous schemes by which the quasi-artistic of the middle classes hope to make art grow when it has no longer any root, and thus I became a practical Socialist.

A last word or two. Perhaps some of our friends will say, what have we to do with these matters of history and art? We want by means of Social-Democracy to win a decent livelihood, we want in some sort to live, and that at once. Surely anyone who professes to think that the question of art and cultivation must go before that of the knife and fork (and there are some who do propose that) does not understand what art means, or how that its roots must have a soil of a thriving and unanxious life. Yet it must be remembered that civilization has reduced the workman to such a skinny and pitiful existence, that he scarcely knows how to frame a desire for any life much better than that which he now endures perforce. It is the province of art to set the true ideal of a full and reasonable life before him, a life to which the perception and creation of beauty, the enjoyment of real pleasure that is, shall be felt to be as necessary to man as his daily bread, and that no man, and no set of men, can be deprived of this except by mere opposition, which should be resisted to the utmost.

Figure 20.1 Peter Kropotkin (1842–1921). Courtesy of the Gallica Digital Library

Figure 20.2 Charlotte Martin Wilson (1854–1944). Charlotte at Newnham College, Cambridge; she is seated in the middle row, left. Courtesy of The Principal and Fellows, Newnham College

20

"Why I Am a Communist," 1894

Editor's introduction

"Why I Am a Communist" was published in *Liberty: A Journal of Anarchist Communism* on February 1, 1894 (vol. 1.2, 13–15). *Liberty*'s editor was James Tochatti, a Hammersmith tailor, union activist, and founding member and campaigner on behalf of the Socialist League.[1] A member of the League's anarchist faction, Tochatti had remained in the League after Morris's departure. Among anarchists of the period he was a relative moderate on the issue of tactics, for the November 21, 1892 *Commonweal* reported his speech at a meeting to commemorate the deaths of the Chicago anarchists:

> Tochatti objected to the wild language. We must not indulge in wild talk about dynamite and pillage (cries of dissent). As for dynamite, he was as ready to use it as any man, when the time came but any talk of its present use was madness. (Oh!) If we want to learn how to preach anarchy let us study the speeches of our Chicago comrades, and learn to explain our noble principles in the same clear and plain fashion (150).

When in late 1893 Tochatti solicited a contribution from Morris for his proposed journal *Liberty*, in the wake of the Walsall anarchist trial and recent terrorist incidents on the continent,[2] Morris asked that he repudiate the doctrine of propaganda by violence:

> I could not in conscience allow anything with my name attached to it to appear in an anarchist paper. . . unless you publish in said paper a distinct repudiation of such monstrosities. . . . I will ask you if you do not think you ought for your own sake . . . and for those who honestly think that the principles of anarchy are right, for I cannot for the life of me see how such principles, which profess the abolition of compulsion, can admit of promiscuous slaughter as a means of converting people—However I don't for a moment suppose that you agree with such propaganda by

> deed: But since I don't think so, that is the very reason why I think you should openly say that you don't. (December 12, 1893, Kelvin, 4.113)

Apparently Tochatti did provide this repudiation, and Morris contributed two essays to *Liberty*, "Why I Am a Communist" and "As to Bribing Excellence" (May 1895). Tochatti reprinted the former in a series of "The Why I Ams" at his Liberty Press the same year, paired with Louisa Sarah Bevington's *Why I Am an Expropriationist.* The manuscript is housed in the International Institute of Social History in Amsterdam (ARCH 00903), and, as Graham Seaman notes in his transcription of this essay on Marxists.org, the Liberty Press pamphlet omits a final paragraph included in the newspaper version in which Morris describes anarchism bluntly as "a negation of society" and a "kind of idealized despair."

The first part of the essay contains Morris's usual clear and eloquent exposition of his view of socialism as a state of "practical equality of condition": "This is its economical basis; its ethical basis is the habitual and full recognition of man as a social being, so that it brings about the habit of making no distinction between the common welfare and the welfare of the individual." Despite the historical progression from chattel slavery through serfdom to a modern-day plutocracy, one constant has remained: "the essential assertion of the necessity for inequality has always been there." Morris spends some time in debunking the notion that those viewed as more worthy are deservedly so: "the functions of the worthy amongst us being directed solely towards their own class; they being otherwise a burden on the *whole* public." Inequality breeds waste, for if one member of the community hoards an excess, "that portion which cannot be used must of necessity be wasted, and the whole Community is impoverished thereby."

Skeptics have asked how a communist society could procure specialists, such as doctors, with the implication that more highly trained persons would need greater compensation.[3] In reply Morris contended that a communal society would provide opportunities for all to exercise their talents, subsidizing the "necessary costs of such opportunities," and since all share in equality of condition, no one would succumb to "the now very serious temptation of pretending to be a doctor when he is not one." This is but one of many ways in which a communist society could render benefits by equal distribution, Morris suggests; greater efficiency in producing utilities, for example, would free citizens for the satisfying pursuits of "art, research into facts [science], literature, the unspoiled beauty of nature . . . the things that make life worth living and which at present *nobody* can have in their fulness."

However, the essay's remaining pages attack what Morris sees as the shibboleths of anarchism: that violence against the state will be effective, that social revolution can be achieved by means of a single event, that workers will support violent revolution rather than immediate reforms, and that the effort to elect socialist candidates is misguided. On the means to establishing a society of equality Morris is quite clear:

> In the first place I do not (who does really) believe in Catastrophical Communism. That we shall go to sleep on Saturday in a Capitalistic Society and wake on Monday into a Communistic Society is clearly an impossibility. Again I do not believe that our end will be gained by open war; for the executive will be *too strong* for even an attempt at such a thing to be made until the change has gone so far, that it will be *too weak* to dare to attack the people by means of direct physical violence.

Moreover, the fantasy that a small minority can effect revolution is destructive; socialism must come by assent: "What we have to do first is to make Socialists."

In addition, changes are already occurring, and socialists should recognize these as hopeful: "the movement towards a communal life has spread wonderfully within the last three or four years; the instinctive feeling towards Socialism has at last touched the working classes, and they are moving toward the great change." Morris's optimism may be based in part on recent working-class efforts toward seizing more power, as manifested by the results of the 1892 general election, in which three working-class men had been elected to Parliament, and the formation of the Independent Labour Party in 1893 from a coalition of socialist and labor groups.[4]

For Morris this stance was a principled concession to current laborite efforts, for he had long advocated for a more revolutionary "one socialist party." He acknowledges what for him are the drawbacks to the aims of this working-class-led activism: "this instinct is not leading them to demand the full change directly . . . Broadly speaking they see that it is possible to wrest from their masters an improved life, better livelihood, more leisure, treatment in short as citizens, not as machines." However, in this context he emphasizes to his anarchist audience the need for active support of such reforms:

> Now to show sympathy with this side of the movement, and to further those who are working for it, is a necessity, if we are to make Socialists nowadays. For again I say it is the form in which the workers are taking in socialism; the movement is genuine and spontaneous amongst them . . . .

At last working people are leading their own movement, "and how important that is, those know best who remember how a few years ago the movement was confined to a few persons, of education and of superior intelligence, most of whom belonged by position to the middle classes."

Reformism is not the end, however, for once workers have gained this initial ground Morris believes they will not stop with the mere extraction of privileges from acknowledged masters: "For the results of the struggle will force on them the responsibilities of managing their own affairs." As he had maintained for more than a decade, Morris stresses that mere lessened inequality is not Socialism: "this period of incomplete Socialism will, I believe, gradually melt into true Communism without any violent change." Under true communism, administration must be "democratic and federative; that is to say there will be certain units of administration, ward, parish, commune, . . . and these units all federated within certain circles, always enlarging."[5] In the absence of the present rivalries of competing parties, debates would cease to be partisan: "the minority would give way without any feeling of injury." Since administration [i.e. bureaucracy] would no longer be a means to power, citizens would seek to reduce it "as much as possible that they might be the freer to use their lives in the pleasure of living, and creating, and knowing, and resting."

Morris's final expurgated paragraph is striking for its blunt attack on the views of its assumed readers: "I must say that I cannot recognize Anarchism (as it has been expounded to me[)] as a possible condition of Society, for it seems to me in its essence to be a negation of society; I rather look upon it as a mood . . . a kind of idealized despair . . ." Instead, one should view recent events with optimism, for "the socio-political movement of today. . . is most certainly setting towards Socialism in its narrower sense, and consequently toward Socialism in its wider sense." Equally important may be the essay's admission that Morris and/or his associates may have altered their views on the real if limited merits of gradualism—"Some time ago we, or some of us[,] scarcely saw it, but growing hope has now pointed it out to us." Morris is also unequivocal about the duty of all who wish an eventual socialism/communism to support "the only possible method for bringing about the great change . . . to equality and general wealth," that is, the existing labor movement.

It is unlikely that Morris would have expressed such favorable views of this movement even three or four years earlier, and when faced with Fabian and Socialist Democratic Federation audiences entirely committed to parliamentary elections, he continued to urge them to focus instead on ends as well as means. After Morris's death

Tochatti published his "Reminiscence of William Morris" in the final, December 1896 issue of *Liberty*. He argued that:

> It is a great mistake to suppose that Morris changed his views with regard to parliamentary action. In a comparatively recent lecture at Kelmscott House he expressed his belief that the people were going that way, but he added with emphasis, 'Don't make the mistake of thinking this, Socialism'. . . . Like his friend Walter Crane, he helped all, being too great a man to be sectarian.

Tochatti promised more reminiscences and an account of Morris's letters to him on the topic of Socialism in the next issue, but *Liberty* ceased publication after December 1896 and these reminiscences did not appear.[6]

Perhaps the matter of interpreting Morris's carefully nuanced views is one of emphasis and timing. In 1894 Morris was in declining health and unable to campaign as vigorously as he might have wished. It seems clear that in "Why I Am a Communist," he uses his position as socialist elder statesman to enjoin those of all factions, including his anarchist friends, to support every plausible, peaceful effort to realize their ultimate shared aims of equality and "liberty."

Notes

1. Stephen Williams and Florence Boos, "James Tochatti: A Little-Known Morris Socialist Comrade," *Useful and Beautiful* 2 (2017): 24–7.
2. Fatal bombings attributed to anarchists had occurred during 1893 in Barcelona and Paris.
3. Tochatti printed a note in the October 1894 issue of *Liberty*, "[A]t a meeting in Hyde Park, we were met with the . . . objection that it would be unreasonable to expect our great men to work at the anvil and like laborious work, in fact it would unfit our poets and artists in their doing fine and delicate work, and our opponent contended that William Morris would be unable to produce the artistic work he now does. Since this is an objection we commonly meet with in propaganda we wrote to William Morris for an expression of his opinion on this subject." Morris's reply is printed in Kelvin, 4.209.
4. Three working-class men had been elected as MPs in 1892 without support from the Liberal Party. Formed in 1893 with Keir Hardie as its first chairperson, the Independent Labour Party's constituency consisted of trade union activists, Social Democratic Federation and Fabian socialists, and members of other labor groups, with a platform committed to the relatively radical program of securing "the collective and communal organization of the means of production, distribution and exchange." Nonetheless its immediate aims were concrete: the eight-hour work day; secular primary and secondary education; unemployment relief and work programs; a minimum wage and the abolition of piecework; welfare programs for orphans, widows, the elderly, and the disabled; school meals and medical care; and the abolition of child labor.

5. For a discussion of Morris and the movement to reform local governments, see Martin Martel, "Romancing the Folk Mote: William Morris, the Socialist League, and Local Direct Democracy," *Useful and Beautiful* 1 (2018): 1–17.
6. The December 12, 1893 letter cited above is the sole Morris letter to Tochatti in Kelvin's *Collected Letters*, so these letters may have been lost.

Objection has been made to the use of the word "Communism" to express fully-developed Socialism, on the ground that it has been used for the Community-Building, which played so great a part in some of the phases of Utopian Socialism, and is still heard of from time to time nowadays. Of Communism in this sense I am not writing now; it may merely be said in passing that such experiments are of their nature non-progressive; at their best they are but another form of the Mediæval monastery, withdrawals from the Society of the day, really implying hopelessness of a general change; which is only attainable by the development of Society as it is; by the development of the consequences of its faults and anomalies, as well as of what germ of real Society it contains.

This point of mistaken nomenclature being cleared off, it remains to ask what real Communism is, and the answer is simple: it is a state of Society the essence of which is *Practical Equality of condition*. Practical, *i.e.*, equality as modified by the desires, and capacity for enjoyment of its various members. This is its economical basis; its ethical basis is the *habitual* and full recognition of man as a social being, so that it brings about the habit of making no distinction between the common welfare and the welfare of the individual.

I am a Communist, therefore, because—1st, it seems to me that mankind is not thinkable outside of Society; and 2ndly, because there is no other basis, economical and ethical, save that above stated, on which a true Society can be formed; any other basis makes waste and unnecessary suffering an essential part of the system. In short I can see no other system under which men can live together except these two, Slavery and Equality.

The first of these two says, some standard of worth having been determined (of course not as a result of the immediate agreement of men living under such and such a system, but of the long development of many centuries) those who have attained to that standard are the masters of those who have not so attained, and live as well as surrounding circumstances, together with a quasi-equitable arrangement amongst the worthy, will allow them, by *using* those who have not come up to the standard above mentioned: in the dealings between the worthy with the non-worthy there is no attempt at any equitable arrangement (I was going to say no *pretence*, but at the present day that would not be quite true); the worthy use their advantage to the utmost, and it is a recognized assumption that the non-worthy are in a state of permanent inferiority, and their well-doing or ill-doing must be looked at from quite a different point of view from that of the worthy. For instance at the present day, the income which would imply ruin and disgrace to a member of the worthy class, would mean success and prosperity to a working man. It must be added that the standard of superiority is always an arbitrary one, and does not necessarily mean any real superiority on the side of the worthy; and that especially in our own days, when the unworthy or disinherited class is the one class which has any real function, is, in fact, the useful class; the functions of the worthy amongst us being directed solely towards their own class; they being otherwise a burden on the *whole* public.

Now this theory of society has been that held for the most part from early historical periods till our own days, though from time to time there have been protests raised against it. The standard of worthiness has varied, but the essential assertion of the necessity for inequality has always been there. In its two earlier phases; birth and race, i.e., the belonging, really or theoretically, to the lineage of the original conquering tribe, conferred the privilege of using the labour of those not so recognized; and Chattel Slavery was the method of using their labour in Ancient, and Serfdom in Mediæval times. In our own days the method of exercising privilege has changed from the use of the arbitrary accident of birth, to the acquirement (by any means not recognized as illegal) of an indeterminate amount of wealth which enables its possessor to belong to the useless class.

It would not be very profitable to discuss which of these three systems of inequality, to wit, Chattel Slavery, Serfdom, or Wage-Earning, is *per se* the better or the worse; it is enough to say that since the present one has come down to us in due course of development from the others, it gives us a hope of progress which could not have belonged to them. And in fact a new theory of Society can now be put forward, not as a mere abstraction, but as a root change in Social conditions which is in actual course of realization.

This theory is Communism; which says: In a true Society the capacities of all men can be used for their mutual well[-] being; the due unwasteful use of those capacities produces wealth in the proper sense of the word and cannot fail to produce it; this wealth produced by the Community can only be fully used by the Community; for if some get more than they need, that portion which cannot be used must of necessity be wasted, and the whole Community is impoverished thereby; and again further impoverished by the necessity for the producers having to work harder than they otherwise need; which in its turn brings about grievous and burdensome inequality; for all men feel unnecessary work to be slavish work. Again, though men's desires for wealth vary, yet certain needs all men have, and since we have seen that it is the *Community* which produces wealth in a true society, to force on any class lack of these needs is to practically thrust them out of the Community and constitute them a class of inferiority; and since we know that they can all work usefully, on what grounds can we do this? Certainly on no grounds that they as men can really agree to. We must *force* them into submission, or cajole them into it. And when force and fraud are used to keep any men in an artificial inequality, there is an end of true Society.

Communism, therefore can see no reason for inequality of condition: to each one according to his needs, from each one according to his capacities, must always be its motto. And if it be challenged to answer the question, what are the needs of such and such a man, how are they to be estimated? The answer is that the habitual regard towards Society as the real unit, will make it impossible for any man to think of claiming more than his genuine needs. I say that it will not come into his mind that it is possible for him to advance himself by injuring someone else. While, on the other hand, it will be well understood that unless you satisfy a man's needs, you cannot make the best of his capacities. We are sometimes asked by people who do not understand either the present state of society or what Communism aims at, as to how we shall get people to be doctors, learned scientists, etc., in the new condition of things.

The answer is clear; by affording opportunities to those who have the capacity for doctoring etc.; the necessary cost of such opportunities being borne by the Community; and as the position of a doctor who has mistaken his vocation would clearly be an uncomfortable one in a society where people knew their real wants, and as he could earn his livelihood by engaging himself to do what he *could* do, he would be delivered from the now very serious temptation of pretending to be a doctor when he is not one.

I might go through a long series of objections which ignorant persons make to the only reasonable form of Society, but that is scarcely my business here. I will assert that I am a Communist because, amongst other reasons, I believe that a Communal Society could deal with every problem with which a Capitalist Society has perforce to deal, but with free hands and therefore with infinitely better chance of success. I believe that a Communal Society would bring about a condition of things in which we should be really wealthy, because we should have all we produced, and should know what we wanted to produce; that we should have so much leisure from the production of what are called "utilities," that any group of people would have leisure to satisfy its cravings for what are usually looked on as superfluities, such as works of art, research into facts, literature, the unspoiled beauty of nature; matters that to my mind are utilities also, being the things that make life worth living and which at present *nobody* can have in their fulness.

I believe in the final realization of this state of things, and now I come to the method by which they are to be reached. And here I feel I shall be dealing in matter about which there may be and must be divers opinions even amongst those who are consciously trying to bring about Communal conditions.

In the first place I do not (who does really) believe in Catastrophical Communism. That we shall go to sleep on Saturday in a Capitalistic Society and wake on Monday into a Communistic Society is clearly an impossibility. Again I do not believe that our end will be gained by open war; for the executive will be *too strong* for even an attempt at such a thing to be made until the change has gone so far, that it will be *too weak* to dare to attack the people by means of direct physical violence.

What we have to do first is to make Socialists. That we shall always have to do until the change is come. Some time ago we seemed to have nothing else to do than that, and could only do it by preaching; but the times are changed; the movement towards a communal life has spread wonderfully within the last three or four years; the instinctive feeling towards Socialism has at last touched the working classes, and they are moving toward the great change; how quickly it is not easy for us, who are in the midst of the movement, to determine; but this instinct is not leading them to demand the *full* change directly; rather they are attacking those positions which must be won, before we come face to face with the last citadel of Capitalism, the privilege of rent, interest, and profit. Broadly speaking they see that it is possible to wrest from their masters an improved life, better livelihood, more leisure, treatment in short as citizens, not as machines. I say from their masters: for there is nowhere else whence it can come. Now to show sympathy with this side of the movement, and to further those who are working for it, is a necessity, if we are to make Socialists nowadays. For again I say it is the form in which the workers are taking in Socialism; the movement is genuine and spontaneous amongst them; and how important that is, those know best who remember how a few years ago the movement was confined to a few persons, of education and of superior intelligence, most of whom belonged by position to the middle classes. Neither need we fear that when the working classes have gained the above-mentioned[1] advantages they will stop there. They will not and they cannot. For the results of the struggle will force on them the responsibilities of managing their own affairs, and mastership will wane before Communal management almost before people are aware of the change at hand.

This will bring us at last to the period of what is now understood by the word Socialism[,] when the means of production and the markets will be in the hands of those who can use them, *i.e.*, the operatives of various kinds; when great accumulations of wealth will be impossible, because money will have lost its privilege; when everybody will have an opportunity of well-doing offered him; and this period of incomplete Socialism will, I believe, gradually melt into true Communism without any violent change. At first indeed, men will not be absolutely equal in condition; the old habit of rewarding excellence or special rare qualities with extra money payment will go on for a while, and some men will possess more wealth than others; but as on the one hand they will have to work in order to possess that wealth, and as on the other the excess of it will procure them but small advantage in a Society tending towards equality, as in fact they begin to understand that in a Community where none are poor, extra wealth beyond the real needs of a man cannot be *used*, we shall begin to cease estimating worth by any standard of material reward, and the position of complete equality as to condition will be accepted without question. I do not say that gifted persons will not try to excel; but their excellence will be displayed not at the expense of their neighbours but for their benefit.

By that time also we shall have learned the true secret of happiness, to wit, that it is brought about by the pleasurable exercise of our energies; and since opportunity will be given for everyone to do the work he is fitted for under pleasant and unburdensome conditions, there will be no drudgery to escape from, and consequently no competition to thrust one[']s neighbour out of his place in order to attain to it.

As to what may be called the business conduct of Communism, it has been said often, and rightly as I think, that it will concern itself with the administration of things rather than the government of men. But this administration must take form, and that form must of necessity be democratic and federative; that is to say there will be certain units of administration, ward, parish, commune, whatever they may be called, and these units all federated within certain circles, always

1. Orig., above mentioned

enlarging. And in each such body, if differences of opinion arise, as they would be sure to do, there would be surely nothing for it but that they should be settled by the will of the majority. But it must be remembered that whereas in our present state of society, in every assembly there are struggles between *opposing interests* for the mastery, in the assemblies of a Communal Society, there would be no opposition of interests, but only divergencies of opinion, as to the best way of doing what all were agreed to do. So that the minority would give way without any feeling of injury. It is a matter of course that since everybody would share to the full in the wealth and good life won by the whole community, so everybody would share in the responsibility of carrying on the business of the community; but this business of administration they would as sensible people reduce as much as possible, that they might be the freer to use their lives in the pleasure of living, and creating, and knowing, and resting.

This is a brief sketch of what I am looking forward to as a Communist: to sum up, it is Freedom from artificial disabilities; the development of each man's capacities for the benefit of each and all. Abolition of waste by taking care that one man does not get more than he can use, and another less than he needs; consequent condition of general well-being and fulness of life, neither idle and vacant, nor over burdened with toil.

All this I believe we can and shall reach directly by insisting on the claim for the communization of the means of production; and that claim will be made by the workers when they are fully convinced of its necessity; I believe further that they are growing convinced of it, and will one day make their claim good by using the means which the incomplete democracy of the day puts within their reach. That is[,] they will at last form a widespread and definite Socialist party, which will, by using the vote, wrest from the present possessing classes the instruments which are now used to govern the people in the interest of the possessing classes, and will use them for effecting the change in the basis of society, which would get rid of the last of the three great oppressions of the world.

[omitted in pamphlet] This is the only road which I can see toward the attainment of Communism. Some time ago we, or some of us scarcely saw it; but growing hope has now pointed it out to us, and it seems to me that we are bound to use it if we are in earnest in wishing to see Communism realized. I am opposed to Anarchism then (among other reasons) because it forbids the use of the only possible method for bringing about the great change from privilege and inequality and property to equality and general wealth. So much for its tactics. As to its theory, I must say that I cannot recognize Anarchism (as it has been expounded to me as a possible condition of Society, for it seems to me in its essence to be a negation of society; I rather look upon it as a mood engendered by the wrongs and follies of our false society of inequality, and which will disappear with them. A kind of idealized despair, surely not justified by the state of the socio-political movement of today; which is most certainly setting towards Socialism in its narrower sense, and consequently towards Socialism in its wider sense, which is what I have been speaking of as Communism.

Valedictory, 1895–1896

Figure 21.1 Orchard Tapestry, 1890. Courtesy of the Victoria and Albert Museum

21

What We Have to Look For

Editor's introduction

Morris delivered "What We Have to Look For" twice in the year before his death: to his beloved Hammersmith Socialist Society, in Kelmscott House on March 31, 1895, and to the Oxford and District Socialist Union at Gloucester Green on October 30, 1895. The lecture was relatively brief and valedictory, but handwritten notes at the end of Morris's manuscript suggest that its Hammersmith delivery may have aroused debate. An account of the second delivery appeared in the November 2, 1895 *Oxford Times* and is reproduced at www.marxists.org/archive/morris/works/1895/look2.htm, along with a report from the Secretary of the Oxford and District Socialist Union, J. Grenfell, published in the November 9, 1895 *Justice*: "William Morris' address was a brilliant success in all ways. Crowded room, excellent lecture, earnest and full of sound advice, a brisk fire of questions answered with much point and brilliancy." May Morris excerpted a section from the beginning and two shorter passages from the end in *William Morris: Artist, Writer, Socialist* (2.357–61), and the manuscript remains in British Library Add. MS. 45,333 (3), ff. 56–68.

Morris's remarks express qualified gratification at the rise of socialist and quasi-socialist sentiments among the general public in recent years, as well as discouragement regarding the probable limitations of worker electoral efforts as a means of true reform. He bluntly chides what he identifies as the two major socialist parties of his day for their unwillingness to combine their efforts, and though he avoids mentioning names, his audience would have clearly recognized his references. Without unity, he warns, the prospect of a true socialist government—and the even happier prospect of the end of economic inequality and arbitrary rule—is unlikely. Even more ominously, in the absence of popular support for the cohesive ideals of socialism, society itself faces the prospect of breakdown and collapse.

Morris is here responding to the failure of the effort at socialist unity which he had strongly promoted during the preceding two years. In early 1893 the Hammersmith Socialist Society initiated an effort to form a Socialist Federation, with Morris as its representative, and the Fabian Society and Social Democratic Federation (SDF) were invited to send representatives. E. P. Thompson relates that the Fabians, as represented by George Bernard Shaw, refused to sign a platform in support of worker ownership of resources, and Henry Hyndman, representing the SDF, objected to permitting participation by the Independent Labour Party (ILP), which had formed in 1893;[1] Thompson summarizes with exasperation, "So ended Morris's most earnest attempt to promote a united party—with the Fabians frightened off by their own *Manifesto*, and Hyndman resolutely closing his eyes to the very existence of the I. L. P."[2]

Though the 1895 July–August general election that brought a Tory victory and the defeat of all twenty-eight ILP candidates had not yet been held at the time Morris first delivered this speech, he may have feared that socialist and labor-allied candidates would not do well in the immediate future. A December 1894 local contest for the London Vestry and Board of Guardians had resulted in the defeat of all Vestry candidates from the "Progressive" slate, including his own daughter May Morris. Although eight candidates from this list were elected to the Guardians, Morris noted that their powers were severely circumscribed.[3] In the absence of a unified socialist effort based on egalitarian principles, he enjoins his hearers to pave the way for future socialist electoral success by continuing to advocate for true socialism—a position consistent with the stance of his lecture's first audience, the members of the Hammersmith Socialist Society.

Accordingly in "What We Have to Look For," Morris argues that the underlying aim of sincere socialists should be to bring about an "end of all politics;" that even socialist political parties are makeshifts as well as dubious means to untrustworthy parliamentary ends; and that no legislation in a capitalist society will bring about more than tenuous palliative changes in ordinary people's lives. This is, of course, a more skeptical view than he had expressed in recent essays such as the 1894 "Why I Am a Communist," or those developed in 1896 in his semi-final publication, "The Present Outlook of Socialism in England," in both of which he suggests that initial working-class parliamentary successes would likely lead to a later period in which workers would demand and achieve more fundamental shifts in power.

Morris began his remarks with an admission that under present circumstances his topic was "a dull job, a dispiriting job[,] because it must necessarily deal with failure and disappointment and stupidity and causeless quarrels, and in short all the miseries that go to make up the degrading game of politics." He notes that this response was in marked and somewhat poignant contrast with the ardor of the early days in the SDF and the Socialist League, when "we had nothing to think of seriously except preaching Socialism to those who knew nothing of it but the name . . . . [W]e gained . . . adherents, and good ones, and that more speedily than might have been expected. . . ." Although early socialists had faced heavy resistance: "[F]rom the depths of their muddling impracticality [audiences] thought our views were impractical," there has been a heartening change: "the number of those [who] can vaguely be classed as socialists has increased enormously, besides a very considerable increase in those who definitely profess Socialism, [and] . . . it has become a common-place that there is little difference between the two parties except that of ins & outs." Or as Old Hammond had put it in chapter 14 of *News from Nowhere*:

> . . . [the two major parties] only PRETENDED to this serious difference of opinion; for if it had existed they could not have dealt together in the ordinary business of life; couldn't have eaten together, bought and sold together, gambled together, cheated other people together, but must have fought whenever they met: which would not have suited them at all. The game of the masters of politics was to cajole or force the public to pay the expense of a luxurious life and exciting amusement for a few cliques of ambitious persons: and the PRETENCE of serious difference of opinion, belied by every action of their lives, was quite good enough for that.

More than 125 years later, these observations sound hauntingly familiar.

Drawing further on his personal experiences in the Socialist League, Morris noted another drawback to political contests: "election times were the very worst times for our propaganda: no one with any political bias could disentangle his thoughts and aspirations from the great party dog-fight which was going on . . . ." As often during this period he predicts that the Liberal Party will soon break apart into two factions, one comprised of potential reactionaries, and the other of potential socialists, a change expedited by the fact that public opinion was no longer credulously trustful of the law of the markets ("the old Manchester school, the utilitarian Laissez faire business"): "everywhere people are shaken as to their views of the eternity of the present system which was once as undoubted a fact to them as the existence of the sun in the heavens."

Another major reversal was that socialists themselves no longer believed in the imminence of revolution: "Almost everyone has ceased to believe in the change coming by catastrophe," a noticeable shift from a period in which

> [he and others] thought that the change we advocated would be brought about by insurrection; and this was supposed even by those who were most averse to violence: no other means seemed conceivable for lifting the intolerable load which lay upon us.

Still, capitalism had not receded: ". . . there are the unemployed. Nothing has been done for them in the mass, and nothing will be done for them"; and worse, the present system remained as before utterly unable to satisfy basic human needs. Even palliatives such as a welfare/workfare system would merely buttress an exploitive wage system for everyone:

> . . . if [it] should [ever] come to be the case that [it] is understood that they who fail in the competition shall have places provided for them by the state, there will be a tendency for wages to fall amongst those who are generally employed . . . . [A]ll those measures for improving the material condition of the working classes without altering their positions . . . [mean] more or less feeding the dog with his own tail.

Faced with this impasse, the pseudo-paternalistic Tories might "make a showy benevolent present (which in the long run will be of no use to you) rather than yield a right however small." Only slightly better, the Liberals under pressure might make "certain improvements in the present creaky and clumsy electoral machinery which will be of some use to you." He makes a further distinction between even complete socialist electoral success and socialism itself: "while the battle for Socialism is going on you can only have the hope of realizing Socialism." So long as such palliatives hold, workers will never be independent; to do well they must "pay the greatest attention to producing exactly what [the] markets demand and at the price they demand."

But such a system is inherently unstable, and at this point Morris makes one of his more important, as well as ominous and troubled, predictions:

> . . . I cannot for the life of me see how the great change which we long for can come otherwise than by disturbance and suffering of some kind. Well, since battle also has been made a matter of commerce, and the God of War must now wear a mantle of bank-notes and be crowned with guineas, . . . since war has been commercialized, I say, we shall . . . not be called upon to gain our point by battle in the field. But the disturbance and the

> suffering—can we escape that? I fear not . . . . Can that combat be fought out[,] again I say[,] without loss and suffering? Plainly speaking I *know* that it cannot.

The elusiveness of these references to "disturbance and suffering . . . loss and suffering" mirror his unease at the political future of "true socialism" as well as uncertainty about the forms such suffering might take—economic collapse, civil war, invasion, environmental loss, the end of national identity, or, far worse, the death of the socialist ideal?

Despite earlier assurances, Morris expresses strong reservations about the tenor of present-day electoral efforts:

> [S]ometimes when I am dispirited I think this is all that the labour movement means: it doesn't mean Socialism at all, it only means improvement in the condition of the working-classes: they will get that in some terms or another—*till the break up comes*, and it may be a long way ahead . . . . *the workmen of this country seem to me to be going so very far from the right road* to winning the slavish peace I have been speaking of . . . . [emphases mine]

It is hard not to see in this passage an admission that "the Great Change" might not come as he had hoped in *News from Nowhere* (1890–1): as a "natural" synergetic result of nonviolent resistance, anger at police repression, and the emergence of new forms of organization and governance in England's green and pleasant land.

Against this bleak prognosis, Morris seizes on some remaining signs of hope. The first is a growing "spirit of antagonism to our present foolish[,] wasteful system . . . and a sense of the unity of labour as against the exploiters of labour . . . ." He finds an indication of this spirit in the surprisingly favorable public response accorded to a recent nominally socialist treatise, Robert Blatchford's 1895 *Merrie England*, which eventually sold more than three million copies in Britain and the United States.[4]

Blatchford (1851–1943) was a professed admirer of Morris, a member of the Independent Labour Party, and an advocate of unity among the various factions of British socialism. Morris's commendation was nonetheless a gracious response to a fellow writer whose popularizations advocated a socialism quite different from "the absolute equality of condition" which Morris had identified as "true socialism" or "communism." For as its nostalgic title might suggest, *Merrie England* sidestepped deep questions of oppression, class conflict, and the means for effecting social change. To see why this wave of popular sentiment (in both senses of the word) must have bemused as well as impressed

Morris, compare Blatchford's rosewater characterization of imperialism (in effect), as the

> present national ideal [which] is to become "The Workshop of the World." That is to say, the British people are to manufacture goods for sale to foreign countries, and in return for those goods are to get more money than they could obtain by developing the resources of their own country for their own use.
>
> My ideal is that each individual should seek his advantage in co-operation with his fellows, and that the people should make the best of their own country before attempting to trade with other people's. (*Merrie England*, chap. 2)

with the following passage from chapter 15 of Morris's *News from Nowhere*:

> The appetite of the World-Market grew with what it fed on: the countries within the ring of "civilization" (that is, organised misery) were glutted with the abortions of the market, and force and fraud were used unsparingly to "open up" countries *outside* that pale.[5]

It was not trade with foreign nations Morris decried, or failure to develop the resources of their own country. It was imperial domination, repression of native culture, and extraction of raw materials for the profit of a small minority.

As for the ideal of a single socialist party (cf. the Wobblies' "one big union"), it might operate on the voluntarily cooperative model of the previously proposed Socialist Federation: ". . . once formed [it] would not break up any existing bodies but include them, [and if so, it] would, it seems to me, have a claim on all genuine socialists . . . ." Morris here calls out the existing socialist parties:

> Well[,] first[,] what are the Socialist forces in the country? Answer two or three—say two bodies partly propagandist[,] partly with electoral views[,] probably of no great strength as to count of noses. More of them I won[']t say at present as I don[']t want to get into controversy as to their relative [merits]; so I will but note that there is at least rivalry between them and sometimes dissension. Besides these two bodies, there are no doubt many pronounced Socialists who are not attached to either . . . .

The "two or three" would likely be the Fabians, the SDF, and perhaps the Hammersmith Socialist Society, with the other "pronounced Socialists" perhaps referring to the Independent Labour Party, whose founding conference in 1893 had affirmed the socialist aim of securing "the collective and communal ownership of the means of production, distribution and exchange." Yet, sadly, these factions even in aggregate are yet "a sect" rather than a party:

> [Y]ou see that we have settled that we want to go into parliament, and for that it seems to me a party is definitely necessary; that declaring ourselves socialists we shall formulate our immediate tactics toward that end: . . . and one thing at least I am sure of[,] *that until it is formed, though we may do good propagandist work we shall do nothing worth speaking of in the political way.* [emphases mine]

A final caution may hint at the factionalism of current socialist leaders: such a future party "will not allow the personal fads and vanities of the leaders (so-called) to stand in the way of real business."

However, given the recent impasses in any attempt to form such a party, Morris counsels that its existence might have to "wait till the general body of socialists see the futility of mere sections attempting to do the work of the whole mass properly organised." Well aware that Fabians, parliamentarians, and members of the SDF would disagree, he enjoined his audience therefore to let others press for

> . . . measures which may be for the temporary good of their class, which are but temporary and experimental, and adapted only for the present state of things, ... Let our liberal and radical . . . friends make these experiments, and take all the responsibility for their failure, for in the long run fail they will.

What he sought for was not a more comfortable "machine life of the useful classes," but a genuine liberation—not a "freedom to sleep under bridges" (in the words of Anatole France) or a freedom to choose one's tenth-generation form of interactive electronic entertainment, but a free social order in which

> those who wish to work happily and unwastefully, to restore that of the earth's surface which is spoilt and keep that which is unspoilt, to enjoy rest and thought and labour without fear or remorse[,] . . . shall be free because we are equal.[6]

Morris was well aware that environmentalism and negative capability come more easily to comfortably situated dissidents ("In these matters I always think what I should do myself; and I find it difficult to answer the question . . ."). But he held firm to his conviction that the ultimate aim for all of us should be "self-respect, happy and fit work, leisure, beautiful surroundings[—]in a word, the earth our own and the fullness thereof."

As his health declined, Morris admitted that he did not know how to break through the barriers of state power and factional impasse. He could only urge his audience to maintain whatever unity was possible, promote their cause through "the old teaching and preaching of Socialism pure and simple," and confront these continuing barriers honestly, candidly, and with a measure of tempered hope.

Notes

1. In 1892 three working men had been successful in a general election. The Independent Labour Party was founded in 1893, with Keir Hardie as chairman, and called for collective and communal ownership of production, distribution, and exchange. When the Labour Party was founded in 1906, the ILP became an affiliate.
2. Thompson, 610. His full account of the episode, "An Approach to Unity," appears on pp. 607–10.
3. Thompson, 619; letter to Georgiana Burne-Jones, December 14, 1894, Kelvin, 4.241. However, after the election he was more positive: "Here they beat us properly; though I didn't think, all things considered, that it was so bad, as we polled about half of what they did." Letter to Georgiana, December 20, 1894, Kelvin, 4.243.
4. *Merrie England* (London: Clarion Newspaper Company, 1895). The preface to the 1895 edition notes that when this edition has been sold out, 875,000 copies will have been sold since its first printing in October 1894, and eventually two million copies were reported as sold in Britain (Laurence Thompson, *Robert Blatchford: Portrait of an Englishman* [London: Victor Gollancz, 1957], 101). In addition, according to Jason Martinek's "'The Workingman's Bible': Robert Blatchford's 'Merrie England,' Radical Literacy, and the Making of Debsian Socialism, 1895–1900," in *New Perspectives on Socialism*, special issue of *The Journal of the Gilded Age and Progressive Era* 2.3, I (July 2003): 326–46, more than a million copies were reportedly sold in the United States.
   Chris Waters has observed in "William Morris and the Socialism of Robert Blatchford" (*Journal of William Morris Studies* 5 [1982]) that "[b]oth [men] shared the conviction that the morally transformed life played a crucial role in the battle for socialism . . . [and] believed that the most important duty of socialists was education, to make more socialists' (22). By 1892 the Hammersmith Socialist Society had begun to sell the *Clarion* at its meetings (21), and when in 1894 Blatchford proposed the founding of a united socialist party, Morris expressed interest, though in the event this group failed to materialize.
5. *CW*, 16.94, chap. 15.
6. MS., what

❧

I do not mean by this what the ideal of Socialism has to offer to us when we have got people[']s heads turned in the right direction, but rather what our present movement may reasonably expect to come across in its progress towards Socialism; it is not prophecy that I am about tonight but a reasonable forecast of the few next moves deduced from the experience of the last few. I consider this a dull job, a dispiriting job[,] because it must necessarily deal with failure and disappointment and stupidity and causeless quarrels, and in short all the miseries that go to make up the degrading game of politics. Still I think it has to be done, in order that we may get on to the next step, and the next and the next till we reach the one where the end of all politics will be clear to us.

Within the last 5 years or so the movement which represents the change from the society of so called free-contract to that of communal organization has undergone a great change[.] In the early days of our movement we had nothing to think of seriously except preaching Socialism to those who knew nothing of it but the name, if indeed they knew[1] that, in the hope that amidst those we addressed our words might touch a few who were sympathetic with the movement, and were capable of learning what we had to teach; or indeed a good deal more. In that hope we were not disappointed. The greater part of the public indeed from the depths of their ignorance thought us mere visionaries, from the depths of their muddling impracticality thought our views were impractical. It must be admitted that behind this propaganda of preaching lay the thought that the change we advocated would be brought about by insurrection; and this was supposed even by those who were most averse to violence: no other means seemed conceivable for lifting the intolerable load which lay upon us. We thought that every step towards Socialism would be resisted by the reactionaries who would use against [us] the legal executive force which was and is, let me say, wholly in the power of the possessing classes; that the wider the movement grew the more rigorously the authorities would repress it. And we were somewhat justified by their treatment of us; for while the movement was yet quite young the said authorities began to think that we were not only foolish but dangerous, which latter we may yet turn out to be, though not in the way which they meant by the word: hence all the stupid police interference with harmless meetings, and Black Monday and Bloody Sunday and the rest of it.

Now there is another thing; we gained, as I said, adherents, and good ones, and that more speedily than might have been expected, because the spirit of Socialism was alive, and on the way, and only lacked, as it does now, the due body which would make it a powerful force. But for a long time we did not touch the very people whom we chiefly wanted to get at,—the working classes to wit. Of course there were many working-men amongst us, but they were there by dint of their special intelligence, or of their eccentricity; not as working-men simply. In fact as a friend of ours once said to me, we are too much a

1. MS., new

collection of *oddities*[.] Anyhow the great body of working men, and especially those belonging to the most organized industries[,] were hostile to Socialism: they did not really look upon themselves as a class, they identified their interests with those of their trade-union, their craft, their workshop or factory even: the capitalist system seemed to them, if not heaven-born, yet at least necessary, and undoubtedly indefeasible.

I don't know if we expected this, but I do not think it dispirited us, partly perhaps because we would not admit it, being sanguine to the verge of braggadocio[.] Well now[,] much of this is changed: the idea of successful insurrection within a measurable distance of time is only [in] the heads of the anarchists, who seem to have a strange notion that even equality would not be acceptable if [it] were not gained by violence only. Almost everyone has ceased to believe in the change coming by catastrophe. To state the position shortly, as a means to the realization of the new society Socialists hope so far to conquer public opinion, that at last a majority of the parliament shall be sent to sit in the house as avowed Socialists and the delegates of Socialists, and on that should follow what legislation might be necessary and moreover, though the time for this may be very far ahead, yet most people would now think that the hope of doing it is by no means unreasonable.

Next it is no longer the case that the working-classes are hostile to Socialism, they even vaguely approve of it generally, and from time [to time] take action through strikes and other agitation which amounts to a claim to be recognized as citizens, and not looked upon as merely part of the machinery for profit-bearing production; [a]nd the number of those [who] can vaguely be classed as socialists has increased enormously, besides a very considerable increase in those who definitely profess Socialism[;] and all this has produced so much impression on the possessing classes, that they are beginning to think of making some concessions in the direction, as they think, of Socialism, so long as it can be done 'safely'.[2]

Another change has taken place outside Socialism amongst the ordinary politicians which has surely some relation to the movement; this is that the old political parties and their watchwords[3] are losing their importance. When we first began our Socialist work in London the two orthodox parties of Tories and Liberals were so completely prominent

2. In *Artist Writer Socialist*, the version used by May Morris adds after "increased" a passage which in the British Library manuscript is placed later: "the condition of one group of workers at the expense of others; and thereby you make a partial content out of general discontent, and hoodwink the people, and prevent their action: 'divide and govern' being a very old maxim of Scoundrels-craft."

3. MS., watch word

that no other possible party was thought of, and it is true that election times were the very worst times for our propaganda: no one with any political bias could disentangle his thoughts and aspirations from the great party dog-fight which was going on at such times. Now on the contrary it has become a commonplace that there is little difference between the two parties except that of ins and outs, and many think even that more in the way of the concessions above said [may come] from the Tory party than the Liberal, which possibly may be the case, though I don't think it will turn out so. On the other hand at present the Liberal party is losing ground and even tending towards break up, perhaps because it includes as nominal members men who may be called semi-socialists. If it does actually break up, the result will obviously be a coalition of the Whiggish Liberals with the Tories, which would make a party strong enough to snap the fingers at socialism and refuse any concessions, and on the other hand the Radical tail setting itself up as a parliamentary party which would be a very weak party while it lasted, and would tend to melt into the general advance of Socialism.

Again whatever else has happened or failed to happen[,] the old Manchester school, the utilitarian Laissez faire business has fallen [in] a very short time after its entire acceptance as an indisputable theory by all would-be intelligent people. Doubtless all this[,] apart from whatever advance in the prospects of labour on which it is founded[,] means a great stir in thought and aspirations apart from the actual Socialist movement. It means that everywhere people are shaken as to their views of the eternity of the present system which was once as undoubted a fact to them as the existence of the sun in the heavens. But what next? There cannot be a great upheaval and ferment in men's minds without something coming of it. But what has come of it as yet? In the first place has any increase in the material prosperity of the workman come of it[?] I do not think so. The strike war[,] taking it widely[,] is necessary certainly, but it has to be paid for. It has been necessary to call attention to the mass of unemployed amongst us. But there are the unemployed. Nothing has been done for them in the mass, and nothing will be done for them, because nothing *can* be done while the present system lasts. That there should be periodically people out of work who can work, is a necessity of the competition for employment under our present system; and surely if [it] should come to be the case that [it] is understood that they who fail in the competition shall have places provided for them by the state, there will be a tendency for wages to fall amongst those who are generally employed[.]

Now you will find that generally speaking this is the case with all those measures for improving the material condition of the working classes without altering their positions; it all means more or less feeding the dog with[4] his own tail; you better the condition of one group of workers at the expense of the others: and thereby you make partial content out of general discontent, and hoodwink the people and prevent their action: divide to govern is a very old maxim of Scoundrelscraft. Now I gave you no reason when I said just now[5] that I did not believe that you would get more out of the Tories than the Liberals; but here is the reason ready to my hand; it is just this sort of concession which the Tories will give you: it is their instinct to make a showy benevolent present (which in the long run will be of no use to you) rather than yield a right however small. Of course from neither party can you expect any measure really socialistic, that is an impossibility, but by pressure you may get from the Liberals certain improvements in the present creaky and clumsy electoral machinery which will be some use to you when you want to get M. Ps. to do your dirty work for you in Parliament.

No[,] I say you are not to expect from the time of the battle [for] socialism any serious improvement in the material condition of the working classes; you can only have that from Socialism, while the battle for Socialism is going on you can only have the hope of realizing Socialism. Indeed meantime I believe that the very upward movement of labour, the consciousness amongst working men that they should be citizens and not machines[,] will have to be paid for like other good things, and that the price will be no light one. I have thought the matter up and down and in and out, and I cannot for the life of me see how the great change which we long for can come otherwise than by disturbance and suffering of some kind. Well, since battle also has been made a matter of commerce, and the God of War must now wear a mantle of bank-notes and be crowned with guineas, since human valour must give way to the longest purse, and the latest invention (which I do not much complain of since it makes it more difficult to exercise the accursed art of destruction and slaughter)[,] since war has been commercialized, I say, we shall as above said not be called upon to gain our point by battle in the field. But the disturbance and the suffering–can we escape that? I fear not. We are living in the commercial epoch of the world; and yet it would appear since I am talking to a socialist society, to an audience mainly socialist, in an epoch when commercialism has not all its own way, in an epoch in short when there is combat between Commercialism, or the system of reckless waste, and Communism or the system of neighborly common sense.

4. MS, "of" added
5. MS., "when I said" repeated

Can that combat be fought out again I say without loss and suffering? Plainly speaking I *know* that it cannot. The rise in condition of life, if not in position of the working classes *must* disturb the smooth going ways of the market, *must* reduce the profits of their employers, *must* reduce therefore their employing power, *must* reduce their spending power, and inspire many forms of the production of useless articles, on which the working men largely live. What harm in that? You may say; none; it would be a gain if we were living in a socialist condition: but as we are now, it would mean the throwing out of work of numbers of industrious men, the greater part of whom, it would be very difficult to find employment for. Take a straw to show which way the wind blows. A few days ago I had a long letter from a lady whom I knew something of, once very rich, and the wife of a very rich manufacturer in Manchester: the drift of the letter was two-fold; 1st complaining of competition, and how they who once made a large profit on their works are now carrying them on at a loss. 2nd expostulating with me for stirring up the men to cry out for higher wages and the like, which injured the power of employment of the masters: the remedy for all being that the men should withdraw their demands [and] work with the employers who loved them so – and so forth and so forth. Well at first when I read the letter I was angry; then I laughed, and thought how true was the old saw: other people[']s troubles hang on a hair: and felt it as difficult to weep for this lady[']s troubles, as she did for the lowered wages of her husband[']s hands and their diminished comforts. But do you know, at last I said to myself: after all she is right from her point of view; yes[,] and perhaps from her men's point of view also; for I shall like to ask them, before I say anything about your tactics and your demands[,] What is it that you really want[?]

Yes, I should above all things like to have a genuine answer to this question; setting aside all convention, all rhetoric and flummery, what is it that you want from the present labour-movement? Higher wages; more regular employment? shorter working hours[,] better education for your children[,] old age pensions, libraries, parks and the rest? Are these things and things like them what you want? They are of course; but what else do you want[?] If you cannot answer that question straightforwardly I must say that you are wandering on a road the outcome of which you cannot tell; you cannot have any helpful politics or tactics. If you *can* answer it, and say yes, that *is* all we want: then I say here is the real advice to give you: Don[']t you meddle with Socialism; make peace with your employers, before it is too late, and you will find that from them and their Committee, the House of Commons, you will get such measure of those things as will most probably content you, and at any rate all that they *can* give without ruining themselves[,] as they phrase it. If this is all you want[,] work with your employers and for them to your best [ability], consider their interests as well as your own[,] be careful not to try the markets over much, make sacrifices today that you may do well tomorrow[,] compete your best with foreign nations; pay the greatest attention to producing exactly what your markets demand and at the price they demand, and I think you will do well. I cannot indeed promise you, that you will bring back the prosperity of the country to the period of leaps and bounds, but you may well stave off the breakdown,[6] which in these last years does really seem to be drawing near. [A]nd at any rate you will make the best of what prosperity there is left us *as workmen* and according to their standard of life.

If that is all you want how can we who are not workmen blame you? In these matters I always think[,] what should I do myself; and I find it difficult to answer the question here, What should I do? Wherefore I must own that sometimes when I am dispirited I think this is all that the labour movement means: it doesn't mean Socialism at all, it only means improvement in the condition of the working-classes: they will get that in some terms or another—till the break up comes; and it may be a long way ahead. And yet the workmen of this country seem to me to be going so very far from the right road to winning the slavish peace I have been speaking of, that I cannot think they mean nothing but that: imperfect, erring, unorganized, chaotic as that movement is, there is a spirit of antagonism to our present foolish[,] wasteful system in it, and a sense of the unity of labour as against the exploiters of labour which is the one necessary idea for those who are ever so little conscious of making toward Socialism. One thing alone would make me think that more is aimed at tha[n][7] the stereotyping of a would be tolerable condition of servitude for the working-classes, and that is the success of our Comrade Blatchford's *Merrie England*;[8] the thousands who have read that book must[,] if they have done so carefully[,] have found out that something better is possible to be thought of than the life of a prosperous mill-hand. For what after all is that something more than a low form of workman's prosperity[,] constant work, to wit, and a 'fair day's wages for a fair day[']s work.' Surely it is nothing less than that which makes life worth living[:] Self-respect, happy and fit work, leisure, beautiful surroundings [–] in a word, the earth our own and the fullness thereof[,] and if nobody really dares to assert that this good life

6. MS., break down
7. MS., that
8. MS., Merry England

can be attained to, [let us maintain this aim] till we are essentially and practically Socialized[.]

So I will indulge my hope that all who[9] call themselves Socialists, Labour Party, and even the fringe of all that would not be contented to make peace with the possessing classes on the terms that all labour questions should be thoroughly considered, that the interests of the working-men should be the first thing sought for, and so on[,] and that they really want to bring about Socialism, and are ready to face what may well be the temporarily disastrous effects of the rise of wages and all the detail that goes to make up the present labour war. And then comes the question; What is to be done? A question all the more necessary to ask since at present we are doing very little.

Now we must take it for granted that the first means[,] so to say[,] is as above stated, to conquer the general opinion of the country and gradually to get a majority in the House of Commons: and you must all remember that before that can be done, the thinking part of the population will have gone Socialist, so that nothing but the last act of the play will remain to be played.

Well that is the end, a long way off doubtless but in nowise an impossible end, a dream without form. What is to be done to get there? Well[,] first[,] what are the Socialist forces in this country? Answer two or three–say two bodies partly propagandist[,] partly with electoral views[,] probably of no great strength as to count of noses. More of them I won[']t say at present as I don[']t want to get into controversy as to their relative [merits]; so I will but note that there is at least rivalry between them and sometimes dissension. Besides these two bodies, there are no doubt many presumed Socialists who are not attached to either, and there are also many who tend towards Socialism, and would be certain to be absorbed by [it] when it takes more definite action than it has yet done; but there is of course no means of finding out how many these unattached socialists and semi-socialists are.

Now what is to be done with these recruits, who are at present not generally acting together, and are for the most part pretty much undrilled? Well[,] are we to be a sect or a party? That is the next question: in that early time I spoke of we were a sect and had no pretence to be a party, and did not need to be one. And mind you I don't mean the word sect to imply any blame or scorn. Sects have before now done a good deal towards forming the world[']s history: but you see we have settled that we want to go into parliament, and for that it seems to me a party is definitely necessary; that declaring ourselves socialists we shall

9. MS., that the all who

formulate our immediate tactics toward that end: such a party once formed which would not break up any existing bodies but include them, would, it seems to me, have a claim on all genuine socialists, and one thing at least I am sure of[,] that until it is formed, though we may do good propagandist work we shall do nothing worth speaking of in the political way. My hope is, and if people really care for socialism *enough*, it will be realized, that we shall do so much propagandist work, and convert so many people to socialism[,] that they will insist on having a genuine Socialist Party which shall do the due work, and they will not allow the personal fads and vanities of the *leaders* (so-called) to stand in the way of real business.

Well[,] it may be some time before we can have that party, because we shall have to wait till the general body of socialists see the futility of mere sections attempting to do the work of the whole mass properly organized. Meantime what should be our tactics? I think that until we can do our party-work effectively, we had better leave off the pretence of doing it at all; that we had better confine ourselves to the old teaching and preaching of Socialism pure and simple, which is I fear more or less neglected amidst the said futile attempt to act as a party when we have no party. I think we have above all to point out to the working men who feel Socialist sympathies, that there are many measures which *may* be for the temporary good of their class, which are but temporary and experimental, and adapted only for the present state of things, and that these are not for genuine Socialists to press forward. Let our Liberal and radical, and, if they will[,] our Tory friends make these experiments, and take all the responsibility for their failure, for in the long run fail they will. Our present system will admit of no permanent change in this direction. Unlimited competition, the laissez-faire of the old Manchester school, the privilege of the possessing class, modified if you will by gifts of the improved work-house kind—in a word once more the machine-life of the useful classes made as little burdensome to them as can be; that is all that can be got out of the present system. And again and again I say[,] if that is your ideal, don't fight against your employers, for you will but waste your livelihood by doing so.

But on the other hand, those who have a wild fancy to be free men, to have their affairs under their own control; those who wish to work happily and unwastefully, to restore what of the earth's surface which is spoilt and keep that which is unspoilt, to enjoy rest and thought and labour without fear or remorse[,] those in a word who wish to live like men, let them say, good wages or bad, good times or bad, let us use them now as best we may, yet not so much for the present profit we may get out of them as for hastening the realization of the new Society, the time when at last we shall be free because we are equal.

[*at bottom of page*:] March 30th, 1895. [*in Sydney Cockerell's hand*]
[*on f. 67v. notations*:]

Tochatti – to use our recruits when we've got them

Mordhurst	the unemployed
Unknown	Henry George and cooperation
Unknown	
Unknown	as to society
Bullock	giving up the problem Mercer
	socialist representatives—
Unknown	conscious or unconsciousness
Clergyman	rather more depressed than I.

Figure 22.1 "Blackthorn" wallpaper, 1892

Figure 22.2 "Double Bough" wallpaper, 1890

22

"Change of Position—Not Change of Condition," 1895

Editor's introduction

Morris published this article in the May 1, 1895 issue of *Justice*, then edited by trade unionist Harry Quelch, who as a delegate for the Social Democratic Federation (SDF) had, like Morris, attended the 1889 International Workers Socialist Congress in Paris (the Second International). "Change of Position–Not Change of Condition" was one of three articles Morris contributed to the SDF newspaper between 1894 and 1896,[1] and along with "How I Became a Socialist" and "The Promise of May," it was included in the SDF's commemorative pamphlet *How I Became a Socialist* (Twentieth Century Press, 1896), published after Morris's death.

For an audience who might be tempted to work chiefly for immediate gains such as the eight-hour day (a plank of the Second International), Morris gets straight to the point: "No good nature of individuals can make a system tolerable which is designed for the benefit of the privileged classes only." His sarcasm neatly mimics the point of view of an imagined capitalist:

> though this Socialist agitation is founded on principles which are wrong, and cannot be carried out in practice, yet it will have given you enhanced wages, reduction of the hours of labour, . . . gas and water galore, and an extended franchise. And then (but I don't know when) you will be happy and contented, and, which is more to the point, so shall we.

The "gas and water galore" seems a possible reference to the municipal aims of the Fabians, who had supported six winning candidates for the 1892 London County Council.

With regret Morris notes the harsh circumstances which prompt workers to seize whatever concessions may be immediately available: "For the present necessities of working people are so great that they must take what they can get. . . ." Nonetheless he insists that workers must concentrate their efforts on gaining the power and control that form the only reliable guarantors of concrete reforms: "all the benefits which [they] know will follow on the abolition of privilege and the realisation of equality." As often during the 1890s Morris envisions a new configuration of British political parties, with a purely socialist (that is, not bourgeois-reformist) party forming a left flank. To this end he enjoins his audience to rise above factionalism, for "the first step towards this consummation [self-determination] is the union in one party of all those in the movement who take . . . the view not of improved condition for the workers but of essentially changed position."

Note

1. After ceasing editorship of *Commonweal*, Morris published in *Justice* two poems, "May Day," (April 30, 1892) and "May Day, 1894" (May 5, 1894); a report of a lecture, "Waste" (March 17, 1894); and three essays, "How I Became a Socialist" (June 16, 1894), "Change of Position—Not Change of Condition" (May 1, 1895), and "The Promise of May" (May 1, 1896). During the same period he also published essays in James Tochatti's *Liberty: A Journal of Anarchist Communism*, thus maintaining ties with both the social democratic and anarchist wings of the socialist movement.

To the Socialist, who is earnest in wishing to stimulate the genuine and practical desire of the workers towards freedom, and who knows well that no mere good nature of individuals can make a system tolerable which is designed for the benefit of the privileged classes only—to the Socialist the aim is not the improvement of condition but the *change in position* of the working classes. For he has full confidence that the change in position must have the immediate consequence of the bettering of condition. I am aware that to many or most of the readers of *Justice* these remarks will seem trite, yet I think some form of the thought in them is necessary to be put before people at present.

For, to say the truth, if I were a non-Socialist, and were interested in the preservation of the society of privilege, I should conceive a hope from the present situation of the possibility of hoodwinking the working men into accepting what I should name (to them) a kind of semi or demi-semi-Socialism, which would do no sort of harm to the society of privilege. I should condescend to Socialism, and pat it on the back. I should say, as indeed, I have heard such worthies say, "Socialism, my friends, cannot give you what it promises, but I am pleased to see you Socialists, because all this labour agitation will call people's attention to the 'condition of the working classes,' and will 'improve it.' You will find that you must work *with* the capitalists and not *against* them, so that you may extend markets, contend successfully with other nations, and improve business. By that means, though this Socialist agitation is founded on principles which are wrong, and cannot be carried out in practice, yet it will have given you enhanced wages, reduction of the hours of labour, more permanency of employment, better housing, gas and water galore, and an extended franchise. And then (but I don't know when) you will be happy and contented, and, which is more to the point, so shall we."

That, I say, will be the sort of line to take for those who wish to keep labour—*i.e.*, usefulness—out of its heritage. And I think it will be taken, I fear not wholly unsuccessfully. For the present necessities of working people are so great that they must take what they can get, and it is so hard for them in their miserable condition to have any vivid conception of what a life of freedom and equality can give them that they can scarcely, the average of them, turn their hopes to a future which they may never see.

And yet if that future is not to be indefinitely postponed they must repudiate this demi-semi-Socialism. They must say: "£2 a week instead of £1; eight hours work instead of nine, ten, twelve; out-of-door relief galore to supplement the out-of-work periods; comfortable (Lord help us!) lodgings found by the municipality—all these are fine things indeed. But we will not even think of them unless we can use them for getting all the benefits which we know will follow on the abolition of privilege and the realisation of equality. That is, in short, what we mean to have. What those benefits may be we cannot imagine in detail; but we know that the sum of them will mean a decent self-respecting life for us all. We are Socialists and believe in Socialism, and the day will come when we shall partly be able to estimate our gains by looking back and wondering that we once thought it worthwhile[1] to strive for such petty advantages as those you have been telling us of."

And again and again it must be said that in this determination we shall be justified when the working-classes make it their determination; and further, for [the] last word, that the first step towards this consummation is the union in one party of all those in the movement who take that view of the movement, and not merely the gas and water and improved trade union view. The view not of improved condition for the workers but of essentially changed position.

1. Orig., worth while

34 THE LABOUR LEADER. [Glasgow, January 25, 1896.

Lastly comes the ethical side of the subject. It has been said that art has nothing to do with the right or wrong of matters; that true art is exercised for art's sake, and that the poet or the painter may attain to his highest perfection quite apart from moral or ethical considerations. This is rather a shallow view. Milton, we are told, reaches his best in depicting the character of Satan. But if that be true it must be principally due to the fact that we live in a world in which rebellion is sometimes the highest virtue.

I have already tried to show that whatever our intellectual prepossessions or theories regarding poetry may be, the heart responds to that which touches the personal everyday feelings readier than to that which appeals to what has been acquired by special intellectual study. The response is unconscious. We see the same unconscious acknowledgment of fundamental ethical facts when they are poetically put, although the whole bent of our received teaching be to the opposite. Burns, so far as I know, stands alone among the poets in asserting, and never forgetting to assert, where the occasion gives opportunity, that our present system of society is a huge lie, a stupid and brutal mistake, the only excuse for which is that we have inherited it and must bear with it till we grow out of it. Nearly all of our old institutions are founded on thoroughly barbarous notions of partiality and privilege, and Burns never fails to challenge them either openly or in an implied way. Burns never departs from a position of stern impartiality in these matters, and I have no doubt that his appreciation of real worth as distinguished from what receives rewards, and honours, and ease, and homage in the world is one of his principal attractions even to the unworthily exalted. We are graded and classified and assorted in such nice distinctions, all recognised and encouraged by habit, custom, religion and law, that one would almost despair of ordinary human brotherly feeling surviving through it all. Burns, however, with a single line can overthrow the whole flimsy arrangement, set up and guarded so carefully, and from one end of it to the other the hearts and intellects of all grades respond to his words. The explanation of this seems to be that the artificial distinctions in society, outrageously false and cruel as they are, though blessed and recognised by the churches, are not really believed in by healthy humanity in any stage in life. Take as an illustration a Burns dinner got up at a price that no man moving in the sphere in which Burns lived could possibly afford to attend! Yet we might be wrong were we to say that the people participating did not appreciate the beauties and the humanising influence of the poet as much as those attending some gathering at one shilling a head. And what are we to make out of the fact that all Burns's keen, cutting satire, at the expense of the learned and the exalted, does not seem to have cost him a single admirer among those who may claim to be either, while the arrows of his wit are as intolerable to-day to the unco guid as when they were first discharged. Many, however, who are still adhering to worn-out ceremonies, observances, and beliefs that the poet has riddled and blown to pieces, do homage to the reforming bard though they still follow the observances their father handed down to them.

Burns' peculiarity is this note of truth founded on exceptional perception and insight, and irresistible power in that he combined in himself the old simple tenderness and wealth of feeling peculiar to the prophets and ancient bards—stronger and tenderer because human intercourse was the highest enjoyment of their lives—with the wit, humour, and subtility of intellect known only in more advanced civilisation. But his supreme excellence to us at the present hour is, that he recognised and asserted the fact that the useful and serviceable members of human society are more worthy and honourable than those who give no equivalent for what they draw out of it; and that he ventured to expend the wealth of his genius in teaching that idea in the hope that he was doing humanity a service.

WILLIAM MORRIS'S CONFESSION.

POLITICAL ACTION.

William Morris, speaking recently in the Holborn Town Hall at a meeting convened by the Social Democratic Federation, said the condition of things into which the English government had got itself was, in his view, due entirely to the general position of labour and capital throughout civilisation. So far as America was concerned, they were in the position that at any time a quarrel might arise which they did not dare to face because they choose to hang on to a colony they had there. If it were not for Canada, who would care anything for America?

He did not believe in any solid danger at the present moment. In some way or another, both America and England would back down, because they were each other's customers, and they could not afford to buy shooting-irons and go shoot their customers.

As far as Africa was concerned, there was a state of desperation among all the nations to "make" something of that "undeveloped" country. And they were "developing" it with a vengeance. When he saw the last account about the Transvaal he almost wished he were a Kaffir for five minutes, so that he could dance round the ring. The position was just that of a pack of thieves quarrelling about their booty. The Boers first stole the land from the people to whom it belonged, then they set about getting somebody to help them to "develope" what they had stolen, and, if they could manage it, they (the English) would steal from the Boers in turn.

But so long as individuals and nations practised stealing for a living those matters were comparatively trifling. What they had to realise and deal with was the fact that all "civilised" States now lived by stealing—*i.e.*, by wasting the labour of all other workmen. If Society were properly organised for labour and the products of that labour fairly and justly divided—*i.e.*, if the workers had what they produced—they would all be able to live a really good life, for by that time they would have pretty well conquered nature, and there would be practically no limit to their power of production if they were working in the only reasonable way—all for each and each for all.

As a result of the growth of Socialism, and of the fringe which always hung about the skirts of a great idea, they must expect to come across a fringe-people who wished to stop at small things. Such were exceedingly lacking in that on which they prided themselves—reason.

The most important political event of last year had been the rout of the Liberal party. He did not regard it altogether as the defeat of Whiggism, but rather as a general rally against all the forward movement, because the defenders of privilege were beginning to see something really serious in the Socialistic movement. It was perfectly natural that the result should be a success for the reactionary party, because those who had the greater part of the money had also the greater part of votes. But so far from being the least disappointed at the result, they ought to look upon it rather as the beginning of Socialism in action as opposed to Socialism in theory. In time gone by, he (the speaker) was not very anxious to see the political side of Socialism pushed forward. Some might consider that an indefensible theory. With him it was merely a matter of tactics. He now distinctly thought the time had arrived for political action. Hyndman's candidature at Burnley he considered a remarkable event, and evidence of the movement forward their ideas were making. But after all he was of opinion, and always had been, that the main thing Socialists had to do was to make other Socialists. There should be no surcease in that direction until the cause was won.

In the meantime they must hit out, and show they were alive. Certain things were talked about, and would be done; but if done altogether, they would not make Socialism in the least. Of course they wanted to "raise the condition of the workers"—like their friends on both sides in the House of Parliament; but suppose that condition raised far above the possibility attainable under the present system. Supposing wages were increased four-fold the present standard, the workers would still be what they were then—slaves, and slaves they would remain until they had their own immediate destinies in their own hands.

Much was talked about the necessity for studying the "ins" and "outs" of Socialism, but he assured them that was not necessary. If they liked the study it was good as an education, and some found it interesting, but after all, what they had to do, if they would be free, was to make up their minds that they would destroy waste, which was poverty. They were all in the grasp of an artificial poverty. Even in England, the richest country in the world, they were obliged to say that so and so could not be done because it was a question of money. They could not make their houses homes, and lives beautiful, they lived in squalor and disorder—why?—because they were so poor. And as a nation they were so poor that even the rich men among them could not have what they desired—self respect.

As he, the speaker, was not a member of the S.D.F. he could praise them for holding aloft the real flag of revolution. They were determined not to stop half way. They knew that whatever efforts they might put forth in the way of amelioration, until the day when Socialism would be realised no true solid gains would or could be won for the workers. Let them try any of the half measures—and to a certain extent they were obliged to countenance such to make the thing go—and they would find that it would mean merely bettering the condition of one group or section of the workers by worsening that of other groups. It could not be helped, because, after all, the workers were not regarded as men, but as machinery to be used for capitalistic production.

The workers were thoroughly and entirely disinherited. Notwithstanding their "vote" they were not citizens of their country; they were as far from that as could be. They were not men but machines. They managed to rub along in a fashion from day to day, but they had not the real lives of people working for their own livelihood.

It was their business to get to be citizens although he did not altogether like the word, for they did not all live, or want to live in cities, and people should be free to live where they liked. The only possibility of getting into that position was to see that they were masters of their time, their tools, and the raw material they had to use. When they had those in their hands they would find that it would be impossible to prevent the civilised world from entering upon a system of society based upon equality. And that was the last word. There were two possible conditions of life for the workers—slavery and equality. Whatever might be said, or however it might be masked, that was the fact. In one age the slavery was a matter of quite obvious force—the iron hand everywhere. At present the force was hidden under a velvet glove, but it was so much the worse for that. They were now under the grasp of a system of capitalistic economy which would beat them and their masters—even if they were so willed—to put them on a better level, save by destroying the system itself.

In conclusion he would urge upon them the necessity for ever keeping before the people the broad, deep, reasonable side of the question, otherwise it would one day come upon them all with suffering, misery and violence, in ways which would be worst instead of best.

Let them gain their cause by reason, *i.e.*, the force of principles and the force of intelligence.

A TRAVELLER FROM ALTRURIA.

Mr. William Dean Howells is a novelist whose name ought to be familiar to all good Socialists. He takes, amongst American writers, a position similar to that occupied by Mr. Grant Allen in this country, but he is a greater artist than our countryman. That, perhaps, may be because he is not so bitterly rebellious—which, again, is a difference of temperament. Howells looks upon the foolishness of life without irritation; the wickedness of it does not make him mad, but unwearying; the wanton injustice of Nature does not drive him to useless wrath, but the note of melancholy underlies the subtle humour of his work. Otherwise he would not be an artist.

The "Traveller from Altruria" and his "Letters" contain the results of Howells' analysis of our unsocial state. They are full of keen perception and ironic humour, yet so kindly that there is no offensive line in the whole. Civilisation, he says in effect, is stupid beneath contempt and vile beyond wrath, but the men and women who suffer under it are not half bad. It is a healthy spirit and a sane way to look at things; it makes one wish that all Socialist writers would cultivate health and sanity. These letters have been running in an American magazine with a circulation of 250,000 for a full year, and were well paid for; that is to say, some 3,000,000 first-class Socialist tracts have been bought, printed, and circulated by capitalists, for capitalists, to the great detriment of capitalism—and all because of a little geniality and wholesome good humour.

The moral is obvious: Less noise, more work; less ranting, more thinking; less bigotry, more kindliness. But the text runs to sermonising.

We have here what are supposed to be letters from an explorer, sent by the State of Altruria to spy out the nakedness of American civilisation. Inasmuch as Altruria is 900 years ahead of modern ideas, he finds plenty of nakedness, and much to disgust and surprise him. The natives are also surprised at some of his ideas, indeed, shocked. He spends the summer at a holiday resort, where the American plutocracy sends its women to recruit themselves after a winter spent elaborately doing nothing. He is taken up by Mrs. Makeley, a fashionable, irrelevant, gushing sort of pretty woman; and he has long talks on economics with an author, a banker, a lawyer, and a clergyman. The banker he makes some impression on, the clergyman is proof against mere logic. At the end of the season he goes up to New York.

The roar and bustle of the place, where ten men strain themselves to do work which might be done by one man and a boy; the railways overhead, the cable cars below, the colossal piracy of the great corporations, the disorganised chaos of life, the muddle of architecture, the dirty streets, the vast slum districts, "smelling of poverty," have all been described many a time, and here again. It is a city where one cannot be Christian without doing harm, nor honest without danger, nor generous without remorse. Pluto reigns supreme, says Mr. Howells.

The American plutocracy is the old oligarchic conception of Government in a new phase, and while it is established and maintained by a community mostly Christian, it is essentially Pagan in its civic ideal. Yet this people, whose civic ideal is Pagan, are, many of them, not only Christian in creed, but Christian in life, so far as their polity and their society permit them to think rightly and act generously. They are people of a fine courage, and they have accesses of a noble generosity, but they have been born and bred in the presence of the fact that each man can alone save himself and those dear to him from want.

There was but one redeeming feature. In the Central Park, one bit of collectivism in the middle of this senseless individualism and beautiful as no European park can be, he finds a bit of Altruria. In spots, that is, Plutocracy had even here planted its paw in the shape of a carriage drive where the wealthy come for fresh air. "To me," wrote the Altrurian, "the lesson of Central Park is that where it is used in the spirit of fraternity and equality the pleasure in it is pure and fine; but where it is invaded by the plutocratic motives of the strife that raves all round it in the city outside, its joys are fouled with contempt and envy."

Of course, the carriage folk were mostly women. Women bear the main burden both of riches and poverty in America; they carry on "society," for which the men have no leisure; they are the reading class; they have fads, and nerves, and no children. Mrs. Makely explained to Mr. Aristides Homos, the Altrurian, that people who lived in flats as they did could not be troubled with children. She did not consider this a trial, and she was very pleased with their flat. She showed it to the stranger with much pleasure, and while talking over it he pleaded guilty to a certain curiosity.

"It is about your servants," I began.

"Oh, of course! Perfectly characteristic! Go on!"

"You told me that they had no natural light either in the kitchen or their bedroom. Do they never see the light of day?"

The lady laughed heartily. "The waitress is in the front of the house several hours every morning at her work, and then both have an afternoon off once a week. Some people only let them go once a fortnight; but I think they are human beings as well as we are, and I let them go every week."

"But except for that afternoon once a week, your cook lives in electric light perpetually?"

"Electric light is very healthy, and it doesn't heat the air!" the lady triumphed. "I can assure you that she thinks she's very well off, and she is!"

"Well, why should you require your servants to go down on a different elevator from yourselves?"

"Why, good gracious!" cried the lady. "Aren't they different from us in every way? To be sure they dress up in their ridiculous best when they go out, but you couldn't expect us to let them use the *front* elevator! I don't want to go up and down with my own cook, and I certainly don't with my neighbour's cook!"

"But if you found yourself beside a cook in a horse car or other public conveyance, you would not feel personally affronted?"

"No, that is a very different thing. That is something we cannot control. But, thank goodness, we can control our elevators, and I should consider it a perfect outrage to ride up and down with the servants."

"In Altruria we hold serving in peculiar honour."

"Well, if you went and got your servants from an office, and had to look up their references, you wouldn't hold it in much honour. It's nothing between us but a question of——"

"Business," suggested her husband.

"Yes," she assented, as if this clinched the matter.

"That's what I'm always telling you, Dolly. Yet you want them to love you, and will try to make them your friends as soon as you get them into the house."

"Well, I can't help it, Dick. I can't live with a person without trying to like them, and wanting them to like me. And then, when the ungrateful things leave me in the lurch, as they do half the time, it almost breaks my heart. But I'm thankful to say that in these hard times they won't leave a good place without a good reason."

"Are there many seeking employment?"

"Well, they just stand around us *thick*! And the Americans are trying to get places as well as the foreigners. But I won't have Americans. They are too uppish. They still expect to be treated as one of the family. I suppose that in Altruria you do treat them as one of the family?"

"We have no servants in the American sense," I answered.

This is a fair sample of Mr. Howells' dialogue; but it would be impossible in a brief notice like this to do justice to his average style. He has a keen sense of the paradoxical, and a logical faculty which is forever amused at the hopelessly illogical nature of the present social system. Combined with a singularly serene and lucid style, this power and patience of insight make his books very grateful reading.

We have not space to do more than glance at these volumes, and recommend all Socialists to get them placed in their local free library. Mr. Aristides Homos carries his remarkable personality and remarkable name through various interesting adventures, and falls in love with a rich widow in the last chapter. The widow loves him, too; but she will not leave her own world and go to Altruria with him. It is almost as if a man should propose to his sweetheart to go with him to heaven. She would not go. So he returned alone to a happier state, yet bearing the sorrow of our epoch with him.

H. C. Rowe.

Figure 23.1 Newspaper clipping for *One Socialist Party*, *The Labour Leader*, January 1896

23

["One Socialist Party"], 1896

Editor's introduction

Morris's last known recorded political speech was delivered in Holborn Town Hall to the Social Democratic Federation (SDF) at a January 3 New Year's meeting ten months before his death. Although the text as reported in the January 25, 1896 *Labour Leader* is untitled, it was likely quite similar to one titled "One Socialist Party" delivered two days afterward to the Hammersmith Socialist Society, for which no text remains. Though the Holborn talk survives only in transcription, the recorder has apparently followed Morris's sequence of thoughts without editorializing, and the ideas as represented seem consistent with his other lectures and writings of the period. The *Labour Leader* was the newspaper of the Independent Labour Party (ILP), edited by Keir Hardie, and so the title and subtitle of the article, "William Morris's Confession / Political Action," may express its editor's satisfaction that Morris has publicly joined the ILP in championing the use of electoral means to gain socialist ends. This stance was only one strand of his reflections, however, as throughout his speech Morris blends tactful praise and concession with admonitions which seem directed toward his specific SDF audience.

It seems fitting that Morris's final political lecture should have been delivered both to the SDF and, most probably, to his own Hammersmith Socialist Society. The relationship between Morris and the SDF continued to be cordial until his death, as on March 21, 1896, *Justice* recorded:

> The Executive Council of the S.D.F. have passed the following resolution: "That this meeting of the Executive Council of the S.D.F. hears with the deepest regret of the indisposition of William Morris, and desires to convey to him its sincere hope that he will speedily be restored to full health and ability to carry on the magnificent work in many directions which he is doing in the interests of the people at large."

When *Justice* mounted an appeal for donations, in June 1896 Morris sent a cordial letter enclosing ten pounds, the largest subscription received.[1]

When writing for an anarchist audience the preceding year, Morris had warned them against violence and a simplistic fantasy of "single-event" revolution, and had urged them to honor the actual choices of working people by supporting the concrete demands of the labor movement. Here by contrast he attacks British nationalism and imperialism (a cause of earlier divergence of opinion between the SDF and Socialist League), gently reproves a tendency to pedantry and dogmatic language, and warns his audience against a tepid support for "[raising] the condition of the workers" without demanding worker control. He reminds them of his own longstanding priority, the continued need for energetic evangelism to "make socialists." Even more fundamentally, he warns of the need to combine with other socialist and socialist-inclined groups into "one socialist party," centered on the demand for worker ownership and autonomy rather than specific benefits. Without this clear aim, he warns, both the socialist movement and society at large will dissolve into chaos and violence.

Morris's opening remarks attempt to dispel excessive concern for possible foreign wars, anxieties which might deflect from alliance with oppressed peoples in other countries. He notes that the current quarrel between Britain and the United States over the Alaskan boundary line would not have occurred had Britain not claimed the right to "own" distant western Canada.[2] Morris is also offended by the naked greed which motivated European powers to seize control of parts of Africa; in particular, the conflict between the British and Dutch settlers over control of South Africa ignores the fact that both groups are eager plunderers of Khoisan land.[3]

Since his audience have directed their energies to recent elections, Morris realizes that they may have been disheartened by the recent electoral victories of the Conservative Party. He offers a more hopeful alternative interpretation; the fact that progressive ideas now evoke greater resistance indicates their increasing influence: "But so far from being the least disappointed at the result, they ought to look upon it rather as the beginning of Socialism in action as opposed to Socialism in theory."

The rest of Morris's remarks balance affirmation and exhortation. In a gentle rebuke of pedantry he suggests that it is less "scientific socialism" which is needed than action:

> Much was talked about the necessity for studying the "ins" and "outs" of Socialism, but he assured them that was not necessary. If they liked the study it was good as an education, and

> some found it interesting, but after all, what they had to do, if they would be free, was to make up their minds that they would destroy waste, which was poverty.

More advocacy is required: "they must hit out, and show they were alive."

Graciously, Morris acknowledges that the time for electoral socialism has come, a view which had been consistently held by his SDF audience. In particular he notes the significance of the 12 percent vote won by their leader, Henry Hyndman, in the recent election in Burnley, the highest proportion of votes yet attained by a socialist parliamentary candidate:

> In time gone by, he (the speaker) was not very anxious to see the political side of Socialism pushed forward. Some might consider that an indefensible theory. With him it was merely a matter of tactics. He now distinctly thought the time had arrived for political action. Hyndman's candidature at Burnley he considered a remarkable event, and evidence of the movement forward their ideas were making . . . .

He further compliments his audience on their open advocacy of true socialism:

> As he, the speaker, was not a member of the S. D. F. he could praise them for holding aloft the real flag of revolution. They were determined not to stop half way. They knew that whatever efforts they might put forth in the way of amelioration, until the day when Socialism would be realized no true solid gains would or could be won for the workers.

Despite these approving words, Morris nonetheless feels the need to remind his auditors of the dangers of mere palliative measures; under a system of competition such gains would be at the expense of others: "Let them try any of the half measures . . . and they would find that it would mean merely bettering the condition of one group or section of the workers by worsening that of other groups." The much-desired suffrage was likewise a limited gain for workers: "Notwithstanding their 'vote'," in economic ways "they were not citizens of their country . . . . they had not the real lives of people working for their own livelihood."

He offers a further warning that mere electoral victories will fail to challenge the present system, and moreover, such a failure may precipitate a horrible cataclysm:

> In conclusion, he would urge upon them the necessity for ever keeping before the people the broad, deep, reasonable side of the

> question, otherwise it would one day come upon them all with suffering, misery and violence, in ways which would be worst instead of best.
>
> Let them gain their cause by reason, i.e. the force of principles and the force of intelligence.

A worst-case scenario would be mass violence, revolution without socialism. Since in past years Morris had criticized Hyndman for attempting to provoke sporadic violence, Morris's appeal to "the force of principles" may encrypt a further warning against counterproductive "actionism." Only moral force—"the force of principles and the force of intelligence"—can effect lasting change.

In summary, Morris's views of the need for "one socialist party" are contingent. If and only if those who now claim the label "socialist" confront capitalism frontally with the demand for equality and self-governance, and are willing to do so in a peaceful, systematic, and united manner, can such a party exist, thrive, and in time dismantle the existing order. Moreover, despite his encouraging words, Morris does not in fact claim that his listeners are doing exactly that.

Notes

1. I am indebted to Frank C. Sharp for these details, letter May 10, 2020.
2. The United States and the Canadian Confederation each laid claim to territory south of present-day Alaska, since both countries desired access to the coast from the Yukon gold fields. The issue was decided by arbitration in 1903.
3. The term used by Morris, Kaffir, is now considered derogatory and Khoisan is used instead. The (Second) Anglo-Boer War (1899–1902) followed a period of conflict between British settlers and the Boer governments of the Transvaal and the Orange Free State in the wake of the opening of diamond mines in the Witwatersrand area of the Transvaal. The ensuing war was notable for its high toll of casualties and British confinement of Boer civilians in concentration camps. The SDF leader, Henry Hyndman, was a supporter of the Anglo-Boer War.

William Morris, speaking recently in the Holborn Town Hall at a meeting convened by the Social Democratic Federation, said the condition of things into which the English government had got itself was, in his view, due entirely to the general position of labour and capital throughout civilization. So far as America was concerned, they were in the position that at any time a quarrel might arise which they did not dare to face because they choose to hang on to a colony they had there. If it were not for Canada, who would care anything for America?

He did not believe in any solid danger at the present moment. In some way or another, both America and England would back down, because they were each other's customers, and they could not afford to buy shooting-irons and go shoot their customers.

As far as Africa was concerned, there was a state of desperation among all the nations to "make" something of that "undeveloped" country. And they were "developing" it with a vengeance. When he saw the last account about the Transvaal he almost wished he were a Kaffir for five minutes, so that he could dance round the ring. The position was just that of a pack of thieves quarreling about their booty. The Boers first stole the land from the people to whom it belonged, then they set about getting somebody to help them to "develop"[1] what they had stolen, and, if they could manage it, they (the English) would steal from the Boers in turn.

But so long as individuals and nations practiced stealing for a living those matters were comparatively trifling. What they had to realise and deal with was the fact that all "civilised" States now lived by stealing—*i.e.*, by wasting the labour of all other workmen. If Society were properly organised for labour and the products of that labour fairly and justly divided—*i.e.*, if the workers had what they produced–they would all be able to live a really good life, for by that time they would have pretty well conquered nature, and there would be practically no limit to their power of production if they were working in the only reasonable way—all for each and each for all.

As a result of the growth of Socialism, and of the fringe which always hung about the skirts of a great idea, they must expect to come across fringe people who wished to stop at small things. Such were exceedingly lacking in that on which they prided themselves—reason.

The most important political event of last year had been the rout of the Liberal party. He did not regard it altogether as the defeat of Whiggism, but rather as a general rally against all the forward movement, because the defenders of privilege were beginning to see something really serious in the Socialistic movement. It was perfectly natural that the result should be a success for the reactionary party, because those who had the greater part of the money had also the greater part of votes. But so far from being the least disappointed at the result, they ought to look upon it rather as the beginning of Socialism in action as opposed to Socialism in theory. In time gone by, he (the speaker) was not very

1. Orig., develope

anxious to see the political side of Socialism pushed forward. Some might consider that an indefensible theory. With him it was entirely a mater of tactics. He now distinctly thought the time had arrived for political action. Hyndman's candidature at Burnley he considered a remarkable event, and evidence of the movement forward their ideas were making. But after all he was of [the] opinion, and always had been, that the main thing Socialists had to do was to make other socialists. There should be no surcease in that direction until the cause was won.

In the meantime they must hit out, and show they were alive. Certain things were talked about, and would be done; but if done altogether, they would not make Socialism in the least. Of course they wanted to "raise the condition of the workers"—like their friends on both sides in the House of Parliament; but suppose that condition raised far above the possibility attainable under the present system. Supposing wages were increased four-fold the over present standard, the workers would still be what they were then—slaves, and slaves they would remain until they had their own immediate destinies in their own hands.

Much was talked about the necessity for studying the "ins" and "outs" of Socialism, but he assured them that was not necessary. If they liked the study, it was good as an education, and some found it interesting, but after all, what they had to do, if they would be free, was to make up their minds that they would destroy waste, which was poverty. They were all in the grasp of an artificial poverty. Even in England, the richest country in the world, they were obliged to say that so and so could not be done because it was a question of money. They could not make their houses homes, and lives beautiful, they lived in squalor and disorder—why? Because they were so poor. And as a nation they were so poor that even the rich men among them could not have what they desired—self-respect.

As he, the speaker, was not a member of the S. D. F. he could praise them for holding aloft the real flag of revolution. They were determined not to stop half way. They knew that whatever efforts they might put forth in the way of amelioration, until the day when Socialism would be realised no true solid gains would or could be won for the workers. Let them try any of the half measures–and to a certain extent they were obliged to countenance such to make the thing go–and they would find that it would mean merely bettering the condition of one group or section of the workers by worsening that of other groups. It could not be helped, because, after all, the workers were not regarded as men, but as machinery to be used for capitalistic production.

The workers were thoroughly and entirely disinherited. Notwithstanding their "vote" they were not citizens of their country; they were as far from that as could be. They were not men but machines. They managed to rub along in a fashion from day to day, but they had not the real lives of people working for their own livelihood.

It was their business to get to be citizens although he did not altogether like the word, for they did not all live, or want to live in cities, and people should be free to live where they liked. The only possibility of getting into that position was to see that they were masters of their time, their tools, and the raw material they had to use. When they had those in their hands they would find that it would be impossible to prevent the civilised world from entering upon a system of society based upon equality. And that was the last word.

There were two possible conditions of life for the workers–slavery and equality. Whatever might be said, or however it might be masked, that was the fact. In one age the slavery was a matter of quite obvious force–the iron hand everywhere. At present the force was hidden under a velvet glove, but it was so much the worse for that. They were now under the grasp of a system of capitalistic economy which would beat them and their masters—even if they were so willed—[gap] to put them on a better level, save by destroying the system itself.

In conclusion he would urge upon them the necessity for ever keeping before the people the broad, deep, reasonable side of the question, otherwise it would one day come upon them all with suffering, misery and violence, in ways which would be worst instead of best.

Let them gain their cause by reason, *i.e.*, the force of principles and the force of intelligence.

Figure 24.1 "William Morris Speaking from a Platform in Hyde Park," May 1894, Walter Crane

24

"Against the Abuses of Public Advertising," 1895

Editor's introduction

Morris's brief remarks at the Royal Society of Arts on January 31, 1896 seconding a motion of the Society for Controlling the Abuses of Public Advertising (SCAPA) apparently comprised his last known public address. Morris had been an early member of SCAPA (1893–1952), along with artists Holman Hunt and John Everett Millais, author Rudyard Kipling (Georgiana Burne-Jones's nephew), and his friends James Bryce, George Howard, and Walter Crane. In his account of the Society (*Media Culture and Society* 3.2 (1981): 179–87), Terry Nevett notes that its founder, Richardson Evans, had sought a professional and upper-middle-class clientele:

> Morris was very much the odd man out in such company. When approached by a member [Eliza Jane Lowalter], with a view to his joining, he wrote in reply: 'To tell you the plain truth, much as they [advertisements] annoy me personally, I cannot help rejoicing at the spectacle of the middle classes so annoyed and so helpless before the results of the idiotic tyranny which they themselves have created . . . . My influence would be of no use as of course it is perfectly well known that I am disgusted by such things; and as I need not tell you I am considered unpractical and am known to be a Socialist' (*A Beautiful World*, x, September 1909 [p. 94]) (letter to Lowalter, Kelvin, 4.98)

The transcript of Morris's 1896 remarks was published in the December 1896 issue (no. 3, 16–18) of SCAPA's publication *Our Beautiful World* (1893–ca. 1922); since a few of the locutions are not entirely congruent with his style, it may be that his statements were transcribed for the periodical by someone else.

Characteristically Morris praises the Society for their choice of a difficult project—the protection of the rural landscape. He notes with satisfaction that the London County Council (then with a majority of Progressive Party members) had recently passed a resolution in favor of protecting historic city buildings from destruction—a result of the work of the Society for the Protection of Ancient Buildings, an organization Morris had helped found and that maintained ties with SCAPA. He hopes that the same Council will grant some protection of the cityscape from offensive displays, a prophecy which would be partly fulfilled at the national level by the 1907 Advertisements Regulation Act, which permitted local authorities to restrict the size of placards and billboards.

By contrast Morris predicts it will be more difficult to focus public opinion on the beauty of the countryside; farmers, for example, are "willing to make a little money, without regard to beauty." Small appeals are inadequate; just as in other venues he had asserted that there were no shortcuts to socialism, so here he notes that "we have to get a majority—an effective majority . . . ." His sympathy remains with difficult but worthy projects: "I must tell you I am not, and never can be, a practical man; but I am perfectly willing to fall in with a scheme which has the slightest chance of success." He uses pithy expressions to point the urgency of action—"while the grass is growing the steed is starving"; when one sees "some pretty piece of scenery disfigured, . . . one says, 'It is horrible; I cannot look at it.'"

From a modern perspective one of Morris's most radical arguments is that, even apart from aesthetic considerations, advertising is wasteful and often unprofitable: "The advertiser must enter into a life and death competition with all the other advertisers. A few succeed and flourish, but the greater part give in. . . ." Though Morris & Co. did advertise its products, these statements may reflect his view that the firm's success had been built largely on referrals, personal ties, and its high reputation, as well as his conviction that only a socialized society could limit the enormous destruction of resources inherent in the competitive system. More than a century later, when advertising and lobbying can metastasize to be the chief form of business overhead, his words still strike home.

Likewise characteristic is Morris's view that the SCAPA resolution under consideration should be broad in scope; for example, the siting of railroads and other disruptive modernizations should be designed to be as little disfiguring as possible. He notes that Mapledurham, one of the spots which Ellen and Guest pass on their boat trip upriver in *News from Nowhere*, has been marred by a great blue wall erected by the Great Western Railway despite the fact that there had been simple and preferable options. The proclamation "That it is of national interest to protect rural scenery from unnecessary disfigurement," reflects the ethos of his pastoral utopia *News from Nowhere* and his deep affection for the Oxfordshire environs of Kelmscott Manor. Perhaps it is fitting that, despite his ill health, Morris made his last recorded public appearance in defense of the natural beauty of his beloved rural countryside.

Let me in the first place say that I think the Society have done absolutely right in pressing the point of the advertisements which disfigure rural scenery rather than making too much of the point of the disfigurement in towns. As soon as you get anything like public opinion to desire some reasonable regulation of advertisements in the towns, there are the municipalities—and some of them, like our own London County Council, would be very anxious, I believe, to do all they possibly could to force public opinion. We owe a debt of thanks to that member of the County Council who succeeded in getting passed the other day a resolution to the effect that the London County Council should take cognisance of every valuable piece of historical building which was threatened with destruction—a most important resolution I think.

Next, we have to remember that the enormous majority of the people of the country do not care one straw about natural beauty. They have, I allow, a certain sort of pleasure in wandering about in the fields and enjoying the fresh air, but, as for looking at nature in detail with anything like observation, it is a fact that the greater part of the people of this country are entirely without eyes! Unless you can use your eyes, and unless the use of your eyes makes you suffer, nothing will be done. Then, the farmers are willing to make a little money, without regard to beauty, and it may be said they are entitled to do that. In point of fact, this is the position: We have to get a majority—an effective majority, which will make enough noise about Reform to get it carried. We have then a very difficult task before us, but in the meantime it is well to consider if we cannot to a certain extent mitigate this evil. I would call your attention to the wisdom—the commercial wisdom—of this matter of advertising.

In the first place, take my word for it, it is only under very peculiar circumstances that advertising ever pays. And yet, my friends, I tell you plainly, people all over the country, in all kinds of businesses, spend enormous sums of money and half ruin themselves in advertising, the result of which is that they do not sell much more. The truth is, it is only on these two conditions advertising pays: the thing must cost little or nothing to make, and it must attract everybody's money. The advertiser must enter into a life and death competition with all the other advertisers. A few succeed and flourish, but the greater part give in, and those that give in—well, their names appear in the *Gazette*. As to those goods which cost nothing to make and a lot to advertise, ought we not to avoid paying for them in hard cash. On the whole, we have a right to see that our money, if we possibly can, should not be wasted.

I cannot help saying that there is nothing for it but for us to slowly build up some kind of public opinion which shall allow us to have our own way, and that, of course, will be a very long job indeed. In these matters, I must tell you I am not, and never can be, a practical man; but I am perfectly willing to fall in with a scheme which has the slightest chance of success, and to give my most whole-hearted support to it, even if it be only an *ad interim* measure. This matter cannot be left from day to day: while the grass is growing the steed is starving.

My resolution says: "That it is a natural interest to protect rural scenery from disfigurement." Now there are a great many things besides placards and so forth that are permanent disfigurements. One permanent disfigurement occurs to me, a disfigurement at Mapledurham, on the Thames, which is no doubt one of the most beautiful spots in England—in the world. There is a sort of bank there. The Great Western Railway wanted more room; it would have been a very easy thing to get that room on the land side, away from the river without spoiling the place, but instead of doing this (which would have been comparatively harmless) they put up a hideous wall of blue brick, to the utter ruin of the view. It was nobody's business, and it went by default.

In taking up this matter of the boards that are stuck about our fields, I think we have done very well. It is very piteous, whilst travelling along the railway, to see some pretty piece of scenery disfigured, and one says, "It is horrible; I cannot look at it."

I also think that the Bill introduced in the last Session was a very right kind of Bill to put before the public. It condemned as a nuisance that which it was worth people's time and trouble to abate if they possibly could, and practically asserted: "That it is of national interest to protect rural scenery from unnecessary disfigurement." That resolution I must cordially sympathise with, and beg to second.

Figure 25.1 "May Day 1890," Walter Crane, published 1890. Courtesy of the Victoria and Albert Museum

25

"The Present Outlook of Socialism in England," April 1896

"The Present Outlook of Socialism in England" was solicited by Hiram Price Collier for his periodical *The Forum* (April 1896, 193–200), a New York monthly that featured serious articles on contemporary topics.[1] The essay was reprinted in 1996 as an appendix to the final volume of Norman Kelvin's edition of Morris's *Collected Letters* (4.393–400), and because it is Morris's last-printed socialist essay I have also included it here. Since the manuscript could have been sent to the *Forum* some time prior to its appearance, one cannot be certain that it constitutes Morris's final message to the world on political topics. However, it is likely a very late essay, since in its views on the urgent need for "one socialist party," it closely resembles the 1895 "What We Have to Look For" as well as his January 1896 speech to the Holborn Branch of the Social Democratic Federation on the topic of "One Socialist Party."

Although the opening pages offer his views on literature, art, and religion rather than politics, on the essay's stated topic of "the present outlook of Socialism in England," Morris's essential message is firm and clear: the workers are increasing in self-direction and power, and socialists must fight elections at every level. Thus far, however, they have failed to do so; and a united campaign by "one Socialist party" must be the path forward for socialists. His words are thus a legacy both of hope and warning.

Morris begins with his usual disillusioned account of the inequities of nineteenth-century England under commercialism. Yet his critiques soon branch into other areas, including religion:

> It is true that in Britain religion lagged behind, and the "free-thinking" which had long been accepted as an essential part of the Whig revolution on the continent, was here revolutionary and unrespectable, as an open and expressed opinion, though even then almost universal amongst intelligent persons. For the deep-seated hypocrisy of our nation (and perhaps race), which

> has often, wrongly as I think, been dignified with the historical title of "Puritanism," would not allow facts to be faced openly on this side of things.

In his 1892 "Communism, i.e. Property" Morris had expressed his view that contemporary religion had nothing to offer socialists—an opinion perhaps sharpened in response to the Christian Socialist movement of the 1880s and 90s[2]—but unlike "The Present Outlook of Socialism" he had not submitted the earlier lecture for publication.

Morris next offers some summary views on nineteenth-century literature and art. Poetry had flourished with the Romantic poets, though in retrospect even Romantic writers of genius avoided immersion in the life around them: "it became once more possible to forget the miseries of real life by burying oneself in the idealities of the great inventors." In his own period, by contrast, literature had survived through its relationship with history:

> [T]he imagination of those who have steeped themselves in the life of serious periods of history, as shown us by their still existing works, can free itself from the ugliness and trivialities of to-day and produce something which is not alien in idea from the living art of the past.

Here he may be referring to the classical and medieval settings of the works of Alfred Tennyson, Robert Browning, and Dante Gabriel Rossetti, the contemporaries whose poetry had most influenced his own writings. Morris's own poetry and romances were likewise heavily historicist, that is, "steeped in the life of serious periods of history"; in works such as *The Earthly Paradise* he sought to create an alternate world freed from contemporary trivialities, and though new in spirit, likewise "not alien in idea from the living art of the past." By contrast, in Morris's view the visual arts suffer more from the constraints of their immediate surroundings, and during the present period alternately lapse into dull conformity or burst forth in assertive alienation: "either their sense of beauty is deadened, or they seek for expression of it in fierce antagonism to the life and thought of the passing time."

Morris also registers his personal distaste for the architecture of the 1850s, which he describes as the expression of "triumphant Whiggery"; this may be a reference to neoclassical styles, as in *News from Nowhere* his narrator expresses distaste for the British Museum in Bloomsbury and St. Martin's Church in Trafalgar Square, both neoclassical buildings. In sum, every sphere of life has been tainted by economic competition: "Commerce, the only thing needful; politics, the slave of the markets;

literature, existing only in rebellion; art forgotten, beauty dead: this, it seemed, was to be the ultimate gain of 'The heir of all the ages in the foremost files of time'" (a line from Tennyson's "Locksley Hall").

As in his previous essays of the decade, Morris avers that public opinion is undergoing a genuine shift: "collective action is admitted everywhere to be the machinery through which we must of necessity strive to make the best of our surroundings. In politics, . . . the word [democratic] has changed its meaning [to] the gathering of opinion of the working classes"—though he is quick to add that this seeming concern is solely motivated by the desire of the governing classes to understand how the latter may be pacified. In poetry and art, as aforementioned, he notes some favorable signs: Tennyson, for example, ("a man, whose poetry was once thought the very acme of wild eccentricity") had risen to become the period's major poet; and the influence of the Pre-Raphaelites has made it more possible for the painters who have followed them to give "their genius free scope." Though he refrains from mentioning his role as a founding member of the Society for the Protection of Ancient Buildings, he expresses satisfaction that architectural works from the Middle Ages are now more appreciated and preserved than previously. Ironically, he notes, this very appreciation has helped lead to a fashion for meretricious neo-Gothic "restoration," the misguided attempt to recreate past artifacts devoid of their original contexts.

In sum, the difficulties which afflict contemporary art and architecture suggest the need for a new society to give birth to a transformed art. Although Morris believes that public opinion is moving toward the desire for a fellowship of equals, he nonetheless offers a cryptic warning: "But unless they [equality of condition and the association of equals] become the root principles of a true society, I for my part can see nothing for it but a continuous degradation of our false society until it disappears in a chaos caused by greed and suffering."

Morris had previously argued in the 1894 "Why I Am a Communist" and elsewhere that a violent revolution ("Cataclysmic Communism") is undesirable and impossible, and that, as workers are able more effectively to gain their demands, they will be able to seize power peacefully. Here, however, he seems to hint at a darker possibility. Though he sees evidence that socialist principles are up to a point gaining ascendancy, *if and only if* workers seek the management of their own affairs will they be successful: "When this lesson is learned thoroughly, I cannot see how the claim can be resisted; and that more especially in a country like Great Britain, the very existence of which depends upon highly organized industries." During the past twelve years workers have begun to demand "at least some recognition of the social rights of . . . *all* workmen, and the upper classes have acknowledged the need for a 'living wage'."

Still—and for Morris there is always a "still"—the present system remains unable to grant what is needed: "The battle must be fought out between the privileged and the useful classes, before the latter can win any solid or lasting benefits for the whole mass." He sees signs of this struggle occurring even in the last election, in which the Tories had gained a resounding victory over the Liberals. Paradoxically, this reaction may be an indirect attack on the socialists, seen for the first time as a serious threat: "It was largely the fear of the reactionists that [Socialism] was becoming a party which caused the successful attack of the election on progress generally."

Sadly the fears of the reactionists remain unjustified. The attacks on socialists have been successful because England lacks a unified socialist party: "its strength, as well as its weakness, lies in its being an *opinion* rather than a party." Without their own party, socialists must beg support from other parties, who may "throw [them] over at any exigency." The response to attack "should be to organize a real definite Socialist party, and, for the sake of the necessary gain, to accept the probable dangers of such a position."

In the face of the existence of at least three self-proclaimed socialist parties at the time—the Fabians, the Social Democratic Federation, and the Independent Labour Party (as well as anarcho-socialists/communists such as the Freedom group)—Morris's statement implies strong reservations: the former may be too meritocratic, the latter two overly focused on immediate demands, and all three, despite their focus on electoral victories, unwilling to combine into "a real definite Socialist party." The constituency of such a "real, definite" party must be a cross-class coalition whose members share a focus on fundamental change:

> This Socialist party must include the whole of the genuine labour movement, that is, whatever in it is founded on principle, and is not a mere temporary business squabble; it must also include all that is definitely Socialist amongst the middle class; and it must have a simple text in accordance with one aim, – the realization of a new society founded on the practical equality of condition for all, and general association for the satisfaction of the needs of those equals. The sooner this party is formed, and the reactionists find themselves face to face with the Socialists, the better.

Morris's final statement is one of qualified hope: "For whatever checks it may meet with on the way, it will get to its goal at last and *Socialism* will melt into *society*." As ever, he is honest: a true socialist party must inevitably transform all relationships, and although such a socialism remains possible for our world, it has not yet arrived. In the final words of *News from Nowhere*, "*if* others can see it as I have seen it, *then* it may be called a vision and not a dream" [emphases mine].

Notes

1. Kelvin, 4.393.
2. Stewart Headlam (1847–1924), the leader of the Christian Socialist movement, founded the Guild of St. Matthew (1877–1909) and edited *The Church Reformer: An Organ of Christian Socialism and Church Reform* (1884–95). A member of the Fabian Society, he published *Christian Socialism: A Lecture* as a Fabian tract in 1895.

The Whig revolution, which began on the fall of medieval society and culminated in the French revolution, on the one hand, and the establishment of the factory organization of production amidst the ruins of handicraft, on the other, seemed in the first half of this century to have stranded the civilized world on a period of academical coma, having some analogy to the great period of the classical civilization inaugurated by the accession of Augustus. In England at any rate a *modus vivendi* had been established between the employers of labor and their "hands," and free-trade and the abolition of the corn laws had so greased the wheels of factory production that, though profits were not made on the extravagant scale which obtained in the earlier years of the century, they were still very large, and the result was to increase enormously the wealth, numbers, and consequent power of the middle classes. In politics the Whigs, under the new name of Liberals, were marching on triumphantly, and of feudal survivals all but the semblance was abolished; and modern democracy, on the basis of irresistible, nay unquestionable, commercialism, seemed to be on the very point of being firmly established. It is true that in Britain religion lagged behind, and the "freethinking," which had long been accepted as an essential part of the Whig revolution on the continent, was here revolutionary and unrespectable, as an open and expressed opinion, though even then almost universal amongst intelligent persons. For the deep-seated hypocrisy of our nation (and perhaps race), which has often, wrongly as I think, been dignified with the historical title of "Puritanism," would not allow facts to be faced openly on this side of things.

As to literature and the fine arts, there had been for some time a stirring amongst the dry bones in the first, and the nonentity of the eighteenth century, of which the dullard Pope was the high-priest, had been invaded early in the nineteenth century by the men of genius of the dawning Romantic school. Poetry began again and it became once more possible to forget the miseries of real life by burying oneself in the idealities of the great inventors.

But literature, less than any of the arts, depends on its surroundings, and the imagination of those who have steeped themselves in the life of serious periods of history, as shown us by their still existing works, can free itself from the ugliness and trivialities of to-day and produce something which is not alien in idea from the living art of the past. Art, in its narrower sense, is not so fortunate, and on all hands can be oppressed by its surroundings. On this side, when the whole world is sick, the men of special talent or genius share the sickness in one way or other; either their sense of beauty is deadened, or they seek for expression of it in fierce antagonism to the life and thought of the passing time, and the present public either corrupts or neglects them. In this period of Whig ascendency, therefore, art was, let us say, lying asleep, and its condition was not ill expressed by the stupidity and emptiness of the London Exhibition of 1851—the first of the series of advertising shows which have since cursed the world with their pretentious triviality. Even the painters of pictures, the producers of art who approach nearer than others to the men of inventive literature, were sunk low indeed. Here and there was a man who rose above his fellows into something like genius, though even his aims were not high, nor his scope wide, as Turner for instance; here and there a man of unquestionable industry and conscientiousness, as Maclise; but, as for the general body of "artists" as they were called, they were about worthy of the somewhat vulgar contempt showered upon them in Thackeray's novels. In short, no man of sense ever troubled himself about "high art," except as a matter of officialism, or as a piece of affectation which his position in society forced upon him.

As for architecture and its kindred arts, people scarcely knew of the existence of such things. Stupid ugliness was worshipped under the name of simplicity or gentlemanly restraint. Beauty or incident was not so much as thought of. Even the active hatred of beauty, which the Philistine cultivates with such single-minded ardor to-day, implies a somewhat better position for the arts than the sordid dullness[1] of the triumphant Whiggery of the "fifties."

1. Orig., dulness

Commerce, the only thing needful; politics, the slave of the markets; literature, existing only in rebellion; art forgotten, beauty dead: this, it seemed, was to be the ultimate gain of "The heir of all the ages in the foremost files of time."

Seemed—but, slowly as the course of events in modern times crawls along, a change has begun to show within the last twenty years. In economics the principle of *laissez faire*, which in the period above spoken of seemed to have been accepted as irrevocable by statesman and dustman alike, has been blown to the winds more in practice even than in theory, and collective action is admitted everywhere to be the machinery through which we must of necessity strive to make the best of our surroundings. In politics, if they have not become more democratic in the old sense of the word, the word itself has changed its meaning, and no longer signifies a consensus of the rich middle classes, but rather the gathering of opinion of the working classes, not, it must be admitted, for the purpose of enabling them to manage their own affairs (*i.e.*, the best method for the production of common utilities), but at least to let the governing or possessing class find out what steps may be necessary to be taken to make the only useful class of the community temporarily contented.

In literature and the arts again there has been some stirring of the dry bones, though I cannot think it has been either deep or widely spread. Yet we have seen a man, whose poetry was once thought the very acme of wild eccentricity, dying a peer of the realm without having to make any considerable recantation; and the Romantic school so successful that it is now rather rebelled against than rebelling. In the arts, owing chiefly to the energy and genius of three young men—Rossetti, Holman Hunt, and Millais,—it is at least possible for painters of pictures to live by giving their genius free scope, if they have it in them, however sore the struggle may be against their isolated position which denies them the support of a reasonable unbroken tradition. Furthermore, owing to the genuine instinct for the study of history which is a birth of these latter days, there has grown up some appreciation of the great architectural works of the Middle Ages, and a certain number of highly educated and refined men have now for some time been struggling against the hideousness of our modern streets by designing buildings which they have striven honestly and not without success to make at once beautiful and useful: though it is true that these buildings must of necessity be more or less imitative of the work of past ages; and also that the movement that has had its rise in the study of historic art has borne[2] with it the disadvantage that the public

2. Orig., born

looks with favor on the preposterous attempt to "restore," as it is called, our ancient monuments, which have suffered so much from the neglect and ignorance of the post-medieval period, to their (supposed) original state; for though we may have learned history enough to cease to look upon our ancestors as a set of savages whose lives and deeds sprang from no visible causes in the past, and led to no consequences in the future, we have not yet grasped the knowledge that these monuments of art sprang from the conditions of society amidst which they were produced; that the art of a people, as distinct from a few ingenious and gifted men living isolated from the people, must of necessity be an essential growth from the life of the epoch.

Indeed, it is because I have so thoroughly learned this lesson myself (as I think), that I must needs look upon the art and literature of these days as but matters by the way, and something without root or organic growth. I believe that they will flourish again, rising maybe from the scanty tradition left us, or maybe from a new birth,—which we now cannot so much as conceive of,—when a new society has been realized, the hope of which (as I deem), is the one bright spot in the century and is now growing clearer to us.

For even now at the bottom of the change above said in economics and politics, in literature and art, lies a great change in opinion, which has produced the visible new birth of Socialism; a new birth dimly foreshadowed at the time of the French revolution by the opinions and attempts of such men as Babeuf[3] and the Utopists. The public opinion points toward a new society founded on equality of condition, and the association of equals. The first of these has been mainly in abeyance since the time of the poverty of tribal society: the second, after playing a principal part in the development of society from the beginning of the great energy of the Middle Ages, fell with them under the triple attack of bureaucracy, political nationalism, and the lust for material advancement. But, unless they are once again to become the root principles of a true society, I for my part can see nothing for it but a continuous degradation of our false society until it disappears in a chaos caused by greed and suffering.

But I repeat that the assertion of these principles is already being made, not merely by small knots of Socialist preachers, but by the working-classes generally. Trades Unionism is losing its old narrowness, and is learning that it must not champion this or that trade or occupation

3. François-Noël Babeuf (1760–97), French revolutionary, early socialist/communist, and editor of *Le Tribun du peuple*, was executed by the French Revolutionary Directory (1795–9) as an insurrectionist.

against the general public; that it must no longer be the carpenters against the public, or the miners against the public,—but the whole body of producers against the non-producers who exploit them; that, in short, the producers must claim the right to manage their own affairs. When this lesson is learned thoroughly, I cannot see how the claim can be resisted; and that more especially in a country like Great Britain, the very existence of which depends upon highly organized industries.

Meantime, I say, the lesson is being learned, doubtless in a rough and unsystematic way enough; yet no one who is conversant with working-class politics can dispute that the attitude of the workmen toward Socialism has quite altered within the last twelve years, and that a claim for recognition as citizens has been put forward by them, to which all classes of society have been forced to pay some attention. Both the theory and practice of even *ultra* Liberals as to the relation of the workmen of the organized industries in Great Britain to their employers, in the days when John Bright was regarded by the prosperous middle class as a dangerous democrat and tribune of the people, was that the workman, as workman, was a part of the machinery of profitable production, that there were certain laws of nature that governed the action of the machine,—always in the interest of those who owned and controlled it, the successful middle class to wit,—and that the members of the machine must submit patiently to any suffering which resulted from the action of those natural laws.

There was little for the workmen to complain of in this, it was thought, because it was not difficult for any of them who were above the average to rise at least into the lower middle class, and most probably into the higher ranks of it; to become in short from a mere "hand" a foreman, the manager of the department, or often enough of a factory itself. As for what was below the average[,] that was *its* lookout, and its complaints would not do anything to turn the course of the "natural law." This, I say, was the theory or practice of such men as John Bright and his party; but the machine for the production of profits has protested against the action of the natural law—which must of necessity degrade every man who could not struggle up into the comparatively few places which were to be had amongst the superintendents of labor,—and by various revolts, strikes and so forth, the claim of citizenship has, as aforesaid, been made by working-men as *living on weekly wages*, and not as workingmen whose savings gave them some share in the privilege of capital.

For a long time the struggle was blind and narrow, but within the last few years it has become a conscious strife for at least some recognition of the social rights of citizens on behalf of *all* workmen willing to exercise their labor power; and, on the other hand, the possessing classes have practically admitted the necessity of a "living wage" for the workmen, even though that must be taken from the profits of the employers. A higher standard of comfort, more leisure, less precarious employment; these things at least, it is admitted, must be granted by the present system to the working-classes,—if the present system can do it—but can it? The answer to that must be found in the answer to another question: Are the interests of the employers and the employed the same? No, must be the answer, they are opposed. And if that be the case, how can the vital questions be discussed and settled with the mutual assent of the two parties to the quarrel? It is clear that they cannot be. When I mentioned the *struggle* of the working classes for citizenship I meant to use the word literally and not metaphorically. The battle must be fought out between the privileged and the useful classes, before the latter can win any solid or lasting benefits for the whole mass. And I have no doubt that it will go on with ever-increasing stress. The concessions made by the privileged classes to the useful ones will grow greater and more important, as the working-men see clearer into their position, and know what it is essential for them to claim; the privileged will concede these with much the same amount of pressure as forces them to yield to present and unimportant demands, some of which at any rate are now used for little else than banners to which to rally those who are yet purblind to the necessities of a real new society. So it will go on till it will be found at last that everything essential has been yielded by privilege, and probably the last opposition will be feeble and formal, and will be easily thrust aside.

It must be remembered that, on the one hand, the tokens that this great change in society is on the way are no longer merely the spread of academic discussion, or the setting forth of Utopias with their roots in the air, but the attempts to deal with "practical" questions concerning the present daily life of the greater part of the population; while, on the other hand, the ideas of a Socialist society are pretty much accepted by those who can by any stretch of language be called thinking people (among whom I do not include the professional politicians). Almost the only opposition offered to them comes from sheer pessimists, or those who are not ashamed to confess their adherence to the sordid cynicism of greed. How can the new society founded on equality and association be brought about? is the real question which is asked by all those who wish for conditions of life in the civilized world which will enable all groups of society to live with self-respect and manly pleasure.

Now I have practically said that, broadly speaking, the change must come about by the useful classes getting gradually educated to a sense of their due claims and responsibilities, and, as a result, going on steadily beating down commercial and economic privilege, as their forerunners the Whigs, whose day culminated in the French revolution, beat down the survivals of feudal privilege.

As to what is going on obviously at present in the world of politics, a few words will be enough on that subject, as I cannot deem it to be of so much importance as many people think. We have recently gone through a general election in Great Britain, the results of which have made the grossest reactionists (the Tories) jubilant, and I suspect have given some pleasure, even amidst their defeat, to the ordinary Liberal politicians.

The overwhelming Tory victory has indeed seemed to some of our party to mean rather a defeat of the Whigs than of the Progressives; but, though this seems plausible in view of some of the incidents of the contest, I should rather put down the victory to a strong rally of all that is reactionary against everything which seems progressive to the reactionists, from mere Whig Liberalism to definite Socialism,—which rally, if properly organized, was sure to be successful: so that it was rather the Liberals who were defeated along with the Socialists than the Socialists along with the Liberals. In other words there was, and is, an instinct amongst the reactionaries that the Socialists have been leading the Liberals and are the real enemies, and it is a true instinct, though politics, like poverty, makes strange bedfellows, and it is rather amusing to see some of our Whig friends dismissed from their seats on the ground of their being the allies of dangerous revolutionaries.

For the rest it was clear that whenever the reactionaries chose to administer such a check to Socialism they could do so with certainty of success, since there is no Socialist party in England; it has indeed ceased to be merely a sect or a "church" as it was some fifteen years ago, but has never gained any organization; its strength, as well as its weakness, lies in its being an *opinion* rather than a party. Yet it was largely the fear of the reactionists that it was becoming a party which caused the successful attack of the election on progress generally. And to my mind the answer to that attack should be to organize a real definite Socialist party, and, for the sake of the necessary gain, to accept the probable dangers of such a position. It is true that a wide-spread opinion cannot be defeated, and need not fear the temporary decision of the ballot-box; but to such a decision it must come at last, unless it is contented to act indirectly through other parties, which may throw it over at any political exigency, and must always be doing hesitatingly and blindly.

To sum up therefore as to the Socialist outlook: There is no progress possible to European civilization save in the direction of Socialism; for the Whig or Individualist idea which destroyed the medieval idea of association, and culminated in the French revolution and the rise of the great industries in England, has fulfilled its function or worked itself out.

The Socialistic idea has at last taken hold of the workmen, even in Great Britain, and they are pushing it forward practically, though in a vague and unorganized manner.

The governing classes feel themselves compelled to yield more or less to the vague demands of the workmen. But, on the other hand, the definitely reactionary forces of the country have woken up to the danger to privilege involved in those demands, and are attacking Socialism in front instead of passing it by in contemptuous silence.

The general idea of Socialism is widely accepted amongst the thoughtful part of the middle classes, even where their timidity prevents them from definitely joining the movement.

The old political parties have lost their traditional shibboleths, and are only hanging on till the new party (which can *only* be a Socialist one) is formed: the Whigs and Tories will then coalesce to oppose it; the Radicals will some of them join this reactionary party, and some will be absorbed by the Socialist ranks. That this process is already going on is shown by the last general election. Socialism has not yet formed a party in Great Britain, but it is essential that it should do so, and not become a mere tail of the Whig Liberal party, which will only use it for its own purposes and throw it over when it conveniently can.

This Socialist party must include the whole of the genuine labour movement, that is, whatever in it is founded on principle, and is not a mere temporary business squabble; it must also include all that is definitely Socialist amongst the middle class; and it must have a simple text in accordance with one aim,—the realization of a new society founded on the practical equality of condition for all, and general association for the satisfaction of the needs of those equals.

The sooner this party is formed, and the reactionists find themselves face to face with the Socialists, the better. For whatever checks it may meet with on the way, it will get to its goal at last and *Socialism* will melt into *society*.

26

"The Promise of May," published in *Justice*, May 1896

Editor's introduction

The third of Morris's articles printed in *Justice* between 1894 and 1896, "The Promise of May," is also his final political essay published in his lifetime, and after his death sections were reprinted by the Social Democratic Federation in the commemorative pamphlet *How I Became a Socialist* (London: Twentieth Century Press, 1896). Morris had previously commemorated May Day in two poems in *Justice* for 1892 and 1894, both later included in the 1915 edition of his *Chants for Socialists*. At the Paris 1889 Second International, May 1 had been declared an official international workers' holiday, and here he summarizes its significance: "May Day is above all days of the year fitting for the protest of the disinherited against the system of robbery that shuts the door betwixt them and a decent life."

Morris condenses his remarks into slightly more than 700 words, conveying his message with simple eloquence: capitalism by definition is waste, and to trust in the potential effects of advancing prosperity is futile; moreover, the defeat of capitalism cannot be easy, for the capitalists' instinct for profit is "an impulse like hunger." As often, he addresses his audience familiarly: "Many of you will smile at this question. . . . My friends, I fear not . . . ." He gently mocks the "trickle down" theory of social progress, that as profit increases the possessors of wealth will be "able to spare more and more from the great heap of wealth . . . so that at last [the producing classes] will have nothing left to wish for, and all will be peace and prosperity." History has repeatedly disproven this hope, he argues, for the advances of organization and science have not helped the disadvantaged since "the end and aim of it all is production of profit for the privileged classes."

As in his speech to the largely Marxist International Workers Congress of 1889, he also warns against a complacently doctrinaire determinism. To those who predict that capitalism will speedily self-destruct under the weight of its own contradictions, he reminds his audience of the power wielded by capitalists in self-defense. Perhaps the chief of these stratagems has been the increasing pursuit of empire through violence: "Look how the whole capitalist world is stretching out long arms . . . and grabbing and clutching in eager competition at countries whose inhabitants don't want them . . . ." Interestingly it is the essay's two paragraphs condemning the ideology and cruelty of imperialism that have been removed from the *Why I Am a Socialist* version.[1]

In his conclusion he asserts that the hunger for appropriation—"the waste of our labour and our lives"—must be resisted by a yet more powerful determination, "the hunger for freedom and fair play for all, both people and peoples." Those now perceived as "hands" must become fully human by an act of will: "we will produce no more for profit but for *use*, for *happiness*, for LIFE." Morris's final published words thus reiterate his long-held faith in radical equality, internationalism, and what might be termed a happiness theory of use value.

Note

1. Henry Hyndman (1842–1921), the leader of the Social Democratic Federation, was a proponent of British imperialism, and one wonders if these paragraphs were excised for ideological reasons. It may be, however, that some excisions were necessary to keep the pamphlet to 16 pages, a convenient size for printing.

Certainly May Day is above all days of the year fitting for the protest of the disinherited against the system of robbery that shuts the door betwixt them and a decent life. The day when the promise of the year reproaches the waste inseparable from the society of inequality, the waste which produces our artificial poverty of civilisation, so much bitterer for those that suffer under it than the natural poverty of the rudest barbarism. For it is undoubtedly true that full blown capitalism makes the richest country in the world as poor as, nay poorer than, the poorest, for the life of by far the greater part of its people.

Are we to sit down placidly under this, hoping that some blessing will drop down from heaven upon us which will bring content and self-respect and a due share of the beauties and joys of the earth to the classes that produce all that is produced, while it will bring no lessening of the dignity and ease and sweetness of life with which the possessing (and wasting) classes are now endowed?

Most of you will smile at that question, but remember that this opinion was not long ago universally held, and is still held by many.

They think that civilisation will grow so speedily and triumphantly, and production will become so easy and cheap, that the possessing classes will be able to spare more and more from the great heap of wealth to the producing classes, so that at last[1] these latter will have nothing left to wish for, and all will be peace and prosperity. A futile hope indeed! and one which a mere glance at past history will dispel. For we find, as a matter of fact, that when we were scarcely emerging from semi-barbarism, when open violence was common, and privilege need put on no mask before the governed classes, the workers were not worse off than now, but better. In short, not all the discoveries of science, not all the tremendous organisation of the factory and the market will produce true wealth, so long as the end and aim of it all is the production of profit for the privileged classes.

Nothing better will happen than more waste and more, only perhaps exercised in different directions than now it is. Waste of material, waste of labour (for few indeed even of the genuine wage earners are engaged in the production of utilities). Waste, in one word, of LIFE.

But again there are some who will say "Yes indeed, the capitalist system can come to no good end, death in a dust-bin is its doom, but will not its end be at least speedy even without any help of ours?" My friends I fear not. The capitalist classes are doubtless alarmed at the spread of Socialism all over the civilized world. They have at least an instinct of danger; but with that instinct comes the other one of self[-] defence. Look how the whole capitalist world is stretching out long arms towards the barbarous world and grabbing and clutching in eager competition at countries whose inhabitants don't want them; nay, in many cases, would rather die in battle, like the valiant men they are, than have them. So perverse are these wild men before the blessings of civilisation which would do nothing worse for them (and also nothing better) than reduce them to a propertyless proletariat.

And what is all this for? For the spread of abstract ideas of civilisation, for pure benevolence, for the honour and glory of conquest? Not at all. It is for the opening of fresh markets to take in all the fresh profit-producing wealth which is growing greater and greater every day; in other words, to make fresh opportunities for *waste*; the waste of our labour and our lives.

And I say this is an irresistible instinct on the part of the capitalists, an impulse like hunger, and I believe that it can only be met by another

1. Orig., least

hunger, the hunger for freedom and fair play for all, both people and peoples. Anything less than that the capitalist power will brush aside, but that they cannot; for what will it mean? The most important part of their machinery, the "hands" becoming MEN, and saying, "Now at last we will it; we will produce no more for profit but for *use*, for *happiness*, for LIFE."

Appendix: List of Morris's Anthologized Essays

The list excludes those listed in Nicholas Salmon's *The Political Writings: Contributions to* Justice *and* Commonweal, *1883–1890.*

Key

Bacon	Alan Bacon, ed., *The Relations of Art to Labour* (London: William Morris Society, 2004)
Cole	G. D. H. Cole, ed., *Selected Writings of William Morris* (London: Nonesuch Press, 1946)
*CW*22 and *CW*23	May Morris, ed., *The Collected Works of William Morris*, vols. 22 and 23 (London: Longman's, 1914–15)
FB	the present volume
Holland	Owen Holland, ed., *How I Became a Socialist* (London: Verso, 2020)
Jackson	Holbrook Jackson, *On Art and Socialism: Essays and Lectures by William Morris* (London: John Lehmann, 1947)
KelAS	Norman Kevin, ed., *William Morris on Art and Socialism* (New York: Dover, 1996)
Kelvin	Norman Kelvin, ed., *The Collected Letters of William Morris* (Princeton: Princeton University Press, 1984–96)
KP	Kelmscott Press
LeMire	Eugene LeMire, ed., *The Uncollected Lectures of William Morris* (Detroit: Wayne State University Press, 1969)
MIA	Morris International Archive (a subdivision of the Marxists International Archive), marxists.org/archive/morris/index.htm, transcribed by Nicholas Salmon, Graham Seaman, and others
MM1 and MM2	May Morris, *William Morris: Artist, Writer, Socialist*, vols. 1 and 2 (Oxford: Basil Blackwell, 1936)
Morton	A. L. Morton, *Political Writings of William Morris* (London: Lawrence and Wishart, 1973)

WMA	Florence S. Boos, ed., William Morris Archive, http://morrisarchive.lib.uiowa.org
WP	William Peterson, ed., *The Ideal Book: Essays and Lectures on the Art of the Book by William Morris* (Berkeley: University of California, 1982)
Zabel	Gary Zabel, *Art and Society: Lectures and Essays by William Morris* (Boston, MA: George's Hill, 1993)

[Against War with Russia] FB
[Art: a Serious Thing] LeMire
A Factory as It Might Be MM2
A Note by William Morris on His Aims in Founding the Kelmscott Press WP
A Review of European Society, introduction MIA, FB
Address at the Cambridge School of Art MIA, FB
Address at the Second Annual Meeting of the S. P. A. B. 1879 MM1
Address at the Twelfth Annual Meeting of the S. P. A. B. 1889 MM1
Address on English Socialism on Behalf of the Socialist League MIA, Holland, FB
Address to English Liberals MM2, MIA
Against the Abuses of Public Advertising FB
An Address at the Distribution of Prizes to Students of the Birmingham School of Art *CW*22, MIA
Art: A Serious Thing LeMire, KelAS
Architecture and History *CW*22, MIA
Art and Industry in the Fourteenth Century *CW*22, MIA, Zabel
Art and Inequality [Address to the Men and Women's College] MM2 [sections], FB
Art and Its Producers *CW*22, Jackson, MIA
Art and Labour LeMire, MIA
Art and Socialism *CW*23, Jackson, MIA, Morton, Zabel
Art and the Beauty of the Earth *CW*22, Jackson, MIA, KelAS
Art and the People: A Socialist's Protest MM2, Zabel
Art under Plutocracy *CW*23, Jackson, Morton, MIA, Zabel, KelAS, Holland
Art, Wealth and Riches *CW*23, Jackson, MIA, Zabel
Artist and Artisan: As an Artist Sees It MM2
Arts and Crafts Essays, Preface MM1
As to Bribing Excellence MM2
At a Picture Show MIA, MM2, Zabel
Change of Position—Not Change of Condition FB, MIA
Commercial War MM2 [sections], MIA [sections], FB

Communism *CW*23, Jackson, Morton
Communism—i.e., Property MM2 [sections], MIA [sections], FB
Dawn of a New Epoch *CW*23, KelAS
Early England LeMire
England and the Turks MM2
Equality sections MM2 [sections], MIA [sections], FB
Feudal England *CW*23
Gossip about an Old House on the River Thames MIA, MM1
Gothic Architecture KP, MIA, WMA, Zabel
How I Became a Socialist Cole, *CW*23, Holland, Jackson, MIA, Morton, FB
How Shall We Live Then MIA, FB
How We Live and How We Might Live *CW*23, MIA, Morton, Holland
Introductory Note to Good King Wenceslas by Dr. Neale MM1
London in a State of Siege MM2
Looking Backward MM2
Makeshift MIA, MM2
Making the Best of It *CW*22, MIA
Manifesto of the Society for the Protection of Ancient Buildings MM1
Misery and the Way Out MM2 [sections], FB
Monopoly: or How Labour Is Robbed *CW*23, Jackson, MIA
Nottingham Kyrle Society, 1881 MM1
Of Dyeing as an Art 1889 MM1
Of the Origins of Ornamental Art LeMire, MIA, KelAS
On the Artistic Qualities of the Woodcut Books of Ulm and Augsburg in the Fifteenth Century MIA
One Socialist Party [newspaper report] FB
Our Country Right or Wrong MM2 [sections], MIA [sections], FB
Paper Read at the Seventh Annual Meeting of the S. P. A. B. 1884 MM1
Preface to Medieval Lore by Robert Steele MM1, MIA
Preface to More's Utopia MM1
Preface to The Nature of Gothic by John Ruskin MM1, MIA
Printing 1888 MM1
Relations of Art to Labour Bacon [sections], MIA [sections], FB
Report of the S. P. A. B. 1878 MM1
Review of Dante Gabriel Rossetti's Poems MM1
Seven Years Ago and Now [report] MIA
Socialism FB
Socialism Up to Date MM2 [sections], MIA [sections], FB
Some Hints on Pattern-designing *CW*22, MIA

Speech at a Meeting of the Kyrle Society, Kensington Vestry Hall, 1881 MM1
Speech at a Picture Show MM2 [sections], FB
Stained Glass MM1
Technical Instruction [an interview with the Royal Commission on Technical Instruction] MM1
Textile Fabrics *CW*22, MIA
Textiles 1888 MM1, MIA
The Aims of Art *CW*23, Jackson, MIA, Zabel
The Art of the People 1879 *CW*22, Jackson, KelAS
The Arts and Crafts of Today *CW*22, Jackson, MIA
The Beauty of Life *CW*22, Jackson, MIA, KelAS
The Coal Struggle: Some Obvious Thoughts Thereon [a letter] MM2
The Deeper Meaning of the Struggle MM2
The Depression of Trade LeMire, MIA
The Early Illustration of Printed Books WP
The Early Literature of the North—Iceland LeMire, MIA
The End and the Means MM2, MIA
The English Pre-Raphaelite School 1891 MM1
The Exhibition of the Royal Academy 1884 MM1
The External Coverings of Roofs *CW*22
The Gothic Revival 1 LeMire
The Gothic Revival 2 LeMire
The Hopes of Civilization *CW*23, Jackson, Morton
The Ideal Book MM1, MIA
The History of Pattern-Designing *CW*22, MIA
The Illuminated Books of the Middle Ages MM1
The Influence of Building Materials upon Architecture *CW*22, MIA
The Lesser Arts *CW*22, Jackson, Morton, KelAS
The Lesser Arts of Life *CW*22, MIA
The Lord Mayor's Show MM2
The Policy of Abstention MM2, MIA, Holland
The Political Outlook MM2 [sections], Holland, FB
The Present Outlook in Politics LeMire, MIA
The Present Outlook of Socialism in England MIA, KelAS, FB
The Promise of May MIA, Holland, FB
The Prospects of Architecture in Civilization *CW*22, Jackson, KelAS
The Revival of Architecture *CW*22, MIA
The Revival of Handicraft *CW*22, Jackson, MIA, Zabel
The Reward of Genius MM2
The Socialist Ideal: Art *CW*23, Jackson, MIA
The Society of the Future MM2, Morton, KelAS, MIA, Holland

The Woodcut Books of Ulm and Augsburg MM1
The Woodcuts of Gothic Books MM1, MIA
Thoughts on Education under Capitalism MM2
Town and Country MIA, FB
True and False Society *CW*23, Jackson, MIA
Under an Elm-Tree; or, Thoughts in the Countryside MM2, Morton
Useful Work versus Useless Toil *CW*23, Jackson, MIA, Morton, KelAS
Waste [report only] MIA
Westminster Abbey *CW*22
What Socialists Want LeMire, MIA
What We Have to Look For MM2 [sections], MIA, FB
Where Are We Now? MM2
Whigs, Democrats, and Socialists *CW*23, Holland
Why I Am a Communist MIA, FB
Work in a Factory as It Might Be: 2 MM2
Work in a Factory as It Might Be: 3 MM2

Index of Titles

A Dream of John Ball, 23, 42, 213n, 268, 288

A Review of European Society, John Sketchley, 153

"A Speech on the Opening of the Dardanelles", 34

"Address at the Opening of the Fourth Annual Loan Exhibition", 119

"Against An Anglo-Russian War", 32, 33

"Against the Abuses of Public Advertising", 367

"An Address to English Liberals", 5, 32–4n

Another Country, Julian Mitchell, 181

"Art and Inequality"/"Of the Popular or Decorative Arts", 4, 10, 14, 74, 76, 315

"Art and Its Producers", 226n

"Art and Labour"/"The Relations of Art to Labour", 5, 94, 133

"Art and Socialism", 3, 11, 26n, 133, 179

"Art for All", 41, 96

"Address at the Cambridge School of Art Prizegiving", 41, 96

"Art under Plutocracy", 133

"As to Bribing Excellence", 324

Beowulf, 1

Biblia Innocentium, 23

"Change of Position—Not Change of Condition", 13, 355–6

"Chants for Socialists", 160, 385

"Commercial War", 8, 14, 91, 159, 160, 179, 206n

Communist Manifesto, Karl Marx, 162

Das Kapital, Karl Marx, 26n, 134, 184n, 316

Decline and Fall of the Roman Empire, Edward Gibbon, 75, 84n, 95

England for All, H. M. Hyndman, 184n

"Equality", Matthew Arnold, 11, 15, 23, 75, 86, 221, 238

Fors Clavigera, John Ruskin, 250

Forty Years of Work Without Wages, Charles Rowley, 277

French and German Socialism in Modern Times, Richard Ely, 134

Garden Cities of To-morrow, Ebenezer Howard, 308

Germania, Tacitus, 75, 84

"Gothic Architecture", 4, 226n

History of Agriculture and Prices, James Edwin Thorold Rogers, 134

Hopes and Fears for Art, 1, 41, 49

"How I became a Socialist", 3, 10, 14, 26n, 203, 315, 355, 356n, 385

"How Shall We Live Then", 9, 12, 15, 243

"How The Change Came", 14, 293

"How We Live and How We Might Live", 133

Land Common Property, John Sketchley, 153

"Manifesto" (Fabian), 19, 338

Manifesto of English Socialists, 242

Manifesto of the Socialist League, 118, 216

May Day, 1894, 356, 37 85, 386

Merrie England, Robert Blatchford, 341–2, 350

"Mine and Thine", 183

"Misery and the Way Out", 91, 133, 159, 163, 179

News from Nowhere, 7, 14, 96, 161, 163n, 181, 185n, 204, 226n, 243–8, 293, 307, 308, 314, 339, 341–2, 369, 374, 377

"Notes on News," 203, 238

"Of the Popular or Decorative Arts"/"Art and Inequality", 74

"On the Origins of Ornamental Art", 226n
"One Socialist Party", 1, 3, 9, 21, 25, 358, 359, 373
"Our Beautiful World", 3, 367
"Our Country Right or Wrong", 5, 6, 33, 48, 49, 154
Principles of Social Democracy, John Sketchley, 153
Psalmi Penitentiales, 23
"Reminiscence of William Morris", James Tochatti, 327
"Slaves and Slave-Holders", 159
"Socialism from the Root Up", 185n, 213, 294n
"Socialism Up to Date", 20, 277, 278, 280
Socialism: Its Growth and Outcome, 23, 26n, 294n
"Speech At A Picture Show", 4, 11, 14, 121
"Tapestry and Carpet Weaving", 226n
The Agricola and Germania, Tacitus, 77, 83
"The Art of Dyeing", 226n
"The Beauty of Life", 96, 167
"The Beauty of the Earth", 96
The Bulgarian Horrors and the Question of the East, W. E. Gladstone, 5, 31
The Crimes of Government, John Sketchley, 153
"The Dawn of a New Epoch", 159
"The Decorative Arts", 41, 74; *see also* "The Lesser Arts"
"The Difficulties of Socialism", John Stuart Mill, 316
The Earthly Paradise, 374
The Exeter Book, 310n
"The Fourteenth Century", 185
The Historical Basis of Socialism in England, Henry Hyndman, 26n, 95, 133, 227n
The House of the Wolfings, 102, 223
"The Lesser Arts", 41, 96; *see also* "The Decorative Arts"
"The Pilgrims of Hope", 160, 268
"The Political Outlook", 26, 203
"The Present Outlook of Socialism in England", 13, 22, 24, 26n, 338, 373–4
"The Promise of May", 26n, 155, 355–6, 385
"The Relations of Art to Labour"/"Art and Labour", 5, 94
The Roots of the Mountains, 102
"The Society of the Future", 243
The Stones of Venice, John Ruskin, 95
The Tables Turned, or Nupkins Awakened, 268, 293
The Turkish Atrocities in Bulgaria, J. A. McGahan, 31
"Town and Country", 307–8
Unto This Last, John Ruskin, 250n
"Useful Work versus Useful Toil", 133
Utopia, Thomas More, 96
"Wake, London Lads", 32
"Wapene Martijn", Jacob van Maerlant, 185n
"War and Peace", 49
"What We Have to Look For", 9, 13, 17, 18, 20, 247, 264, 337–8, 373
"Why I Am a Communist", 16–18, 323, 338, 375

Subject Index

abolition
- of central power, 256
- of child labor, 327n
- of classes, 93, 130, 183, 200, 214, 263
- of compulsion, 323
- of piecework, 327n
- of private profit, 200
- of private property, 183, 248, 251, 261, 279, 293, 305
- privilege, 13, 214, 287, 299, 356, 357
- of slavery, 95
- of the feudal system, 115, 283, 377
- of the House of Lords, 139

abolition of waste, 333
absolutism, 6, 35
actionist, 362
administration, 49, 247, 256–7, 261, 301n, 326, 332–3; *see also* bureaucracy; organization
advertisement, 52, 161, 211, 279, 285, 367, 368–70, 378
aesthetics, 42, 267, 273, 368
Afghanistan, 6, 26n, 51, 65, 68, 70, 72, 162
Africa, 6, 10, 49, 64n, 65, 160, 162, 360, 363
aggression, 49, 50, 51
agriculture, 100, 102, 111, 134, 137, 164n, 254, 266, 271n, 296n, 301n, 308, 310
Alaska, 360, 362n
Alexander, Keith / Thomas, William Keith, 60
America, 9, 22, 26n, 64, 52n, 125, 212, 272, 305n, 363; *see also* United States
anarchists, 12, 15–17, 50, 60n, 185, 292, 264, 268, 294n, 316, 318, 323, 325, 327, 346, 356n, 360
anarchy, 33, 35, 57, 70, 172, 323
appropriation of property, 386
Arabs, 162, 174
Arch, Joseph, 163, 266, 271
architecture, 2, 3, 4, 78, 80, 94, 98, 103, 110, 219, 226n, 374, 375, 378, 379; *see also* building; monument
aristocracy, 23, 82, 106, 115, 139, 154, 156, 165, 195, 210–217, 222–3, 228, 230, 236, 278, 289, 296; *see also* accident of birth
Aristotle, 95, 100, 301
army, 57, 70, 108, 127, 140, 144, 174, 145, 171–2, 175, 218, 222, 230, 256, 279, 284
Arnold, Matthew, 75, 86
art, 76, 78–9, 80, 103–4, 114, 119, 254, 375, 378
- worthy art, 75, 85, 114

artisans, 106, 134, 138, 139, 290, 312
artists, 8, 42–7, 106, 107, 110, 160, 161, 170, 321, 327n, 378; *see also* craftsmen; handicraftsmen
Arts and Crafts Movement, 268
arts, 5, 8, 10, 11, 14, 17, 33, 41–7, 49, 74–88, 91–3, 94–107, 100, 110–14, 117, 119, 121–3, 127–9, 130, 133, 141, 161, 169, 179, 180, 182, 190, 193, 204, 208, 222, 226n, 235, 246, 250, 251, 252–5, 266, 267, 268, 277, 307, 317, 320, 321, 324, 331, 348, 374–5, 378–80
- building arts, 254
- decorative arts, 76, 77, 352, 268; *see also* arts: popular arts
- disagreeable arts, 255
- domestic arts, 246, 254, 268
- fine arts, 84, 180, 190, 255, 378; *see also* arts: intellectual arts

industrial arts, 100
intellectual arts, 100, 102, 110, 255
lesser arts, 47, 80, 100, 102, 255
minor arts, 253
open air arts, 254
ornamental arts, 92, 103, 110
popular arts, 41, 77–80, 83, 85, 87, 88, 91, 93, 96, 110, 250
workshop arts, 254
aspirations, 10, 16, 50, 54, 73, 75, 78, 84, 85, 141, 177, 193, 218, 221, 226, 293, 315, 339, 347; *see also* passion
association of equals, 13, 375, 380; *see also* fellowship
associations (political), 13, 22, 105, 192, 209, 246, 268, 289, 295, 296, 316, 376, 382, 384
Ancoats Brotherhood, 74, 277, 307
Ancoats Recreation Committee, Manchester, 20, 277
Ayrshire Miners Union, 263
Birmingham Republican Association, 153
Bloomsbury Socialist Society, 263
Bloomsbury Working Men's College, 179
Chichester Liberal Association, 32
College for Men and Women, London, 74
Democratic Federation, 91, 92, 315, 318; *see also* Social Democratic Federation
Eastern Question Association, 5, 31, 75, 206
Electoral Labour Association, 263
Fabian Society, 10, 19, 23, 133, 136n, 155, 204, 228n, 243, 244, 247, 268, 326, 327n, 338, 342, 343, 355, 376, 377n; *see also* Progressive Association
Fulham Liberal Club, 226n
Hammersmith Liberal Club, 203
Hammersmith Socialist Society, 19, 20, 23, 178, 289, 307, 337, 338, 342, 344n, 359
Labour Electoral Association, 272
Labour Emancipation League, 159
Labour Reform League, 153
Labour Representation League, 206
Leeds Philosophical and Literary Society, 94, 95
Leicester Radical Club, 243,
Liberty and Property Defence League, 302
London Patriotic Club, 179
London Vestry, 20, 338
National Agricultural Labourers' Union, 163, 266, 271n
National Secular Society, 133, 179, 302n
Northampton National Secular Society, 179, 302n
Nottingham Socialist Club, 225n
Oxford and District Socialist Union, 337
Peckham and Dulwich Radical Club, 179
Positivist Society, 302,
Progressive Association, 133, 136n; *see also* Fabian Society
Royal Society of Arts, 320n, 367
Scottish Labour Association, 263
Scottish Land and Labour League, 133
Social Democratic Federation (SDF), 1, 9, 18–20, 21, 25, 31, 32, 91, 116n, 120, 123, 153, 154, 155, 159, 178, 225n, 226n, 227n, 244, 267, 274, 293, 315, 316, 327, 338, 339, 342, 343, 355, 359, 360–2, 373, 376, 385, 386n
Socialist Labour League, Edinburgh branch, 226n
Socialist League, 1, 15, 18, 19, 25, 116, 118, 133, 152, 153, 159, 160, 162, 178, 179, 203, 204, 208, 225n, 226n, 242, 243, 244, 263, 265, 266, 267, 268, 271, 272n, 274, 276, 287, 291, 292, 323, 339, 360
Society for Controlling the Abuses of Public Advertising (SCAPA), 367, 368
Society for the Protection of Ancient Buildings, 3, 308, 368, 375
University Settlements Association, 74, 119, 126n
West Bromwich Institute, 74

Athelstan, 310
Atilla, 200
Australia, 272
Austria, 31, 56n
autonomy, 19, 20, 265, 360; *see also* freedom; liberty

Babeuf, Francois-Noel, 380
Balkans, 6, 31, 36, 37, 53n, 56–7, 65, 83, 95, 100–5n, 162, 166, 165, 174, 194, 235, 236, 296, 297
ballot-box, see also election; suffrage; vote, 22, 73, 291, 292, 304, 383
barbarian, 8, 35, 44, 51, 57, 68, 70, 75, 76, 78, 82–5, 102–4, 175, 176, 223, 225, 235, 247, 251, 261, 308, 310, 319, 386, 387
Barnett, Rev. Samuel Augustus, 119, 126
Bateson, Dr. W., 41
Bax, Ernest Belfort, 23, 26n, 185n, 213n, 244, 289, 294n, 316, 318, 319n
Beaconsfield, Lord, 6, 37n, 63n, 64, 70; *see also* Disraeli, Benjamin
beauty, 42–5, 47, 71, 76, 79, 82, 87, 95–6, 98, 100, 103, 107, 110–11, 114, 119, 121–4, 128–9, 139, 141–3, 149, 161, 165, 166, 169, 265, 268, 274, 298, 308, 309, 310, 312, 313, 317, 319, 321, 324, 331, 343, 350, 364, 368, 369, 370, 374, 375, 379, 386
Bedford, Duke of, 181
Bell, Sir Lothian, 134
Benthamite, 11
birth
  accident of birth, 223, 236, 281, 295, 299, 329; *see also* aristocracy
  new birth, 79, 104, 114, 182, 184, 196, 247, 380; *see also* great change
Blatchford, Robert, 341, 342, 344, 350
bourgeoisie, 172, 173, 205, 206, 209, 211, 212, 214, 215–17, 219, 265–7, 270, 272, 273, 356
Bradford, 133, 203
Bradlaugh, Charles, 302
Bright, John, 185, 267, 273, 381
Browning, Robert, 374
brutality, 46, 75, 82, 83, 88, 101, 108, 113, 122, 123, 130, 142, 165, 183, 197, 218, 225, 233, 271
Bryce, James, 367
building, 96, 103, 110, 138, 191, 254, 310, 328, 368, 369, 374, 379; *see also* architecture; monument
bureaucracy, 236, 267, 272, 326, 380; *see also* administration; organization
Burne-Jones, Edward, 3
Burne-Jones, Georgiana, 344n, 367
Burnley, Lancashire, 361, 364
Burns, John, 132, 280, 294n

Cairnes, John Elliott, 234
Cambridge, Guildhall, 41, 96
Canada, 9, 360, 362n, 363
capital, 92, 99, 106, 144, 148, 156, 157, 164, 168, 170, 173, 174, 177, 183, 188, 191, 193, 195, 200, 201, 206, 212, 213, 217, 219, 285, 320n, 362, 381
capitalism, 6, 9, 159, 160, 161, 162, 175, 183, 206, 225, 234n, 317, 331, 340, 362, 385, 386
capitalists, 9, 14, 16, 60n, 82, 102, 106, 120, 125, 126, 127, 133, 156, 160, 161, 162, 163, 166, 168, 175, 176, 177, 180, 181, 182, 183, 184, 186, 191, 194, 195, 201, 213, 217, 222, 225, 236, 263, 270, 272, 282, 283, 287, 325, 330, 331, 338, 346, 355, 357, 364, 365, 385, 386, 387, 388
Carlyle, Thomas, 75, 77n, 85, 316, 319
Carpenter, Edward, 264, 268
Carruthers, John, 26, 158
centralization, 244, 247, 256–8, 261, 267, 272
Cetewayo, 51, 65, 68
Champion, Henry Hyde, 227n
Charles V, 78
Chartism, 154, 156, 195
Chartist, 18, 153, 154, 155, 156, 201, 270
chauvinism, 225, 267, 273; *see also* nationalism
cheating, 56, 83, 167, 170, 172n, 214, 339
church, 71, 107, 169, 204, 213, 312, 374, 383

citizens, 53, 55, 58, 70, 95, 100, 101, 104, 122, 165, 166, 194, 235–36, 259–60, 277, 283, 290, 291, 297, 303–4, 308, 324, 325, 326, 331, 346, 348, 361, 364–5, 381
citizens not machines, 138, 174, 177, 213, 291, 303, 325, 331, 348, 365
citizenship, 300, 305, 381–2
city, 68, 96–7, 101–4, 126, 149, 236, 258, 296n, 207, 307–8, 310, 368; *see also* town(s)
civilization, 8, 35, 42, 45, 46, 47, 51, 56–7, 62, 66–8, 74–5, 76, 78–80, 82, 83–5, 88, 98, 100, 101, 102, 110, 124, 127, 128, 129, 136, 140, 142, 143, 161, 165, 169, 175–6, 182, 187, 192, 193, 196, 198, 212, 222, 223, 225, 230, 235, 236, 239, 251, 252, 264, 282, 283, 285, 290, 296, 297, 303, 310, 311, 317, 319, 320, 321, 342, 362, 363, 365, 377, 382, 383, 386, 387
class(es)
  abolition of classes, 183, 200, 263, 283
  capitalist class, 125, 205, 263, 387
  commercial classes, 115, 116, 194; contented classes, 142, 155; possessing classes, 189, 190–1, 333, 345, 346, 351, 352, 379, 382, 387; privileged classes, 190, 237, 239, 284–5, 355, 356, 382, 385, 387; producing classes, 140, 283, 385, 387; *see also* middle class
  cultivated classes, 11, 119, 128
  educated classes, 270
  employing class, 180, 184, 190-1, 199, 201; *see also* employer(s)
  exploited classes, 272
  gentlemen class, 298
  governing classes, 375, 384
  hanger-on, 134, 142
  master-class, 297
  middle class, 22, 93, 94, 97, 109, 115, 116, 119, 120, 129, 130, 139, 140, 143, 144, 155, 176, 194, 195, 196, 199, 200, 205, 211, 217, 223–4, 235, 236, 266, 267, 270, 272, 278, 283, 285, 296, 297, 301, 319, 321, 326, 332, 367, 376, 377, 379, 381, 384
  non-producing class, 164–5, 200
  oppressed class, 115, 188
  rich class, 180–1, 186, 188, 190, 192, 218, 234, 283
  system of classes, 5, 120, 130, 198, 234n
  upper classes, 14, 148, 192, 194, 201, 285, 376
  useful classes, 200, 282, 284, 329, 343, 352, 376, 379, 382
  useless class, 192, 200, 282, 329
  wage-earning classes, see also proletariat, wage-earning, 107, 133, 144
  well-to-do classes, 113, 137, 241
  working classes, 5, 8, 9, 11, 14–15, 92, 98, 106, 116, 127, 133, 134, 135, 143, 146, 154, 155, 159, 160, 170, 176, 179, 180, 182, 184, 190, 194–5, 196, 199, 201, 205, 212, 217, 224, 239, 266, 267, 269, 277, 280, 281, 291, 299, 300, 302n, 305, 325, 327n, 331, 332, 338, 340, 341, 342, 346, 348, 349, 350, 356, 357, 375, 379, 380, 381, 382
class allegiance, 120
class distinctions, 263
class division, 133
class domination, 156
class hierarchy, 11, 95, 265
class of ability, 259
class of laborers, 126, 134
class of toiling slaves, 142
class of workers, 126, 139, 180, 182, 195, 196
class society, 184, 187, 194, 200, 205
class violence, 187
class-struggle (or war), 150, 190, 195, 266, 270
classical period, 95, 97, 100, 102, 103, 104, 124, 193, 289, 290, 296, 297, 377
coalition, 162, 206, 325, 347, 376
Cobbett, William, 301
Cobden-Sanderson, Thomas, 134
Cobden, Richard, 185
Collier, Hiram Price, 373

colonies, 5, 9–10, 65n, 111, 176, 205, 362
Colvin, Sydney, 41
commerce, 14, 17, 42, 64, 67, 83, 97, 99, 107–11, 116, 120, 125, 144, 159, 166, 169, 173, 185n, 192, 212, 218, 256, 257, 284, 309, 340, 348, 374, 379
commercial, 8, 14, 24, 91, 96–7, 99, 108, 111, 115–16, 124, 126, 130, 147, 160, 161, 163, 164n, 165, 167, 172, 173, 175, 188, 194, 195, 210, 212, 215, 217–18, 224, 237, 239, 257, 267, 270, 272, 279, 282, 283, 285, 311, 340, 348, 369, 383
  War Commercial, 126, 127, 129; *see also* commercial war
commercial liberals, 8, 175; *see also* Manchester School
commercialism, 24, 110, 156, 160, 170, 173, 174, 175, 197, 217, 237, 348, 373, 377
commodity, 108, 146, 161, 173, 179, 195
Commonweal, 1–3, 153, 159, 183, 185n, 203, 235n, 238n, 243, 264, 268, 274, 292, 294n, 323, 356n
commonwealth, 109, 183, 198, 221, 229, 315, 317, 318, 320
communal, 7, 9, 156, 172, 184, 200, 224, 278, 280, 291, 301, 305, 308, 311, 316, 324, 325, 327n, 330–2, 333, 343, 344n, 345
commune, 256, 257, 326, 332; *see also* Paris Commune
Communism, 10, 12, 15, 16, 18, 20, 23, 24, 244, 259, 270, 289, 293, 294, 300, 305, 316, 325, 326, 328, 329, 330, 331, 332, 333, 334, 341, 348, 356, 374, 375
cataclysmic or catastrophic Communism, 15, 16, 18, 163, 247, 325, 331, 361, 375; *see also* violent revolution
Communists, 12, 16, 17, 18, 26n, 216, 230, 243, 251, 289, 293, 294, 295, 316, 323, 324, 325, 327–33, 338, 375, 376, 380n
communitarian, 289
community, 14, 42, 68, 105, 114, 116, 148, 163, 169, 173, 176, 183, 187, 189, 197–8, 201, 204, 209, 221, 229, 230–2, 233, 247, 253, 254, 255, 256, 259–60, 289, 295, 300, 313, 324, 328, 330, 332, 333, 379
competition, 8, 15, 106, 110, 114, 115, 116, 120, 123–5, 129, 130, 146–7, 150, 159, 162, 163, 164n, 166, 167, 168, 170, 171, 175, 180, 189, 190, 191, 200, 201, 205, 212, 217, 224, 229, 234–5, 237–9, 241, 257, 266, 279, 282, 284–5, 309, 326, 332, 340, 347, 349, 350, 352, 361, 368, 370, 374, 386, 387
conflict, 14, 33, 160, 163, 176, 179, 180, 195, 196, 204, 341, 360, 362n
congress
  Berlin Congress, 31, 53n, 56n, 64n, 71n, 154
  International Socialist Workers Congress or Second International, 11, 155, 263–4, 268, 272, 355, 385
  International Trades Union Congress, 238–9
conscience, 26n, 61, 73, 91, 93, 145, 187, 212–13, 270, 318, 323, 278
Conservative party, 22, 26n, 37, 49, 360; *see also* political parties; Tory Party
Constantinople, 80; *see also* Byzantine Empire
consumption, 145, 161, 171, 173, 189, 200, 223, 232, 234, 285
continent, 24, 26n, 115, 154, 156, 197, 217, 238n, 271, 323, 373, 377; *see also* Europe
cooperation, 19, 97, 130, 230, 237n, 270, 282
cooperative, 20, 76, 97–8, 109, 115, 161, 172, 180, 194, 253, 254, 257, 280, 282, 342
Corn Laws, 185n, 273n, 301n, 377
corporations, 105, 109, 224, 245, 247, 249, 261, 311
corruption, 8, 15, 37, 43n, 53n, 69, 100, 102, 103, 169, 173, 193, 217, 219, 222–5, 228, 230, 235–6, 256, 296, 378

council(s), 25, 65n, 67, 247, 248n, 256, 266–7, 271, 355, 359, 368–9
countryside, 8, 71, 162, 177, 266, 267, 269, 271n, 305n, 308–10, 311, 312, 368–71; *see also* fields; landscape; scenery
court (royal), 37–8, 212
coward(s), 36, 55, 63, 91, 93, 112, 145, 154, 156, 204, 208, 217
crafts, 60, 105, 107, 110–11, 126, 129, 188, 246, 253, 268, 269, 346, 348
craftsmen, 50, 58, 105, 106, 109–10, 127, 279, 285, 296–7, 310; *see also* artists; handicraftsmen; workmen
Crane, Walter, 152, 319, 327, 368, 367, 372
creativity, 43, 222, 266, 267, 293
criminal, 136, 138, 186, 201, 224, 230, 240
cultivation, 8, 11, 36, 38, 44, 78–9, 81, 92, 95, 100–2, 108, 119, 122, 124, 127–8, 142, 162, 177, 197, 219, 236, 258, 310, 321, 378; *see also* education; instruction; learning
culture, 74, 75, 76, 80, 95, 119, 211–13, 266, 238–9, 277, 342
Cyprus, 31

Darwinists, 224, 237n, 247
decentralization, 244, 247, 256–7, 258; *see also* federation; region
deception, 36, 122, 135, 144, 166, 172n, 227, 303
degeneration, 76, 261
degradation, 11, 13, 15, 75, 77–8, 79, 80, 82, 91, 92, 98, 122, 136, 163, 171, 177, 184, 187, 192–3, 201, 209, 213–14, 223, 225, 235, 247, 250, 264, 281, 282, 305, 309, 339, 345, 375, 380, 381
democracy, 6, 24, 51, 69, 70, 204, 201–11, 212, 214–15, 216, 217, 223, 227, 228, 232, 235, 347, 248n, 256n, 291, 300–1, 321, 328n, 333, 377
democratic, 14, 76, 105, 201, 204, 205, 206, 210n, 214, 216, 228n, 269, 293, 326, 332, 356n, 375, 379
democrats, 215, 381
dependence, 13, 149, 223, 234–5, 238, 265, 267, 271, 273, 274, 278, 281, 296
depression, 77n, 91, 93, 173, 198, 199, 205, 206, 219, 308
desire(s), 7, 12, 22, 25, 37n, 43, 44, 46, 52, 54, 64, 72, 73, 76, 77, 78, 82, 85, 88, 99, 114, 129, 147, 150, 148, 169, 170, 174, 183, 206, 210, 218, 219, 222–3, 229, 230, 231, 233–4, 244, 245, 247, 248, 249, 251, 255, 259, 260, 278, 279, 281, 286, 287, 293, 294, 295, 300, 305, 308, 309, 310n, 313, 315, 319, 321, 328, 330, 356, 361, 364, 369, 375; *see also* necessaries; necessities; needs; wants
destruction, 5, 8, 9, 14, 17, 50, 59, 61, 68, 71n, 75, 84, 95, 99, 101, 104, 108, 110, 121–3, 131, 133, 142, 144, 146, 159, 163, 173, 181, 184, 186, 199, 201, 209, 232, 239, 283, 298, 308, 310, 320, 325, 348, 361, 364, 365, 368, 369, 384, 385
Devonshire Great Consols, 160, 163n, 181, 185n, 238n
Dickens, Charles, 211, 317
discontent, 45, 69, 92, 99, 121, 130, 134, 136–7, 139–42, 145, 150, 155–6, 182, 186, 195, 204, 207, 216, 236, 251–2, 270, 272, 278, 283, 316, 319, 346n, 348
disease, 80, 123, 187, 214, 246, 254, 255, 286; *see also* sickness
Disraeli, Benjamin, 6, 31, 33, 34n, 64n, 67n, 71n, 163n, 289; *see also* Lord Beaconsfield
distribution, 106, 126, 135, 147, 148, 173, 180, 189, 190, 205, 231, 250n, 254, 255, 264, 267, 293, 308, 324, 327n, 343, 344n
domination, 101, 103, 105, 148, 156, 162, 191, 237n, 265, 267, 273, 342
drudgery, 138, 214, 255, 261, 332; *see also* toil
duty, 43, 52n, 54, 55, 68–9, 76, 80, 81, 84, 88, 91, 97, 104, 129, 130, 161,

162, 164, 169, 188, 215, 279, 283, 296, 326, 344n; *see also* responsibility

East, 46, 78, 80, 82–3, 103, 300; *see also* Ottoman Empire
Eastern Question, 31; *see also* Balkans
ecological, 96, 308
economic, 8, 12, 91, 95, 96, 106, 115, 116n, 135, 138n, 145n, 150, 153, 161, 163, 164n, 194, 199, 203, 206, 212, 216, 217, 239, 265–6, 267, 272, 290, 317–18, 320n, 324, 318, 337, 341, 361, 374, 383
economic progression, 96–7
economics, 26n, 167, 179, 181, 185n, 212, 222, 233, 249, 293, 316, 318, 379, 380
economy, 139, 204, 208, 233, 365
Edinburgh, Queen Street Hall, 133, 226n
Education Acts, 71n, 112n
education, 7, 11, 20, 23, 44, 47, 51, 52, 59, 68, 71, 71, 95, 97, 112–14, 115, 128–9, 134, 135, 137, 140, 141, 143, 144, 145, 149, 159, 161, 164, 176, 180, 183, 186, 190, 201, 204, 206, 207, 208, 213, 217–18, 222–4, 228, 232, 236, 244, 246, 253, 261, 270, 278, 279, 282, 286, 302, 318, 326, 327n, 332, 344n, 349, 360, 364, 379, 392; *see also* cultivation; instruction; learning
egalitarian, 7, 10, 13, 94, 95, 181–2, 184, 221, 243, 247, 269, 338
Egypt, 154
election, 5, 6, 19, 21–3, 25, 26n, 49, 52, 53n, 57n, 65, 71, 72, 73n, 156, 227n, 265, 266, 268, 269, 271, 280, 291–2, 293, 294, 304, 325, 326, 327n, 337, 338, 339, 340, 341, 342, 344n, 347, 348, 351, 359, 360, 361, 373, 376, 383, 384; *see also* ballot-box; suffrage; vote
Ely, Richard, 134
emancipation, 52n, 130, 148, 263, 266
emigration, 269n, 270, 278, 282
Empire(s), 5, 31, 57, 75, 78, 83–4, 102–4, 154, 162, 215, 223, 235, 267, 273, 310, 386
  British Empire, 215, 267, 273
  Byzantine Empire, 78, 103–4
  Ottoman Empire, 5, 31, 35–7, 154
  Roman Empire, 75, 83–5, 95, 101–4, 223, 235–6, 310–11; *see also* Italy
  see also imperialism
employer(s), 106, 120, 121, 125, 126, 139, 148, 155, 174, 179, 182, 188, 190, 194, 195, 199, 206, 222, 230, 234, 235, 238n, 271, 281, 290, 297, 349–50, 352, 377, 381–2
employment, 41, 106, 116, 120, 125–6, 129, 134, 138n, 141, 147, 160, 176, 180, 188–90, 194–5, 199, 203, 212, 223, 235, 238, 269n, 282, 285, 327n, 340, 347, 349, 353, 357, 382
Engels, Friedrich, 235, 244, 289, 294n
England, 9, 13, 14, 18, 20, 22, 24, 26n, 32, 34–7n, 46, 50, 51, 54, 55, 64, 67, 68, 70–3, 75, 80, 85, 96, 101, 102, 105, 106, 108, 111, 115, 116, 124–6, 134, 139, 155, 156, 162, 164, 174–6, 184n, 188, 195, 197, 212–16, 225, 234, 244, 267, 270–4, 303, 308, 310, 311, 315, 338, 341, 342, 344, 350, 363, 364, 370, 373, 376, 377, 377, 383, 384; *see also* Great Britain
enjoyment, 13, 184, 198, 201, 219, 252, 278, 281, 301, 303, 317, 319, 320, 321, 328, 343, 352, 369
enlightenment, 60, 61, 69–70, 211, 224
environment, 3, 224, 261, 309, 317, 341, 343, 369; *see also* surroundings
equality, 1, 4, 5, 6, 8, 10–14, 15, 16–17, 18, 22, 23–5, 42–3, 47, 75–7n, 82–4, 86–8, 95, 101, 106, 107, 116, 120, 128, 149, 150, 159, 169, 177, 181, 183, 184, 187, 190, 192–4, 209, 221, 222, 223, 225, 228–9, 232, 234–9, 241, 243, 244, 251, 256, 258–60, 266, 267, 272, 279, 283, 286–7, 289, 290, 291, 293, 294–301, 303–5, 315, 317, 318, 324–30, 332–4, 337, 341, 343, 346, 353, 356, 357, 362, 365, 375, 376, 380, 382, 384, 386
  radical equality, 5, 10, 24, 42–3, 243, 267, 386

equality (of condition), 12–13, 22, 84, 239, 244, 258, 259, 297, 324, 328, 376, 384
equal rights, 97, 121, 130, 131; *see also* rights
equals, 12, 13, 22, 129, 215, 223, 224, 233, 236, 239, 256, 289, 295, 375, 376, 380, 384
establishment, 135, 159, 283, 377
ethics, 12, 26n, 104, 179–80, 184, 185n, 204, 206, 208, 247, 260, 301n, 302, 315, 316, 320n, 324, 328
Europe, European, 5, 9, 10, 14, 15, 37, 38, 67, 76, 78, 80–3, 85, 102, 103, 106, 107, 115, 138n, 153, 165, 175, 176, 199, 206, 210, 212n, 223, 235, 264, 267, 268, 269, 290, 299, 360, 383; *see also* continent
Evans, Richardson, 367
evil, 11, 14, 35, 42, 47, 60–1, 68, 75, 79, 84, 86, 120, 123, 127, 129–30, 133, 135, 138, 181, 187, 192, 194, 199, 204, 207, 208, 211, 226, 240, 245, 247, 282, 286, 300, 320, 369
executive, 16, 57, 63, 216, 292, 304, 325, 331, 345; *see also* government; parliament
exploitation, 8, 9, 14, 51, 60n, 99, 102, 163, 169, 175, 176, 180, 181, 205, 272, 279, 290, 296, 340, 341, 350, 381

fables, 176, 268
factionalism, 19, 20, 25, 203–5, 265, 280, 291, 323, 327, 339, 341, 343–4, 356
famine, 80, 219, 246, 252, 279, 286; *see also* hunger; starvation
farmers, 140, 271, 278, 368, 369
federation, 19, 101, 247, 256–7, 261, 293, 295, 326, 332; *see also* decentralization; region
fellow-men, 35, 58, 72, 100, 117, 121–3 125, 134, 138, 141, 143, 150, 155, 174, 182, 183, 186, 188, 191, 192, 198, 212, 214, 222, 311, 342, 378
fellowship, 10, 11, 12, 18, 23, 181, 192, 221, 224, 225, 239, 289; 293, 295, 375; *see also* association of equals
feudalism, 23, 92, 96–7, 103, 104, 105, 107, 109, 115, 156, 180, 188, 194, 214, 221, 228, 236, 279, 283, 289, 296, 297, 311, 377, 383,
fields, 8, 9, 121, 162, 177, 183, 199, 252, 310, 369, 370; *see also* countryside
force of intelligence / of principles / of reason, 18, 362, 365
Fourier, Charles, 155, 204, 268, 273, 316, 318
France, 31, 54, 57–9, 126, 134, 139, 212, 256, 265, 271, 316
France, Anatole, 180, 343
franchise, 115, 138, 267, 273, 290, 300, 355, 357
free contract, 188, 205, 214, 215–16, 290, 297, 298, 345
freedom, 11, 13, 23, 32, 37, 38, 56, 57, 75–6, 79, 88, 95, 101, 104, 106, 107, 107, 115, 130, 140, 151, 161, 184, 188, 194, 201, 214, 215–16, 217, 228, 233, 236, 237n, 247, 252, 260, 273, 290, 300, 307, 309, 333, 343, 356, 357, 376, 386, 388; *see also* autonomy; liberty
Freedom Group, 376; *see also* political parties
free men, 12, 15, 52, 73, 124, 223, 232, 235, 254, 259, 291, 295–6, 304, 208, 310–11, 352
Frere, Sir Henry Bartle Edward, 65
Froude, James Anthony, 109
future, 13, 26n, 33, 35, 42–3, 45, 76, 77, 79, 86, 123, 127, 150, 153, 182, 185n, 187, 219, 245, 249, 251, 252, 268, 279, 285, 286, 294, 316, 320, 341, 357, 380

gambling, 60, 73, 83, 108, 116, 147, 180, 181, 190, 192, 339
Garden City movement, 308
Garibaldi, Giuseppe, 57
Gascoyne-Cecil, Robert/ Lord Salisbury, 26, 64
Germany, 31, 83, 105, 115, 126, 134, 139, 212, 235n, 256, 265, 269n
Gibbon, Edward, 75, 83–4, 95
Giffen, Robert, 145, 150

Gladstone, William Ewart, 5, 6, 31, 36, 37n, 49, 56n, 65
Glasgow, 94
God, 17, 54, 87, 95, 101, 124, 139n, 163, 165, 176, 200, 211, 221, 229, 252; *see also* religion
God of War, 17, 340, 348
government, 14, 23, 49, 52, 53n, 57, 65, 67–72, 92, 105, 145n, 197, 211, 215, 218, 221, 228, 229–30, 244, 247, 248n, 256, 269n, 291, 293, 296, 328n, 332, 333, 337, 346n, 348, 362, 375, 379, 381, 387; *see also* executive; parliament
Great Britain, 1, 4–10, 18–20, 22, 24–6, 31, 49–51, 53n, 54, 56n, 64–5n, 67–8n, 70n, 71n, 75, 96, 116, 145n, 154, 160, 162, 185n, 203, 205, 218, 227n, 238n, 263, 265, 267–9, 271n, 273, 279, 290–1, 294, 302n, 310, 341–2, 344n, 356, 360, 362n, 373, 375, 377, 381, 383, 384, 386n; *see also* England
great change, 11, 16–17, 43, 84, 108, 111, 115, 130, 209–10, 228, 244, 246, 247, 294, 297, 307, 317, 320, 325–6, 331, 333, 340, 341, 345, 348, 380, 382; *see also* new birth
Great Charter, 154
Great Exhibition of 1851, London, 378
Great Western Railway, 369, 370
Greeks, 56, 78, 95, 100–3, 162, 166, 174, 235, 236, 296n, 297
Grenfell, J. G., 337
guilds, 105–6, 109, 257, 269, 290, 296, 297, 298, 308, 311, 377n
  craft-guilds, 105–6, 109, 257
  merchant-guilds, 105–6

handicraft, 24, 104, 105, 301, 310, 377; *see also* manufacture
handicraftsman, 42, 47, 83; *see also* artist; craftsman; workman
hanger(s)-on, 124, 125, 134, 140, 141, 142
happiness, 10–13, 26, 32, 44, 47, 52, 57, 60–2, 66, 67, 68, 72, 73, 98, 101, 114, 124, 127, 130, 134, 136, 138, 141, 142, 145, 150–1, 166, 176, 180, 181, 185n, 187–8, 192, 193, 196, 197, 212, 224–5, 228, 234, 239–40, 246, 249, 252–3, 258, 260, 268, 274, 281, 293, 300, 303, 307, 319, 332, 337, 343, 350, 352, 355, 357, 386, 388; *see also* enjoyment; joy
Hardie, Keir, 280, 294n, 327n, 344n, 359
Harrison, Frederic, 158, 162, 164n, 165n, 170, 205, 206n, 210, 212, 214–15
Hegelian, 76, 237n
Helots, 216, 296; *see also* Sparta
Henderson, Fred, 202, 268
Henry VII, 108
Henry VIII, 109
heritage, 9, 146, 273, 279, 282, 285, 301, 309, 312, 357
hideousness, 44, 82, 102, 107, 108, 123, 219, 235, 270, 370, 379
hierarchy, 11, 12, 23, 38, 95, 104, 105, 124, 134, 165, 183, 188, 210, 225, 228, 229, 236, 250n, 265m, 296, 298
Highland clearances, 160
history as a progress(ion), 76, 266, 324
Hobbes, Thomas, 1
Homer, 320
Home Rule, 9, 26n, 49, 64n, 266, 302n; *see also* Irish question
honesty, 53, 76, 91, 93, 108, 200, 201, 227, 233, 241, 248, 250, 273, 377, 379
House of Commons, 17, 64, 210n, 222, 230, 349, 351; *see also* parliament
House of Lords, 139, 222, 230; *see also* parliament
Howard, Ebenezer, 308
Howard, George, 367
humanity, 23, 51, 60, 63, 75, 153, 162, 165, 171, 174, 181, 185n, 192, 204, 206n
human race, 58, 77, 97, 114, 160, 170, 186, 251; *see also* mankind
hunger, 6, 71, 102, 145, 180, 214, 279, 284–5, 385–8; *see also* famine; starvation
Hunt, Holman, 367, 379
Huxley, Thomas Henry, 320

Hyndman, Henry Mayers, 9, 19, 26n, 95, 132, 133, 184, 227n, 228n, 316, 318, 319n, 338, 361, 362, 364, 386n
hypocrisy, 10, 23, 24, 26n, 34, 37, 63, 150, 165, 215, 219, 272, 290, 300, 373, 377

Icelandic sagas, 75, 223
idealism, 25, 269, 272, 273
idealized despair, 324, 326, 334
ideals, 11, 21, 22, 25, 41, 52, 73n, 129, 150, 172–3, 177, 181–2, 184, 205, 212, 215–17, 221, 224, 225, 228, 237, 239, 244, 248, 256, 258–9, 260, 261, 265, 267, 268, 272, 274, 290, 300, 307–8, 313, 316–19, 321, 341–2, 337, 344, 352; *see also* visions
imagination, 7, 33, 50, 55, 59, 60, 121, 172, 248, 311, 357, 374, 378
imperialism, 5, 10, 14, 18, 26n, 33, 49, 159, 162, 163, 176, 265, 267, 342, 360, 386; *see also* Empire
imperial wars, 6, 9, 24, 51, 75, 160, 161
independence, 31, 56n, 96, 102, 144, 168, 224, 239, 266–7, 273, 340
Independent Labour Party (ILP), 19, 21, 280, 294n, 325, 327n, 338, 341, 342, 344, 359, 376; *see also* political parties
India, 65, 70, 154, 212n, 227n, 231, 302n
Indian Rebellion, 154
individualism, 102, 302, 302, 384
individuality of character, 95, 101
industrialism, 75, 170–1, 175, 180, 189, 193, 198, 265, 267, 317
industries, 111, 115, 126, 173, 195, 238n, 270, 271, 308, 311, 346, 375, 381, 384
industry, 35, 38, 56, 64, 104, 141, 143, 168–71, 191, 212, 234, 278, 280, 282, 289, 316, 349
inequality, 6, 8, 10, 12, 14, 16, 41–2, 74–87, 159, 177, 184, 187, 190, 222, 225, 229, 230, 232, 234–7, 239, 241, 245, 278, 279, 283, 286, 289, 290, 294–5, 297–9, 300, 301, 303, 324, 326, 329–30, 333–4, 337, 386
inequities, 181, 268, 278, 309, 373
injustice, 45, 53, 55, 56, 58, 70, 71, 83, 88, 92, 97, 101, 116, 122, 129, 135, 148, 177, 184, 190, 201, 250, 267, 273, 278, 283
instruction, 45, 47, 62, 71n, 121, 156, 206, 211, 213, 216, 217, 253; *see also* cultivation; education; learning
intellect, 23, 37, 81, 82, 142, 145, 228, 254, 299, 300
Internationalism, 10, 22, 225, 247, 265, 386
Ireland, 6, 26n, 49, 70, 203, 205, 215, 218, 240n, 256, 267, 305n
Irish, 215, 222, 230, 240
Irish question, 69, 266, 271; *see also* Home Rule
Italy, 80, 87, 101, 102; *see also* Rome; Roman empire

Jingoism, 7, 8, 53, 55, 175, 267, 273
journeymen, 105–7; *see also* workers
joy, 12, 50, 54, 76, 88, 187, 188, 224, 232, 239, 267, 315, 318, 386; *see also* enjoyment; happiness
Joynes, James Leigh, 268
Judaism, 26n, 34n, 290
Justice (newspaper), 1–3, 13, 20, 25n, 26n, 155, 227n, 268n, 274n, 315n, 316, 319n, 337, 355, 356, 359–60, 385
justice, 7, 36, 38, 39, 42, 44, 51, 52, 55, 56, 61, 63, 72, 109, 145, 148, 183, 187, 225, 290, 298
Justinian, Emperor, 78

Kant, Immanuel, 184
Keats, John, 60
Kelmscott House, Hammersmith, 49, 73, 159, 178, 185n, 226n, 289, 327, 337
Kelmscott Manor, 306, 308, 369
Kipling, Rudyard, 367
Kitz, Frank, 263, 272n
knowledge, 8, 45, 70, 75–6, 77, 79, 80, 84, 88, 100, 103, 128, 139, 141, 150, 160, 170, 213, 253–4, 286, 380
Kropotkin, Peter, 237n, 322

labour, 10, 13, 42, 47, 66, 67, 83, 84, 86, 92, 95, 97–9, 100, 102–17, 121, 125–8, 130–1, 133, 135, 139, 144–8, 150, 153, 156–7, 165–8, 171, 173, 179, 180–1, 183, 186–95, 198–200, 206, 212, 218, 219, 222, 229–30, 232–3, 234–5, 237, 241, 246–7, 252, 255, 258, 260–1, 263, 267, 268, 269n, 273, 277–9, 280–7, 289–92, 296–7, 299, 301, 303–4, 310, 313, 316, 320, 325, 327n, 329, 341, 343, 347, 350–1, 352, 355, 357, 362, 363, 376–7, 381–2, 384, 386, 387
labourers, 8, 20, 96, 102, 105, 106, 109, 114, 120, 126, 134, 137, 140, 147, 148, 164n, 189, 192, 194, 224, 236–7, 266, 271, 278, 284, 290, 297, 298, 302
labour-market, 125, 191
labour movement, 5, 22, 280, 326, 341, 348–9, 350, 360, 376, 384
labour system, 99, 111, 307–8
Lafargue, Paul, 265
laissez-faire, 26n, 115, 185n, 205, 218, 290, 3302n, 339, 347, 352, 279
landlords, 108, 215
landscape, 119, 121, 268, 309, 368; *see also* countryside; scenery
Lankester, Edwin Ray, 261
Lansbury, George, 20
Latimer, Hugh, 96, 108
law, 71n, 101, 104, 106, 109, 121, 164, 173, 180, 187, 194, 213, 237, 295, 297, 339
law of nature (and life), 73, 76, 79, 101, 115, 381; *see also* natural law
learning, 96, 110, 145, 180, 224, 236, 246, 253, 277, 330, 345; *see also* cultivation; education; instruction
Leeds, 34n, 83, 94, 95, 133, 203
legislation, 97, 108, 206n, 338, 346
leisure, 7, 11, 52, 58, 72, 88, 97, 112–14, 123, 127, 129, 138, 140, 149, 159, 161, 164, 165, 166, 167–8, 169, 199, 200, 222, 232, 240, 246, 257, 259–60, 280, 282, 286, 307, 325, 331, 343, 350, 382
Leviathan, 160
Liberal Party, 4, 5, 6, 7, 31, 33, 37, 49, 56n, 73n, 182, 203, 205, 216, 277, 280, 291, 327, 339, 347, 363, 384; *see also* reactionists; Whig party; political parties
liberalism, 270, 383
liberals, 35, 36, 38, 52, 55, 143, 144, 149, 162, 185, 196, 205, 219, 227, 266, 267, 273n, 302, 340, 343, 346–8, 352, 376, 377, 381, 383; *see also* Liberal Party
  commercial liberals, 8, 14, 163, 175–6
libertarian, 153, 316,
liberty, 50, 75, 84, 162, 166, 174, 218, 327; *see also* autonomy; freedom
Liebknecht, Wilhelm, 265
Linnell, Alfred, 220, 224, 240
literature, 95, 98, 161, 167, 182, 193, 204, 208, 235, 251–3, 255, 266, 268, 274, 324, 331, 373–5, 378–80; *see also* poetry
livelihood, 17, 101, 106, 108, 120, 123, 125, 129, 137, 149, 169, 171, 174, 180, 189–90, 191, 193–4, 198, 200, 230, 232, 251, 257, 259–60, 261, 271, 284, 296, 299, 303, 305, 321, 325, 330–1, 352, 361, 365; *see also* standard of life
Local Government Act (1888), 266
London, 11, 15, 20, 31–2, 34n, 42, 44, 50, 51, 58, 59, 68, 74, 76, 83, 87, 88, 96, 112, 113, 119–21, 123, 136n, 137, 140n, 154–5, 159, 177, 178, 179, 203, 225n, 226, 227n, 238, 240, 243, 257, 270, 271, 272n, 308, 311, 338, 346, 355, 359, 362, 368–9
London County Council, 355, 368–9
London Vestry and Board of Guardians, 20, 338
lords, 104, 105, 124–5, 170, 219, 222, 279, 296, 311
Lowalter, Eliza Jane, 367
Lushington, Vernon, 206n, 302n
luxury, 45, 82, 87, 100, 102, 122, 129, 134, 145, 147, 187, 188, 192, 194, 222–3, 230, 231, 234–6, 260, 281, 284, 286, 313, 339

McGahan, Januarius Aloysius, 31, 36n
machine industries, 111, 115, 126
machinery, 67, 95, 100, 111, 138, 153, 167, 168, 170, 182, 183, 195, 200, 230, 261, 270, 272, 283, 286, 304, 340, 346, 348, 364, 375, 379, 381, 388
machines, 110, 112, 113, 135, 138, 148, 163, 168, 174, 176–7, 187, 189, 194, 199, 206, 211, 213, 219, 248, 255, 284, 291–2, 303, 304, 325, 331, 343, 348, 352, 365, 381; *see also* citizens not machines
MacMahon, Marechal Patrice, 57, 58
Madise, Daniel, 378
Maguire, Tom, 268
Mahdists, 154–62
Malleson, Elizabeth, 74
Malleck, William Hurrell, 301
Malthusianism, 201, 270
management, 181, 233, 234, 250n, 291, 304, 308, 315, 318, 332, 375, 379, 381
managers, 180, 191, 381
Manchester School, 175, 183, 185n, 200, 339, 347, 352; *see also* commercial liberals
Manchester, 9, 20, 74, 83, 175, 183, 185n, 199, 200, 277, 307, 339, 347, 349, 352
mankind, 42, 47, 60, 61, 80, 101, 159, 161, 164, 176, 182, 193, 194, 204, 207, 251, 263, 283, 320, 328; *see also* human race; humanity
Mann, Tom, 272
manufacture, 97, 111, 112, 146, 175, 223, 257, 258, 271, 308, 310, 311, 342; *see also* handicraft
manufacturer(s), 82, 116, 161, 167, 168, 175, 200, 213, 349
manufacturing districts, 112, 246, 257–8
Mapledurham, Oxfordshire, 368, 370
market(s), 6, 16, 96, 99, 106, 108, 109, 111, 125, 138, 146, 147, 159, 161, 162, 164n, 166, 173, 175, 176, 188–9, 191, 195, 205, 215, 217, 222, 233–5, 255–6, 273, 295, 305, 311, 332, 339, 340, 342, 349–50, 357, 374, 379, 387
marketing, 254
Marx, Eleanor Aveling, 235, 287
Marx, Karl, 6, 8n, 26n, 134, 146n, 162, 163, 168, 179, 184–5, 213, 261n, 316, 318, 320n
Marxist, 95, 154, 181, 237n, 244, 264, 267, 279, 316, 385
master(s), 11, 13, 17, 104–7, 110, 113, 114, 116, 128, 135, 139, 141, 142, 146, 148, 149, 151, 156–7, 165, 168, 170, 171, 174, 180, 181, 182, 188–90, 192, 194–6, 199, 200, 201, 211, 213, 217, 219, 238, 240, 250n, 255, 265, 273, 290, 296–9, 303–4, 310n, 313, 318, 325–6, 328, 331, 339, 349, 365
mastery, 9, 11, 80, 150, 175, 206, 228, 317, 320, 333
material, 82, 103, 106, 107, 109, 111, 114, 128, 170, 171, 258, 271, 290, 312, 387
  material advancement, 123, 380
  material advantage, 227, 236
  material gain, 129
  material nature, 23, 150, 299, 300
  material needs, 232
  material poverty, 75, 82, 340, 347, 348
  material progress, 12, 260
  material prosperity, 75, 155, 347
  material reward(s), 243, 332
  material riches, 75, 82
materialism, 232
May Day, May 1st, 385–6
mechanical, 62, 85–6, 97, 116, 173, 214, 232, 256, 300, 317, 319–20
medieval, 23, 96, 166, 180, 188, 206, 213n, 236, 290, 300, 308, 311, 374, 377, 380, 384
merchant, 60n, 247, 272n, 297
Middle East, 49
middle-ages, 106, 114, 140, 296
middlemen, 106, 110, 179
militarism, 18, 50, 52
Mill, John Stuart, 316, 318, 319
Millais, John Everett, 367, 379
minority, 16, 38, 292, 304, 325, 326, 333, 342

misery, 13, 15, 18, 25, 44, 60, 81, 91, 96, 103, 109, 111, 121, 122, 127, 130, 133–49, 151, 159, 161, 163, 169, 179, 182, 187, 192–3, 196, 207, 225, 231, 236, 240–1, 264, 266, 270, 298, 300, 317, 320, 338, 342, 345, 357, 362, 365, 374, 378
Mitchell, Julian, 181
modern, 42, 74, 76, 78, 81, 84–5, 87, 88, 93, 95, 99, 100, 102, 106, 123–4, 145, 165, 166, 174, 184, 188, 200, 201, 204, 208, 217–18, 232, 245, 251, 256–7, 268, 272, 274, 280–1, 283–4, 296, 298–9, 310, 311, 312, 319, 321, 324, 377, 379
modernization, 368
money, 8, 53n, 56, 60, 93, 112–13, 123, 138, 147, 161, 162, 165, 166, 168–9, 177, 188, 191, 213, 278, 282, 296, 332, 342, 363, 364, 368–70; *see also* prosperity; wealth
monopolist(s), 25, 102, 169, 174, 176, 239, 245, 249, 257, 358–9, 279, 299; *see also* profit-grinder(s)
monopoly, 23, 96, 111, 116, 135, 148, 168, 192, 203, 211, 247, 248, 257–8, 260, 279, 382–4, 286–7, 290, 293, 300, 305
  monopoly of trade, 111, 116
monument(s), 380; *see also* architecture; building
moral force, 362; *see also* principles
morality, 43, 62, 70, 74, 96, 101, 142, 145, 160, 166, 170, 173, 179, 185n, 187–8, 192, 207, 211–12, 223, 235, 237, 239, 241, 278, 281, 316, 344n
Moralization of Capital, 164
Mordhurst, C. Henry, 353
More, Sir Thomas, 96, 108
Morgarten, Switzerland, 162, 163n, 174
Morris, Jane, 27, 31, 32
Morris, Jenny, 32
Mowbray, Charles, 272
municipal government, 105, 247, 248n
municipal socialism, 310
Munster Anabaptists, 300
murder, 31, 70, 75, 85, 222, 225, 231, 240, 241; *see also* revenge

Napoleon Bonaparte, 57
nation, 14, 24, 26n, 37, 49, 50, 53–5, 57, 60–3, 65–6, 69, 70, 76, 81, 96, 104, 111, 126, 171, 175–7, 258, 273, 310n, 341–2, 350, 357, 363–4, 369, 371, 373, 377
national, 71, 171, 174, 190, 247, 264, 265, 266
nationalism, British, 154, 360,
nationalism, 49, 380; *see also* chauvinism
National Vain-glory, 6, 50, 53–5, 62, 63, 67, 69
natural order, 23, 100, 146
nature, 8, 11, 23, 42, 43, 46, 54, 55, 77n, 80, 86–8, 92, 96, 98, 101, 105, 107, 123, 128, 141, 143, 144, 146, 147, 150, 165, 170–1, 172, 186, 187, 188, 193, 212, 228, 230, 232, 233, 237, 246, 250, 252, 255, 260, 286–7, 290, 295, 299, 300, 301, 308, 310, 312, 324, 331, 363, 369, 381
  natural law, 115, 381; *see also* law of nature
necessaries, 106, 168, 188, 230, 232, 259, 287, 295; *see also* desires; wants
necessities, 62, 100, 123, 127, 145n, 199, 217, 230–1, 257, 279, 281, 283, 286, 299, 313, 355, 357, 382; *see also* desires; wants
needs, 13, 22, 68, 153, 168, 173, 177, 180, 183, 197–8, 198–9, 211, 214, 222–3, 225, 229–32, 235, 243, 258–60, 286, 299, 309, 330, 332, 333, 340, 376, 384; *see also* desires; wants
neo-classicism, 96, 374
neo-Gothic, 375
New Islington Hall, Ancoats, 277
newspaper(s), 33, 50, 52, 59, 159, 161, 167, 175, 266; *see also* press
Nicholl, David, 292
Nottingham, Secular Hall, Beck Street, 225n

O'Connor, Thomas Power, 271
opposition, 5–6, 10, 16, 18, 38, 49, 50, 115, 138, 162, 163n, 165n, 177, 185n, 187, 191, 196–7, 203, 256,

264, 270, 271, 273n, 291, 297, 302n, 311, 317, 321, 333, 360, 363, 382, 384
oppression, 10, 18, 37, 42, 44, 76, 80, 83, 86, 88, 96, 99, 111, 113, 115, 122, 124, 133, 134, 137, 141, 142, 154, 156–7, 163, 180, 192, 214, 247, 258, 266, 281–4, 293, 311, 319, 333, 341, 360, 378
organization, 8, 15, 16, 19, 20, 21, 22, 24, 78, 92, 95, 105, 107, 110, 135, 163, 164n, 168, 172–3, 182, 188–9, 194, 196, 19, 201, 217, 228–30, 232, 235, 239, 255, 264–6, 268, 271n, 272, 279, 283–4, 289, 291, 292, 293, 294n, 299, 300, 303–5, 310–11, 315–17, 320, 327n, 341, 345–6, 350, 352, 363, 375–7, 381, 383–4, 385, 387; *see also* administration; bureaucracy
organized misery, 161, 317, 320, 342
overproduction, 176, 183, 199–200, 205, 224; *see also* production
Owen, Robert, 155, 162, 172, 185n, 204, 270
owners, 101, 104, 121, 165, 1889, 259, 281, 303
ownership, 16, 20, 138n, 146–7, 183, 188, 224, 248, 278–80, 283, 291, 309, 338, 343, 344n, 360, 381; *see also* proprietorship
Oxford, 86, 206, 311, 337
Oxfordshire, 369

palliative(s), 12, 14, 24, 81, 92, 119, 123, 181, 187, 192, 196, 226, 266, 273, 338, 340, 361
Paris, 25, 257, 263, 269n, 327n; *see also* Second International Socialist Workers Conference
Paris Commune, 14, 160, 206, 218n, 256n
parliament, 17, 20, 21, 34n, 37, 56n, 64, 65, 69n, 87, 154, 191, 196, 206, 209–10, 211, 216, 218–19, 266–7, 271–2, 273, 280, 294n, 325, 327, 338, 343, 346–8, 351, 364; *see also* government
parliamentarianism, 247
parliamentary, 203, 209
  candidates, 21, 291, 361
  election, 326
  reform, 266
  representation, 71
  system, 196, 211
party
  European socialist parties, 264, 269
  moderate Party, 217–18
  old parties, 182, 196, 218, 271, 300, 301, 346, 384
  one socialist party, 3, 5, 9, 18–19, 21, 25, 203, 280, 325, 344n, 356–8, 359–65, 373, 376; *see also* socialist unity
  political parties, 97, 116, 182, 196, 203, 207–8, 209, 216, 251, 273, 280, 315, 228, 338, 346, 356, 384; *see also* Conservative Party; Freedom Group; Independent Labour Party; Liberal Party; Tory Party; Whig Party
  progressive party, 22, 215, 219, 368; *see also* progressive(s)
  reactionary party, 205, 217, 218, 291, 300, 363, 384
  socialist party, 13, 14, 15, 18–22, 26n, 206, 228, 264, 265, 280, 292, 304, 333, 337, 342, 344n, 352, 376–7, 383, 384
party of Moderation, 205, 217; *see also* Whig Liberals
passion, 7, 45, 52, 62, 72, 319, 320; *see also* hope
patriotism, 50, 53, 55–6, 63, 162, 166, 174, 215, 236
patronage, 71, 82, 85, 270
pauper(s), 63, 186, 284, 310; *see also* poor people
peace, 6, 7, 22, 25, 39, 50, 52, 56, 58, 66, 72, 73, 76, 79, 97, 103, 116, 120, 124n, 126, 127, 150, 172, 182–3, 200, 219, 250, 327, 341, 349, 350, 351, 362, 385, 387
peaceful revolution, 5, 14–18, 20, 196, 291–3, 304, 375
Peace with Honour, 64n, 71

Pericles, 95, 100
periodical(s), 3, 16, 20, 22, 26n, 159, 161, 167, 206n, 268, 367
Persia, 80, 103, 154
pessimism, 188, 211, 251, 260, 320, 382
Plantagenet kings, 299
Plato, 43, 301
pleasure, 42, 44, 46–7, 64, 71, 76, 78, 84, 88, 101, 111, 112, 137, 140, 142, 149, 149, 161, 162, 164, 192, 198, 200, 219, 222, 224, 232, 246–7, 250–2, 253, 254, 259, 260, 261, 278, 279, 282, 283, 285, 286, 310, 317, 320, 321, 369, 382, 383
pleasure of life, 98–9, 107, 110, 114, 117, 127, 251–2, 279, 285, 326, 333
poetry, 43n, 75, 88, 95, 97, 98, 268, 374–5, 378, 379; *see also* literature
Poland, 56n
political, 7, 12, 21–3, 50–1, 72, 95, 101, 139, 154, 156, 176, 182, 193, 201, 203–6, 208–9, 211–12, 214, 216–9, 221–2, 227, 233, 234n, 235–6, 244, 256, 263–4, 268–71, 273, 286, 290–1, 300, 304, 309, 315, 318, 334, 339, 341, 343, 347, 352, 359, 361, 363–4, 373, 380, 383
politician(s), 1, 74, 85, 205, 211, 212, 267, 273n, 346, 382–3
politics, 12, 13, 50, 72, 139, 161, 165n, 167, 196, 201, 203–4, 207, 209, 211, 215, 225, 235, 247–8, 249, 264, 269, 271, 291–2, 301n, 315, 319, 338–9, 345, 349, 373, 374–5, 377, 379, 380, 381, 383
poor people, 10, 23, 45, 81, 82, 83, 97, 109, 112, 113, 117, 119, 123, 128, 135, 136, 137, 144, 5 148, 161, 162, 164–5, 167, 168, 169, 170, 176, 179, 186, 188, 191, 194, 201, 212–13, 214, 222, 224, 232, 234, 237n, 240, 259, 279, 283, 284, 285, 290, 297, 298, 300, 308, 311, 313, 317, 318, 319, 320, 332, 364, 386; *see also* pauper(s)
Positivists, 162, 164–6, 204, 205, 206n, 210, 228n, 301n, 302n
possession(s), 113, 114, 141, 146, 148, 164–6, 173, 180, 184, 188–9, 191, 197, 200, 254, 302, 303, 305, 332; *see also* classes: possessing classes; property; resources
possessors, 146, 329, 385
Pottier, Eugene, 224
poverty, 62, 75, 82, 108, 119, 135, 137, 144, 167–8, 169, 183, 187, 197, 198, 205, 206, 218, 223, 231, 235, 267, 270, 271n, 273n, 278, 281–3, 296, 298, 301, 324, 330, 361, 364, 380, 383, 386
power(s), 8, 9, 14, 15, 16, 20, 31, 35, 43, 50, 62–3, 67, 71, 92, 96, 105–6, 107, 109, 110, 111, 123, 125, 130, 135, 144, 146, 147–8, 154, 159, 161, 162, 166, 171, 173, 176–7, 183, 188–92, 194–5, 197, 201, 205–6, 213, 215–17, 225, 237n, 244–5, 252, 263, 265, 266, 267, 271, 272, 274, 283, 291–3, 296, 297, 299–301, 304, 317, 319, 320, 325, 326, 338, 344–5, 349, 356, 360, 363, 373, 375, 377, 382, 386
power of capital(ists), 161, 168, 206, 213, 217, 219, 388
practical arts, 307
practical movement, 204, 317, 320; *see also* socialism, practical
preaching, 18, 21, 116, 135, 138, 145, 147, 179, 192–3, 201, 226, 266, 268, 270, 323, 331, 339, 344–5, 352, 380
press, 56n, 68, 161, 176, 271; *see also* newspaper(s)
principle(s), 13–14, 15, 18, 21, 22, 33, 51, 63, 65, 67, 68, 73, 86, 88, 98, 110–11, 115, 139, 153, 154, 156, 179, 186, 188, 216, 247, 256, 280, 304, 315–16, 323, 325, 338, 355, 357, 362, 365, 375, 376, 379, 380, 384; *see also* moral force
printing-press, 73
privilege(s), 13, 16, 42, 106, 109, 115, 146–7, 148, 191, 195, 197–8, 206, 214, 218, 222, 237–9, 241, 278, 279, 283–6, 287, 290, 299, 326,

329, 331, 332, 333, 352, 356, 357, 363, 376, 381–3, 384, 387; *see also* classes: privileged classes
producer(s), 183–4, 200, 213, 279, 281, 284–6, 304, 330, 378, 381
production, 9, 16, 17, 24, 44, 67, 82, 85, 87, 98, 103, 108, 102–4, 107–8, 110, 111, 117, 123, 147, 159, 164–8, 170–1, 173, 176, 177n, 180, 183, 188–94, 196, 198–200, 205, 212, 213, 217, 223–4, 229–31, 233, 239, 245, 246–9, 252, 263, 267, 270, 272, 277, 281, 283–6, 295, 296n, 293, 295, 297, 299, 301, 303, 305, 316, 307, 320, 324, 327n, 329, 331–3, 340, 343, 344n, 346, 349, 350, 363–4, 374, 377, 378–81, 385–8; *see also* overproduction
profit(s), 6, 13, 24, 96, 97, 101, 104, 108, 110–13, 125–6, 129, 169, 174–6, 177, 180–1, 182, 190, 191, 195, 199, 200, 201, 237, 238, 247, 256–8, 272, 282, 287, 290, 304, 309, 316, 331, 342, 346, 349, 352, 368, 377, 381–2, 385–8
profit-grinders, 99, 111–13, 116, 176, 212, 285; *see also* monopolists
profit-mongering, 109, 147
progress, 11, 12, 15, 24, 50, 61, 65, 69, 76, 78, 81, 84, 95–7, 101, 114, 115, 129, 131, 140, 142–4, 150, 154, 155, 156, 165, 171, 177, 192–4, 196, 204, 211, 213, 217, 221, 228, 236, 237n, 260, 267, 279, 285, 290, 317, 319, 321, 329, 344, 376, 383, 385
progressive(s), 20, 23, 44, 133, 153, 196, 213, 218, 261n, 328, 338, 360, 383; *see also* progressive party
proletariat, 106, 107, 205, 211, 245, 257–8, 270, 290, 301, 310, 387; *see also* class; wage-earning
propaganda, 91, 92, 93, 159, 161, 270, 318, 323, 327n, 339, 345, 347
propagandist(s), 21, 342, 343, 351–2
property, 15, 16, 18, 20, 23, 108, 121, 131, 146, 160, 164, 171, 180–1, 183–4, 191, 192, 197, 200, 205, 214–16, 251, 259, 261, 267, 272, 270, 289–305, 308, 311, 333, 374, 387; *see also* possession; resources
proprietorship, 270; *see also* ownership
prosperity, 65, 68, 75, 83, 96, 97, 111, 140, 145, 155–6, 173, 176, 185n, 187, 195, 213, 214–15, 267, 272, 284, 293, 309, 316, 329, 347, 350, 381, 385, 397; *see also* commonwealth; money; wealth
puffery, 161, 167

Queen Victoria, 33, 34n, 37n, 64n, 68n
Quelch, Harry, 319, 355

race, 9, 24, 26n, 44, 50, 54, 55, 56n, 58, 62, 77, 81, 97, 100, 175, 198, 211, 216, 329, 373, 377; *see also* humanity
  progress of the race, 165, 177, 192
  superior race, 9, 75, 81, 231
race for money, 123, 127, 139, 176
race to destruction, 123
racism, 8
radical democracy, 247, 256n
radical reformation, 85, 180, 244
radical socialism, 12, 271,
radical transformation, 14
radical(s), 10, 31, 33, 35, 74, 85, 129, 133, 153, 165, 179, 182, 196, 205, 206n, 212, 214, 216–17, 221, 222, 240n, 247, 270, 273n, 291, 300n, 301n, 302n, 327, 343, 347, 352, 368, 384
radicalism, 23, 69n, 214, 227–9, 318
Ragnarók or Twilight of the Gods, 163, 176
reactionaries, 256, 339, 345, 383
reactionary forces, 14, 384
reactionary governments, 14
reactionary party, 205, 291, 300, 363–4
reactionists, 6, 22, 35–8, 57, 74, 85, 139, 177, 196, 206, 216–19, 267, 271n, 272, 304, 376, 383, 384
reason, 6, 18, 22, 33, 35, 37, 45, 57, 61, 87, 104, 109, 121, 123, 128, 129, 149, 188, 198, 201, 206, 219, 233, 245, 249, 278, 281, 295, 311, 317, 321, 330, 361–2, 363, 365; *see also* force of intelligence

reason(s) for discontent, 137, 139–40, 142
rebellion, 5, 52n, 105, 139, 146, 154, 163, 165, 177, 188–9, 240, 319, 375, 379
reform(s), 6–7, 25, 33, 37, 49, 52, 56n, 66, 72, 73, 97, 119, 130, 205, 210n, 218–19, 244, 258, 261n, 264–6, 273n, 293, 309n, 325, 328n, 337, 356, 369
reformer(s), 76, 80, 119, 226, 269,
reformist(s), 10, 12, 162, 180, 201n, 203n, 326, 356
region, 138n, 247, 268, 280; *see also* decentralization; federation
religion, 9, 14, 23–4, 46, 71, 97, 116, 120, 128, 164, 170, 172, 175, 181–2, 185n, 187, 192, 193, 204, 208, 210, 236, 289, 290, 294, 298, 301, 320, 373–4, 377; *see also* God; worship
religion of city worship, 96, 102
religion of humanity, 23, 162, 165, 181, 185n, 206n
religion of socialism, 26n, 181, 184, 315
rent, 138n, 180, 190–1, 199, 212, 215, 311
representation of the People Act (Third Reform Act), 138n, 205, 294n
reproduction, 46, 95, 98, 125, 144, 237n, 255, 285
resistance, 13, 17, 37n, 38, 52, 55, 87, 102, 105, 115, 120, 130–1, 135, 146, 148, 157, 162, 163, 174, 175, 196, 201, 206, 214–15, 217, 219, 259, 261, 280, 290, 321, 339, 345, 360, 375, 381, 386
resistance, peaceful, 16, 341; *see also* peaceful revolution
resource(s), 19, 175, 215, 233, 257, 267, 280, 286–7, 291, 297, 338, 342, 368; *see also* possession; property
respect and self-respect, 52, 62, 72, 82, 86, 95, 173, 223, 234, 268, 280, 281, 291, 304, 343, 350, 364, 382
responsibility, 20, 37, 38, 61, 80–1, 86, 101, 141, 144, 176, 221, 222, 224, 229–30, 233, 239, 244, 255, 256, 258, 273, 278, 280, 281, 283–4, 287, 291, 304, 326, 332, 333, 343, 352, 383; *see also* duty
revenge, 36, 50, 51, 55–6, 61, 63, 68, 73, 76, 81, 225, 310; *see also* murder; vengeance
reverence for the life of man, 119, 121–2, 123, 128
revolt(s), 15, 20, 37, 100, 106, 122, 188, 213n, 217, 266, 292, 304, 381
revolution, 15, 16, 20–1, 24–5, 26n, 60n, 76, 95, 99, 100, 102, 104, 111, 115, 130, 140, 142, 150, 153, 182–3, 193, 195–7, 200, 204–6, 208–9, 217, 218, 219, 221, 223, 225, 226, 247, 292, 304, 321, 325, 339, 360, 361, 364, 373, 377, 383
  French Revolution, 24, 84, 115, 153, 297, 377, 380, 383–4
  nonviolent or peaceful, 18, 22, 275, 293; *see also* peaceful resistance
  social revolution, 14, 17, 121, 129, 131, 155, 208, 244, 251, 256, 257, 269, 291, 315, 320, 325
  violent revolution, 292, 325, 362, 375; *see also* cataclysmic Communism
Ricardo, David, 318
rich(es), 23, 45, 47, 62, 69, 75, 80–3, 86n, 96, 97, 110, 112–13, 117, 120, 122, 123–5, 127–30, 134, 136, 138, 141–5, 147–8, 160, 164–5, 167, 170, 176, 181, 186, 188, 190–2, 194, 199, 205, 213, 214, 215, 217, 218, 222–4, 231–2, 235, 237, 260, 278, 279, 281, 283–7, 290, 296–300, 311–13, 317–18, 320, 349, 364, 379, 386; *see also* prosperity; wealth
right(s), 6, 51, 55–7, 61–2, 70, 73, 97, 101, 104, 121, 131, 136, 160, 182, 187–9, 198, 218, 222, 229, 266, 272, 283, 290, 293, 294n, 340, 348, 360, 370, 376, 381; *see also* equal rights
robbery, 32, 99, 108, 164, 214, 222, 230, 232, 240, 295, 304, 385, 386,
Rogers, James Edwin Thorold, 134, 213
Romantic school, 378–9

Rome, 78, 84, 101, 103, 165, 194, 235–6, 298; *see also* Italy
Rome, fall of Rome, 15, 75, 223, 235
Rooke, Thomas, 3
Rossetti, Dante Gabriel, 374, 379
Rowland, Harriet, 119
Rowley, Charles, 277
ruler(s), 66–7, 69, 82, 83, 104, 140, 148, 156, 206, 219, 233, 237, 290, 295, 299, 304, 337
Ruskin, John, 74, 75, 86, 95, 98, 223, 250, 267, 269n, 277, 279, 316, 319
Ruskinian, 95, 223, 267

scenery, 368–71; *see also* countryside; landscape
Scheu, Andreas, 158, 268, 316, 318
science, 8, 43, 160, 170, 179, 204, 208, 235, 252, 267, 324, 385, 387
Scotland, 71n, 112n, 133, 145n, 177n, 263, 303Scott, Walter, 215, 237n
serf(s), 100, 104–6, 109, 115, 124, 165–6, 193–4, 289, 296–7, 324, 329; *see also* slave(s)
servitude, 133, 144, 350
Shaw, George Bernard, 202, 242, 244, 251, 252, 274, 338
shopkeeper(s), 140, 255
sickness, 35, 46, 76, 80, 95, 99, 142, 183, 189, 198, 232, 238, 251–2, 286, 318, 378; *see also* disease
Sketchley, John, 153–6
skill(s), 83, 100, 120, 126–7, 134, 137–9, 146, 168, 188–9, 212–13, 237n, 246, 253, 265, 279, 283, 284, 285, 287, 301, 316
slave(s), 8, 12, 15, 50, 55, 63, 73, 95, 100–2, 104, 112, 121, 124, 129–30, 135, 141, 142, 146, 148–9, 151, 156–7, 159, 160–1, 163–6, 176–7, 182, 188, 189, 194, 206, 208–9, 217, 219, 222, 223, 233–4, 235–6, 237, 240–1, 254, 257, 259, 271, 272, 273, 281, 282, 285, 289, 291, 295–8, 303–4, 364; *see also* serfs
slaveholder(s), 124, 159, 222, 230, 233–4
slavery, 8, 12, 52n, 75, 81, 82, 87, 95, 97, 99, 100–3, 104, 121, 123, 124, 131, 135, 140, 148, 150, 156, 160, 170–1, 180, 182, 193, 213, 218, 222, 227n, 229, 236, 238, 246, 254, 258–9, 261, 291, 293, 297, 300–1, 310, 313, 324, 328, 339, 365, 374, 379
Smith, Adam, 164n, 318
Smith, Frank, 294
social democracy, 321, 293
social order, 43, 160, 179, 222–3, 343
social relations, 17, 97, 298
social revolution, 14, 121, 129, 131, 155, 315, 320, 325
social transformation, 25, 263, 269, 294
socialism
  American socialism, 272
  democratic socialism, 204
  egalitarian socialism, 7, 94
  electoral socialism, 293, 361
  English socialism, 26n, 243, 263–74
  European socialism, 264, 268–70, 316
  Fourierist socialism, 155, 204, 316, 318
  militant socialism, 257
  Owenite socialism, 155, 204, 270
  practical socialism, 204, 208, 244, 251, 318–21, 351; *see also* practical movement
  Scientific socialism, 154–6, 360
  Utopian Socialism, 328
socialist(s)
  "Little-England" socialist, 225
  Christian socialists, 374, 377
  electoral socialists, 293, 361
  gradualist socialists, 243
  making of socialists, 25
  revolutionary socialists, 208–10
socialist ideal(s), 25, 52, 301, 341
socialist principles, 21, 153, 375
socialist propaganda, 91–3
Socialist Radicals, 271
socialist society, 11, 13, 21–3, 309, 348, 382
socialist unity, 5, 9, 13, 18, 337; *see also* one socialist party
socialist(ic) movement, 5, 20, 25, 248, 266, 268, 269, 274, 347, 356, 360, 363, 364, 377
socialize, 263, 351, 368

society
basis of society, 15–16, 99, 114, 161, 164, 182, 196, 226, 263, 270, 283, 292, 296, 333
capitalist society, 166, 330, 338
commercial society, 42, 224
communal society, 9, 278, 280, 324, 330–1, 333
communist society, 294, 324
contemporary society, 4, 8, 42, 320n
egalitarian society, 184, 243
just society, 50, 52
medieval society, 213n, 377
new birth of society, 104, 182, 184, 196, 247, 380
tribal society, 289, 380
solidarity, 9, 52, 157, 180–2, 184, 224–5
Sparta or Lacedaemon, 296
Spencer, Herbert, 237, 302
standard of life, 116, 125–6, 138, 148, 151, 174, 191, 213, 230, 259, 284, 305, 350; *see also* livelihood
standard of worth, 295, 299, 328, 332
starvation, 8, 32, 67, 96, 101–2, 104, 109, 139, 159, 161–2, 164, 177, 184, 198, 200, 231, 257, 259, 273–4, 368, 370; *see also* famine; hunger
Stephens, James Fitz James, 212
Strongbow/ de Clare, Richard FitzGilbert, 6, 70
struggle(s), 45–6, 56, 58, 63, 78, 79, 97, 104–7, 109, 115, 116, 120–1, 123, 126, 130, 139, 142, 150, 170–1, 183, 188, 190, 192, 195, 197, 206, 213, 218, 232, 237, 239, 247, 257, 261, 270, 281, 284, 296, 297, 320, 326, 332–3, 376, 379, 381–2
stupidity, 9, 38, 51–3, 59, 60, 62, 68–9, 71, 72, 129, 146, 148, 167, 169, 199, 256, 264, 281, 312, 338, 345, 378
subsistence, 144, 180, 188–90, 194, 198, 290, 296n
suffering, 8, 14, 15, 17–18, 23, 25, 53, 101, 111, 116, 126, 136, 242, 144, 163, 165–6, 175, 177, 196, 199, 218, 223, 228, 231, 235, 249, 281, 298, 308–9, 312, 318–19, 328, 340–1, 348–9, 362, 365, 369, 374, 375, 380, 381, 386
suffrage, 101, 154, 156, 205, 280, 291, 294, 302n, 361; *see also* ballot-box; election; vote
surplus produce of labour, 297
surplus profit, 290
surplus value, 179, 185n, 199, 200, 279
surplus wealth, 9, 199, 299
surroundings, 110, 112–13, 120, 121, 128–9, 135, 145, 169, 180, 234, 240, 246, 260, 282, 297, 307, 312, 328, 343, 350, 374, 375, 378, 379; *see also* environment
survival of the fittest, 224, 237n
syndicalism, 224
system, 8–9, 11–13, 77n, 91, 112, 114, 116, 120–1, 123–4, 126–7, 129–30, 134–5, 140–3, 147, 148, 157, 163–4, 168, 177, 180, 182, 184, 185n, 190, 193–4, 196, 198–201, 204, 211, 215, 223, 231, 234, 244, 291, 296, 310, 317, 328, 339–41, 347–8, 352, 355–6, 361, 365, 276, 382, 385–6
capitalist system, 92, 99, 106, 110–12, 126, 144, 157, 164, 307, 346, 365, 387
feudal system, 97, 104, 114, 283, 308
profit-driven system, 97, 99, 113
system of classes, 5, 120, 130, 133, 198, 234n, 282
system of commerce, 24, 91, 124, 127, 130, 160, 163, 172, 175, 212, 256, 283, 285–6, 385
system of competition, 15, 114, 116, 120, 124, 130, 135, 140–3, 147, 148, 200, 361, 368
system of cooperation, 194, 230
system of inequality, 303, 329
system of production, 244, 252, 252

Tacitus, Publius Cornelius, 75, 83, 84
Tarleton, H. B., 272
technology, 163, 267, 268
Tennyson, Alfred, 56, 56, 66, 374, 375
Thackeray, William Makepeace, 378
thrift, 137, 139, 143, 146–7, 169, 174, 187, 270, 282

Tochatti, James, 158, 272, 323, 324, 327, 328, 356n
Tochatti, Louisa, 272
toil, 42, 43, 47, 57, 60, 62, 64, 112, 133, 137, 142, 149, 165, 240, 261, 282, 333; *see also* drudgery
Tory Party, 6, 35, 37–8, 64, 67, 69, 71, 135, 196, 205, 214–16, 227–9, 256, 266, 272, 291, 338, 340, 346–8, 352, 376, 383, 384; *see also* party: political parties; Conservative Party
Toryism, 228–9, 300
town(s), 8, 44, 82, 105, 112, 122, 141, 162, 177, 181, 191, 246, 248n, 258, 266–7, 268, 271, 279, 284, 307–13, 369; *see also* city
trade, 9, 104–5, 109, 120, 125–7, 137, 140, 171, 175, 185n, 189, 190, 199, 213, 271, 302, 342, 377, 380
trade depression, 9, 116n, 173, 109–200, 205, 212, 213
trade(s) union(s), 115–16, 126, 133, 138, 143, 144, 154, 156, 180, 182, 185n, 188, 190, 195–6, 201, 206n, 238, 263, 271, 297, 323, 327n, 346, 357
  reactionary trades unionism, 238n
tradition, 23, 109, 110, 285, 290, 300, 379, 380, 384
transformation, 4, 14, 15, 25, 182, 205, 221, 223, 227, 229, 235, 238, 263, 269, 281, 292, 294, 344n, 375, 377
transition, 15, 135, 150, 194, 196, 223, 228, 244, 252, 259, 295, 318
tribal society, 289, 294n, 380
tribe(s), 53, 83, 102, 105, 175, 194, 236, 290, 295–6, 299, 329
Turkey, 6, 26n, 31, 35, 37, 56n, 62, 176; *see also* Ottoman Empire
Turner, J. M. W., 378
two-stage hypothesis, 248n
tyranny, 8, 101, 124, 129, 165, 169, 172, 175, 177, 184, 188, 197, 201, 210, 215, 218–19, 222, 232, 235, 236, 281, 284, 367

ugliness, 44, 81, 82, 96, 99, 100, 103, 110, 122–3, 142, 169, 312, 320, 374, 378; *see also* hideousness; vulgarity
unionism, 271n
unionization, 134, 271
unit(s) of administration, 247, 257, 261, 326, 332
United States of America, 9, 138, 153, 227n, 341, 344n, 360, 362n; *see also* America
unity, 117, 135, 205, 218, 240n, 264, 289, 295, 297, 303, 337
  socialist unity, 5, 13, 18, 20–1, 337–8, 341–2, 344, 356, 357, 373
  unity of the working classes, 224, 239, 341, 350, 362
utopia, 96, 98n, 193, 204, 225, 248n, 273, 309n, 328, 369, 380, 382

value(s), 2, 12, 42, 43, 138n, 160, 180, 181, 183, 191, 198–9, 209, 278–9, 301n, 320n, 386; *see also* surplus value
vengeance, 14, 76, 81, 363; *see also* revenge
Victorian, 95, 223, 248n
violence, 5–7, 10, 14–18, 20, 24–5, 33, 37, 45, 49, 56, 58, 62, 76, 134–5, 141, 148, 182, 187, 196, 206, 217, 219, 224, 225, 237, 247, 267, 273, 278, 281, 292–4, 304, 323, 324–6, 331, 332, 340, 341, 345–6, 360, 362, 365, 375, 386–7
vision, 36, 42, 135, 143, 203, 246, 345, 377; *see also* ideal
vote, 7, 16, 33, 52, 65, 71, 72, 87, 138, 154, 156, 205, 227n, 247, 264, 271, 273, 293, 294n, 333, 361, 363, 364; *see also* ballot-box; election; suffrage
voting rights, 160, 294n
Voting Rights Act, 160, 267
vulgarity, 42, 45, 75, 77n, 82, 205, 308–9, 311, 312, 320, 378; *see also* hideousness; ugliness

wage(s), 13, 61, 106–7, 112, 116, 127, 134, 136, 138, 143–4, 146, 149, 164, 168, 180, 185n, 188–90, 193, 195, 213, 238, 277, 282, 283, 287, 291, 304, 327n, 340, 347, 349, 350–2, 355, 357, 364, 376, 381–2

wage-earning, 100, 106, 107, 125, 133, 144, 166, 189, 283, 329, 387; *see also* proletariat; wage-earning class
wage-slavery, 95, 182, 218, 237, 241, 291
Walker, Emery, 39n, 202
wants, 45, 108, 199, 230–1, 330; *see also* desires; necessaries; necessities; needs
war-party, 6, 34–5, 37–8
war(s)
  civil war, 15, 58, 182, 196, 341
  class-war, 227n, 266, 270
  colonialist wars, 205
  commercial war, 8, 14, 91, 99, 147, 159–60, 163, 166-8, 170–1, 172, 173, 175, 177, 179, 206n, 284–5
  foreign war(s), 6, 8–9, 33, 37, 50, 360
  imperial wars, 6, 9, 24, 51, 161
  national wars, 247
  necessary war, 57–8, 61, 63
  of choice, 5
  of civilization, 62
  of exploitation, 8, 175
  of liberation, 57
war(s) (specific)
  Anglo-Afghan wars, 6, 26n, 49, 51, 65n, 70, 154
  Anglo-Persian, 154
  Anglo-Russian, 6, 31–3, 49, 50, 163n, 271n
  Anglo-Zulu, 154
  Ashanti wars, 154
  Bhutan (Indian) war, 154
  Crimean War, 154
  First Boer War, 26n, 64n, 154, 362n
  First World War, 26n, 31
  French war, 116
  Mahdist war, 154
  War of the Roses, 108
  Russo-Turkish war, 31, 53n
  Second Anglo-Marri (Pakistan) War, 154
  Second Opium War, 154
  Tory War, 6, 35
waste, 8–9, 13, 15, 26n, 35, 46, 53, 103, 121, 126n, 138, 147, 161, 166–7, 169–71, 172–3, 182, 183, 184, 192–3, 196, 197, 199, 222, 225, 230, 232–5, 241, 248, 252–3, 258, 261, 266, 271, 279, 285, 298, 299, 303–4, 317–18, 320, 324, 328–30, 333, 341, 343, 348, 350, 352, 356n, 361, 364, 368, 370, 385–7
wealth, 2, 9, 16, 20, 42, 61, 82, 85, 96–7, 106, 109, 112, 135, 136, 147, 164–6, 173, 179, 180, 181, 183, 187–90, 192–4, 197–9, 230–1, 233, 236, 241, 259–69, 263, 279, 281–3, 285–6, 290, 295, 296, 298–9, 301, 307–8, 312–13, 317, 326, 329–33, 377, 385, 387; *see also* money; prosperity; rich(es)
Webb, Philip, 158
well-being, 41, 131, 329, 333
Whig party, 24, 26n, 205, 214, 216–17, 270, 319, 320, 347, 363, 372–4, 377, 378, 383–4; *see also* Liberal Party; party: moderate party
Wilson, Havelock, 280, 294n
women and children, 50, 54, 168, 188, 189, 191
Wordsworth, William, 64
workday, 113, 130, 189, 194, 233, 244, 271, 312, 327n, 349, 355, 357
worker(s), 13–20, 24, 74, 95, 97, 99, 106, 110–12, 113, 116, 119, 120–1, 127, 130, 133–5, 139, 147–8, 150, 154, 156–7, 160, 162, 164, 168–9, 170–1, 173–4, 176–7, 180, 182–4, 189–92, 195, 196, 199–201, 205–6, 217–19, 222–5, 233–5, 237–9, 241, 255, 261, 263, 265–6, 268–74, 278–9, 280, 281, 282, 284–7, 290–3, 299, 307, 309, 313, 318, 325–6, 331, 333, 337–8, 340, 346n, 348, 355–7, 360–1, 363–5, 373, 375–6, 385, 387; *see also* journeymen
worker aristocracy, 154, 278
workhouse, 127, 138, 146, 149, 180, 189, 190, 211n, 298, 303, 310
working-men, 15, 92, 116, 130, 139, 141, 143, 169, 195, 196, 206, 212, 216, 217, 270, 282, 291, 301, 303–4, 313, 319, 329, 344n, 345–6, 348–9, 351, 352, 356, 381, 382
working people, 154, 224, 291, 326, 355, 357, 360

workmen, 105–7, 1091, 114, 120, 125–8, 135, 138, 139, 146, 147, 149–50, 168–9, 174, 186, 188, 190, 191, 192, 194–5, 198–9, 213–14, 222–4, 228n, 230, 234–5, 238n, 239, 270, 271, 273, 279, 282–5, 296–7, 321, 341, 347, 350, 363, 376, 381–2, 384
world, 9, 11, 33, 35, 36, 42, 44, 45, 46, 47, 55, 57, 58, 62, 63, 66, 68, 69, 70, 75, 77–9, 81, 82, 85, 87, 92, 95, 96, 97, 101, 108, 109, 111, 212, 121, 122, 130, 139, 142, 145, 147, 148, 150, 165, 166, 175, 176, 180, 182, 183, 184, 185n, 188, 189, 193, 197, 200, 206, 207, 208, 218, 221, 222, 224, 228, 229, 230, 235, 239, 246, 249, 252, 254, 274, 279, 285, 286, 290, 291, 297, 301, 307, 309, 312, 319, 333, 342, 348, 364, 370, 374, 386
  ancient world, 150, 236–7, 298, 300
  Bourgeois world, 205–6, 211, 216, 219
  capitalist world, 386, 387
  civilized world, 57, 67, 78–9, 83–4, 101, 142, 251, 297, 320, 365, 377, 382, 387
  egalitarian world, 87, 95
  history of the world, 57, 61, 100, 141, 351
  modern world, 184, 189, 201, 298
  new world, 229, 239, 247, 260, 269n, 282
world-market, 256, 273, 342
worship, 95–6, 101–2, 103, 116, 124, 164n, 211, 221, 229, 378; *see also* God; religion

yeomen, 108, 109, 169, 235, 236

EU representative:
Easy Access System Europe
Mustamäe tee 50, 10621 Tallinn, Estonia
Gpsr.requests@easproject.com

www.ingramcontent.com/pod-product-compliance
Lightning Source LLC
Chambersburg PA
CBHW060612100726
47907CB00006B/1585

* 9 7 8 1 3 9 9 5 4 8 5 1 9 *